1017040423

951.056 CHI   MAY 1 7 2006

The Ch**WITHDRAWN**

revolution as history / edi

MERRITT LIBRARY

The Chinese Cultural Revolution
as History

D0555052

THE WALTER H. SHORENSTEIN
ASIA-PACIFIC RESEARCH CENTER

Studies of the Walter H. Shorenstein Asia-Pacific Research Center
Andrew G. Walder, General Editor

The Walter H. Shorenstein Asia-Pacific Research Center in the Freeman Spogli Institute for International Studies at Stanford University sponsors interdisciplinary research on the politics, economies, and societies of contemporary Asia. This monograph series features academic and policy-oriented research by Stanford faculty and other scholars associated with the Center.

ALSO PUBLISHED IN THE
SHORENSTEIN ASIA-PACIFIC RESEARCH CENTER SERIES

Prospects for Peace in South Asia
edited by Rafiq Dossani and Henry S. Rowen (2005)

Ethnic Nationalism in Korea: Genealogy, Politics, and Legacy
by Gi-Wook Shin (2006)

The Chinese
Cultural Revolution
as History

Edited by Joseph W. Esherick,

Paul G. Pickowicz,

and Andrew G. Walder

Stanford University Press

Stanford, California

2006

Thompson-Nicola Regional District
Library System
300-465 VICTORIA STREET
KAMLOOPS, BC   V2C 2A9

Stanford University Press
Stanford, California

© 2006 by the Board of Trustees of the Leland Stanford Junior University.
All rights reserved.

No part of this book may be reproduced or transmitted in any form or by any means, electronic or mechanical, including photocopying and recording, or in any information storage or retrieval system without the prior written permission of Stanford University Press.

Printed in the United States of America on acid-free, archival-quality paper

Library of Congress Cataloging-in-Publication Data

The Chinese cultural revolution as history / edited by Joseph W. Esherick, Paul G. Pickowicz, and Andrew G. Walder.
    p.   cm.—(Studies of the Asia-Pacific Research Center (Stanford University))
    Includes bibliographical references and index.
    ISBN 0-8047-5349-0 (cloth : alk. paper)
    ISBN 0-8047-5350-4 (pbk. : alk. paper)
    1. China—History—Cultural Revolution, 1966–1976.
I. Esherick, Joseph.   II. Pickowicz, Paul.   III. Walder, Andrew G. (Andrew George), 1953–   IV. Series.

DS778.7.C4563   2006
951.05′ 6—DC22

             2005026557

Original Printing 2006

Last figure below indicates year of this printing:
15   14   13   12   11   10   09   08   07   06

1017040423

Contents

Acknowledgments

This volume is the result of a year of group research activity that culminated in a conference entitled "The Chinese Cultural Revolution as History" convened at the University of California, San Diego, on June 8–9, 2003. In preparation for the conference, members of the group benefited enormously from visits to research libraries at Stanford University and at the San Diego, Los Angeles, and Berkeley campuses of the University of California. We thank the highly professional staffs of those libraries for their keen interest in the project and their timely assistance in providing rare materials.

In addition to the authors contributing to this volume, several other outstanding young scholars participated in the research project and presented papers at the conference. We wish to thank Joel Andreas, Elizabeth Dorn, Matthew Johnson, and Shinichi Tanigawa for sharing their research findings and participating in the larger project. The entire project was highly collaborative, and all of the essays presented here benefited from the active participation and constructive suggestions by all members of the group.

We are grateful to several prominent China scholars and Cultural Revolution specialists who visited the group and provided invaluable feedback during the months leading up to the conference: Roderick MacFarquhar, Richard Madsen, Stanley Rosen, Susan Shirk, Matthew Sommer, Yeh Wenhsin, and Zhang Yingjin. During the conference itself, David Jordan, Barry Naughton, Naomi Oreskes, Richard Madsen, Cecily McCaffrey, Stanley Rosen, Elena Songster, Xiao Zhiwei, and Zhang Yingjin served with remarkable effectiveness as formal discussants of the individual papers.

Special thanks are due to Michael Schoenhals. Not only did he visit the research group at a crucial early phase of the project, unselfishly sharing his encyclopedic knowledge of the Cultural Revolution, he also read and critiqued the individual papers at multiple stages of their development, directed researchers to important but untapped primary sources, and provided an invaluable review of the entire volume at a key stage of its preparation for publication. Richard Gunde did an exceptionally careful and professional job in copyediting the manuscript, for which we are most grateful.

We are pleased to acknowledge the generous financial support for the research, conference, and editorial phases of the Cultural Revolution as History project provided by the Asia-Pacific Research Center at Stanford University and the following organizations at the University of California, San Diego: The Center for the Humanities, the Department of History, the Council of East Asian Studies, the Hsiu Endowment for Chinese Studies, and the Program in Chinese Studies.

ONE

The Chinese Cultural Revolution as History: An Introduction

Joseph W. Esherick, Paul G. Pickowicz, Andrew G. Walder

The Cultural Revolution had a riveting impact on the fledgling field of contemporary China studies. When the red guards first made their appearance, research on the People's Republic was still in its infancy. Early studies of its polity, economy, and society described the organizations put in place near the end of the 1950s to mobilize the population for political campaigns and rapid economic growth. They also emphasized the distinctive ideology that shaped these organizations and the regime's efforts to indoctrinate the population and conduct ambitious political and economic campaigns. Divisions among the elite were already evident, and were expressed in several purges and campaigns against intellectuals. The operational codes of party and government bureaucracies—which struggled to balance the tension between political loyalty and professional expertise—were just becoming clear.[1]

Yet shortly after these distinctive institutions were established, they were torn apart in the unprecedented upheavals that began in June 1966. The nation was rent by waves of civil strife that lasted more than two years, followed by harsh military repression and campaigns of political persecution that accelerated in intensity until they began to wane in the early 1970s. China remained unsettled politically in the immediate aftermath. Continued jockeying among elite factions coincided with frequent strikes and protest movements in the period prior to Mao's death in September 1976, and aftershocks reverberated into the early 1980s.[2]

The effect on China scholarship was immediate. Franz Schurmann's monumental study of the regime's systems of internal communication and control, *Ideology and Organization in Communist China*, appeared in 1966, just as the Cultural Revolution began. He immediately amended his influential synthesis in an expanded edition two years later. His lengthy "Supplement" to the new edition began with a self-criticism, and is worth quoting at length:

> The forces of Chinese society are equally as important as those coming from the structure of state power. I do not believe that this indicates a resurgence of the old social system, but rather that China's major social classes (workers, peasants, and intellectuals) exert great pressure on the ideology and organization which direct that country. If revolution makes ideology and organization necessary to refashion society, the passage of time leads to a resurrection of the forces of society. . . . If I were to give the book a new title today, I would call it *Ideology, Organization, and Society in China*. The original title testifies to the weight I assigned ideology and organization, and to China's Communist character. However, due weight must now be given to the resurgence of the forces of Chinese society.[3]

Michel Oksenberg concurred with this assessment and articulated a research agenda that guided much of the next fifteen years of social science scholarship on contemporary China, most of which focused on the decade after 1966.

> The Cultural Revolution provided a remarkable opportunity to view the structure of Chinese society in the 1960s. Prior to 1965, that view was obscured by the carefully nurtured image of a monolithic society led by a unified, cohesive elite. In 1966–67, the image was destroyed, revealing that the rulers were deeply divided and locked in bitter struggle. As the rulers lost their ability to provide unified, coherent guidelines to the nation, the various segments of society became more able to pursue their own interests. As a result, the Cultural Revolution made it possible to analyze the concerns of the major groups in society and their relative abilities to achieve their interests.[4]

This new emphasis was already evident in Ezra Vogel's *Canton under Communism*, an account of the new regime's efforts to consolidate political control and reorganize the society and economy of Guangdong: the book culminated in a chapter on the Cultural Revolution that interpreted the upheaval in precisely these terms.[5]

While few doubted the sharp divergence of China under Mao from the patterns of Soviet Communism, students of the Soviet bloc were already critical of scholarship that emphasized regime ideology and mechanisms of political control. Independently of events in China—and before the Cultural Revolution—they called for attention to the conflict and pluralism behind the façade of totalitarian conformity.[6] Without dramatic material of the kind provided by the Cultural Revolution, however, students of the Soviet bloc could fully pursue this agenda only in studies of the Hungarian revolution of 1956, the Prague Spring of 1968, or periodic upheavals in Poland.[7] Among students of China, the Cultural Revolution bred a more intense engagement with the organization of society and the political forces that sprang from it.

Work inspired by this agenda continued to appear well into the 1980s. Scholarship about China during the Mao era was notable for its emphasis on the structure of society and what would later be termed state-society relations. Students of political participation examined the ways in which individuals and groups could pursue their interests within the evident constraints of political institutions.[8] Students of political institutions looked closely for evidence of bargaining among bureaucratic interests and mass constituencies, both in the process of policy making and policy implementation.[9] Students of the educational system and the occupational structure examined the career incentives that drove individuals into patterns of cooperation with or withdrawal from regime-sponsored political activity.[10] Students of grassroots politics and economic institutions explored the ways that state institutions bred social networks and personal loyalties that served to extend the power of the state while at the same time blunting or diverting it.[11] Others looked more closely at earlier periods of the People's Republic for evidence of collective protest of the variety that was so evident in the late 1960s.[12] The result was a specialized scholarly literature that looked remarkably unlike anything connected with the term totalitarianism.

Although these studies were decisively shaped by the Cultural Revolution, they did not deal directly with the Cultural Revolution itself. This became a thriving sub-topic that focused particularly on the upheavals of 1966–68, and especially on the most visible protagonists: student red guards, worker rebels, and the mass organizations engaged in factional struggles. A major theme of this work—which appeared with greatest frequency from the mid-1970s to the early 1980s—was that the political struggles of the late 1960s expressed the conflicting interests of identifiable groups in Chinese society. Schurmann himself signaled this new emphasis on the importance of social forces when he spoke of the red guards: "in the Cultural

Revolution, I believe that, no matter how much the students were guided from above, they basically expressed forces deriving from their own social class."[13] Gordon White elaborated the idea in his lengthy analysis of a red guard tabloid that created controversy by taking aim at the political class labels employed by the regime and the hierarchy of status and privilege that they created.[14] Hong Yung Lee found that the class background of students shaped their factional affiliation in the political struggles of the late 1960s, and Chan, Rosen, and Unger further elaborated the argument while taking issue with some of the specifics of Lee's formulations.[15] This work inspired detailed studies of the structure of the educational system and the pattern of educational attainment, and in particular the system of class labels and its impact on education, student strategies, and careers.[16]

Hong Yung Lee synthesized the underlying conception that united work in this vein: the Cultural Revolution created an opportunity for social groups to pursue their interests, and the conflicts expressed social differences that had emerged under Communist Party rule.[17] Lee's work was firmly in the tradition of interest group politics: elite factions representing radical versus conservative tendencies made common cause with mass groups whose interests were aligned with elites seeking either to transform or preserve the status quo. Mass factionalism therefore expressed a struggle between the "haves" and "have nots": conservative factions were drawn from those close to the regime or who had benefited the most from its policies, and radical factions were drawn from those alienated from the regime or relegated to subordinate or disadvantaged positions within it.[18] The significance of the Cultural Revolution was that it provided a window of opportunity for these underlying tensions to surface, and the conflicting interests to be expressed—even though the pursuit of group interests was masked in a political rhetoric that sought to justify private ends in the language of political ideals.

This agenda was pursued enthusiastically throughout the 1970s and early 1980s. The Cultural Revolution proved a rich source of material on disadvantaged groups that briefly mobilized to redress their grievances: demobilized soldiers who had been shipped to remote state farms instead of receiving the urban job assignments they had expected;[19] urban youth who had been part of the first wave sent down to the countryside in the early 1960s;[20] and contract and temporary workers who were excluded from the pay and benefits enjoyed by those permanently attached to urban work units.[21] Intellectual life was portrayed as a continuing contest between critical voices with patrons in the top leadership and establishment intellectuals with different patrons who encouraged their attacks on the critics.[22] This was a portrayal of a China seething with social divisions and conflicts, with citizens eager to seize available opportunities to express their interests, mobilize to advance or protect them and, if necessary, do battle with their opponents. In order to penetrate to this underlying reality, one had only to look beneath a rather fragile façade of political rhetoric and totalitarian control.

In hindsight, there are two striking features of this first wave of scholarship on the Cultural Revolution. The first is how firmly "society-centered" it was, and its sensitivity to the ways in which Chinese citizens at all levels consciously pursued their interests and participated willingly in the conflicts of the period. These conflicts were used as a window through which one could "read backwards" to the structure of the underlying society and its hidden tensions.

The second is how remarkably thin the evidence was for these interpretations. One has to admire the ingenuity with which authors reconstructed patterns of inequality and conflict from a relatively small number of interviews with émigrés, and from scattered copies of red guard tabloids, critical wall posters and pamphlets, transcripts of radio broadcasts, and rare issues of local newspapers.[23] All of this work proceeded without the benefit of the kinds of sources that scholars take for granted today: direct local interviews and oral histories with key participants; extensive collections of tabloids, pamphlets, speeches, and wall posters; published local histories, reference works, and official compendia of social statistics; and even survey research with retrospective questions.

Events in China after Mao soon pushed the study of the Cultural Revolution off center stage. For more than a decade it was the most topical of subjects, highly relevant to questions about the nation's current condition and future prospects. But after Mao's death China's unfolding transformation redirected the attention of the field: first to the tumultuous events from the Democracy Wall movement of 1978 to Tiananmen Square in 1989, and then to the accelerating economic and social transformation of China into the present century.

New Trends in Cultural Revolution Research

In the decades since the initial heyday of Cultural Revolution scholarship, the landscape for research on the subject has shifted dramatically, largely due to changes in China. Taken together, five trends have laid the foundation for a vigorous new scholarship on the Cultural Revolution that inevitably will look very different from the research of the first generation. First, there has been a steady increase in the documentation relevant to the activities of the elite in central and local bureaucracies: publications of entire series of formerly internal documents, organizational histories, diaries and chronologies of important officials, transcripts of their speeches and of meetings, and related reference works, diaries, and biographies. It is now possible to bring the political elite—and its extensive and intensive connections to grassroots organizations and individuals—back into the picture in a way that was never before possible. The regime-centered agenda of pre–Cultural Revolution scholarship can be pursued much more successfully than ever before, while synthesizing insights from this with the later society-centered perspectives. Second, there has been a steady cumulative increase in the availability of all the highly prized and once-scarce unofficial sources of information—"red guard materials" and accounts by ordinary participants—that were the staple of the first generation of research. The quantity of available documentation of this type has increased by several orders of magnitude. The third trend is the outpouring of revelations that began in the late 1970s and continued well into the 1990s about violence, torture, and murder. The victims, whose experiences were remarkably obscured in the first wave of research, have been forced back into the center of our attention, requiring extensive changes in our understanding of the politics of the Cultural Revolution and its social impact. Fourth, thousands of official histories and chronologies of provinces, cities, counties, districts, and universities have been published since the mid-1980s, and many of these cover in some detail the events of 1966–76. And last, but not least, a significant Chinese-language scholarship on the Cultural Revolution has appeared in recent years in the form of research articles, academic monographs, and reference works.

DOCUMENTATION OF ELITE ACTIVITIES AND
BUREAUCRATIC OPERATIONS

Although the Cultural Revolution provided students of contemporary China with their first insights into the structure of society and its underlying social tensions, it also provided researchers interested primarily in the organization of the regime and its internal politics with an unprecedented view of this subject. Red guards and rebels dug deeply into official archives and published accounts of past debates and policy disputes designed to illustrate the perfidy of those being purged as capitalist roaders. These materials were the staple of the scholarly literature on regime-level politics for much of the next decade.[24]

One of the unfortunate yet unavoidable features of scholarship on contemporary China is the relentless demand for a present-centered kind of "relevance": the need to understand where China is today and where it will likely go in the future. China has changed so rapidly that events even a few decades old soon appear irrelevant to the present. Leadership splits and maneuverings in the late Mao period seemed increasingly arcane in a rapidly unfolding political scene under Deng Xiaoping and his successors, with most of the principals long since imprisoned or dead. The subject seemed even more remote in the post-Deng, post-Jiang era.

It is largely for this reason that social scientists have generally failed to take advantage of the increased availability of information about the workings of the regime in the late Mao period, particularly the structure of the bureaucracy, mobility and career patterns, and the activities, conflicts, and maneuverings behind the scenes that were almost completely obscured twenty years ago.[25] The late 1980s and 1990s saw an upsurge of publication of organizational histories, documentary collections, and biographical materials of a kind never enjoyed by the first generation of scholars. These materials permit researchers to construct a clear picture of the structure of government and party organizations, the membership of key committees, and the movement of individuals via promotions and purges through specific party and government posts. The most noteworthy are the hundreds of organizational histories (literally, "Materials on Organizational History" or *zuzhi shi ziliao*) published at the national, provincial, and local level. These compendia cover the periods from the first activities of the Communist Party in the region to the late 1980s or early 1990s.[26] They describe in minute detail the successive reorganizations of party and government, and provide complete lists of those in leadership posts and members of leadership committees, figures on the number of personnel in various bureaus and commissions, compilations of documents that issued from the work of these committees, and statistical tables on party and government personnel, often tabulated by year according to age, educational level, and gender.[27] Although less extensive in their coverage, similarly detailed materials on such subjects are often found in local gazetteers (*difang zhi*) published at the municipal, county, city district, and even organizational level.[28] More specialized reference works attempt to convey this kind of information in more abbreviated form.[29] Somewhat different in focus are biographical dictionaries that provide capsule summaries of the background and careers of individual office-holders.[30] These materials afford scholars a clear view of the offices held by individuals at specific points in time, their careers through the bureaucracy, who they worked with, and who was promoted and who was purged in successive political campaigns. All of these things were obscure in the first generation of scholarship on regime-centered politics. The guesswork and speculation that once characterized work on the topic are largely a thing of the past.

A different range of sources focuses on the daily activities of specific prominent individuals. Detailed "chronological biographies" (*nianpu*) of the professional lives of such key leaders as Zhou Enlai, Liu Shaoqi, He Long, Chen Yi, Nie Rongzhen, Wang Jiaxiang, and Chen Pixian, for example, have been published in recent years.[31] A similar type of source is the "collected manuscripts" of such figures as Mao and Zhou Enlai: a record of their letters, directives, and written comments on reports on a day-by-day basis.[32]

More vivid and detailed are memoirs that have been published with increasing frequency in recent years by some of the key actors on both sides of the political struggles of the period. Wang Li, Liu Zhijian, and Mu Xin, key early members of the Central Cultural Revolution Group who were purged in 1967 for various errors, have published memoirs or detailed accounts of specific episodes.[33] Li Xuefeng, acting first party secretary of Beijing in the summer of 1966,[34] and Wu De, a party secretary and mayor of Beijing from 1966,[35] have left accounts of key episodes during the Cultural Revolution that they observed first-hand. Wang Dongxing, the head of Mao's security detail,[36] and General Yang Chengwu, appointed acting chief of the general staff of the People's Liberation Army (PLA) in 1966,[37] have both left accounts of key episodes. Zhang Chengxian, a member of the Hebei Province Secretariat and leader of the work team sent to Beijing University in 1966,[38] and Guo Yingqiu, party secretary of People's University who succeeded Deng Tuo after his May 1966 suicide and who was put in charge of the work teams sent to schools in June and July 1966,[39] have recently recorded their accounts for posterity. Xu Jingxian, an associate of Zhang Chunqiao and Yao Wenyuan, who became the chairman of Shanghai's Revolutionary Committee in 1967, has published a book-length memoir.[40] A related genre are memoirs published in remembrance of major political figures by their personal secretaries, relatives, or other associates. Recent examples are accounts of the activities of Liu Shaoqi and Zhou Enlai during the Cultural Revolution written by their aides.[41]

More tendentious but often revealing are the internal case histories of the activities of individuals denounced after Mao's death for their "anti-party activities" during the Cultural Revolution. These materials often resemble the denunciations of leading "capitalist roaders" during the Cultural Revolution, but they are more detailed, more voluminous, and more widely available. Excerpts were published in mass circulation venues in the late 1970s and early 1980s, but compendia compiled as study materials by regional party schools in the 1980s contain detailed accounts of specific factional activities that greatly deepen our understanding of elite politics in the period.[42]

A final type of source is the transcripts of talks by national and local leaders at rallies, meetings, and receptions during the period from mid-1966 to late 1968. Scattered samples were available to researchers during the first wave of Cultural Revolution research. By the late 1990s, however, hundreds of them were widely available, affording a much more complete and detailed portrait of the interactions of top officials with mass organizations. Some of these speeches are carried in the larger collections of red guard tabloids that have been published in recent years (more on this below). Others are available in bound collections of leaders' speeches or "reference materials" widely published and circulated at the time.[43] Many of these collections are readily available at second-hand book stalls in China, and some of them have formed the basis for collections compiled independently and produced for sale abroad. One of the most useful is the book-length index and CD-ROM produced by the Chinese University of Hong Kong, which contains the text of close to 2,000 such meetings and speeches and which can be searched with keyword phrases.[44]

These materials promise a clearer understanding of the role of officials in the Cultural Revolution, both as active political agents and as victims.[45] More important, however, is the potential implication of these sources for past portrayals of mass politics as relatively autonomous expressions of social forces. The intensive interaction between elites and masses suggests a more nuanced interpretation of mass politics and the course of the movement as a product of the unpredictable interplay between elite and masses, determined neither by the structure of the regime nor the interests of any of the parties to the conflict.[46]

THE ACCUMULATION OF UNOFFICIAL SOURCES

The second development is an exponential increase in the availability of the same unofficial materials that were the staple of the first generation of Cultural Revolution scholarship: wall posters, handbills, newspapers, pamphlets, and reference collections compiled by work units and red guard and rebel organizations. In the mid-1970s all extant copies of such materials available in government archives and libraries in English-speaking countries were collected in a twenty-volume library edition that contained 6,743 pages of material.[47] Two eight-volume supplements issued in 1980 and 1992 added another 8,822 small-format pages of material, although this came too late to benefit the first wave of scholarship on the Cultural Revolution.[48]

Two massive reprint collections have recently multiplied several-fold the available materials of this type. The first, a twenty-volume collection of red guard newspapers from Beijing and other regions, added 9,644 large-format pages in 1999.[49] The second, a forty-volume collection of newspapers exclusively from Beijing, added 15,926 pages in 2001,[50] and another collection of similar magnitude from the provinces is being prepared. If we restrict our count solely to the material available in these standard library reprint editions, students of the Cultural Revolution now enjoy access to more than six times as many pages of material as researchers at the end of the 1970s.

This, however, is only a fraction of the sources of this type that are now accessible. Other reprint services offer hundreds of documentary collections for sale to libraries and individuals.[51] Used book stores and dealers of Mao-era memorabilia in China have provided another source, and purchases from these sources have been photocopied and informally circulated among researchers. Private collections held by individuals and work units in China are occasionally available, and significant collections of internal documents from the period, including written confessions by those accused of crimes, are held in the archives of many universities, research institutes, and government agencies. Although these materials are not yet widely accessible, their existence is well known.[52]

One of the most valuable sources of information in the first generation of Cultural Revolution scholarship was interviews with former red guards and other participants in the events of the period. Conducted almost exclusively in Hong Kong, the scholarship that resulted focused heavily on events in Guangzhou.[53] This same source of information is far more widely available today, both in China and abroad. Thousands of former red guards have emigrated abroad after completing their higher education, and the faculties of universities and office staff of work units throughout China are filled with a generation of individuals—now more than fifty years old—with direct experience in the events of those years, an abiding interest in those formative years, and often real enthusiasm about sharing their recollections. Although such oral histories are inevitably affected by the vagaries of memory and often colored by self-serving reconstructions internalized over the course of decades of political study, it is now much easier to do retrospective interviewing within China of the kind conducted among émigrés in Hong Kong thirty years ago. Potential informants are far more abundant and it is much easier to test the veracity of accounts by finding several people to report about a single place or event.[54]

Published memoirs by red guards were also an important source of insight for the first generation of researchers. Those available through the 1980s were based exclusively on the accounts of politically active but relatively marginal figures in the provinces about what they personally witnessed, and they were indeed valuable.[55] These individuals, however, were never able to report directly about key events in well-publicized struggles in the nation's capital of the type that captured the attention of those chronicling the subject. This has begun to change. Some of the key participants in these events have been interviewed and their accounts published either in China or abroad, and some have begun to publish books of their own.[56]

In short, the same unofficial sources that fueled the first wave of Cultural Revolution scholarship are far more abundant than ever before, and will become more so as archives in China gradually become more accessible. This material will permit a far more concrete, detailed, and textured portrayal of the events of those years. This will inevitably lead scholars to confirm, elaborate, correct, or challenge the line of interpretation established by the first generation of scholars who worked with far more limited sources of information, and will surely lead to new lines of historical interpretation or social science inquiry.

THE HUMAN COST: CHRONICLES OF VICTIMIZATION

The arrest and subsequent public trial of the "Gang of Four" touched off a campaign designed to reveal them as conspirators and criminals who promoted the cruelty and violence of the Cultural Revolution. There were several dimensions to this campaign, which began in the late 1970s and continued into the show trial of 1980 and its immediate aftermath.[57] The first was the "literature of the wounded," or "scar literature" (*shanghen wenxue*), short stories and novels that portrayed the cruelty and violence of the period in unvarnished terms. Translated quickly into English, these accounts had the greatest early impact on outsiders' views of the human toll of the Cultural Revolution.[58] The second dimension was "reportage literature" (*baogao wenxue*) or fictionalized narratives based on real cases,[59] and "reports" (*baogao* or *baodao*), or lightly dramatized accounts of persecution and suffering during the Cultural Revolution based on official case investigations or the work of investigative journalists.[60] The third dimension was a series of articles that appeared between 1978 and 1981 in mass circulation newspapers that reported on particularly violent episodes that could be attributed to the machinations of one of the "Gang of Four" or their local associates.[61] These seemingly unending tales of cruelty, imprisonment, torture, and murder did not necessarily challenge the thrust of a scholarly literature that focused on conflict and the pursuit of individual and group interest. However, embarrassingly little of this underlying reality of political life in China during the Cultural Revolution was reflected in published scholarship, even scholarship about the red guards themselves. Clearly there was a yawning gap in scholarship about this dimension of the Cultural Revolution experience—one that has yet to be adequately filled.

The thousands of investigations of "false cases" and the accompanying rehabilitations of victims (sometimes posthumously) and their families generated material that found its way into publications during the 1980s and early 1990s. Local histories—at the provincial, county, city district, and even university level—regularly cite statistics on the numbers killed, wounded, imprisoned, or otherwise persecuted during the period from 1966 to 1972. The format of these statistics makes clear that they are derived from investigations to reverse "false cases" and rehabilitate those who were wrongly accused, especially local officials. Often these sources provide considerable detail on the investigations that generated these figures, or on the activities that generated the casualties. Perhaps best known is Zheng Yi's accounts of the horrific local violence in Guangxi Province, where the highest casualty figures were recorded.[62] The sources indicate that these accounts draw on more extensive records held in local archives, which have yet to be exploited by researchers.[63]

A separate line of investigation is the accumulation of personal testimony that memorializes specific individuals and provides some detail about the way in which they met their untimely end. Wang Youqin, for example, has interviewed scores of individuals about instances of torture and murder, and has collected accounts conducted by others, and has posted transcripts of these oral accounts on a website and published an indexed book that records this information.[64] These accounts have formed the basis of articles on beatings and deaths of high school teachers and officials.[65]

Victim-centered scholarship is only the first step in coming to grips with this dimension of the Cultural Revolution, of which there was barely a hint in the first generation of research. Although knowledge about the human toll of the period has been widespread among scholars for more than two decades, this awareness has yet to be integrated with a supposedly "society-centered" perspective that treated politics in the Cultural Revolution era as something akin to interest groups in a pluralistic setting. Was the violence simply a by-product of the pursuit of group interests, or are there dimensions of the regime and society during that era with which existing scholarship has yet to come to grips? Intellectual agendas are determined in large part by our understanding of what happened, and in retrospect much of the first generation of scholarship seems to have missed what is probably the most profound question of all. This presents a major challenge for future research: how do we explain the magnitude of the human toll, and how do we square this historical reality with intellectual perspectives that strained to analyze China in the Mao period in pluralistic terms?

OFFICIAL HISTORIES OF REGIONS, LOCALITIES, AND ORGANIZATIONS

During the past twenty years thousands of official histories of regions, localities, and organizations have been published, representing our fourth trend. These publications are official overviews reflecting orthodox party interpretation of events, and they rarely treat any subject in considerable depth. They vary greatly in quality, focus, and degree of detail. However, some of them provide surprising levels of detail about certain topics directly or indirectly related to the Cultural Revolution, and due to the large numbers of such accounts their cumulative impact on our knowledge can be considerable.

The provincial-level histories in the *Dangdai Zhongguo* series are an example: specialized volumes cover the history of individual provinces and separate functional areas of the national bureaucracy. They can provide surprising detail on certain events of the period—the numbers of cadres who lost their posts or who were accused of political crimes, or the numbers of deaths due to political persecution.[66] Similar materials can be found in brief histories of provinces and cities published in recent years.[67] A variant of this genre is the "chronicle of events" (*dashiji*) for a city or province. These sometimes cover the entire post-1949 period,[68] but some are specifically devoted to the Cultural Revolution.[69]

Far more numerous are the local gazetteers published by counties and districts. More than two thousand have been published since the mid-1980s, and while hundreds are available in libraries abroad,[70] virtually all of them are easily accessible in Hong Kong, Shanghai, and Beijing.[71] Like the other local histories, these vary greatly in quality and detail, but they sometimes contain remarkable material about a variety of subjects. County gazetteers for Shaanxi and Shanghai, for example, are unusually detailed and often contain lengthy narrative accounts of local events.[72] Gazetteers for Guangxi Province are also relatively detailed, and contain surprisingly specific information about the region's unusually extensive violence.[73] The gazetteers also contain valuable information about the structures of party and government, incumbent office-holders, and basic data about population, party membership, and living standards. Although these sources have already received considerable attention in the scholarly community, less well-known are the large numbers of analogous university histories that have been published since the 1980s, some of which contain similarly detailed information about the Cultural Revolution on their campuses, school enrollment figures, information about party organizations and membership, and chronicles of events.[74]

CHINESE-LANGUAGE SCHOLARSHIP

Finally, a significant Chinese-language literature on the Cultural Revolution has recently emerged, and although the research community in China is still relatively small, it is active and is producing very valuable work. This scholarship had its origins in the early 1980s campaigns to expose the crimes of the "Gang of Four" and educate the population to "thoroughly repudiate the Cultural Revolution."[75] These early studies had a clear didactic purpose and were firmly shaped by the dictates of the 1981 resolution on party history and related documents, but they often revealed information that was new at the time.[76] Historical accounts that appeared in the 1980s—both official and unofficial—drew on much of the denunciatory materials, and also began to draw systematically on archival materials in support.[77]

Since that time Chinese scholarship has developed in two directions. The first, stronger in research institutes attached to the government, party schools, or departments of party history, is a regime-centered literature that focuses on the activities of leading officials and certain key events of the period. Though sometimes still strongly wedded to official interpretations, in recent years the didactic impulse has become less explicit, and scholars have begun to explore new directions that are tangential to the emphases of official orthodoxy. Representative of this trend are recent general histories of the Cultural Revolution,[78] and research articles that reexamine the impact of crucial party plenums or specific turning points in elite conflict.[79]

The second direction is stronger among researchers who work in universities and research institutes. This is a literature that is more focused on events in such basic-level units as the major universities, or on the red guard and rebel movements themselves. Research on the red guard movement has grown rapidly in recent years. Among the more important contributions are two major books,[80] and specialized articles on red guard factionalism,[81] the burning of the British diplomatic offices in Beijing,[82] the organization of red guard groups and their publishing activities,[83] and the origins of the first high school red guards.[84] The elite maneuverings behind Nie Yuanzi's famous "first Marxist-Leninist wall poster" at Beijing University on May 25, 1966, have produced an attentive literature, and are a subject of some controversy.[85] Recent edited collections have pulled together a mixture of academic and nonacademic writings that provide a quick overview of the range of work being produced, and some of the areas of disagreement and debate.[86] Also noteworthy are independently produced dictionaries and reference works that provide students and researchers a quick entrée to some of the more arcane terms and events of the period.[87]

Taken as a whole, these five trends have gradually reversed a situation that was both a truism and a tired lament only two decades ago: the paucity of sources. In fact, in terms of the written documentation generated at the time by participants both inside and out of party and government, and in terms of the collection, compilation, and publication of documentary materials by official agencies in the ensuing decades, the Cultural Revolution is unusually well documented for such a period of upheaval. One would be hard-pressed to name political movements or instances of rebellion in which the participants were so obsessively oriented to the written word, each group producing reams of wall posters, handbills, newspapers, pamphlets, and even their own historical accounts of the major events.[88] The anticipated opening of archives of materials held by local governments, research institutes, and universities will only further improve the situation.

Toward a Field of Historical Scholarship

What is the significance of referring to the Cultural Revolution as "history"? This means, most importantly, that the study of the late Mao period is now so far into the past that it is no longer burdened by the demand for relevance to the country's current evolution. Inevitably, the questions with which scholars from any discipline approach the topic will be different than what we find in the first generation of research. We can now approach the period from the perspective of the disciplines of history and historically oriented social science. Social science writings on the Mao era were in some ways a "first draft" of the history of the People's Republic. But they were more than that, because they left behind a trail of ideas, arguments, and generalizations that were never subjected to prolonged examination, as the contemporary China field's span of attention moved forward temporally with the march of time. The early interpretations serve to focus subsequent research and challenge the next generation of scholarship to reexamine, elaborate, modify, and propose alternatives. In so doing, the study of the Cultural Revolution, and the entire Mao era, increasingly becomes a more sustained reflection on the nature of the Chinese revolution and its long-run consequences for Chinese society—whether this comes from extensive examination of archival material, new memoirs, or the analysis of retrospective survey data on the life trajectories of individuals.[89]

So what is the agenda for this field of history? The first task is to address gaps in the scholarly literature that became increasingly evident in the post-Mao era. The most obvious need is to address more directly the human cost of the period, which was largely ignored in the first wave of scholarship. How do we reconcile what we now know about this human toll with the earlier emphasis on the social sources of political conflict? Are these views incompatible? A related issue is raised by our greater access to the activities of the political elite in bureaucratic organizations. Might a closer examination of the activities of elites, and their intense interactions with non-elites, breed a different interpretation that is better able to account for this enormous human toll?

Another way to think about gaps in our knowledge is to identify areas that have received relatively little attention. Our review of scholarship on the Cultural Revolution makes clear that the first wave focused very heavily on the period of mass mobilization, from 1966 to 1968. Remarkably, however, there is almost no research literature that covers the ferocious persecution campaigns of 1968 to 1971, a period during which we now know that by far the greatest numbers of victims were claimed. Why was the period after the end of the mass movements so much more violent than the first? This period came to a close after the death of Lin Biao—a pivotal event still shrouded in mystery, although recent publications have finally begun to provide well-grounded and plausible interpretations.[90] This turning point marked a period of renewed protest and unrest, which attracted a great deal of attention for a brief period, but which is still a much neglected topic. The mid-1970s themselves were a crucial transitional period between the darkest period of the Cultural Revolution and the historical turning point at the end of the Mao era: the decision to push forward with reform and opening at the elite level, and the first vigorous stirrings of a democracy movement at the mass level. A close examination of the late Mao era may not have direct relevance for charting China's future, but it will certainly shed light on what has emerged as one of the major historical questions of our time: the sharply divergent path of the Chinese Communist Party and Chinese society from the Soviet bloc over the past two decades.

As these topics are explored in depth, their immense complexity will become more apparent. Existing studies of the Cultural Revolution in different regions make clear that events of the period proceeded at a different pace and the conflicts took remarkably different forms. In some ways it will appear as if there were different Cultural Revolutions in different parts of the country: the pace and structure of conflict is already known to have varied considerably across large cities and between cities and countryside.

We are also likely to discover variations across institutions even within a single locality. And a closer look at localities will undoubtedly lead to surprises: conflicts, for example, that had little to do with the presumed group interests that preoccupied the first wave of research. Indeed, as the sources permit us to look more closely at local events and the actions and relationships of individuals, we are likely to find that there were many motives and interests other than those readily attributable to occupational categories, rank, or family status. Although the literature on the Cultural Revolution has always emphasized strategic action, we are now likely to discover strategies and motives that were obscured or ignored in earlier scholarship. We can now explore this central question in ways that were impossible two decades ago.

EXPLORATIONS

The essays in this volume reflect a new era of research by younger scholars who have immersed themselves in the many new sources on the history of the Cultural Revolution. Their topics range from red guards at an elite Beijing university to political violence in a distant village, from popular paleoanthropology to the protection of cultural treasures, from a model village favored by Mao's wife to a small-town schoolteacher plucked from obscurity when the Chairman suddenly answered his letter. The temporal span of these studies extends from the earliest stage of red guard attacks on "old" culture to the mid-1970s efforts to consolidate and institutionalize the revolution. Reflecting established methodologies in historical studies, the authors focus on particular localities or case studies to provide detailed analyses of the complex interface and ever-shifting dynamics of state-society interactions during the several phases of the Cultural Revolution.

While recognizing that political elites commanded impressive institutional resources and ideological weapons, the essays highlight the very real limits on the ability of Mao and the party elite to manipulate their legions of followers and impose their will on society. Similarly, while acknowledging the resilience and creativity of social forces operating at the grass roots, the authors doubt the capacity of social actors to express their collective will in autonomous political movements. The explanation for the Cultural Revolution's unique combination of anarchy and dictatorship, of strident popular rebellion and coercive state action, lies in the often unscripted and unpredictable interplay between state and society. Different levels and factions within the party-state sought to mobilize, manipulate, or constrain social actors, but were rarely able to do so with any predictable efficacy. Social actors sought to take advantage of opportunities provided by the policies, campaigns, rhetorical strategies, or political infighting of the state, but the fate of their initiatives was typically quite different from the original intent. The high politics of the Cultural Revolution will require a separate volume, and a forthcoming study by Roderick MacFarquhar and Michael Schoenhals will soon fill that gap.[91] The chapters in this book focus on the local and the particular, probing the multiple intersecting, interpenetrating, and interacting relations between state and social actors. These studies suggest that neither the structures of the Maoist regime nor the focused agendas of particular social interest groups were decisive in shaping the course of the Cultural Revolution. Only the contingent and shifting interaction of these and other factors explains the history that we see.

The first and most dramatic phase of the Cultural Revolution was the explosive red guard movement of 1966–68. In a manner unprecedented in communist-ruled states, young middle school and university students were unleashed to attack cultural symbols of the old society, academic representatives of "bourgeois" scholarship, and party leaders allegedly infected with revisionist ideas. In most instances, the red guard movement quickly fractured into fiercely conflicting factions, and the sources of this red guard factionalism have been the focus of much past scholarship.[92] Xiaowei Zheng's research on student activism at Qinghua University utilizes newly available red guard publications and memoirs, as well as extensive interviews with former red guards, including the Qinghua rebel leader Kuai Dafu. Recent detailed studies of red guard factionalism have questioned the earlier sociological interpretation depicting conflict between conservative factions led by the children of party cadres arrayed against radical factions recruited from more disadvantaged groups.[93] Zheng suggests that the social background and academic experience of red guards did influence their behavior, but there was far more involved than a simple struggle between conservative "haves" and radical "have nots." Students whose parents were high officials wanted more political respect. The "academically challenged" students of rural and working-class origins disliked the emphasis placed on technical expertise. Student cadres—the political favorites of the campus party machine—were widely resented by political outsiders, especially middle-class students who had less-than-red class backgrounds.

Zheng's careful narrative of the first years of the red guard movement shows that students' background did influence their political choices, but they were also constantly interacting with state agents: President Liu Shao-qi's wife joined the Qinghua work team; Premier Zhou Enlai was dispatched for a secret pre-dawn meeting with the radical leader Kuai Dafu. But as political divisions deepened in the central party leadership, lines of authority crossed and snapped and political signals became impossible to read. In this context, Zheng argues, students had to make their own choices, and their political choices were not always "rational" or consistent with their class or status group interests, and passion, ideals, and serious ideological debate were important in guiding their decisions.

Destructive raids by red guards in the first months of the Cultural Revolution are among the best known aspects of the movement. Radical students burned books, smashed antiques, defaced shrines, and destroyed old buildings. Dahpon Ho reexamines the Destroy the Four Olds campaign of 1966–67, reminding us that much of the passion and violence of the Cultural Revolution was actually about culture. Most importantly, he calls our attention to the many efforts of elites and ordinary people to resist the campaign of destruction. At the highest level of state power, Zhou Enlai and others intervened to save important monuments, and Central Committee directives warned that many famous sites were "state property" and should be protected as products of the genius of working people from China's past. Even the most radical central leaders of the Cultural Revolution had a soft spot for ancient Chinese culture, as bibliophiles protected rare books and antique lovers pilfered confiscated artifacts from state warehouses for their private collections.

The intricate dynamics of center and locality, of state and social actors, are dramatically chronicled in Ho's account of the heroic efforts of local cadres and residents to defend the Confucius temple complex in Qufu from a determined assault led by red guards descending from Beijing. Based in part on field research and interviews in Shandong, his analysis of the three-month siege in 1966 describes complicated shifting alliances, explosive confrontations, popular perceptions and motives, and the intervention of such leading Maoists as Chen Boda and Qi Benyu on the side of those who fought to spare the temple.

The red guard mobilization of the early Cultural Revolution brought some of the most visible and unforgettable acts of violence and destruction, but much of this early violence was against property rather than people. The much publicized assaults on teachers and party cadres were certainly cruel, painful, and deeply humiliating, but fatalities were the exception rather than the rule.[94] The greatest number of fatalities came in the middle period of the Cultural Revolution, the period from the formation of the revolutionary committees in 1968 to the death of Lin Biao in 1971. The next two chapters cover this period, and seek explanations for the mass violence that plagued many areas of rural China. In a comparative study of three provinces—Guangdong, Guangxi, and Hubei—Yang Su focuses on rural violence in the form of organized mass killings, a phenomenon rarely seen in the cities. Based on a careful statistical analysis of data from newly published official county-level accounts, Su shows that these massacres were not the work of crazed mobs, but were systematically organized by village militia or mass organizations. They were, furthermore, inspired by directives from the state center urging "preemptive attacks" on "class enemies" who opposed the restoration of order following the factional conflicts of 1966–67. When local zealots failed to find any real conspirators, they attacked the usual suspects: toothless "class enemies and bad elements" left over from the prerevolutionary past.

Yang Su's account, however, is not just a story of brutal violence by unaccountable state agents. His comparative analysis shows that the detailed Cultural Revolution records from Hubei reveal little of the mass killing seen in Guangdong and Guangxi. The provincial power structure was a critical factor explaining the extent of rural violence, and here the key variable was the exclusion of the rebel faction from the new revolutionary committees. Where they were excluded (as in Guangdong and Guangxi), the unchecked power of the victorious faction was more likely to condone violence against imagined enemies. His analysis is thus another powerful example of the way in which the interaction between state structures and local sources of social conflict helps explain the dynamics of the Cultural Revolution.

The next chapter, by Jiangsui He, continues the discussion of rural violence in this middle period of the Cultural Revolution, but instead of a broad comparison of several provinces, He offers a microscopic picture of violence in a single Chinese village—Yangjiagou, in northern Shaanxi Province. In contrast to Yang Su's focus on mass killings and the political circumstances that produced them, Jiangsui He examines in intimate human detail the murder of a single individual—landlord Ma Zhongtai. Her account challenges the standard party narrative that emphasizes intense class hatreds as the catalyst for land reform and revolution in the 1940s. Drawing her data from a Beijing University oral history project in the village, He argues that prerevolutionary Yangjiagou enjoyed considerable multi-class harmony. The Ma landlords dominated politically and economically, but the villagers appreciated their many welfare and security services. It was not class hatred that motivated the murder of Ma Zhongtai. Replicating in microcosm the pattern that Yang Su discovered in southern China, He finds that the beating death of Ma and the subsequent suicide of his wife were directly related to the formation of revolutionary committees and the Cleansing of the Class Ranks campaign that followed in 1969. We also see how the death of this elderly and harmless former landlord in an isolated Shaanxi village was linked to national political struggles, for Ma Zhongtai was the brother-in-law of a prominent party official who had come under attack in northeast China. When those attacks began, Zhongtai was sent back to his village, where the presence of a PLA unit and a series of fortuitous events left him hounded, assaulted, and killed by young toughs and local militia members. In Jiangsui He's account, Ma's death left the village traumatized and still in moral ruins in the 1990s—the prerevolutionary legacy of village community in shambles and the effort to instill a new revolutionary morality failed.

One of the least understood phases of the Cultural Revolution unfolded in the early and mid-1970s. The most violent excesses of the movement were now over; revolutionary committees had been formed in every locality, school, office, and factory to reestablish order and consolidate the revolution; and the Ninth Party Congress in 1969 had proclaimed the CCP's unconditional loyalty to the Thought of Chairman Mao. Then two years later, Lin Biao, vice-chairman of the party and Mao's "closest comrade in arms," perished in a mysterious plane crash and was denounced as a traitor. The fierce factional struggles that wracked the party became manifest, as radicals continued to promote a politics of "class struggle" while moderates focused on economic development and opening to the West, which began with Nixon's visit to China in 1972. The next three chapters use a variety of newly accessible official, unofficial, and archival sources, together with on-site field research, to shed light on this period.

In Chapter 6, Jeremy Brown takes us to the village of Xiaojinzhuang, which Mao's wife, Jiang Qing, cultivated as a rural model embodying the radical spirit of the Cultural Revolution. As a result, obscure Xiaojinzhuang was widely publicized in the national media, and countless groups made revolutionary pilgrimages to the village. In contrast to the chaotic and unscripted red guard movement of the early Cultural Revolution, the Xiaojinzhuang phenomenon looks like an elaborate theatrical production, complete with script writers, directors, stage managers, publicists, and performers. Culture is once again at the center of radical politics, and villagers were so busy performing that soldiers had to be brought in to do routine farm work. As Brown explains, the producers of this political drama were urban radicals who, in effect, colonized the village. This was not all top-down political manipulation, however, as some rural cadres and talented female performers and athletes seized the opportunity to escape the drudgery of agricultural toil. In the end, the death of Mao and the arrest of Jiang Qing brought the Xiaojinzhuang production to an abrupt halt. This cultural theme park failed miserably because self-serving urban elites made impossible demands, and because few were convinced of the authenticity of the model. This did not prevent the local beneficiaries from being cruelly scapegoated by new leaders once the fraud was exposed.

Sigrid Schmalzer's chapter on popular science in the 1970s explores another aspect of the politics of culture. Examining the politically charged arena of paleoanthropology—the study of human origins—Schmalzer takes seriously the Cultural Revolution's announced goal of promoting a new working-class epistemology. This implied a shift from "disseminating" scientific knowledge to the superstitious masses to developing a new kind of "mass science" in which "the people" played an active, even leading, role. Paleoanthropology had a special place in socialist science because it was inspired by Engels' notion that "labor created humanity," and because field research on human origins required a great deal of back-breaking physical labor. These special characteristics made it easier for nonspecialists to contribute to the scientific process. In the early 1970s, mass participants led expeditions; peasant workers were credited with finding, reporting, and protecting valuable fossils; and some amateur scientists eagerly criticized the work of their intellectual partners. In the end, however, neither the radicals nor the scientific elites took seriously the idea that workers, peasants, and soldiers possessed efficacious "knowledge forms or mental orientations" by virtue of their class position. The masses were seen as basically superstitious, and any understanding they had of science was viewed as the product of successful "dissemination." Here, of course, Schmalzer's chapter resonates with Brown's study of Xiaojinzhuang. Urban intellectuals, including Cultural Revolution radicals, continued to believe in the superiority of their own elite knowledge and proved unable to incorporate peasant wisdom into scientific inquiries of significant technical complexity.

In Chapter 8, Elya J. Zhang provides a dramatic example of the utterly unpredictable ways in which state actors and local agents interacted in the later Cultural Revolution. Her focus is Li Qinglin, an ordinary rural school teacher, a "nobody" who rose in helicopter-like fashion in the last years of the Cultural Revolution. Political "helicopters" were a common Cultural Revolution phenomenon, and the "helicopter" metaphor was pervasive. Mao needed radical allies to check the machinations of old-style party bureaucrats who had survived the early years of the Cultural Revolution and were now returning to power. The ranks of competent rebels were sparse, however, so it was necessary to identify, recruit, and swiftly promote people who might play the radical role.

Zhang's study of Li Qinglin, based on new documentary, archival, and interview data, including talks with Li himself and his family, is a compelling case study of the tragic (though sometimes comic) rise and fall of a very ordinary Chinese citizen. Li was a small-town teacher in Fujian. He was neither a party member nor a political activist. Li's life changed drastically when Mao penned a brief reply to his respectful letter complaining about the harsh conditions his two sons endured as sent-down youth in the countryside. Remarkably, despite Mao's repeatedly expressed interest in Li's case, local and provincial party members managed to deflect the Chairman's inquiries and block any investigation of wrongdoing. This stonewalling only ended when the provincial leaders' factional rivals championed Li's case in order to topple their adversaries. Li was rapidly inducted into the party and promoted in the provincial apparatus, where he responded eagerly to his new-found prominence. Once the Cultural Revolution ended, however, his fall was even more rapid than his rise. He was dismissed from all posts by the veteran party bosses, identified as a criminal follower of the Gang of Four, paraded and abused before countless mass rallies, subjected to various trumped up charges, and finally sentenced to life in prison.

Zhang's research, like the other studies in this volume, seeks to understand the Cultural Revolution as it was experienced at the local and personal level. Central party leaders and state actors are never absent from these accounts, but they were not in a position to control events. Insignificant local actors like Li Qinglin, the Qinghua red guard radical Kuai Dafu, or the village poet in Xiaojinzhuang were provided opportunities to advance their agendas and for a time they pursued them zealously. The newly available archival, documentary, and oral history sources allow us to follow these local actors, and their complex interactions with the contending levels and factions of the state. None of these local actors enjoyed a happy fate, but their stories tell us a great deal about the dynamics of the Cultural Revolution and its enduring historical legacy.

The Cultural Revolution ended in 1976. Or did it? This is the subject taken up by Liyan Qin in the final chapter of this book. Addressing the complicated legacies of the Cultural Revolution, Qin examines the ways in which former sent-down youth recalled their experiences in the countryside. Her careful analysis of widely read post–Cultural Revolution literary sources reveals ambiguity, denial, nostalgia, and ongoing debate. In the 1980s, many former red guards were drawn to the enormously popular novella *Snowstorm Tonight* by Liang Xiaosheng. Liang describes the urban activists sent to the frigid Northeast in the late 1960s as decent, idealistic, true believers who willingly sacrificed their youth in response to the call of Chairman Mao and the motherland. Liang's vivid portrayal captured the mood of nostalgia prevalent among sent-down youth who returned to the cities in the late 1970s and early 1980s. Feeling out of place in the brave new world of the post-Mao urban sector, they desperately sought meaning for their lives in their Cultural Revolution experiences of sacrifice and suffering.

By contrast, Wang Xiaobo's *Golden Age*, published in 1994, condemns any inclination to "aestheticize the ugliness of the past," and insists that it is a virtue to admit that one has been duped. Set in the lush borderlands of Yunnan, Wang's account downplays political theatrics in favor of intimate treatments of private life, sexuality, and the sent-down youths' profound alienation from the Maoist political system. Reflecting the mood of the 1990s, *Golden Age*, according to Qin's analysis, rejects the "hero-villain" binary so pronounced in nostalgia fiction, and presents instead protagonists who are full of contradictions: self-indulgent, narcissistic, cynical, but more recognizably human than the self-pitying characters in *Snowstorm Tonight*. As Liyan Qin's analysis of recent Chinese fiction suggests, China has not yet broken the hold of the Cultural Revolution on the imaginations and identities of those who lived through those turbulent years. Memory of the Cultural Revolution, like its history, remains a highly contested field.

CONTRIBUTIONS AND QUERIES

Taken as a whole, these studies reveal the multiple advantages of approaching the Cultural Revolution as history. The passage of time has permitted fresh perspectives and allowed us to see how the dynamics of political and social conflict have played out as an ongoing historical process. The accumulation of published and archival, official and unofficial sources, together with the availability of extensive oral history accounts permits a new level of detail and nuance that was impossible in the earlier generation of Cultural Revolution scholarship. Viewing the movement from some distance allows us to escape the categories and rhetoric of the day and look at the movement with fresh analytical lenses.

Nowhere are these advantages clearer than in the analysis of the social actors in the studies collected here. The first generation of Cultural Revolution studies was very much trapped in the discourse of the movement, as red guards were classified according to class background or the political status of their parents. These categories play a strikingly minor role in the analyses presented here, as it is now possible to describe key protagonists in much more human detail, with biographical backgrounds that are far more helpful in explaining their behavior than the stark classifications of "bourgeois intellectual" or "revolutionary cadre's children." A compelling analysis of the social forces acting in these years is possible precisely because we now begin to see Chinese society under Mao in its real complexity, rather than relying on the regime's imposed framework of "class struggle" between revolutionary and revisionist lines.

The passage of time permits and indeed compels us to consider the cultural consequences of the Cultural Revolution. Several of the chapters here remind us that culture mattered in the struggles of the 1960s and 1970s. Ordinary people fought to protect their local cultural monuments. Jiang Qing made cultural production the central theme of her model village. Ironically, however, more Chinese culture is being erased in the post-Mao China of shopping malls and skyscrapers, McDonald's and Starbucks, Hong Kong music and "hooligan literature." By and large this is happening with little political debate, and one wonders if this is a reaction to the politicization of culture in the Cultural Revolution, or whether the decade-long interruption of cultural transmission in schools and public rituals, the drastic thinning of the ranks of cultural elites through death and political persecution, so attenuated the vitality of the living tradition that it had little ability to resist the hedonism and nihilism of the present era.[95]

The studies collected here challenge the old conventional wisdom that the Cultural Revolution was fundamentally an urban phenomenon.[96] Yang Su's study of mass killings and the chapters on individual villages by Brown and Jiangsui He all bring rural China back into the picture. These and other studies noted above decisively document the spasms of violence that affected many parts of the Chinese hinterland.[97] Significantly, however, the few dissident academic voices who still defend aspects of the Cultural Revolution tend to focus on the rural areas, especially the spread of basic education and advances in health care, and their contributions to economic development.[98] Clearly mass violence did not happen everywhere, and the regime's attention to rural welfare (and the dispatch of millions of educated youth to the countryside) seems to have benefited some villages. The contrast between the Cultural Revolution experience in urban and rural China is but one aspect of the significant patterns of regional diversity in this era and more research is certainly needed to clarify the logic behind these patterns of spatial difference.

One of the greatest challenges and sources of fascination in the history of the Cultural Revolution is the remarkable combination of dictatorship and anarchy. The highly ideological atmosphere in which any personal act or expression could have political meaning led to a stifling uniformity in political rhetoric (loyalty to Mao, opposition to all forms of "bourgeois revisionism"), in culture and entertainment (the eight model operas), in dress and adornment (drab unisex clothing, short hair, no makeup for women). Any transgression of the stringent limits on personal or political expression could have the direst of consequences, and most urban residents had to be constantly on guard against giving offense to the defenders of revolutionary orthodoxy. On the other hand, since the party organization was paralyzed and the security apparatus overburdened, people were making their own decisions on how they should act within the ideological parameters laid down by the central Cultural Revolution leadership. The intense factional conflict that broke out among the red guards is graphic evidence of the fact that students were making their own (and different) decisions about the correct standards of political behavior. In a very real sense, participants in the Cultural Revolution were both victims and agents.

By treating Cultural Revolution actors as real human beings with complex backgrounds and conflicted motivations, the chapters in this volume help us to identify and remedy the simplifications of some past scholarship as we probe the choices people made. But we shall need more studies of this nature to fully understand how political authority was exercised by agents of the fractured and factionalized state, how individual social agents strategized to deal with the confusing yet deadly serious politics of this era, and the types of social bonds or networks that survived or were newly formed to help people cope with threats (and opportunities).

It is now almost forty years since the outbreak of the Cultural Revolution. The young men and women who grew up in this era are now the middle-aged leaders of China. Indeed, China's current president and general secretary of the Communist Party, Hu Jintao, was a student at Qinghua University, living through the events described in the chapter by Xiaowei Zheng. Because this was an age in which young people had to make choices for themselves, in a context where the political signals were not at all clear, they experienced a unique coming of age. Exactly how the Cultural Revolution affected this generation is still unclear. But the chapters in this volume bring us one step closer to understanding some of the grassroots dynamics of a most unusual historical era.

TWO

Passion, Reflection, and Survival: Political Choices of Red Guards at Qinghua University, June 1966–July 1968

Xiaowei Zheng

On June 3, 1966, probationary Communist Party member and first-year Qinghua University student Wang Fan spent a whole afternoon in the university amphitheater, pondering the implications of several recent provocative articles in *People's Daily*. For Wang Fan, the official endorsement of Nie Yuanzi's aggressive big character poster attacking the party authorities at Beijing University and the militant editorial "Smashing All the Ox Devils and Snake Spirits" augured the arrival of a violent political storm. Wang Fan, who came from an intellectual family and had studied at Shanghai's best high school, was a top student, an activist, and the chairperson of his class. Full of enthusiasm, he wanted to respond to Chairman Mao Zedong's clarion call to rebel against the "capitalist roaders"—the party authorities at his own university. However, the frightening notion that criticizing the party organization was equal to rightism was deeply entrenched in his mind; besides, he had just been cautioned by his department chair. Looking at the sunset, Wang Fan finally made up his mind. He persuaded several friends who were also student cadres in his class to join him, and together they drafted a big character poster for display on June 5. In the poster, Wang and his friends called the decision of the Qinghua party committee to build a separate canteen for female students a revisionist crime since no group should receive special privileges. Though the students could not, for the moment, identify any other serious errors of the school party committee, they expected that they would uncover serious faults one by one, just as the *People's Daily* editorial suggested. They believed that their poster would contribute to this exciting new campaign launched by Chairman Mao.[1]

Because of his bold condemnation of the school party authorities, Wang Fan became the Cultural Revolution leader in his class when an outside work team entered the campus four days later, on June 9. However, the work team's repressive and controlling style revealed over the following ten days made Wang Fan and his comrades doubt its origin and authority—did not Chairman Mao say that the masses should be entrusted with ultimate power during this movement? Without any insider information, these students inquired at the State Council's reception office and were told that the work team was sent by Mao himself. As a result, Wang apologized to the work team leaders for having doubts. To Wang Fan's surprise, the work team immediately branded him a counterrevolutionary for "organizing evil plots to damage the work team," and removed Wang and his comrades from their leading positions in the movement. Wang Fan was incarcerated and put under around-the-clock surveillance. At the time, he believed that he would be sent to a labor camp or the countryside for the rest of his life.[2]

At the same time, Wang Fan's older classmate, third-year chemical engineering student Kuai Dafu, was also imprisoned in an isolation cell because of his brash complaints about the work team. Born into a poor peasant family in Jiangsu, Kuai was the only one of six children that his family could send to college. Also a good student, Kuai's photo had appeared in a 1963 *People's Pictorial* as a role model for peasant children hoping to go to college.[3] Very outspoken and with a strong sense of social justice, Kuai once spent a summer investigating the devastating effects of the Great Leap Forward in his village and reported on the exploitive behavior of rural cadres to the National People's Congress. In the movement to study the nine commentaries critiquing Soviet revisionism published in *Red Flag* in 1965, Kuai had again become a model for his active role in "exposing unreliable thoughts" (*baolu huo sixiang*) and his eagerness to thoroughly rectify "selfish thoughts." Once the Cultural Revolution began, Kuai wrote posters to criticize the school's party leaders. Like Wang Fan, he was initially promoted by the work team to lead the movement in his class, but after openly expressing his dissatisfaction with the work team, he too was labeled a counterrevolutionary.[4]

At this moment, Kuai Dafu and Wang Fan, two students with very different backgrounds, were in the same boat and shared the same counterrevolutionary label. After they were released from confinement, Wang joined Kuai's tiny red guard organization and became one of Kuai's best writers. Later, however, they would choose different paths. When Kuai's group expanded and became dominant at Qinghua, Wang bailed out. He joined an opposing faction because he could not agree with Kuai's methods and approach in conducting the revolution. In the April 1967 ideological debate on rehabilitating the Qinghua cadres, Wang vigorously challenged Kuai's point of view, and in the bloody armed battle to come, the two fought each other at the risk of their lives.

In fact, like Wang Fan and Kuai Dafu, thousands of Qinghua students were seriously thinking and searching for what they believed would best represent Chairman Mao's cause, genuinely seeking and articulating their political ideals. The goal of this chapter is to shed light on the political choices of red guards at Qinghua University. At every crossroads of the Cultural Revolution between 1966 and 1968, what decisions did students make and what were their reasons? What were their underlying motives and how did these motives impel their political choices? This chapter uses fresh data—including interviews of former red guard leaders and activists—to explore why students were provoked to join the Cultural Revolution, and explain the immediate causes and longer-term origins of factional divisions among red guards.

Literature Review

The red guards have been a hotly contested topic in Cultural Revolution research. The dominant sociological approach developed by Stanley Rosen, Anita Chan, and Jonathan Unger emphasizes the importance of social groups, especially official class designations, in leading students to enlist in rival mass organizations.[5] Focusing on secondary schools in Guangzhou, the authors assert that after the early 1960s, the increasingly difficult prospect of moving upward, along with the shifting criteria for university admission and Youth League recruitment, exacerbated the competition between students from "red" class backgrounds and "middle" class backgrounds. After 1962, the antagonism grew so strong that it became the most crucial variable affecting factional alignment in the Cultural Revolution.[6]

The political approach of Andrew Walder, on the other hand, posits that it was students' differing responses toward the work teams that forced them into opposing groups.[7] Using evidence from Beijing's universities, Walder finds that during the work team period, because of the unclear political circumstances and scarce, misleading, and constantly changing information, students' positions and status before the Cultural Revolution provided no clear guide to their behavior during the Cultural Revolution. Red guard factions emerged when students from similar social backgrounds responded differently to the work teams. Later on, students of different factions struggled to justify their earlier actions and avoid the wretched fate of political victims—the red guards "were fighting not to lose."[8]

In part, the divergence between the political interpretation and the sociological approach reflects the distinction between university and high school red guards and the different geopolitical locations of Beijing and Guangzhou. Rosen, Chan, and Unger's data are still compelling in linking factionalism to class labels in Guangzhou's secondary schools. Far away from the political center, Guangzhou's students were much less sensitive to or even unaware of the center's constantly changing political signals. Moreover, Guangzhou's secondary school red guard organizations were formed with the direct help of Beijing's secondary school red guards, who used the bloodline theory of family class status as their organizing principle.[9] In fact, when Guangzhou red guards Dai Hsiao-ai and Liu Guokai wrote their memoirs in the 1970s, they repeatedly stressed the importance of the bloodline theory, indicating the actual influence of class labels on students' choices in becoming red guards.[10]

On the other hand, Walder correctly argues that static pre–Cultural Revolution group interests based on class labels did not play an obvious role in universities. Indeed, different attitudes toward the work team were the direct and the most obvious basis for the initial factionalism in universities. There was no simple one-to-one correspondence between students' backgrounds and their factional affiliation, especially in a school like Qinghua, where the impact of class background had been greatly reduced in the stricter political investigation (*zhengshen*) after 1963. However, why exactly did students respond to the work team at Qinghua so differently? Why did people like Kuai Dafu and Wang Fan, despite their favored political position, challenge those in power? How do we explain the 1967 split between people like Wang and Kuai, who had no need whatsoever to justify their behavior toward the work team?

There is one early study by William Hinton of the Cultural Revolution at Qinghua. Based solely on interviews conducted under the Workers' Propaganda Team occupation of Qinghua in the early 1970s, Hinton's understanding was compromised by limited access to alternative voices while the

Cultural Revolution was still in progress.[11] Now it is time to look back at this important university again.

This chapter hopes to complicate the story that Walder tells about faction formation in the universities. It is certainly true that during the movement, students were constantly engaged in opportunistic speculations in unpredictable political circumstances. However, students did not base their actions solely on self-interested calculations of the center's signals. Their passions and political convictions also played a crucial role. Passion and convictions, in the extremely volatile political atmosphere of the first fifty days of the Cultural Revolution, emboldened student activists to behave according to their own thinking and offered them the much needed confidence to pit themselves against various overbearing authorities. Later, convictions were fine-tuned ideologically. It was these increasingly crystallized ideological standpoints that redefined the groupings of the Qinghua students. Such ideologies were genuine and important: they were almost the sole resource allowing the out-of-favor faction to stick to its cause. Though ideologies might have developed through struggle, they were not simply added on as rhetoric or "legitimation."

The focus here is on the experiences of student leaders and activists in the movement. In the Cultural Revolution, followers switched organizational affiliation according to which way the political wind blew; leaders and activists, who had invested much more in a particular course of action, showed greater commitment and consistency. Thus, it is mainly through the latter that one defines the different ideas and actions of the competing factions.[12]

The Qinghua Dilemma: Stuck between Redness and Expertise, Obedience and Independence

Qinghua University was meant to be a model institution producing graduates who were both "red and expert." Even before this slogan was officially proposed by Mao in 1958, Qinghua party secretary Jiang Nanxiang declared his intention in 1952 to build Qinghua into a "cradle of red engineers."[13] Mao Zedong later proclaimed that education was supposed to make students develop their morality, knowledge, and physical condition as a whole, and to create laborers with both knowledge and socialist beliefs.[14] Quickly, Jiang Nanxiang followed Mao's lead in drafting his concrete plan for Qinghua. In moral education, students should learn Marxism, Leninism, and Mao Zedong Thought, participate in production, and learn from peasants and workers. As for expertise, students should master calculus, basic scientific theories, experimental skills, and at least one foreign language; they should conduct research and solve problems independently. In addition, physical training should prepare students to work in good health for their country for at least fifty years.[15]

In large part, Qinghua achieved these goals. From 1958 to 1966, fifty-nine new laboratories were built and 4.6 billion yuan were allocated to the school.[16] The curriculum was rigorous: a complete undergraduate education included theory classes, discussion and problem-solving, laboratory experiments, project design, practical training, testing, and thesis design.[17] With a faculty made up of China's best scientists and engineers, Qinghua shaped students to become experts in their fields. In 1959, at an average age of only twenty-three and a half, Qinghua students designed and manufactured China's first nuclear reactor.[18] Qinghua students were red, too. In 1961, Jiang Nanxiang defined redness as "the two upholds and one obedience," that is, "to uphold the Communist Party's leadership and socialism" and "to obey the state's orders on job assignments."[19] This definition was clear-cut and enforceable—it put the issue that concerned students most, job allocation, completely under state control. Many interviewees reported that the political education was persuasive and successful, and each year Qinghua graduates were sent to every corner of the country, hoping to contribute to the motherland.[20]

On the surface, redness and expertise seemed successfully combined. The Qinghua party leadership made clear that the only way to become a student cadre was to be both red and expert. Students were stratified according to this dual standard. At the top were student cadres, with excellent academic credentials and at least fair class labels, or whose political performance was excellent while their studies were decent.[21] With regard to the composition of the school cadres, the Qinghua leaders also tried their best to combine redness and expertise. Since all department party secretaries and chairs were required to be full professors or at least associate professors, the best minds at Qinghua were recruited into the party machine and nominally became part of its political elite.[22]

Nevertheless, beneath the surface, the tension between redness and expertise remained intense. Many students felt trapped: "The emphasis on expertise urged us to judge people according to their true ability, while the general emphasis on class background held against this view."[23] In fact, not just the students, but the entire school was suffering from the same predicament. Even though Jiang Nanxiang always claimed that the university's 108 professors were "the most precious treasures of Qinghua" and it was true that these professors received an average monthly salary as high as 267 yuan, many were often put in a precarious position by Jiang and his Qinghua party committee.[24] Often, politically suspect professors and teachers became the targets and scapegoats of political movements. In the 1957 Anti-rightist campaign (*fan you*), Jiang and his party apparatus arbitrarily identified 571 rightists, many of whom were faculty members.[25] During the Great Leap Forward, the Qinghua leadership's statement that "we should be too left rather than right toward the teachers" was cited by Mao as a model for all China's schools. Again, in the 1959 Anti-rightist-tendency campaign (*fan youqing*), teachers were harshly criticized.[26] Thus, as one teacher later argued in the Cultural Revolution, professors who earned 200 yuan were not as privileged as cadres who earned 70 yuan. When the cadres abused their political power, they were more reactionary than the professors.[27] These inherent conflicts between party cadres and teachers in the Qinghua structure became so prominent that they became a focal point in the later split among red guards.

Despite Jiang Nanxiang's attempt to balance redness and expertise, the school's party organization was dictatorial and oppressive. Before the Cultural Revolution, the Qinghua party organization (proudly called a "leak-proof engine" by Jiang) was the school's absolute ruler.[28] With frequent group study sessions held by each unit, party leaders ensured the rigorous supervision of each party member in the 18 general party branches (*zongzhi*) and 238 party branches (*zhibu*).[29] In order to control students more effectively, in 1953, Jiang Nanxiang initiated a political counselor (*zhengzhi fudaoyuan*) system, which selected party or Youth League students who excelled in both academics and politics to become counselors.[30] Political counselors were usually seniors or graduate students. Counted as half-time paid cadres, these counselors organized politically active students to attend short-course party schools, selected student cadres in each class, arranged political educational programs, and helped to identify "backward" students who had either moral or academic problems and reported them to the school authorities.[31] Through the counselor system, the commands of the school authorities could reach every single student, fortifying the absolute control of the party.

Remarkably, the school's rigid political control did not prevent students' independent intellectual adventures, largely due to the school's dual emphasis on both expertise and redness. As Wang Fan eloquently put it thirty years later, "Even though the state and the school party organization forced us to be obedient tools, the academic training encouraged us to love exploring and to seek truth with an independent spirit."[32] The university provided a three-year course on Marxist-Leninist theory and numerous talks on domestic and international politics.[33] The course provided students with a sociological vocabulary to analyze society, while the various talks equipped them with a solid grasp of political conditions and fostered a strong political consciousness. Even in the dry theory course, students applied their truth-seeking spirit. They seriously discussed national affairs and diligently honed their debating skills. To a great degree, it was Jiang Nanxiang's education that empowered students to think and make their own independent judgments. Ironically, the Qinghua students, pining for a more active role in a participatory politics, made the party authorities their first political target as their passions were unleashed in the Cultural Revolution.

A left wind blew hard after 1962. Following Mao Zedong's 1962 Beidaihe speech emphasizing class struggle, Qinghua was pressured to recruit more students with "good" class backgrounds and higher political reliability.[34] However, because of Jiang Nanxiang's special standing in the Education Ministry, the school still had leeway in deciding quotas for each province and made its own admission decisions.[35] As a result, Qinghua had a disproportionally large number of undergraduates from the three places that provided the highest quality students: Beijing, Shanghai, and Jiangsu.[36] Though class origin became increasingly important, whenever the pressure let up a bit Qinghua would recruit academically first-tier students. For example, in 1962, when political performance was emphasized over class origins, Qinghua adjusted its original admission plan by 20 percent so as to admit more students with high scores.[37]

As the atmosphere outside the university became increasingly politicized, Qinghua's consistent emphasis on study made it seem revisionist. On February 13, 1964, the first day of the lunar New Year, Mao held a meeting of national educators to reform China's educational system. He harshly criticized the school system, saying that too many courses were killing students and the tests were like ambushing enemies. He ordered that the length of schooling be shortened and the number of courses be cut in half.[38]

Jiang Nanxiang reacted quickly. He actively grasped Mao's directive to combine schooling with production and used Qinghua's school factory as a way to show his adherence to the Maoist line. Also, after discussing the curriculum with some trusted teachers, he changed the six years of Qinghua schooling to five and a half years, but protected the important basics. Instead of radically changing the existing structure, Jiang did his best to maintain the strict schooling by tinkering with nonessential matters and argued that Mao's words needed to be interpreted before applying them to science and technology schools like Qinghua.[39] However, Jiang could not save Qinghua when Mao became angrier with the education system. In his famous May 7, 1966 letter to Lin Biao, Mao alleged, "the phenomenon of capitalist intellectuals dominating the schools must not continue!"[40] It was now impossible for Jiang to maintain Qinghua's system by making a few minor corrections. Still, Jiang made a last attempt to defend the university against Mao's charges. In a speech addressed to Qinghua's cadres, Jiang declared he would "lead his boat of ten thousand people against the wind" (*kai wanren dingfeng chuan*).[41] By doing so, Jiang put himself in great danger.

By this time, Qinghua's students were agitated. The constant political study on opposing and preventing revisionism (*fan xiu fang xiu*) and the incessant calls for readiness against a possible world war made everyone vigilant. Crucially, Mao's 1964 proposal regarding the five standards for revolutionary successors pushed students even more into politics and fanned their passion for political careers.[42] After 1964, a group of students, distinguished by their political enthusiasm and deep concern for matters of national importance, emerged and became increasingly active. They came from different class backgrounds (both red and middle classes) and occupied different positions in the Qinghua hierarchy, but their zealousness in applying Mao Zedong Thought to everything brought them together. Some of them were student cadres, but despite their favored status bestowed by the school's party organization, they held to their strong opinions and challenged the school authorities.[43] Jiang Nanxiang's "against the wind" stand irritated the enthusiasts who found their school head inactive in implementing Chairman Mao's call. For these "revolutionary successors," the Cultural Revolution offered a long-awaited liberating moment to break away from Jiang Nanxiang's dictatorial control and finally pursue political dreams of their own. Soon, everyone at Qinghua was thrown into an unprecedented political storm.

Passion in the First Stage: June–September 1966

On receiving the Central Committee's May Sixteenth Circular concerning the Cultural Revolution, the Qinghua party leaders found Mao's intentions by no means clear.[44] They understood that the Cultural Revolution was another political movement that they had to lead. But, who were the "representatives of the capitalists" and how was this group to be defined? And what was the goal of the movement?[45] As for the Qinghua students, most were overwhelmed by the flood of forceful editorials in *People's Daily* beginning in June 1966. The editorials incited them to take action: "Whether you truly support socialism will be judged by your activities and performance in this current Cultural Revolution."[46]

In this chaotic, confusing, and anxious climate, the first group of big character posters denouncing Jiang Nanxiang appeared on June 2.[47] Faced with criticism, the party quickly reacted. Cadres warned students not to criticize Jiang Nanxiang and equated student critics with the 1957 rightists. Furthermore, the school authorities mobilized their highly efficient party organization to orchestrate a poster-writing campaign by student cadres to counterattack the critics.[48] Under the direction of the party, the political counselors also ordered student cadres to work against the students who had criticized the Qinghua party apparatus.[49] On June 3, in one day, ten thousand big character posters allegedly appeared at Qinghua defending the Qinghua party leadership for sticking to the socialist line. The writers were the obedient student cadres. Feeling a sense of duty, they carried out their routine task of attacking those who criticized party authority.[50]

Classes stopped on June 3. At that moment, only the children of high-level cadres had any knowledge of what was going on. As soon as Nie Yuanzi's poster criticizing the Beijing University party leadership as a black gang was sanctioned and published in *People's Daily* on June 2, Liu Tao (daughter of China's president Liu Shaoqi) and He Pengfei (son of Marshal He Long) were summoned home by their parents, informed that Jiang Nanxiang had been labeled a capitalist roader by the Politburo, and urged to be active.[51]

On June 4, Liu Tao and He Pengfei each wrote a poster harshly criticizing Jiang as a revisionist. The tone of these two posters was trenchant and condescending, but because of the special positions of Liu and He, the posters had a huge impact on campus. At the outset, in addition to these children of high-level cadres, another group of students also stood out. This was the group of political enthusiasts who were excited about the movement and eager to contribute—both Wang Fan and Kuai Dafu belonged to this group. They, together with the high-level cadres' children, provided the momentum in this very first stage of Qinghua's Cultural Revolution. Responding to Mao's instruction to fight revisionism and impassioned by Nie Yuanzi's bold poster, these students condemned their school leaders as revisionists and black gang elements.

In these first seven days of Qinghua's Cultural Revolution, those who dared criticize the Qinghua party leaders all had the credentials to participate for they all came from "good" or "fair" class backgrounds. Students of "bad" class backgrounds were silent because life had taught them not to "consider political movements as a way to achieve anything."[52] They had no credentials to speak out. Thus, at this moment, student activism required both decent class status and a strong motivation to join in, but the motivation could be derived either from having high-level cadres as parents or from political passion.

Jiang Nanxiang was flexible. On June 5, as soon as he noticed the strangely identical actions of the children of high-level cadres, he took a proactive tack. One day after Liu Tao and He Pengfei's posters, Jiang made an impressive self-criticism—he welcomed all the posters and swore to follow the example of the students. He again organized the political counselors to write posters, this time ostensibly to criticize the Qinghua party leadership. However, despite his best efforts to follow and control the students, Jiang could not save himself and his comrades.[53] Party rule at the university ended on June 9, when an outside work team comprising 513 members entered Qinghua. Under the work team regime, the former power-holders became the objects of dictatorship (*bei zhuanzheng*). In one-on-one interrogation sessions, the work team forced teachers to inform on each other. It classified the 2,450 teachers of Qinghua into twenty-seven categories. One hundred thirteen cadres were identified as capitalist roaders, sixteen professors as reactionary academic authorities (*fandong xueshu quanwei*), and fifty other teachers as ox devils and snake spirits. From June 12 to 16, 103 cadres were forced to parade around the campus to be humiliated in public. Political counselors were labeled "black lackeys" (*hei zhaoya*) and student cadres as "black sprouts of revisionism" (*xiuzhengzhuyi hei miaozi*).[54] They were removed from their positions by the work team.

The work team utilized the red class children and the anti-Jiang enthusiasts as its power base.[55] These students were assigned to Cultural Revolution committees at different levels to lead the movement. The work team granted students the right to humiliate their former school leaders. With the sanction of the work team, the students' activities became violent. Teachers and party cadres were humiliated and, for the first time at Qinghua, some were beaten. Political counselors who carried out everyday party management became the direct targets of the radical students.[56] However, bearing in mind the out-of-control result of the Hundred Flowers movement, the work team became afraid that the movement would veer off track. It then demanded absolute control of the movement by identifying the targets and determining the format of each struggle meeting.[57]

Among the new beneficiaries in the work team regime, some were content with the power granted by the work team and submissive to its orders. However, the dictatorial style of the work team did not satisfy everyone. Some of the political enthusiasts, who had just been liberated from the previous rulers of the school and were eager to make revolution in their own way, felt disillusioned. They hated the work team's overbearing manner and its "sneaky" methods of using secret inquisitions to carry out the movement.[58] Instead, they wanted an open revolution and wanted to lead it themselves, and they did not hesitate to express their antagonism toward the work team.

Kuai Dafu was the leading figure of this anti–work team action. Although handpicked by the work team to lead the Cultural Revolution committee in his department, Kuai challenged the authority of the work team by alleging that "it was not likely to have been sent by Chairman Mao" and that the members of the work team were actually conservatives.[59] On June 16, Kuai Dafu openly interrogated the work team in a poster entitled "Where Is the Work Team Going?" In this poster, he rejected the work team slogan that "we should infinitely trust the work team" and claimed that "we will struggle against those who oppose Mao Zedong Thought, no matter how high he stands or who he is."[60] On June 21, Kuai commented on an anti–work team poster: "The key to revolution is power. We succeeded in seizing power from the school party. Now, we have to think whether the current power-holders really represent us. If not, we have to seize power from them again!"[61] The conflict intensified on June 22 when work team member Wang Guangmei (Liu Shaoqi's wife) failed to show up at a discussion meeting planned for Kuai's class. Feeling fooled, Kuai reacted drastically by posting a provocative poster addressed to the work team's leader: "Comrade Ye Lin, What Is Going On?" In this poster, Kuai and his ten diehards questioned the work team's political intentions and its seriousness in conducting revolution.[62] Kuai told the work team leader: "We can conduct the Cultural Revolution by ourselves. Before you came, we had already been doing that for a long time!"[63]

Kuai then asked for a school-wide debate to be held on June 24 on whether to support the work team. At the meeting, Kuai argued powerfully against the work team, lacing his speech with quotations from Mao. He accused the work team of disregarding the masses and constraining their revolutionary actions.[64] Outraged and humiliated, the work team decided to make Kuai their major target and started persecuting "Kuai-type people" (*Kuaishi renwu*). Hundreds of posters appeared the day after the debate, all generated by the work team to criticize Kuai. On June 26, Kuai went to the State Council and Party Central Committee to complain, but his efforts were to no avail. Kuai was identified as a counterrevolutionary and deprived of his Youth League membership. He was put into an isolation cell two days later.[65] Just as they treated Kuai, the work team also attacked Wang Fan, labeling him a Kuai-type person, and jailed him.[66]

There was something unique about these Kuai-type people. In general, they were fervent political enthusiasts who wanted to be "revolutionary successors." Many also held a strong sense of social justice. They noticed the oppressive bureaucratism of the party organization and sincerely believed that its injustices must be fixed. For instance, as a high school student, Kuai Dafu had written a letter to the National People's Congress, reporting the sufferings of ordinary peasants in his hometown in Binhai, Jiangsu. Believing that the local party organization had gone rotten, he exposed the cadres' exploitive and oppressive behavior to the National People's Congress and begged the center to send down able leaders to fix the situation.[67] Passionately, people like Kuai longed for a movement of their own and abhorred the work team for treating them like meek sheep.[68]

Importantly, Kuai-type people had strong political credentials because of their previous revolutionary activities against the school authorities and their impeccable class background; some had been put in important positions by the work team. But these students also dared to follow their own interpretation of Mao's call, no matter who the power-holders were or what they thought. While the well-informed high cadres' children were satisfied with controlling Qinghua and some academically disadvantaged students were pleased to see the downfall of the previous school leadership, these Kuai-type people kept advancing their own cause and were determined to lead the political movement in their own way. A characteristic of these students was their audacity. Most Kuai-type people were first- or second-year undergraduates at Qinghua—they had only a shallow understanding of the earlier 1957 Anti-rightist campaign and were so confident that they freely pointed out the problems of the work team. It was their political passion to lead the movement that pulled them into the torrent of Mao's plan to dismantle the party-state apparatus and push the movement on.

In its anti-Kuai movement, the work team divided the students. It made some students its supporters; at the same time, it identified fifty counter-revolutionary Kuai-type people, namely, students who opposed the work team.[69] Five hundred people were criticized and asked to provide drafts of their anti–work team posters and letters. Two tried to commit suicide: one died and the other was left permanently handicapped. People who had supported Kuai, signed Kuai's posters, or even applauded Kuai during a debate, were investigated, accused, and forced to confess by the work team.[70]

The political wind changed suddenly after July 18, 1966, when Mao came back to Beijing. Kuai Dafu and others were freed and the emphasis of the Qinghua movement switched back to attacking the Qinghua party authorities. On July 23, 25, and 26, Chen Boda, Kang Sheng, and Jiang Qing attended consecutive meetings at Beijing University, discussing the mistakes of the work teams.[71] On July 27, a poster by Wang Xiaoping, daughter of the Central Cultural Revolution Small Group (hereafter, Central Group) vice-head Wang Renzhong, appeared on the Qinghua campus and openly criticized the work team for following a "mistaken line" (*luxian cuowu*).[72] Two days later, at a meeting of Cultural Revolution activists, Liu Shaoqi and Deng Xiaoping made self-criticisms for dispatching work teams. Also on the same day, the work team started to withdraw from Qinghua.[73]

Still, the political signals at the Qinghua campus were mixed. Even though Mao had Kuai Dafu specially summoned to attend the meeting of Cultural Revolution activists and secretly sent Premier Zhou to speak with Kuai on July 30 and again on August 1, power-holders from the work team period were the absolute majority of the Qinghua delegates to the July 29 activists' meeting.[74] On the one hand, more students dared to show their dissatisfaction with the work team and display their sympathy for Kuai after Qinghua's loudspeakers broadcast the July 29 activists' meeting on July 30. On the other hand, the work team's former supporters, especially the children of high-level cadres, still held "official" power. Led by Liu Tao and He Pengfei, they dominated the Qinghua Cultural Revolution Preparatory Committee, an executive organ established by the work team as its successor. To solidify their base, Liu Tao formed an association of poor peasants, workers, and revolutionary cadres (Pinxie) on August 2. However, the association did not win widespread support among Qinghua students; rather, many regarded it as simpleminded and meaningless.[75]

Hence, there was a disparity between Mao's directive and the actual understanding of it at Qinghua. The work team problem remained unsolved: no work team leader had conducted a thorough self-criticism and no official rehabilitation had been granted to the Kuai-types. For the persecuted Kuai-type people, the situation was no better even after Premier Zhou's visit to Qinghua. On August 4, Zhou led a large convoy of limousines carrying central and provincial leaders to Qinghua for a meeting that supposedly rehabilitated the Kuai-type people and praised their "rebellious spirit." The premier claimed that the work team had severe faults, but he also rebuffed requests to discuss the work team's problems and directed that the Preparatory Committee left by the work team be recognized as the leader of Qinghua.[76] As a result, the Kuai-type people were still stigmatized by the accusations made by the work team, whereas the Preparatory Committee announced on August 7 that it would "concentrate fire on attacking the black gang and black line."[77]

Antagonism between students continued unabated. On August 8, a dozen students who wanted to continue discussing the work team problem and fully reinstate the Kuai-type rebels organized the August Eighth Liaison (hereafter, Eights). The cofounders, Wu Dong, Tang Wei, and Chen Yuyan, were all from "good" class backgrounds. Offended that the work team had not publicly admitted its mistakes, the Eights insisted the work team return to Qinghua to apologize so that the students with a rebellious spirit (*zaofan jingshen*) could be truly rehabilitated.[78] One day after the founding of the Eights, Wang Guangmei urged the Preparatory Committee to form a mass organization, the August Ninth Liaison (hereafter, Nines), as its power base.[79] As the beneficiaries of the work team, leaders of the Nines refused to deal with the work team's faults. Since the Nines were organized by the Preparatory Committee, which held power on campus, the struggle with the Eights became a fight over power. The process of organized factional division at Qinghua had begun.

The external political situation favored the anti–work team group. On the afternoon of August 8, just after the formation of the Eights, the sixteen points of the Central Committee, which clearly criticized the policies of the work team as misguided, were broadcast at Qinghua.[80] On August 15, Mao's poster "Bombard the Headquarters," which accused the work team of unleashing a "white terror" on campus, appeared at Qinghua.[81] Remarkably, however, inside Qinghua, the pro–work team August Ninth Liaison still dominated. Some children of cadres among the Nines formed a picket corps. They wore their parents' intimidating army uniforms to show off their sense of superiority and power. Ordinary students felt much safer joining the Nines because the group had been initiated by Qinghua's power-holders, that is, the Preparatory Committee, which had been sanctioned by Premier Zhou on August 4. As a result, the Nines became the overwhelming majority, while the Eights were only an intrepid minority. In promoting their agenda, the Eights decided on August 17 that they had to openly rehabilitate Kuai to affirm their "rebellious spirit." The Eights initiated a school-wide discussion on August 19 in an effort to refute what they felt were rumors about the Kuai-type people. In the middle of the meeting, the Nines' picket corps rushed into the meeting hall and beat people who made favorable statements about Kuai, shouting "Revolutions are for leftists only, and rightists should not even think of shaking the sky!" They occupied the meeting hall and ended the debate.[82] In this first major clash between the two groups, which was later called "the August 19 incident," the Nines trampled the Eights by resorting to violence.

Tension between the two groups intensified after Mao's August 18 red guard mass rally in Tiananmen Square, which stimulated the formation of red guards nationwide. On August 20, the Nines organized their key members into the Qinghua University Red Guards, with Liu Jufen, daughter of Liu Ningyi, chair of the National Federation of Trade Unions, as their leader. The members of this group were exclusively children of cadre background.[83] On August 22, the Eights formed a hard-core red guard group, the Mao Zedong Thought Red Guards. Unlike the elitist Nines' red guards, not only did it include the children of middle peasants and professionals, but the majority were children of ordinary peasants and workers.[84]

The political winds encouraged the Eights to establish their own red guards. On August 22, the very day that the Mao Zedong Thought Red Guards were founded, Premier Zhou Enlai went to Qinghua a second time. During the visit, the premier officially informed the students that the work team had followed "a mistaken line" and exercised "a capitalist dictatorship." The work team leader, Ye Lin, publicly apologized to the students.[85] Even so, the Eights and their Mao Zedong Thought Red Guards were few in number and often in danger. Leaders of the Eights had not been persecuted by the work team; thus the formation of the Eights and their Mao Zedong Thought Red Guards cannot be reduced to self-interest. Repeatedly overwhelmed and trampled by their antagonists, the Eights still insisted on splitting from the powerful majority for they believed that they had the correct grasp of the Maoist cause of the Cultural Revolution, that the masses should be given absolute power and be the major force of the movement. As an Eights' leader articulated their position in his August 22 poster,

> When truth is first discovered, it is always believed only by a minority. Being a member of a minority is enormously difficult, for one has to constantly scrutinize one's thoughts to see if they represent those of Chairman Mao. . . . A minority must have faith in the masses. They must sympathize with the masses' initial difficulties in understanding Mao and endure the pain this entails. . . . Being in the minority also requires breaking free from one's ego, because if one puts self-interest first, one will be too afraid to remain true to one's convictions. . . . The minority must have the courage to stand up for what it believes. . . . We denounce those who only follow the political wind, and we must fearlessly fight against all kinds of attacks in order to pass on Mao's thoughts!

At the end of this poster, the author titled himself "a fighter for Mao Zedong Thought," wrote down his name, address, and class background, and welcomed people to join him.[86]

The formation of the two hard-core red guard organizations led to even more intense antagonism. On August 24, two days after the establishment of the Mao Zedong Thought Red Guards, the pro–work team Qinghua University Red Guards launched a "red terror." Allied with red guards of cadre background from eleven middle schools, they tore down all the posters of the Mao Zedong Thought Red Guards and all that attacked the central leaders who had sent the work team; they also savagely beat some members of the Mao Zedong Thought Red Guards. They then conducted their version of revolutionary action by beating the cadres. The Qinghua University Red Guards and their allies demolished the symbolic school gate built in 1911, and that night they forced 200 cadres out of their homes and made them carry heavy stones. The cadres were ordered to stand in a line carrying big rocks while the red guards stood on both sides, whipping them mercilessly with leather belts.[87]

The violence of the loyalist Qinghua University Red Guards drove many students toward the Mao Zedong Thought Red Guards. After the withdrawal of the work team, the Preparatory Committee and the Qinghua University Red Guards organized the school's former party and administrative cadres for hard, punitive manual labor. Seventy percent of the Qinghua cadres were subjected to hard labor. After the red terror, the Qinghua University Red Guards made the cadres work even harder, forcing them to labor under the scorching sun without being permitted to speak or even take a drink of water. Some cadres were put into temporary cells and interrogated.[88] This inhumane treatment of former cadres greatly alienated many students, especially the former student cadres, from the Qinghua University Red Guards. Moreover, the Qinghua University Red Guards' repeated assertion of the importance of class origins drove away those who were either from non–red class backgrounds or disgusted by the mindlessness of it all.[89] This was also the first official split involving a large number of Qinghua students—the Eights and the Kuai-type people on one hand, fighting against the Nines on the other.

Up until this point, a peculiar form of activism constantly pushed Qinghua's Cultural Revolution onward. This activism came from the political enthusiasts who had seriously participated in the movement and insisted on conducting it according to their own readings of Mao. Convinced that they had truly grasped the essence of the Maoist line, the Kuai-type people rose up since they believed that the work team was violating Mao's teaching that the masses should be given ultimate power. Also holding to what they believed to be the Maoist line, the Eights carved out their own way of fighting for a fair handling of the mistreated and a genuine vindication of their rebellious spirit, despite their overbearing and often violent antagonists. Their zeal in making revolution brought them together and led to their decision to form an anti–work team faction. Without any insider information or much thought of the consequences, they allowed their convictions, which sometimes threatened their own interests, to be the key driving force in the decisions they made. Therefore, for both the Kuai-type people and the Eights, this passion—derived from their worship of Mao Zedong Thought, their effort to understand Mao, and their yearning to put these understandings into action in what they considered a truly democratic fashion—was the main impetus of their activism.

It is true that in the first two months of the Cultural Revolution almost all the activists came from "good" or at least "fair" class backgrounds. The most prominent players—the steadfast rebels such as the peasant's son Kuai Dafu, the ordinary revolutionary cadres' children such as Wu Dong and Chen Yuyan, and the staunchest work team supporters such as the high-level cadre's son He Pengfei—all came from red class backgrounds. Many of them were already party members. Thus, neither political status nor class labels decided students' political orientation. What also needs to be noted is that in this very first stage of the Cultural Revolution, the political behavior of students was not simply a matter of deciphering political signals. Before August 8, the message that "the work team had done wrong" was too weak and vague at Qinghua to determine the anti–work team students' political stand.

At this point, the political behavior of students was not consistently or consciously a matter of pursuing self-interest. Students had not discovered the structural reasons for their different school experiences and located their interests. It was later, through the debates on the Qinghua cadres, that students learned to identify their positions in the pre–Cultural Revolution days and developed ideas about how to behave politically in the newly volatile atmosphere. Only then would Qinghua students systematically reflect upon the social implications of the Cultural Revolution and become more aware of their positions and interests.

Factions Redefined: Politics and Ideology, September 1966–May 1967

By September 1966, the signals from the center were too clear to mistake. Though trying their best to suppress the Mao Zedong Thought Red Guards' criticism of the work team, under heightened political pressure from Mao, the loyalist Qinghua University Red Guards shifted ground by sacrificing

Wang Guangmei.[90] The deepening accusations at the center against Liu Shaoqi and Deng Xiaoping led directly to the demise of the Qinghua University Red Guards. According to Mao's sixteen points, the major targets of the Cultural Revolution were the "party leaders taking the capitalist road."[91] This put the Qinghua University red guards in a terrible bind, for some of the so-called capitalist roaders were their parents. On September 6, the Third Headquarters of Beijing College-Level Red Guards (hereafter, Third Headquarters), made up of rebel red guards, was founded and it soon gained the favor of the Central Cultural Revolution Small Group. Zhou Enlai met with Third Headquarters representatives on September 26 and stated that they were true proletarian leftists and that the charges made against them by the work teams and the factions that opposed them were mistaken. The leadership committee of the Qinghua University Red Guards resigned on September 29.[92]

By the end of September, the Mao Zedong Thought Red Guards had become the biggest faction at Qinghua. Now that their common enemy was gone, the festering disagreements between the Mao Zedong Thought Red Guards and Kuai-type people came to a head. Though the Kuai-type people were supposedly rehabilitated by the Mao Zedong Thought Red Guards, they had never been able to make their own voices heard. Dependent, they could not really resume their leading position and reestablish their reputation. Moreover, many members of the Mao Zedong Thought Red Guards, especially the former student cadres (many of whom had joined the Eights relatively late) distrusted the Kuai-type people. They disliked some Kuai-type people's defiance of authority and thought they were just chasing after fame.[93] However, such latent and unarticulated dislike was soon buried by another onslaught of politics.

After the establishment of the Third Headquarters, Kuai Dafu became its deputy chief and, on September 24, under the direct encouragement of the Central Cultural Revolution Small Group, Kuai established his own Qinghua organization, the Jinggangshan Red Guards.[94] At first, Jinggangshan had only a dozen members, made up mainly of Kuai-type people, including Wang Fan.[95] The new group's organizational principles were noteworthy: "Political performance is the most vital criterion for recruitment; though we generally require our members to have 'good' class backgrounds, we by no means rely on class origins alone."[96] Anyone who "has a sincerely rebellious spirit and acts according to Mao's thoughts and the sixteen points can join."[97] Even more surprising was the ominous quality of the group's declaration: "The two-line struggle has been intense from the outset of the Cultural Revolution. In June and July *some* party leaders at the center followed the wrong class line, and even up to this day Chairman Mao's sixteen points could not be implemented. . . . We will dare to remove any person from his position, no matter how high, if he defies Mao Zedong Thought."[98] Only one week later, the Central Group took aim at the "bourgeois reactionary line" (*zichan jieji fandong luxian*) and Kuai Dafu became one of its most stalwart vanguards.

On October 6, 1966, all the central party leaders (except for Mao and Lin Biao) attended a mass meeting to formally launch the campaign against the "bourgeois reactionary line." At the meeting, Zhang Chunqiao announced an urgent directive from the Central Military Committee, demanding once again the rehabilitation of those labeled counterrevolutionaries by the work teams and stressed that this directive was "applicable to every school."[99] This clearly showed that the targets of this campaign were power-holders like Liu Shaoqi, who was blamed for sending the work team. At this crucial meeting, it was Kuai Dafu who led one hundred thousand university students in swearing an oath to attack the capitalist roaders. Overnight, Kuai became a superstar.

Back at Qinghua, Kuai's originally tiny Jinggangshan Red Guards soon became the largest organization at Qinghua. Kuai's unmatchable position and his group's loose admission requirements attracted all kinds of "impure" people: the rank and file of the former Nines, and even students with bad records or family problems. All this made the former student cadres of the Mao Zedong Thought Red Guards very uneasy over Kuai's burgeoning power. Even within the Jinggangshan Red Guards, veteran rebels such as Wang Fan could not agree with this hasty growth of his own group.[100] Starting on December 1, Kuai attempted to unify Qinghua's three major red guard groups, Jinggangshan and two subsections of the Mao Zedong Thought Red Guards.[101] Jiang Qing and her allies greatly hastened the process of unification. On December 18 Zhang Chunqiao was sent to urge Kuai to be more vigorous in uniting all of Qinghua's students. Zhang also informed Kuai of the Central Group's specific target in the movement and asked Kuai to take the lead.[102] Just one day after Zhang's visit, a unified Qinghua University Jinggangshan Corps was established with Kuai as its commander in chief.

Clearly, the rise and fall of red guard factions was strongly influenced by the sponsorship of central political figures. The once-powerful Qinghua University Red Guards suddenly crashed and burned, while the formerly humbled Kuai Dafu now led the majority of Qinghua students. But even under direct manipulation by the center, differences among students and distrust of the stigmatized students by former student cadres persisted and gradually became more pronounced after the establishment of the Jinggang-shan Corps.

The first "feat" of the newly founded Jinggangshan Corps was the "December 25 Great Action." On the early morning of December 25, six thousand Qinghua students and teachers, dominated by Jinggangshaners, entered the center of Beijing via five different routes. They posted anti-Liu and anti-Deng posters, shouted "Down with the reactionary capitalist line," and sang propaganda songs.[103] This was an enormously influential mass action that publicly criticized Liu Shaoqi.[104] Its sensational display realized the hopes of the Central Group. On December 30 Jiang Qing and Yao Wenyuan personally went to Qinghua to congratulate Jinggangshan for its revolutionary enthusiasm and leadership.[105]

However, despite the outside recognition of the group's accomplishments, the action aggravated the group's inner tensions. Once the Jinggangshan Corps was established, Kuai built up his own circle, including his old dissident comrades from the work team period and others who had recently gained his personal favor. Kuai's ego was swelling. He soon ordered a special group of Jinggangshaners to compile the *Collected Works of Kuai Dafu*, much on the pattern of eminent central party leaders.[106] Faced with a string of Kuai's egotistic acts, only five days after the Jinggangshan Corps was founded, the former Eights' founder Tang Wei and three close associates withdrew. A young man of strong opinions, Tang Wei could not agree with Kuai on the December 25 Great Action. He considered it ill-advised and shallow that Kuai, instead of criticizing the mistakes of the reactionary headquarters, focused on humiliating Liu Shaoqi.[107] When Kuai rejected Tang Wei's advice, Tang resigned. In Tang's public resignation letter, he criticized Kuai's dictatorial work style and growing ego, the corps leaders' factionalism, and their disrespect for the masses.[108]

Tang Wei's criticism of Kuai's showy and radical style resonated with other former Mao Zedong Thought Red Guards, especially former student cadres. Although they had supported Kuai in criticizing the capitalist reactionary line, these student cadres found the newly formed Kuai clique too defiant and thuggish. For instance, the clique dared to ignore Premier Zhou Enlai's admonition and tricked Wang Guangmei back to Qinghua for a struggle session.[109] Moreover, these critics were concerned that Jinggangshan included too many people of "impure" class background and felt that the backgrounds of the Kuai clique (mainly the newcomers) were too "complicated" to be reliable. Some newcomers launched fierce attacks on the former school authorities. One person in the Kuai clique claimed that all Qinghua party members were rotten and needed to be removed because "they obtained their party membership simply by flattering leaders."[110] Such a raging tone perturbed many of Kuai's earlier supporters, especially the former student cadres who were drawn to the Eights and Kuai due to their revulsion over the Nines' maltreatment of Qinghua's cadres. Even Kuai's veteran allies, like Wang Fan and Sun Nutao, left him.[111] Resentment of Kuai and his clique was mounting. In fact, the first school-wide meeting after the foundation of the corps turned out to be a gathering to air complaints about Kuai. Many thought Kuai had gained his position too easily and that "only authority gained through real effort can be respected."[112]

Barely two weeks after the Jinggangshan alliance, these frustrations led to the open establishment of five regiments (*zongdui*), made up of the former Eights' leaders, which challenged Kuai's dictatorship.[113] Antagonism toward Kuai intensified when "his men" mistakenly attacked the Central Group advisor Kang Sheng. Kuai's core group claimed that Kang Sheng was a reactionary, which deeply irritated Jiang Qing and her Central Group allies. On January 22, 1967, Chen Boda telephoned Kuai twice, angrily ordering him to end the struggle against Kang Sheng.[114] Jiang Qing charged Kuai with "living off his past gains" (*chi laoben*).[115] The Central Group worried that as soon as the students gained power, they would slide off the track. In response to this criticism, Kuai on the one hand immediately distanced himself from the attack on Kang Sheng and warned his people away from the Kang Sheng issue. On the other hand, he stuck with his comrades, claiming that they had acted out of good intentions.[116]

For the anti-Kuai regiments, Kuai's blunder supplied a golden opportunity to take further action. On January 24 regiment leaders requested that the corps's headquarters be "rectified," and eight battle teams from different regiments established a liaison to rectify the Kuai clique's actions. Kuai regarded this as a personal challenge and overreacted by calling his critics Trotskyites angling for power. He then initiated a campaign against Tang

Wei and other former Eights leaders who were now in the regiments. The Trotskyite label was so vicious that it threatened to disrupt the unity of Jinggangshan, which concerned Jiang Qing. Jiang Qing ordered her secretary to tell Kuai of her position and two days later, on February 7, Kuai had to admit his mistake at a mass meeting and eventually rescinded the Trotskyite charge.[117] Of course, this did not quell the antagonism.

Having committed serious political mistakes and being challenged on campus, Kuai was still the golden boy in the eyes of the central leaders. On February 26 when Vice-Premier and Public Security Minister Xie Fuzhi received a Shanghai "power seizure committee," he urged Kuai, who accompanied him, to build a stable power base at Qinghua.[118] After *People's Daily* publicized the Guiyang Cotton Factory model of uniting each workshop and *Red Flag* publicized Mao's directive calling for a "triple alliance" of revolutionary cadres, students, and soldiers, the pressure on the regiment leaders was intense and it was increasingly difficult for them to survive as separate groups.[119] Faced with Kuai's demand that all groups above the level of a class (*banji*) be disbanded, the regiment leaders rolled them back into separate battle teams organized at the class level. At this point, the uneasiness about Kuai's radical and defiant manner was strong but still not openly articulated. The leaders of the regiments had been unable to come to terms with their concerns about Kuai; they remained helpless until the contentious issue of how to deal with cadres rose to the fore.[120]

On March 30, 1967, a *Red Flag* article specifically condemned the work team's reactionary policy at Qinghua and claimed that most of the Qinghua cadres were good.[121] The faltering regiment leaders quickly took notice, since the article resonated perfectly with their views on the former Qinghua cadres and they could finally absorb the cadres into the power center to replace Kuai's dictatorship. They soon plunged into the debate on Qinghua's cadres, which had been the focal point for Qinghua cadres and teachers for about a month after a March 1 *Red Flag* editorial entitled "We Must Treat Cadres Correctly."[122] These Qinghua cadres, who had never been rehabilitated after being removed by the work team, began to request the restoration of their rights. But many Qinghua teachers, who had been ruled and controlled by the party cadres before the Cultural Revolution, did not want to let the cadres off too easily. During the Cultural Revolution, these teachers had been liberated from the previous school party's dictatorship and sided with Kuai.[123]

The first step in the counterattack against Kuai's group was to lash out against the relatively vulnerable teachers' organization that supported Kuai. The reticence of the teachers to liberate the cadres could be interpreted as reactionary and was used to discredit Kuai. Regiment battle teams made up of former student cadres led the rhetorical assault on the teachers' organization for arguing that "all of Qinghua's cadres were rotten" and "professors who earned 200 yuan were more revolutionary than cadres who earned 46 yuan."[124] Shen Ruhuai, who had emerged as the most adamant regiment leader and had been the party secretary of his class before the Cultural Revolution, also turned his criticism toward the teachers' organization.[125] These regiment leaders had strong connections with the former Qinghua cadres. With this new national focus on Qinghua's cadres, they wanted to liberate the former cadres and at the same time discredit Kuai Dafu.[126]

Their chance came on April 12 when Kuai's clique made another serious gaffe, alleging that the March 30 *Red Flag* article on liberating the Qinghua cadres was erroneous.[127] Taking this opening, on April 14, Shen Ruhuai and other regiment leaders formed the April Fourteenth Liaison (hereafter, Fourteens) and called themselves the Liberating Cadre Liaison, a name that reflected a cause they truly cared about.[128] At this point, the second serious factional split among Qinghua students started.

The repercussions of this split were huge. After the divide, Qinghua cadres joined the Fourteens, which greatly enhanced this fledgling faction. On April 29, 147 Qinghua cadres posted a public letter, "To All Revolutionary Cadres and Cadres Who Want to Be Revolutionaries." In this letter, they claimed that the Fourteens followed Mao's teachings and were the most resolute group in fighting against the capitalist reactionary line.[129] As the former leaders of Qinghua, these party and administrative cadres were quite influential. Kuai and his followers were furious. On May 1 his group fired back, labeling the cadres' letter an attempt to restore the old Qinghua.[130] Such a strident stand by Jinggangshan drove these cadres and their student sympathizers to support the Fourteens, whose ranks grew rapidly.

From December 1966 to April 1967, the antagonism of the former student cadres toward the Kuai clique came into sharper relief as the movement developed. Soon, an ideological agenda was spelled out, which prepared the foundation for a powerful mass organization counteracting Kuai's corps. Starting at the end of April, ideological debates on Qinghua's cadres were passionately carried on by both sides. The Fourteens launched the first salvo, arguing that the Cultural Revolution had now reached a new stage and, following Mao's new "triple alliance" formula, that the task of the revolution should turn to building a new regime instead of advancing continuous seizures of power.[131] Since the majority of cadres were good, they should be included in the new regime.[132] On the other side of the debate, Kuai and his fellows blasted this "new-stage argument."[133] They maintained that if cadres were to be absorbed into the alliance, they must be carefully scrutinized and tested. The pro-Kuai teacher's organization, composed of some who were once mistreated by the cadres, also contributed to Kuai's cause. Following Kuai's argument that the Qinghua party members were rotten, they claimed that the cadres of the old Qinghua were corrupt as well. They maintained that since Liberation in 1949, the cadres had become the new privileged class. Though the cadres did not necessarily earn more than professors, their political privileges made them overbearing and oppressive. They were the social base of the capitalist Liu-Deng headquarters.[134]

Because cadres represented political authority in the old Qinghua system, the discussion of their role raised questions about how to evaluate the old Qinghua of the first seventeen years of the People's Republic, which in turn decisively affected one's understanding and assessment of the Cultural Revolution. The corps gave a rather negative evaluation of Qinghua's past seventeen years, while the Fourteens gave the past more credit—they disliked the corps's iconoclastic attitude of "repudiating everything and overturning everything" of the past.[135] These debates stemmed from deeper contradictions in the previous Qinghua hierarchy and the sociopolitical structure of the previous seventeen years. It was through such debates that the stratified nature of the previous power structure became clearer. Many interviewees recalled that such debates led them to reflect on the early People's Republic power structure and their own positions in it, and that these reflections influenced their later decisions.

Students began to understand their positions in the past more clearly and began to switch their initial affiliations as the debates deepened. Rapidly, the Fourteens expanded from around seven hundred people in the middle of April (before the debate) to about two thousand at the end of May.[136] The former student cadres overwhelmingly flowed to the Fourteens: an investigation by the Jinggangshan Corps revealed that by April 26, among all the student cadres of the eight departments surveyed, over 60 percent had joined the Fourteens and less than 20 percent had joined the corps.[137] According to the Fourteens, many of those who stuck with Kuai had been disadvantaged students in the past system—that is, they had either poor academic performance or "bad" class origins—and preferred a radical change.[138] At this point, the more articulated political analyses of the contending groups allowed students to make thoughtful and conscious political choices on factional affiliations. For the Fourteens, the ideological debates prepared a powerful foundation for the crueler organizational split to come.

Remarkably, there was a distinct group of idealist students who, despite their disadvantaged positions in the old sociopolitical structure, held strong beliefs that the first seventeen years of the People's Republic were dominated by the "red" line and "good" people. The Cultural Revolution, they believed, should not deny everything from the past. These idealists, including the Fourteens' theorist and key leader Zhou Quanying, played a crucial role in the group and ardently led the movement forward.[139]

The conflict intensified when, after May, the struggle to form a revolutionary committee became the dominant issue. A revolutionary committee was meant to represent a legitimate, formal, and long-term regime, and it was to possess the resources to eliminate any antagonistic force. Kuai took this as an opportunity to throw out the Fourteens once and for all, while the Fourteens were determined to fight back. Vice-Premier and Public Security Minister Xie Fuzhi was deeply concerned over the escalating confrontation between the two groups and he even summoned the leaders of Jinggangshan and the Fourteens and demanded they unite. But Xie was dreaming if he thought his pleas would solve anything. On May 21 Xie personally drafted a four-point document mandating an alliance. His plan allocated seven seats in the Preparatory Revolutionary Committee to Kuai and six to the Fourteens. Thus, the document actually granted Kuai control over the committee.[140] Naturally, leaders of the Fourteens flatly rejected the pact.

While Kuai's Jinggangshan had already established an election committee for the new regime and was preparing to celebrate its founding on May 28, in Yuanmingyuan, the nearby former imperial park, the agitated Shen Ruhuai and his diehards held a secret meeting. The situation, Shen stated, was that "either the fish dies in the net or the net is torn to pieces. Kuai is already contracting the net. The only way for the Fourteens to survive is to break our way out!"[141] In the early morning of May 29, 1967, Shen and other leaders of the Fourteens announced the establishment of the April

Fourteenth Headquarters, which marked the official organizational split from Kuai. The establishment of the April Fourteenth Headquarters had a great effect. The originally planned founding meeting of Qinghua's revolutionary committee did not happen because Zhou Enlai refused to attend due to the factional divisions at the school. This humiliation deepened the Jinggangshaners hatred of the Fourteens.

As we have seen, aside from the egos and political ambitions of some group leaders who wanted to lead the Cultural Revolution, there were deep ideological reasons for ordinary students to join the Fourteens. After teachers and cadres (who were more aware of their interests than the students) plunged into the students' debates, the previous Qinghua hierarchy became clearer. Students developed their ideas about this power structure and took sides in the better articulated debates. With an idea of how they would carry on the Cultural Revolution, though in a definitely weaker position and without any official backing from central leaders, the backbone of the Fourteens still stuck with their leaders and fought against Kuai, which required no uncertain commitment.

During these ideological debates, students gradually recognized their own interests; many switched affiliations according to their newly recognized identities.[142] It is true that many students' strongly held ideas were influenced by their past experience and social status in the pre–Cultural Revolution Qinghua system. However, there were idealists who chose sides according to neither status nor interests, but because of their opinions about Qinghua and socialist society in general. When red guards of both factions found that the larger discourses partially resonated with their own ideas, they believed that Mao shared their beliefs, which gave them confidence to carry on. As Ji Peng stated years later,

> Both sides were confident in their ways of carrying out the revolution and both sides actually found ammunition in Mao's statements. The Fourteens depended on Mao's new directive on alliances and his earlier argument on preserving a certain part of the old regime. On the other hand, Kuai's corps utilized Mao's theory of continuous revolution, which they interpreted as justification for their radicalism.[143]

Revolution in Practice: The Last Stage,
June 1967–July 1968

Zhou Enlai's no-show for Kuai Dafu's revolutionary committee crushed
Kuai's attempt to become the absolute leader of Qinghua. It also made both
factions understand the importance of central leaders' support when trying
to solve their internal problems. Trying to act on the signals sent by central leaders, both factions shifted their focus to the world outside Qinghua.
Such actions surged in July 1967 during the campaign to "drag out a small
handful in the army" (*jiu jundui yi xiaocuo*). Soon after the July 20 incident, when the Wuhan military district commander Chen Zaidao detained
Central Group members Wang Li and Xie Fuzhi, Kuai announced that he
would lead Jinggangshan troops to attack the capitalist roaders in the army,
"the armed Liu-Deng line."[144] He sent his Jinggangshan members to seize
power in many provinces and their newspapers endlessly denounced army
leaders. On July 29, hoping to ferret out more army reactionaries, Kuai led
his red guards to search the house of Xu Xiangqian, the chairman of the
military Cultural Revolution committee, and confiscated classified documents.[145]

In the meantime, the Fourteens also sent loads of followers to the provinces to struggle against the army.[146] They did not want to seem backward.
Besides "dragging out a small handful in the army," both factions followed
other calls from the center. They protested in front of the British embassy
when Britain allegedly mistreated Hong Kong residents.[147] On August 22,
1967, it was the milder Fourteens who aggressively burned down the British
embassy. Even though many members of the Fourteens questioned the sack-
ing of the embassy, the competitive pressure from Jinggangshan led them
to do so.[148] Students were stretching hard in their actions and rationaliza-
tions to over-fulfill the expectations of the central leaders so as to win their
support. In this stage of the movement, students were even more open to
manipulation from the center, which they were trying to please. This also
led them to deviate from their main goals and political convictions.

Although the students' actions were often inconsistent, their ideologies
grew to be increasingly systematic. Both factions displayed great theoretical
interest in pursuing the social implications of the Cultural Revolution. By
using Marxist class theory and terminology, they offered their own creative
interpretations of the upheaval and the preceding seventeen years. In August
1967 the Fourteens' theorist Zhou Quanying wrote one of the most famous

polemics of the Cultural Revolution period, "The Fourteens' Spirit Shall Win!" After being attacked by Jinggangshan's nationally circulated newspaper for weeks, Zhou's article influenced numerous red guards all over the country and was perused by Mao.[149] The article proclaimed the Fourteens' rationale. The Cultural Revolution, Zhou stated, "was a revolution led by the proletariat, who were also the leading class of the preceding seventeen years." As for the preceding seventeen years of the socialist regime, the overall class line "was correct and stable . . . and those who dominated were from the 'good' classes and the dominated were from the landlord, capitalist, and other 'bad' classes." Thus, Zhou opposed the idea that the Cultural Revolution should be a reversal (*da fan'ge*) of the past and that wealth and power should be redistributed. The article maintained that although there were problems with the central political regime, changes should be moderate and must not overhaul the entire sociopolitical structure.[150]

On the other side were the radical Kuai supporters who called on their followers to "smash the old Qinghua completely" (*chedi zalan jiu Qinghua*). Their principle was "wherever oppression is worst, revolution is strongest." For them, all Qinghua cadres were corrupt because Jiang Nanxiang had set up his successors among the young party cadres.[151] Thus, though the university leaders had already fallen, the danger from the second and the third generations of cadres persisted. In order to overthrow the past rule completely, Jinggangshan refused to give any power to the former cadres and insistently denounced the past seventeen years.[152] As we have seen, in this stage even though students at times acted irrationally and inconsistently in their effort to win the favor of higher-ups, and even though there was indeed a gap between their deeds and goals, they were still seriously thinking and reflecting upon the past.

By the end of 1967, Mao had backed off from supporting rampage and anarchy and the newspapers started to urge students to return to school. After the focus of the two factions shifted back to campus, the competition between Jinggangshan and the Fourteens degenerated into armed skirmishes. Jinggangshan persecuted several cadres who supported the Fourteens. In response, the Fourteens aggressively lashed out against some teachers siding with Jinggangshan. Although both sides suffered casualties, neither would stop fighting.[153] The trigger came in March 1968, when Nie Yuanzi incited an armed fight at Beijing University, devastating her enemy and opening the way to the establishment of her own revolutionary committee. Soon after that, in an April 1968 *People's Daily* article, Mao called on people to "never concede" when facing class enemies.[154] Inspired by Nie's success and encouraged by Mao's new order, on April 26, 1968, Kuai Dafu started the famous Hundred Day War in Qinghua.

Mao could not understand why his repeated orders to Qinghua students to stop fighting had no effect.[155] In the end, Mao turned to the method that he had earlier so harshly criticized—he sent in an outside work team. At noon on July 27, a Workers' Propaganda Team made up of more than six hundred workers and soldiers marched onto the Qinghua campus to halt the students' armed fights. The embattled Fourteens welcomed the team whole-heartedly, while Kuai, in an overwhelmingly dominant position, ordered his troops to open fire on the intruding force that had placed his final victory out of reach. As a result, five workers died and 731 were wounded. During the fight, Kuai sent a telegram to Mao. Appealing for help, he wrote: "At the direction of an unknown black hand, a force of one hundred thousand people entered Qinghua and was slaughtering the Jinggangshaners."[156]

Shocked and furious at what Kuai's group had done to his work team, on July 28, several hours after Kaui's followers had opened fire, Mao summoned five prominent red guard leaders to the Great Hall of the People and presided over a meeting that dragged on from 3:30 a.m. to 8:30 a.m. All the important Cultural Revolution leaders attended this meeting at which Mao made clear his determination to stop the armed battles in China's universities once and for all. At first, Kuai Dafu did not show up. Mao wondered why and asked sarcastically, "Isn't he trying to find the black hand? . . . How can he hunt it out? The black hand is me!"[157] For Mao, his original plan for a revolution in education was dashed by the very students he had hoped would carry it out. Mao said, "it has been two years since you vowed to struggle, to criticize, and to transform [the school system], but now, you do not struggle, criticize or transform. . . . When you struggle, you are just carrying out armed fights with each other!"[158] Mao had high expectations for Kuai Dafu, but the young leader had deeply disappointed him. But even at this moment, Mao still thought highly of Kuai: "In my eyes, Kuai Dafu is a good guy . . . [but] he was manipulated by some bad people around him." For Mao, using the work team to "oppress" Kuai was his only choice. In contrast, Mao labeled the Fourteens as "anti–Cultural Revolution." He especially resented a sentence in Zhou Quanying's famous polemic. Mao declared: "The Fourteens claim that 'The 414 Spirit Shall Win.' I am not delighted. They say that the people who won power could not maintain it. Does this mean that the proletarian class gained the regime but should give it up to the Fourteens?!" But Mao never interrupted the Fourteens' growth and even ordered Zhou Quanying to be released from prison.[159]

At this point, Mao had certainly changed his attitude and strategy toward using the red guards. Instead of allowing students to wreak havoc at all levels of the party-state, he wanted a more stable situation and hoped to begin reconstruction of the regime. He worried that his orders would not be carried out because so many pockets of armed conflict had popped up. Jinggangshan's blunder made Mao decide to abandon the use of red guards: "Now the young revolutionary generals are committing mistakes" (*xianzai shi xiaojiang fan cuowu de shihou le*).[160] Following the fate of Qinghua's red guards, workers' propaganda teams occupied all the schools in China and the once shining red guards were pushed off the stage. This also ended the spectacular history of Qinghua's red guards and their factional confrontations.

As we have seen, in this brutal last stage of Qinghua's red guard movement, ideological differences between the two factions were still developing and students kept pondering the ideological meaning of their struggle. However, the intense competition between the two factions distorted their behavior. In trying so hard to win support from the higher-ups, the students engaged in actions that became increasingly detached from their convictions. Later, during the intensive armed fights, survival and helping one's group and friends to survive took precedence. When Mao decided to eliminate the red guards, students were utterly vulnerable. There was little they could do but watch as the red guard movement quickly evaporated.

Conclusion

It seemed that the hatred between Jinggangshan and the Fourteens would last forever, especially after members on both sides had been killed or severely wounded. However, shortly after the Workers' Propaganda Team entered the campus, students calmed down. It was time for many students to leave school after these two intense years of Cultural Revolution. Hatred abated quickly when real-life problems—job allocations—demanded their attention. The sad and abrupt abandonment by Mao made some red guards realize the absurdity of their fights. As a red guard poem noted, "the Nines disintegrated with no gain; the Eights disappeared into nothing."[161]

Nevertheless, the absurdities and distortions of the students' behavior in the last stage do not mean that their choices came from nowhere or were patternless. Past studies of red guard factionalism have argued that the divisions lay in either different class labels or different relations to the work team. However, neither the political nor the sociological understanding of the red guard movement acknowledges a key characteristic of the Qinghua students during this time: they did have ideals and they did think. They did not simply develop factions based on their reactions to events or their perceived self-interest based on their situation in the pre–Cultural Revolution era. Rather, students were seriously developing their political understanding, pursuing what they thought were the right causes, and striving to realize their ideals through action.

This chapter stresses the role of passion and ideological convictions. At the opening of the Cultural Revolution, far from knowing accurately where their interests resided and acting accordingly, students tended to think rather abstractly about the correct course of action. In particular, the Kuai-type people and the Eights insisted on conducting the movement according to their own understandings of Mao. They rose up against their daunting enemies for they wanted to carry out the Cultural Revolution on their own and believed that the masses should be given ultimate power and trust, as Mao had said. It was this passion—derived from their worship of Mao, their striving to understand Mao, and their burning desire to apply this understanding in action—that led to the first division among students in Qinghua.

As the movement continued, the ideological debates about the previous school and sociopolitical structures played an increasingly crucial role in students' decision making. Starting from the debate on whether to rehabilitate the former cadres, clearly opposed political doctrines finally emerged after April 1967 and students' self-perception about what they were fighting for became clearer. Ideological standpoints were developed and clarified through struggle; they were not simply added on as "legitimation." Here, students' previous positions and experiences in the old school system tended to influence their behavior and students regrouped accordingly. Notably, it was this hierarchy of the Qinghua microcosm rather than the officially propagandized hierarchy composed of different bloodline labels that exerted more influence over students' decisions. Still, the link between their pre–Cultural Revolution positions in the school and their later factional

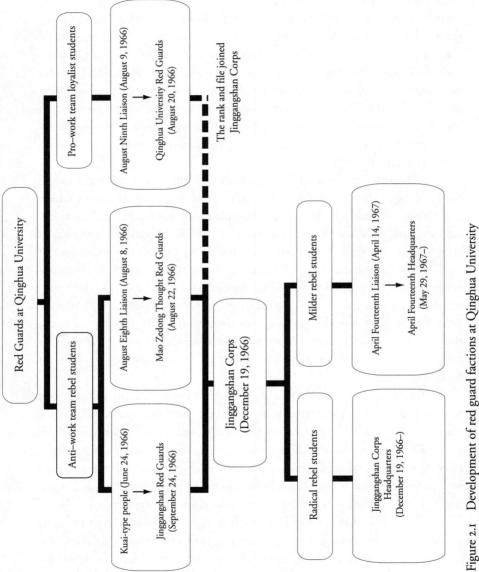

Figure 2.1   Development of red guard factions at Qinghua University

choices was not a one-to-one correspondence, as demonstrated by the political idealists.

In short, the activism and divisions of Qinghua's red guards arose from passion, political convictions, and their groups' efforts to survive; each carried varying weight in different stages. At first, the young students did not have mature and articulated political theories; later through debates they came to reflect on and understand the sociopolitical structure in which they lived and recognized their positions; and in the end, they desperately fought for the survival of their groups. Under ambiguous and changing circumstances, the reasons for factional divisions evolved through time. Nevertheless, ideals and conscious thinking were significant. Red guards at Qinghua made thoughtful political decisions in the face of unclear circumstance and did not base their choices solely on personal interests. Rather, they pursued what they thought were the right causes while struggling hard to adapt to ever-changing political circumstances.

THREE

To Protect and Preserve: Resisting the Destroy the Four Olds Campaign, 1966–1967

Dahpon David Ho

For the Mao Zedong Thought Red Guards who limped away from the Confucius Temple complex, the humiliating defeat of August 26, 1966, must have tasted worse than any bitter pill—it was blasphemy. The intrepid young warriors were supposed to "sweep away all ox ghosts and snake demons" and smash the old world to smithereens. Instead, they got an old-fashioned drubbing from officials and residents of Confucius's hometown of Qufu (Shandong Province) who had joined forces to protect the most "feudal" site in China. Even the poor and lower-middle peasants—whom the red guards claimed to represent—had not only refused to raise arms against the Confucius Temple complex but had even formed their own mass organization to *defend* it. The final straw was that for all their efforts the red guards were labeled a "little black gang" and forced to write self-criticisms. Somehow, the unthinkable had happened: "feudal old culture" had trounced Mao Zedong Thought. This confrontation, later known as the August 26 incident, was the opening salvo of a battle that might have roused even Confucius from his grave. When the red guards returned with a vengeance months later, they showed no mercy to the Kong family graveyard.[1]

Studies of the Cultural Revolution have, with good reason, focused on the destructive acts of red guards and the cries of "smash, burn, fry, and scorch" that accompanied them.[2] There is no question that destruction of cultural relics occurred on a massive scale during the high tide of iconoclasm in 1966–67. In Beijing alone, at least 4,922 of the capital's 6,843 officially classified historical sites were damaged or destroyed from mid-Au-

Figure 3.1.   Buddhist sculptures ablaze on the streets of Hefei, Anhui Province, in September 1966. The image calls to mind the words of Neal Hunter's poem (see Michael Schoenhals, *China's Cultural Revolution*, 187): the golden passengers sit real still / meditating on China burning buddhas / China setting fire on fire.

gust to September 1966. Valuable classics, paintings, and antiques ransacked from 33,695 Beijing households were fed to the flames, and an estimated 1,700 people were beaten to death. Zealots in Shanghai were even more efficient at their handiwork—the fifteen days from August 23 to September 8, 1966, were sufficient for seek-and-destroy attacks on 84,222 households.[3] As the "Declaration of War on the Old World" spread like wildfire, red guards stormed Uighur mosques in Xinjiang and torched Korans, pillaged some sixty Buddhist temples on Shanxi Province's Mount Wutai, and trampled on the grave of folk hero Yue Fei in Hangzhou, among other exploits.[4] Young rebels declared in one manifesto that they would use "Mao Zedong's great invincible thought" to "turn the old world upside down, smash it to pieces, pulverize it, create chaos and make a tremendous mess, the bigger the better."[5] The crusade to wipe out China's "old thought, old culture, old customs, and old habits" continued nationwide for over a year. For Chinese and foreign observers alike, mere mention of the Destroy the Four Olds (*po sijiu*) campaign conjures up vivid images of burning buddhas, desecrated temples, and mounds of books ablaze in the revolutionary fires of red guards on the rampage.

It is clear, however, that "not all Chinese succumbed to mass hysteria."[6] If the Cultural Revolution was truly "a nationwide all-round civil war," as Mao Zedong boasted on his seventy-third birthday (December 26, 1966), then actors and agendas running counter to the red guard tide cannot be ignored. The defenders of the Confucius Temple complex in Qufu, and others like them, dared to oppose the self-proclaimed "destroyers of the old world," Chairman Mao's "most militant troops, the mortal enemy of the 'four olds.'"[7] All over China relics of "old, feudal, or bourgeois" culture were reduced to ashes, but that so much survived in spite of the red guards' best efforts suggests a deeper story of protection and resistance whose surface has scarcely been scratched.

Resistance is generally thought of as public opposition. However, for a more comprehensive understanding of resistance it behooves us to consider, as James Scott does in *Weapons of the Weak*, "forms of struggle that stop well short of outright collective defiance."[8] Even if their intentions perfectly coincided, a top-level party official and an average Chinese urban or rural resident would have had different means at their disposal. Thus, central documents and statements of party leaders must be placed alongside the "ordinary weapons of relatively powerless groups: foot dragging, dissimulation, desertion, false compliance, pilfering, feigned ignorance . . . and so on."[9] What kinds of people resisted the Cultural Revolution's onslaught against traditional Chinese culture, and what tactics did they use? Were villagers who buried an ancient temple bell of like mind with Premier Zhou Enlai, who "talked a young zealot out of destroying the historic lineage of the garden city of Hangzhou" over long-distance telephone?[10]

Moreover, how does the dispute over the fate of old culture shed light on the meaning of the past in the *Cultural* Revolution? As early as 1940, drawing inspiration from the iconoclasm of the May Fourth movement, Mao Zedong's essay "On New Democracy" had sounded the death knell of old culture: "Reactionary culture serves the imperialists and the feudal class and must be swept away. Unless it is swept away, no new culture of any kind can be built up. There is no construction without destruction, no flowing without damming, and no motion without rest; the two are locked in a life-and-death struggle."[11] Red guards held these words high as they bombarded everything old under the sun, but apparently not all Chinese were convinced. To protect and preserve cultural relics was to stake claim to a past that was somehow valued more than the "new world" proposed by the Cultural Revolution.

Studying the Cultural Revolution as history invites us beyond the rubble-strewn footpaths of "four olds" infamy to inquire about those who obstructed the revolution's attempts to extirpate the artifacts of Chinese history. Let us consider, then, those would-be defenders of China's cultural heritage, and begin the task of telling their stories.

New Words to Protect the "Old": Central Actions and Rhetorical Strategies

These days Premier Zhou Enlai has become in essence, though not in name, China's patron saint of cultural relics. On August 18, 1966, he posted sentries in front of the Imperial Palace (Gugong) in Beijing to repulse the advance of red guards bent on wreaking havoc.[12] Zhou issued orders for the protection of Beijing's Ancient Observatory (Gu guantai), Changsha's Mawangdui tombs, the relics at sacred Mount Tai, Hangzhou's Lingyin Temple, the Banpo Neolithic site in Xi'an, the Han tombs at Mancheng Lingshan. It is also believed that Dunhuang's Mogao Grottoes and Bingling Temple, Tibet's Panchen Lama monastery, and even less well-known sites like the Kaiyuan Temple in Quanzhou, Fujian, owe their preservation to the respected premier.[13] As recently as 1999, tourist entry passes and a commemorative sign at the Potala Palace in Lhasa, Tibet, were inscribed with words honoring Premier Zhou's personal orders to the local military district to protect the palace at all costs.[14] Similar notes of high praise can be heard throughout China.

Indeed, acknowledgments of the premier's accomplishments during the Cultural Revolution are sometimes so laudatory that one must consider them with care. Although many of Zhou's contributions have a clear basis in fact, there is a tendency to associate Zhou Enlai's name with everything positive that occurred in the Cultural Revolution, just as the "Gang of Four" is vilified for every calamity.[15] But whether or not Zhou personally protected every site that claims him as savior, it is evident that his efforts made a lasting impression on cultural workers, and that for many, his name became the aegis and symbol of cultural preservation itself.

It was unusual during the Cultural Revolution for anyone to maintain power and prestige while so actively giving orders running counter to the radical tide. Notwithstanding Zhou Enlai's personal charisma and authority, such direct resistance to the Destroy the Four Olds campaign was simply impracticable on a wide scale. After all, power-holders at all levels were being criticized and toppled for less. It has been argued that Zhou's reputation and political savvy gave him considerably more maneuvering room than most of his compatriots. For example, Zhou's order to prohibit a mass influx of red guards into Beijing on October 26, 1966, was interpreted by Li Tien-min as a sign that Zhou was "the only one who criticized and restricted certain actions of the Red Guards."[16] Zhou also remained unscathed despite a speech in which he defended the republican revolutionary Sun Yat-sen and publicly "slammed the Red Guards of Shanghai for breaking into Sun's widow's home: 'Some youngsters have acted like hooligans.'"[17] But not even Chairman Mao himself (had he so wished), much less Premier Zhou, could have ordered the People's Liberation Army to safeguard every cultural site in China. Some other type of resistance was needed if the destructive tempests were to be curbed.

On October 15, 1966, Zhou tried to persuade a group of eleven Tibetan students to take the slow road. Struggling against religion was necessary and good, Zhou said, "but the principle of wiping out superstition is long-term. Unless there is new thought to replace them, superstitious thoughts cannot be wiped out in one stroke; this requires long-term transformation."[18] He continued, "At present, Tibet is 'destroying the four olds,' striking monasteries and temples, breaking the power of the lama institution—this is all very good. However, would it be possible not to destroy monasteries and temples, but to convert them to schools instead, or utilize them as storehouses? As for Buddhist icons, if the masses demand their destruction, it's fine to destroy a few, but you must think about preserving some of the great temples. Otherwise, our elders will be resentful of us."[19] In name, Zhou Enlai praised the battle against the "four olds," but he attempted to steer the movement's iconoclasm to a moderate course by appealing to notions of pragmatism and filial respect, arguing for careful treatment of "great temples" without appearing counterrevolutionary.

Zhou Enlai negotiated the perilous rapids by tugging at the heartstrings of even the most strident iconoclasts. Roderick MacFarquhar once likened him to a "superb horseman attempting to stay on and ultimately control

a bolting horse."[20] Zhou pointed not to the oppressive products of an en-
slaved feudal past, but rather to the architectural and artistic feats of the
Chinese people. Such cogent arguments appealed to the nationalistic pride
of many Chinese. In 1971, when the first groups of American scholars began
to trickle into China, their tour guides delighted in showing off the splen-
dors of the Imperial Palace. When asked why such "feudal" sites were toler-
ated during the Cultural Revolution, the guides proudly explained that they
were fruits of the genius and creative power of the Chinese masses![21] Zhou
was also credited with making the "clever suggestion that the Red Guards
emulate the Long March by making their journeys on foot instead of by
train, thus releasing locomotives and carriages for economic work while at
the same time tiring out the young radicals before they could do too much
damage."[22] Words were not necessarily more potent than sentinels, but in
some circumstances they could go where no guard could tread. Zhou, however, hardly had a monopoly over such rhetorical tactics.

On March 16, 1967, the Central Committee, State Council, and Central
Military Commission jointly published a "Circular concerning the protection of state property and the practice of economy while making revolution."[23] The document began by criticizing a host of offenders—"small
handfuls of party persons in authority taking the capitalist road, landlords,
rich peasants, counterrevolutionaries, bad elements and rightists"—for having "instigated some people to sabotage state property." Although "some
people" (*yibufen ren*) remained unnamed, the document was clearly aimed
at red guards engaged in destructive acts. If all the usual suspects cited above
were the ones *instigating* "some people" to destroy state property, what
possible culprits were left? In any case, the government wanted such acts
stopped immediately. "Proletarian revolutionaries" were urged to "struggle
against all deeds of sabotaging state property . . . and take concrete measures
to protect state property."[24] Hostile acts would be dealt with as "conspiracies
and plots of the class enemies."

Of course, the general term "state property" (*guojia caichan*) denoted
more than just cultural relics. As the circular made clear, industrial equip-
ment, school property, farm tools, collective grain and seeds, draft animals,
houses and machinery, means of transport, public funds, and just about
every public good was potentially "state property." But article four stated
in no uncertain terms: "Management and protection of cultural relics and
books must be strengthened; under no circumstances may they be wantonly

disposed of or destroyed." This "revolutionary" document urged all citizens to follow Chairman Mao's directive to "practice economy while making revolution" and oppose the reprobates who "sabotage the state's economic construction and the Great Proletarian Cultural Revolution." In truth, it was a reprimand from China's highest authorities calling for an end to wanton destruction by red guards. Few could have missed this message, which was issued to virtually every party committee and posted extensively in urban centers, villages, and military and work units.[25]

Just shy of two months later, the central authorities decided that perhaps they had not made themselves sufficiently clear. They offered further explication on May 14, 1967, with the publication of "Regarding several suggestions on protecting cultural relics and books during the Great Proletarian Cultural Revolution."[26] In this document, the Central Committee appealed to pride in China's long history and claimed that the wealth of cultural relics and books were part of the nation's glorious "revolutionary tradition." "These cultural relics and books are all state property; in the midst of the Great Cultural Revolution, we should strengthen our protection and management work," the document declared. Article seven broadened the scope of concern to include "cultural relics and books stored in all museums, libraries, cultural management bureaus, cultural work teams, culture stations, relic shops, and classical bookshops, all of which are state property."[27] Once again, the Central Committee hammered home the term "state property." Red guards, on the other hand, knew these things by another name: "four olds."

Regardless of what they were called, what good were such items in the topsy-turvy world of continuous revolution and rebellious youth? Party central tried to explain. According to article two, "feudal" buildings, religious sculptures, and the like warranted preservation so that they might someday be used as "public spaces for condemning the crimes of the ruling classes and imperialists, and for educating the masses in class struggle and patriotism." Likewise, article four reasoned that old "poisonous books should not be burned indiscriminately, but preserved as negative educational materials for further criticism."[28] These less than laudatory remarks seem like bizarre ways to defend and honor what the document initially referred to as China's "outstanding legacy." However, only these sorts of arguments would have had suitable currency in the iconoclastic political atmosphere of 1966 and 1967. Had the Central Committee expounded in print on the aesthetic beauty or inherent worth of "feudal" relics, it would have simply added fuel to the fire stoked by red guards.

It would be erroneous to ascribe all of these central initiatives to Zhou Enlai. As head of the State Council, he certainly had a hand in drafting these pronouncements. He was also adept at employing Maoist rhetoric, as shown from his frequent use of Mao's dictum "use the past to serve the present" (*gu wei jin yong*) as a justification for promoting cultural preservation and archaeological studies in the 1960s.[29] But the March 16 circular bore the stamp of the top three organs of state. There were undoubtedly sympathetic ears in high places in Cultural Revolution China. It is likely that at least Chen Yi and Li Xiannian, Zhou's allies at the party center, were involved. After the Cultural Revolution, Li Xiannian played an important role in allocating state funds for restoring cultural sites like the Imperial Palace and Zhalan cemetery.[30]

Even at the highest level, cultural preservation was an issue that had to be clothed in exhortations to "protect state property," "practice economy while making revolution," and other legitimizing Mao quotations. Moreover, these types of directives could not be enforced by central power alone. Authorities in Beijing had to appeal for the cooperation of banks, smelting plants, paper mills, and "recycling centers" (*feipin shougouzhan*) in turning over relics to the local cultural bureaus for appraisal and safekeeping. Support from local revolutionary and military committees was also essential if the items confiscated during red guard house searches were to be collected and cataloged. In an interesting twist of fate, cultural relics that had once been owned privately suddenly became "state property" upon confiscation by red guards bent on wiping them from the face of the earth. Indeed, article five of the May 14 document implored local agencies to take stock of all the precious new items strewn about government warehouses so that they would not be scattered and lost.[31] The indirectness and general furtiveness of these efforts reveals something about the tenuous state of central authority in the Cultural Revolution.

But what of the earlier troop dispatches and similar direct rebuffs aimed at red guards? Let us return to Beijing's Imperial Palace—colossal, incontrovertibly "feudal," and right in the center of the national capital. Zhou Enlai's commands may have succeeded in blocking red guard entry on August 19, 1966, but it is unlikely that those acts alone would have sufficed to forever quell assaults on the palace. The palace, which housed a treasure trove of cultural relics accumulated from centuries as the imperial axis of China, could not be banished from sight with a snap of the fingers.

It could, however, be rendered inoffensive. A look at Figure 3.2 helps explain the strange turn of events whereby Beijing red guards stopped clamoring for wrecking balls and started defending the old palace from more sinister enemies. In October 1967 Peng Zhen, the disgraced former mayor of Beijing, became a punching bag in a series of diatribes that linked his "revisionist" city planning with schemes to destroy the Imperial Palace. Peng's vision of Beijing from the early 1960s, based on a three-pronged program of "stateliness, beauty, and modernity," was reviled in Beijing red guard newspapers as being utterly "revisionist" and "taking the capitalist road."[32] All of the abuse heaped on Peng stemmed from a comment Chairman Mao supposedly made in the early 1960s: "It's not good to have cities too big." Peng Zhen, who allegedly advocated a population of ten million for the nation's capital, was castigated for defying Chairman Mao with his trademark "big-city-ism" (*da chengshi zhuyi*) and "big-road-ism" (*da malu zhuyi*).[33] Thereafter, the insults increased.

Figure 3.2 illustrates how Peng Zhen's alleged "big city, big road, and big park" ideas were equated with purported delusions of a "new imperial palace." This red guard diagram, reproduced from "black materials" gathered on Peng, shows the original Imperial Palace torn down and replaced by a modern government complex, wide avenues, parks, and a "new Tiananmen." Chugging at the head of Peng's long train of heresies was his plan to tear down "our Great Leader Chairman Mao's living and working area—Zhongnanhai—and convert it into a rear flower garden for his 'new palace!'"[34] Red guard caricatures sealed this image of Peng as a counter-revolutionary schemer. One cartoon, which depicted Peng lounging on a chair and propping his foot on a model of the palace, bore the following caption: "Traitor Peng ordered 'Imperial Palace revisions.' . . . He dreamed of becoming an emperor himself!"[35]

It is difficult to say exactly how much cultural preservationists at the party center contributed to spreading the image of Peng as an evil mastermind plotting to ruin the Imperial Palace. Nonetheless, the image effectively silenced those calling for the destruction of the palace.[36] As Elizabeth Perry and Li Xun have noted, "the strategy of wrapping oneself in revolutionary colors at the same time that one painted the opponent in counterrevolutionary hues was one element in a whole repertoire of debating techniques

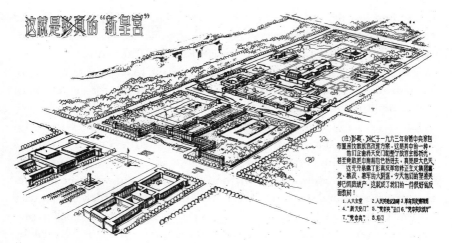

Figure 3.2.   Red guard diagram of Peng Zhen's "New Imperial Palace." From *Shoudu yuanlin pixiu lianluozhan, Yuanlin geming, di san qi, Bei batian: Peng Zhen zhuanji* [Parks in revolution, third issue, Beijing hegemon: Peng Zhen special collection] (August 1967), 6–7. Thanks to Michael Schoenhals for this source.

that marked Cultural Revolution discourse."[37] Thus, in a dramatic reversal, the red guards sloughed off their former vows to smash through the palace's maroon walls and sweep away its vault of "four olds"; instead, they excoriated the impudent class enemy who had dreamed of bulldozing it. No one wanted to be identified with "counterrevolutionary revisionist" Peng Zhen.

The Cultural Revolution had more than its fair share of ironies. If even the specter of Beijing's deposed mayor could be twisted into evidence for saving the Imperial Palace, the other surprising voices emanating from the party center were no less revealing of the quandaries surrounding cultural relics. Chen Boda, then editor of *Red Flag* and director of the Central Cultural Revolution Small Group, was hardly the likeliest contender for the title of cultural protector. However, Jiang Qing later recalled with annoyance how Chen stood up for "three curious little caves," the triple arches that once stood before the Gate of Heavenly Peace (Tiananmen).[38] Chen Boda, Yang Zizhen, and others countermanded Jiang's order to demolish the three feudal arches. Chen refused to budge even though Jiang complained that the arches caused traffic accidents. The argument dragged on until 1971, when a compromise was reached: the arches were not to be destroyed, but removed to a park called Taoyuanting, on the outskirts of Beijing. Still,

Jiang Qing insisted on getting the last word. "That act of preservation did *not* enhance the arches' meager historical significance, she added pointedly," in her conversations with historian Roxane Witke in 1972.[39] As Jeremy Brown illustrates in his riveting chapter on the roller-coaster politics of Xiaojinzhuang, Jiang Qing had her own forceful program for the reform of Chinese culture (see Chapter 6).

Chen Boda's colleague on the Cultural Revolution Small Group, Qi Benyu, was arrested and purged for various "ultra-leftist" crimes in January 1968, but not for his soft spot for classics and cultural relics. In public, he was ever the red-blooded radical. Behind closed doors, however, he met frequently with cultural workers and exhorted them to try harder. On January 27, 1967, Qi Benyu conferred with a group of "revolutionary rebel" representatives from book departments and cultural units. Qi opened his talk by urging everyone to "grasp the work of cultural relics management, see what problems exist, and put forth some solutions."[40] On being told that books were being burned by fearful households, that libraries were dealing with the overflow of confiscated books by carting them off to wastepaper mills, and that no one dared to store or buy books anymore, Qi retorted: "Well, I want to buy them, some must be read!" Then, jabbing a finger at the China Bookshop representative, Qi said: "So there's no space to store books, well I'll fix that. Any books the libraries send, you'd better take them in. The Beijing Library's books are state property, so no one is allowed to tamper with them—this is the property of the masses!" Qi further implored his audience: "Your paper milling units can call a joint conference with the Institute of History, Cultural Relics Bureau, Beijing Library, China Bookshop, and the Academy of Sciences Library. Do not worry about paying a little money to get these old books. . . . You must take good care of them. Do not burn them, appraise them first; make this a principle for me!" In that meeting with the "revolutionary rebels," Qi the "ultra-leftist" appears to have taken backstage to Qi the historian.[41]

Of course, Qi Benyu's arguments for preserving cultural relics were couched in all the appropriate revolutionary rhetoric. When the Beijing Library representative reported that classics were being pulverized in paper mills, Qi swiftly interjected a politically correct warning about "those destructive acts of some power-holders within the party taking the capitalist road."[42] As with the central documents published later that year, no finger of blame was pointed at the red guards. But when it came to conservation,

Qi had little patience for indecision. At one point, the China Bookshop representative asked what to do if outsiders sent books but there were no storage areas left. "Take them in anyway," Qi said. "China is so big, and there's no place to store a few books? You can use the Confucian temple [in Beijing]. If that's not enough, then we'll talk." Such "old things," Qi stressed, were crucial educational materials for the future. "People like Wu Han and Jian Bozan used old things to oppose the party and oppose socialism. For the proletariat to continue struggling with them, we need to make use of these things for criticism," he reasoned.[43] These rhetorical strategies combined nicely with Qi's emphasis on cultural relics as state property, a pattern that was echoed in the May 14 circular. Qi may well have played an active role in crafting that central document.

But was Qi simply mouthing the rhetoric of class struggle, or did he truly want to preserve cultural relics only as material for communist education? Qi spoke to cultural workers at the Imperial Palace on December 1, 1966, and stressed three times that the old palace—a "feudal dynastic den and old landlords' nest"—had to be revamped into a revolutionary model like the Rent Collection Courtyard (Shouzu yuan) in Sichuan Province.[44] The Rent Collection Courtyard, "a series of sculptural tableaux done in sinified socialist realism," graphically condemned the terrible crimes of the ruling classes.[45] Seizing upon that model, Qi demanded a new and "revolutionary Imperial Palace, an exhibition hall of the people's class struggle." However, he quickly added that burning was a cheap shot, not a sign of real commitment to revolutionary change. "Of course, I repeat: I do not advocate that you destroy the cultural relics here," he said. "These things must be preserved, because they were confiscated by the people. Things confiscated by the people must be protected. Although there are items you cannot publicly display, *do not take the easy way out and burn them*. I have faith that you will not take such an easy course of action."[46]

Whatever his personal feelings may have been, Qi Benyu made it clear that he was also speaking on behalf of Chen Boda and Kang Sheng, his comrades in the Cultural Revolution Small Group. On one occasion, Qi snapped, "I don't care what faction you're from, all of you must comply. If any books are to be burned, you'd better come up with a list and send it to Comrade Boda for approval."[47] Acting in concert, these three leaders could have posed at least as strong a challenge to acts of red guard destruction as Zhou Enlai. Kang Sheng's ulterior motives, however, complicated the picture.

To call Kang Sheng's "borrowing" of cultural relics anything more than cunning theft requires a stretch of the imagination. Calling it "resistance" seems ludicrous. Nevertheless, Kang Sheng took concrete steps to ensure the safety of cultural relics, lavishing loving attention on them after he had seized them for his private collection. Exploiting the fact that private property confiscated by red guards had effectively become "state property" during the chaos, Kang avidly perused the holdings of state warehouses as if they were extensions of his own library.[48] He also went bargain-hunting at the Imperial Palace Museum and the Beijing Cultural Relics Bureau, where he spent many productive hours "researching" the former possessions of "ox ghosts and snake demons" like Deng Tuo, A Ying, and Qi Baishi.[49] At the start of the "four olds" campaign Kang issued explicit orders to Beijing cultural workers that no matter what tumult the red guards caused, the collection of acclaimed connoisseur Zhuan Xihua was not to be scattered or destroyed. No doubt distraught at the prospect of red guards torching some valuable items, Kang asked repeatedly about the Zhuan Xihua collection for three years. On the morning of October 18, 1969, Kang finally got word that the coveted items had been secured in a state warehouse. He spent the whole day poring over the treasures before carting many off to his home.[50]

Kang Sheng's act of pilfering aside, this episode reveals that many confiscated or otherwise offensive items were being sent to state warehouses instead of being burned outright.[51] Kang must have appreciated Qi Benyu's efforts on behalf of "old things." He would not have been able to plunder without the efforts of cadres to collect and preserve collections that might otherwise have been destroyed. Moreover, Kang Sheng's relationship with red guards was ambivalent at best. He opposed their acts of wanton destruction because of his ulterior motives, but at the same time red guard attacks on the "four olds" gave him ample opportunity to heist confiscated goods. Kang justified his appropriations by stamping the items with his three-fold seal of approval: "Returned to the public" (*gui gong*), "Everything for the public, nothing for the self" (*da gong wu si*), and finally "Kang Sheng."[52] Apparently, some of the highest party elites had their own conflicting motives for opposing outright destruction of the "four olds." After the Cultural Revolution, a Japanese visitor to Kang's house of treasures mused, "Who says China has no millionaires? Isn't Kang Sheng one of them?"[53]

There is no adequate measuring stick to judge the effectiveness of these central actions and rhetorical strategies. Some accounts credit encouragement from the party center with inspiring cultural workers to persevere in their defense of cultural relics; others claim that central directives were relatively ineffectual.[54] Central proclamations could help shield key sites and act as guideposts for protecting cultural relics, but resistance ultimately had to come from the local areas, where real battles over the "four olds" were being fought.

Burials, Closures, and Cover-ups

The Cultural Revolution turned the work of archaeology upside down—cultural relics were as likely to be buried or covered up as they were to be unearthed and made public. Sweating it out in an atmosphere of iconoclasm and radical rhetoric, local officials and residents were generally not well situated to directly countervail red guard activities by means of public debate and media criticism. Concealment became the predominant mode of preservation at the local level. Concerned residents in the remote Shaanxi village of Sigou (literally, "temple gulch") could not call on the army or central directives to safeguard their village namesake, but they made the most of the limited means at their disposal. Red guards wrecked the Xitiangufo Temple in the closing months of 1966, but failed to locate the bronze temple bell. Thirty years later, when the temple was finally rebuilt in Sigou, an anonymous donor returned the bell and revealed that it had been buried to avoid the hostilities above ground.[55]

Nearby Yangjiagou also had a legacy to hide when red guards came tramping through the center of the village. Two Qing dynasty memorial tablets commemorating the meritorious deeds of the Ma family landlords vanished in plain sight when villagers pitched in to cover them with bricks and clay. Overnight, the village got a convenient blank wall for pasting big character posters. Passing by in 1969, PLA unit 4785 added a dash of color by painting a portrait of Chairman Mao dressed in military garb.[56] Perhaps Mao would have been proud of the "ingenuity of the rural masses." The tablets, scrubbed clean of their protective layers, remain a village landmark today. The Ma family of Yangjiagou suffered its own travails, however, as Jiangsui He shows in Chapter 5.

Tactical subterfuge and redirection were the order of the day. In fall 1966 caretakers at the Summer Palace (Yiheyuan) worked their way down the ornately decorated walkways bordering the palace's Kunming Lake, whitewashing the traditional Chinese murals. "When youthful militants came by, they found the offensive scenes already obliterated and left the corridor unharmed."[57] Quick-thinking abbots barred their doors and swathed temple gates in Mao posters—red guards would have to choose between mutilating the chairman's portrait and seeking less troublesome targets. Cultural workers in Chengdu seized upon the fact that Chairman Mao had paid a visit to Du Fu's thatched cottage (Du Fu caotang) on March 7, 1958. Not only had Mao lingered to savor Du Fu's poetry, but he had read aloud a Qing dynasty couplet honoring Du Fu, smiled, and pointed to it while exclaiming: "Good!" (*hao!*) In honor of this ultimate seal of approval, local cadres erected signs proclaiming: "Chairman Mao visited the thatched cottage" and "Chairman Mao's poetic atmosphere."[58] The young rebels decided to live and let live. Who would deny the Great Helmsman the right to enjoy a little classical poetry?

Considering the Cultural Revolution's xenophobic atmosphere, it is intriguing that even some relics of foreign heritage were protected locally. In 1967, foreign visitor Louis Barcata asked a Chinese Catholic priest in Shanghai how he managed to maintain his church and small congregation despite the shrill rhetoric prevailing in the streets. To Barcata's surprise, the priest explained that he himself was a salaried employee of the "Anti-religious Combat Office" of the Shanghai municipal party committee.[59] Evidently, going through the motions of being an iconoclast allowed one to serve a wholly different agenda. This was illustrated in an interesting episode at Zhalan, the oldest Catholic cemetery in Beijing.

Zhalan, a gift from the Wanli Emperor to the Jesuits in 1610, was home not only to a Catholic church and cemetery, but also the Beijing Communist Party School that opened in September 1956.[60] The party school and the Church of All Saints had peacefully coexisted on the Zhalan grounds for years, and the tombs of Matteo Ricci, Adam Schall, and Ferdinand Verbiest (the three most famous Jesuit missionaries to the imperial court) were protected by the Beijing Cultural Relics Bureau. Zhou Enlai had personally ordered that the three tombstones remain undisturbed in their original places. These facts did not deter red guards of the nearby Beijing Construction School from confronting Gao Yimin, principal of the party school, in August 1966. They demanded to know why the tombs had not been demolished and issued a three-day ultimatum. Seeing that the municipal party committee and the Religious Affairs Bureau were already paralyzed, a custodian at the party school concocted a plan. He greeted the frustrated red guards on the third day and said, "We were waiting for you to come. Let's dig a hole and bury the steles, and tell them they may never come up again, okay?" The students then worked all day to dig three pits over a meter deep, carefully pulled down the steles with ropes, and buried them with earth. They departed sweaty but content, and the steles of Ricci, Schall, and Verbiest were preserved. In 1979, after an expenditure of 10,000 yuan, the steles were unearthed and restored.[61]

With all of the bonfires, big character posters, rallies, and endless cacophony of rebellious shouts occupying national attention, it is safe to say that museums were not the most popular places to while away idle days. The welcome mats were gone anyway. Simon Leys wrote in the 1970s: "Until quite recently the would-be visitor nearly always ran into locked doors with a notice saying 'Closed for Repairs.'"[62] The Museum of Chinese History and the Imperial Palace Museum in Beijing were closed to avert damage to relics and exhibits, as were the Shandong Provincial Museum, Shanghai Municipal Museum, and other institutions throughout China.[63] "Perhaps we shall find pilgrims subtle enough to unearth from this a new philosophy of the 'closed museum,'" Leys remarked wryly. "After all this may be an original, not to say revolutionary conception of the museum, its nature and its function."[64] At the least, closure kept "feudal" objects safely out of public view. Relics in private collections and public spaces generally "had a less happy fate: the Red Guards served them up as a gigantic burnt offering."[65] It was no doubt because the Imperial Palace Museum was insulated from public view that Kang Sheng was able to "borrow" so many treasures from its vaults.

Locals also called down the big guns whenever they could. The most common entreaties to higher authorities took the form of phone calls and letters to Zhou Enlai, who was seen as the court of final appeal. According to David and Nancy Dall Milton, "millions of Chinese believed that he was the only man in that enormous country capable of solving the problems in which they all found themselves entangled."[66] In the Hubei city of Hanyang, head monk Chang Ming's letter of appeal to Zhou on behalf of Guiyuan Temple prompted the Wuhan military district to dispatch troops to protect the temple.[67] Whether the hundreds or thousands of such appeals actually reached the premier is debatable, but apparently some higher-ups were listening.

This is not to say, however, that local residents simply waited for salvation from the party center. On the contrary, they often had to initiate their own collective action, as in the aforementioned cases of Yangjiagou and Sigou. The streets of Beijing after August 20, 1966, were in complete disarray—random beatings, house raids, and gleeful smashing of relics made many residents fear for their families and property. Some banded together to protect their homes and relics in shifts. "When night fell, groups of old women and children, armed with sticks, gathered before their houses or patrolled the *hutung*," one observer wrote. "They were protecting themselves against 'bad elements,' though no one could say who these really were. . . . The strange spectacle of these old people and children in the darkness, dressed in their traditional clothes, took the onlooker straight back to the nameless terrors of the Middle Ages."[68] Cultural workers also labored to retrieve and catalog relics from paper mills, recycling centers, and smelting plants. Local actions like these helped preserve items that would not have caught the attention of the busy leaders in Zhongnanhai.[69]

In fall 1966, red guards in Tibet raised a ruckus at the gates of the Juela Temple, which housed a priceless jewel from Princess Wencheng of the Tang dynasty. The resident lama, Mimaciren, refused to open the gates, but his own son Lobu climbed the wall and opened the main door from inside. Mimaciren rushed to the Tang hall, seized the jewel, and stuffed it in his mouth, determined to swallow it if the red guards asked any questions. Luckily for him, they did not, though they bashed some of the larger temple relics.[70] In Luoyang, once the capital of many Chinese dynasties, the thousand-year-old Baima Temple narrowly escaped the torch thanks to members of the Luoyang party committee, who went straight to the local military garrison on July 20, 1966.[71] Precious days could have flitted by had they appealed to the central party apparatus for reinforcements. As it turned out, the temple structure was saved, but many of the Buddhist relics inside were seriously damaged. Present-day gazetteers from places like Hubei also report that locals hustled on their own accord to stanch the torrent of destruction.[72] After the Cultural Revolution, a former mayor of Quanzhou, Fujian, was even overheard "bragging" that he had taken the initiative to save a few sites.[73]

Local leaders also coordinated their resistance and rhetorical strategies with those of the party center. The debate over the fate of the Lingyin Temple in Hangzhou, for example, bounced between municipal leaders and the

State Council. Once the order came down to preserve both the temple and the nearby Feilai Cliff, the municipal caretakers built a wall at the entrance of the gorge to further guard against vandalism.[74] In another instance, Duan Wenjie, curator of the Mogao Grottoes, recalled: "Premier Zhou gave instructions that the safety of the monuments should be ensured at all costs. We, at the Academy, issued circulars and explained to Red Guards about the historic and artistic value of the monuments."[75] We may remember that the two central documents did not elaborate on cultural value; rather, they stayed in the clinical realm of class struggle and "state property." When combined with local efforts, however, central authority could embolden cultural workers to try their hand at persuasion.

Persuasion was a dangerous game in the heat of the Destroy the Four Olds campaign, but it was successful on some occasions. In Shanghai, as in most large cities, items confiscated from house-to-house searches were sent to recycling centers and smelting plants for disposal. Near the end of 1966, Shanghai cultural workers discovered that a Ming dynasty religious sculpture from Baiyunguan Temple was about to be melted down for scrap metal. They rushed to the Yongsheng smelting plant and issued leaflets supporting the worth of cultural relics. In the process, they managed to convince the factory head to transfer the bell to the local cultural bureau for safekeeping. "Gold and silver have a price, but cultural relics are priceless," the factory head told his workers.[76]

Verbal support for "old culture" was possible mainly because local pride still appealed to red guards. Despite their stated iconoclasm, many of the young revolutionaries closely identified with aspects of their local heritage. Red guard Gao Yuan from Hebei, for example, was proud that his town was once the home of Zhao Yun, a heroic general from the classic *Romance of the Three Kingdoms*. He also bragged that his father, Gao Shangui, had saved the town's ancient city wall from destruction.[77] In August 1966, a Tibetan red guard called Bandan Zhaxi made the long pilgrimage to Beijing bearing a traditional white *hada* from his hometown. The long strip of cloth, inscribed with the names of everyone in his town in both Tibetan and Chinese, was intended as a gift for Chairman Mao. Before he left Beijing, Bandan Zhaxi ran up to the walls at Tiananmen, grabbed a fistful of earth from its base, and wrapped it carefully for safekeeping. "I shall bring this red earth from the base of Tiananmen back with me to Tibet, and sprinkle it at the base of the Potala Palace," he declared. "Tiananmen and the Potala Palace are the two most precious and venerable sites for the Tibetan people."[78] He did not mention, however, that Tiananmen (the "Gate of Heavenly Peace" leading to the Imperial Palace) and the Potala Palace were focal points of the "feudal ruling classes." Local pride had a definite place in the hearts of even the most publicly ardent iconoclasts.

National pride carved out its own little niche as well. In spite of the "four olds" rhetoric, archaeological workers continued to unearth artifacts during the Cultural Revolution. New discoveries from all around China were sent to Beijing by local cultural bureaus. An exhibition called "Cultural Relics Unearthed during the Cultural Revolution" debuted in the Imperial Palace on July 1, 1971, and went on a worldwide tour the following year.[79] Even Jiang Qing expressed pride in these cultural treasures, which she said "belong not only to the Chinese people, but to the people of the whole world."[80] Perhaps protectors of "old culture" did not have to look as far and wide for support as it has been assumed—feelings of pride ran straight to the top echelons of Chinese society.

In August 1966, Gao Yuan and his "army of Monkey Kings eager to make havoc under heaven" were confronted by a company of soldiers who had set up camp at the Dafo Temple in Yizhen, Hebei Province.[81] An army officer held aloft a "little red book" and cautiously approached the students. "Little revolutionary generals," he said, "this temple is on the national register of cultural relics. It does not belong to the category of the four olds. Please leave and find your four olds elsewhere." When pressed with complaints that the temple's Celestial Kings were "superstitious monsters," the officer responded: "These statues are the work of ancient artisans. They are the wealth of the people. We should not destroy them." The officer led the skeptical red guards to the hall of the Goddess of Mercy and told them the story of why only two of the statue's forty-two arms were made of real bronze. "The Japanese aggressors sawed off the other forty arms and melted them down to make bullets to kill the Chinese people," he explained. Several of the red guards were enraged and began to shout, "Death to the Japanese devils!"[82]

The officer was adept at working a crowd. Although he had a detachment of troops at his disposal, he resorted first to persuasion. His attempt to draw a line between nationally protected cultural relics and the "four olds" is instructive—quite possibly this line of reasoning was being used at famous sites nationwide, like Duan Wenjie's placards at the Mogao Grottoes. His defense of artifacts as "the wealth of the people" resonates with the "state property" and "property of the masses" rhetoric so often used in central documents. The story about World War II channeled the red guards' ire toward the "Japanese aggressors," effectively making the temple a museum for condemning "imperialist crimes" instead of just another feudal relic. Finally, the officer spun a tale about the painstaking labors of Liao dynasty Chinese craftsmen that had the red guards gazing at the bronze Goddess of Mercy with "new admiration." "Do you still think we should smash these cultural relics?" the officer asked.[83]

Despite the officer's persuasive efforts, the red guards of Yizhen Number One Middle School had little time to answer his plea. While most had remained spellbound before the Goddess of Mercy, other students had regrouped outside and pulled all four Celestial Kings down at once, smashing the clay figures. The demolitionists only retreated when the officer ordered a platoon of soldiers to link arms and blockade the main hall. "Nobody wanted to clash with the People's Liberation Army," Gao Yuan recalled.[84] It seems that cultural power, too, grew out of the barrel of a gun.

Then again, sticks and stones in the hands of local vigilantes were also forces to be reckoned with. In August 1966, sixteen red guards from Amoy University planned to raze the nationally renowned Nanputuo, the Temple of the Goddess of Mercy of the Southern Seas.[85] They tied ropes to the Four Guardians and pulled down one and part of another, scraping off several kilograms of gold powder for themselves. The temple monks rushed to the scene in a fury, forcing the outnumbered Amoy University red guards to retreat. Ken Ling, who was a middle school red guard at the time, recalled: "The incident shocked all Amoy. Nan Pu To was a cultural landmark, once designated for special protection by the Council of State. . . . It was a beautiful, solemn place, and many took pride in it." Outraged by the attack, "the citizens of Amoy demanded severe punishment for the culprits. Angry workers from several factories left their jobs and went together to the Amoy University student dormitories, wielding clubs and threatening to kill those Red Guards," Ling wrote. "They ransacked the dormitories in search of them. The sixteen Red Guards were so badly frightened that they changed their names and fled." That incident, Ling concluded, "made me understand that we were really not free to destroy the four olds as we wished, without fear. Above, we would run into the opposition of the Party Central; below, we would encounter the indignation of the people."[86]

Brazen and destructive though they were in their war with the "old world," red guards were not omnipotent. Emotions ran high and tempers were on a short fuse, as the youths from Amoy University discovered. But local pride and public anger were not limited to Amoy. War drums rumbled in Qufu, the hometown of Confucius, in autumn 1966.

"China's Holy Land" under Siege: The Battle over Qufu's Three Confucian Sites

On August 24, 1966, faced with reports of troublemakers coming to attack the Three Confucian Sites (San Kong), forty-four-year-old Qufu county secretary Li Xiu still had the poise to smile and conjure up an appropriate Confucian adage. "As the old saying goes, let's properly escort [these barbarians] out of our lands" (*li song chu jing*), Li declared.[87] The audience smiled back, though the air remained tense at the hastily convened conference. Greater ebullience prevailed outside the Confucius Temple complex, where a makeshift army of local peasants and students was munching on a hearty repast of steamed buns and salted soup.[88] Volunteers from the municipal cultural relics management committee kept busy cooking for the hungry crowd. Having spent the whole day sealing off vulnerable temple doors, putting up wall posters, and patrolling the grounds, the defenders welcomed a good meal.

Like any competent leader, Li conscientiously rallied his troops with words and kept their appetites sated with food and drink. He also urged them to vigilantly resist, but refrain from violence: "When the red guards come, let us open up a great revolutionary debate, reason with them, and send them away safely."[89] Secretary Li certainly made it sound easy. In all, it seemed an auspicious prelude to yet another successful campaign, in a city well accustomed to political movements.[90]

No one expected a bitter three-month siege. Li Xiu's hope of properly sending the "evildoers" packing proved as misguided as the red guards' dream of effortlessly "washing away all the muddy waters left behind by the old society."[91] Filled with extreme rhetoric, tactical deception, and shifting loyalties, the Qufu siege was as intense as any scene from *The Water Margin*, complete with song and verse. At the outset, peasants, students, and militia members toiled alongside county officials to protect their local heritage. In later reversals, some Qufu residents joined the red guard chorus of "smash,

smash, smash . . . kill, kill, kill!"[92] Outsiders at various levels further complicated the scene and forced people to take sides. The battle that engulfed Qufu exposed the dilemmas of a local community caught in the blistering cauldron of the "four olds" campaign.

Thirty-seven years after his "sending off the barbarians" speech, Li Xiu recalled how he felt imbued with a distinct historic mission. "At that time, we felt that even a few hundred years of restoration would never be enough to repair a few days of destruction," he said. "The Three Confucian Sites were treasures of China—we weren't defending Confucius, we were defending our country's cultural relics. Entrusted with such a responsibility, I would not have shirked it even to save my life."[93] For Secretary Li and the Qufu county leaders, what was really at stake during the Cultural Revolution was not some abstract notion of honoring sages long dead, but a real sense of urgency in defending China's cultural heritage.

Many Qufu residents were proud of their town's cultural renown as the "home of Confucius and Mencius." Today, local gazetteers refer to Qufu as the "Holy Land of the East" (*Dongfang shengdi*).[94] When red guards from most of Qufu's secondary schools first took to the streets to "destroy the four olds" in August 1966, they had a riotous time burning old books and paintings, pounding statues of deities, changing street names and shop signs, cutting off "bourgeois" braids and pigtails, and searching the homes of "bad elements," but strangely, none of them showed an interest in the most "feudal" site of all—the Confucius Temple standing right before their eyes.[95] If it were simply an oversight, it would have been one of the most extraordinary examples of negligence in the entire Cultural Revolution.

The seeming blindness of Qufu red guards must have been grounded in local pride. The Three Confucian Sites, renowned as "nationally protected cultural sites," were fundamental to local identity and were inextricably tied to Qufu's image nationwide.[96] In his speech, Li Xiu had appealed to these feelings by emphasizing the fame of the relics: "They are the Chinese people's outstanding cultural legacy, the fruits of the sweat and wisdom of the laboring masses. They are treasures of the world, and pillars of the East's cultural florescence."[97] Local pride stirred in the veins of the construction workers who confronted red guards outside the gates of the Confucius Mansion shortly before the August 26 incident. "The Confucius Mansion and Confucius Temple were built with the blood and sweat of countless generations of laboring masses. How can you even speak of destroying them?" one worker asked. Another old worker huffed: "Chairman Mao never said the Confucius Mansion was one of the 'four olds.' . . . All I know is that this has been the work of my ancestors for generations. If you want to destroy it, you'd better have some documents!"[98]

The old worker was right about one thing—Mao Zedong had not explicitly said that the Three Confucian Sites were to be obliterated as "four olds." Mao had toured Qufu on October 28, 1952, and never requested bonfires to light up the city's landmarks.[99] Until the outbreak of the Cultural Revolution, nothing had seriously threatened the foundation of Qufu's fame. Even the November 1962 conference to "debate Confucius" (*taolun Kongzi*) in Ji'nan city had been largely inconclusive. In his closing remarks, Shandong provincial vice-secretary Yu Xiu had simply announced that another big debate on Confucius would be needed in three to five years. "I believe that it will reap an even greater harvest than the present conference," he said.[100] Yu could not have known the prescience of his words. Four years later, he would be pushed to the ground and forced to watch as red guards ransacked the Kong family tombs.

The fireworks began on August 24, 1966, when students at the Qufu Normal Institute vented their frustration: "All over the country people are enthusiastically destroying the 'four olds,' yet the worst of the 'four olds,' the Three Confucian Sites, are still standing right next to us! We have done nothing, as if we were compelled to wait for outsiders to come and rebel— this is our shame!"[101] The students united under the banner of the Mao Zedong Thought Red Guards and prepared to bring mayhem to the front steps of the Confucius Temple complex. They would soon get their wish, though the outcome was not to their liking.

The August 26 incident was an important confrontation in which local pride came to blows with outside forces. The Qufu Normal Institute was not part of the city proper. Situated outside Qufu's western gate, with campus grounds not much smaller than the Qufu city center, the institute operated independently from the municipal party committee. Hence, Qufu residents regarded the Mao Zedong Thought Red Guards as arrogant outsiders who had no respect for the local peace.[102] The locals had formed their own mass organization, the Red Rebels (Hongse zaofan dui), led by Qufu cadre Zhang Fuhai. When the red guards came shouting in the night and thumping on the east gate of the Confucius Temple complex on August 26, the Red Rebels and local residents decided that enough was enough.

Irate local militia, members of the Qufu Communist Youth League, and poor and lower-middle peasants from South Gate Village (Nanguan dadui) joined the Red Rebels in defense of the Confucius Temple complex. Even the local military district sent a token detachment of troops as tensions escalated. A militia member spotted a Qufu native (*bendiren*), a university student, among the red guards and shouted at him: "Why you little son of a counterrevolutionary bad element! So even you are seizing this chance to cause chaos!"[103] Angry Qufu residents shoved the student back and forth and cursed him as a traitor.

Outnumbered and surrounded, some of the red guards were beaten, while others had their clothes torn. Some were yanked into the Confucius Mansion for further struggle sessions. A few red guards fought back, ripping off some of the soldiers' insignia in the scuffle. "Set up our Red Rebel sign right here!" roared Zhang Fuhai, planting himself at the east gate. The beleaguered students were finally saved by the arrival of county vice-secretary Zhang Yumei, who urged residents to be lenient. It was already three o'clock in the morning when the last red guard squeezed through the encirclement and trudged back to Qufu Normal Institute, leaving behind the unscathed Confucius Temple complex and the laughter of its victorious defenders.[104]

After the August 26 incident, things seemed to quiet down in Qufu. County officials ordered the miscreants of the "little black gang" to submit self-criticisms, but this was just a slap on the wrist.[105] While the Red Rebels continued to vigilantly stand guard, most Qufu residents turned their attention to the autumn harvest. But the red guards of Qufu Normal Institute were not to be vanquished so easily. Although they refrained from direct assaults on the Confucius Temple complex, they persisted in their criticisms and looked for cracks in the complex's defenses. During this lull in the storm, the red guards were busy making contacts with their compatriots nationwide and appealing their case in Beijing.

Five students from Qufu Normal Institute had gone up to Beijing as representatives at the national red guard rallies. On August 26, just hours before their comrades began collecting bruises at the doorstep of the Confucius Mansion, these five visited the National Cultural Relics Bureau to discuss the "four olds." The official in charge advised them to think carefully about their actions. "The purpose of preserving cultural relics and historical sites," he said, "is to serve the workers, peasants, and soldiers, to serve the socialist revolution and socialist construction." The official proceeded to lecture them: "Since the movement has just started, don't be in such a hurry to smash and destroy things; instead, we can seal them up for now and open a mass debate." He cited the example of the Imperial Palace, which he gave a new revolutionary name: "Our Beijing 'Blood and Tears Palace' (Xieleigong) has been handled in precisely this way—it's still sealed, and the results have been quite good."[106]

If the students from Qufu Normal Institute were hoping for backing in their fracas with the "four olds," they would not get it from the National Cultural Relics Bureau. Still, they found many sympathetic ears in Beijing. During the "great linkups" (*da chuanlian*), red guards from the capital and all over China streamed into Qufu. Most famous of all was Tan Houlan, leader of the Jinggangshan regiment from Beijing Normal University, who loudly declared her support for the Qufu Normal Institute. Two hundred Beijing red guard reinforcements marched into Qufu on November 9, 1966, to the tune of "Very good" (*Hao de hen*) and "Obliterate Confucius's Manor" (*Daohui Kongjia dian*).[107] The noose tightened.

The Qufu party committee had also scrounged for allies. Since the start of the "four olds" polemics, Li Xiu had tried to enlist the help of a wide range of Qufu residents. His August 24 meeting and early propaganda efforts had won the support of many residents and students from two local schools, Qufu First Middle and Qufu Normal School.[108] In a bid to deny public poster space to other groups, the students had covered the Confucius Temple complex with big character posters declaring: "Resolutely oppose the destructive acts of class enemies!" They also threatened swift retribution if anyone removed their posters. Such efforts were pitched at deterring outside red guards from interfering in Qufu affairs. "What makes them think they can just come over here and smash the Three Confucian Sites?" demanded a local student.[109] During the August 26 incident, students from Qufu First Middle made a long distance phone call to the State Council office. The official who answered their call was noncommittal about central aid, but his words were sympathetic to cultural protection. The middle school students promptly issued flyers announcing the State Council's "support" for the Three Confucian Sites and pasted them all over the city.[110]

Although the night of August 26 had ended in victory for the local guardians, open defiance was swiftly becoming untenable. Daily reports of more and more red guards descending on Qufu worried the local party officials. Soon the Red Rebels would be outnumbered, and local residents were growing fearful of the swelling horde of militant youth. Moreover, there was sobering news that the Longmen Buddhist sculptures, also a celebrated national treasure, had been smashed in the ancient city of Luoyang (Henan Province). How long could the defenders hope to hold out?

Qufu officials were familiar with the kinds of rhetorical strategies, false compliance, closure, and subterfuge that were common currency at the central and local levels. "The Three Confucian Sites are going through internal restructuring, so they are closed indefinitely. This is a high level directive," said one cultural worker, though no such directive existed.[111] Local party leaders like Li Xiu, Cui Xuyi, and Wang Huatian also constantly used the rhetoric of "state property" as a defensive weapon. In September and October 1966, Qufu leaders threw themselves into painting walls red and plastering Mao quotations everywhere. As part of this so-called Red Sea (*hong haiyang*) campaign, the two prominent stone lions that flanked the Confucius Mansion's main gate were carefully measured and covered with wood paneling. The wooden boxes were then painted with the brightest revolutionary red and inscribed with the highest mantle of protection, a pair of Mao quotations. Workers ensconced the complex's most valuable relics in the recesses of rear halls and flower gardens; on the pretext of "reforming" the Confucius Temple complex, the doors were sealed to all except cultural workers and cadres.[112]

But the red guards refused to be duped by what they called "false revolution, actual protection" (*jia geming, zhen baohu*).[113] Too many eyes were fixated on the Confucius Temple complex for it to be boxed up and hidden away. In many ways, the arrival of Tan Houlan and the red guards from Beijing Normal University was a harbinger of doom for the resistance. The emboldened red guards formed a grand alliance called the Denounce Confucius Liaison (Tao Kong lianluozhan) and spread the word to rebels nationwide that they would not rest until the "four olds" in Qufu were crushed to dust. In the "Denounce Confucius Battlefield Report" (*Tao Kong zhanbao*), they reviled Li Xiu for "spreading false rumors and inciting the peasants against us" and compared his suppression of students to the 1956 Hungarian incident.[114] The students also publicly criticized the State Council for not revoking the Three Confucian Sites' national protection status. Tan Houlan, who had ties to the Central Cultural Revolution Group and national fame as one of Beijing's top five red guard leaders, brought enormous prestige to the red guard cause. On November 9, defectors from Qufu

First Middle and Qufu Normal School were among those welcoming Tan with shouts of "Learn from the red guards of Beijing Normal University!"[115] When Tan led an assault on the Confucius Temple complex the next day, Zhang Fuhai's swaggering Red Rebels dispersed like gas out of a deflating balloon.

On November 10, 1966, the Qufu party committee had little choice but to capitulate. Red guards marched into the Confucius Temple complex and claimed to have discovered an old Nationalist Party flag, which they triumphantly seized as proof that the place festered with "counterrevolutionary activities."[116] That night, officials like Cui Xuyi desperately tried to bury some more relics. "In that moment, all I could think was: these belong to our country, we absolutely must protect them," Cui later recalled. However, many of the relics were soon detected by the red guards, who had an informant in the temple complex.[117] Assistant secretary Zhang Yongnian made one last phone call from the Qufu office to the party center in Zhongnanhai on November 11, hoping beyond hope for a response. He got two.

"Do not burn the Confucius Temple, Confucius Mansion, or the Confucius Forest," read Chen Boda's November 12 telegram. "Preserve them as feudal museums of the Kong family landlords, like the Rent Collection Courtyard. The Confucian graves can be dug up." Qi Benyu's telegram, which arrived soon after, was a bit more specific. "Han dynasty monuments should be preserved, as should anything up to the Ming. Qing dynasty relics can be smashed," Qi wrote. "You may transform the Confucius Temple into something like the Rent Collection Courtyard. The Confucian graves can be exhumed. Find someone knowledgeable in cultural relics to appraise the goods."[118] When Chen and Qi's instructions were publicized, the Qufu cadres had mixed feelings. If the central directives were followed, the Three Confucian Sites would largely be spared from the flames. However, red guards were being given a free hand to smash many relics and engage in what quickly devolved into grave robbery.[119]

Some of the more zealous iconoclasts might have been disappointed that central leaders were unwilling to completely destroy the old world. On November 13, red guards forced Zhang Yumei to make a county-wide radio broadcast encouraging the masses to rise up and smash Confucius forever, but Zhang played an "underhanded trick" (*shoujiao*) to make the broadcast inaudible in most areas.[120] Irritated but unfazed, the red guards proceeded to interpret the orders as they saw fit. Chen Boda and Qi Benyu had said nothing about the State Council stele that declared the Confucius Temple a nationally protected cultural site. Local officials prized the stele as a symbol of central government support, whereas red guards clamored for the demolition of this "'protective umbrella' of ox ghosts and snake demons."[121] Once the stele was destroyed in the great November 15 red guard rally, the road was clear for virtually anything. Even Zhang Fuhai and some of the Red Rebels joined in the looting of the Confucian graveyards.[122] It hardly seemed to matter whether the graves belonged to the Han, Ming, or Qing dynasties. Old authorities and social inhibitions, just like old culture, were symbolically smashed during the Cultural Revolution.

Zhang Hongsen, a retired army doctor living on the west side of the Confucius Temple, felt his hopes crumble just like the State Council stele on November 15. "All lost, all lost . . . even our country is lost! You may not want it, but I do!" he cried, seizing a piece of the stele on which the words "Chinese people's . . . " (*Zhonghua renmin*) could still be made out. Clutching the stone fragment and murmuring, "I want it, I want it," Zhang carried it home. The next day, red guards from Qufu First Middle banged on his door and issued an ultimatum for its return. Zhang hurled the stone into the city moat that very night. Then he posted an anonymous message to the people of Qufu on the Drum Tower gate: "Comrades, think for a moment, what is Tan Houlan doing here? She is aiming spears at our people's government and Premier Zhou!" The red guards were livid and demanded that the local security bureau find the culprit. The search was also on for the "black hand" who had secretly tacked up this criticism during the great November 15 rally: "This gang from Beijing Normal University is doing the bidding of the Nationalist reactionaries and warlords. By destroying Confucius, these criminals want our children and grandchildren to forget class struggle!"[123] Apparently, there was still resentment against the outside red guards. But in the heat of victory, the victorious "little generals" found such defiance little more than a nuisance.

Tan Houlan left Qufu on December 3, 1966. Some have suggested that she was called back to Beijing by Zhou Enlai to prevent further desecration of Qufu's cultural relics.[124] Others attribute her departure to tensions in the party center and the Central Cultural Revolution Group.[125] Both possibilities hint at further outside intervention in the Qufu feud, which had long since swelled beyond being just a local crisis. Before exiting the stage, Tan's deputy commander, Zhang Daoying, ordered that the campaign against the

Three Confucian Sites be carried out in accordance with Chen Boda's guidelines. Although they were "four olds," the buildings were not to be burned. After making sure the remaining red guards understood these instructions, the outsiders who came, saw, and conquered pulled out of Qufu.

Ultimately, the red guards claimed a total victory over the Three Confucian Sites. As 1966 drew to a close, their exploits included smashing some 6,618 relics, pulling down 1,000 stone tablets, and looting or defacing more than 2,000 graves.[126] The attempt at protection thus ended in failure. Or did it? The Confucius Temple complex, though damaged, was not incinerated as the red guards had threatened in all their battle hymns. Like the Baima Temple in Luoyang, the Confucius Temple lost many relics and steles, but much, including the buildings themselves, remained intact. Today, Qufu tour guides point out not only the cracks in the restored tablets where red guard sledgehammers did their worst, but also the untouched Ming dynasty tablets on which a faint red "save" (*liu*) can still be made out. Legend has it that Tan Houlan wrote the red characters herself, but whether she did so freely or out of respect for Qi Benyu's directive remains a mystery.

The Destroy the Four Olds campaign in Qufu, with its diverse cast of Qufu officials, local residents, Beijing red guards, and party elites like Qi Benyu and Chen Boda, was an important stage on which local and central tensions played out a complex drama. Like many such dramatic moments in the Cultural Revolution, the great trial of Qufu ended not only in tragedy, but also on a note of irony. In 1966, red guards toiled day and night to eradicate Confucius, even going as far as digging up his grave to declare him safely "dead." Yet the old sage survived to be dragged out once more in the Criticize Lin Biao and Confucius (*pi Lin pi Kong*) campaign eight years later. The great debates of 1974 were held at the Confucius Temple complex, where Li Xiu had first pledged to defend the relics.[127] Try as it might, the Cultural Revolution simply could not "sweep away" the Chinese past.

Dragging Out the Past, for Good or for Ill

By using a variety of tactics to protect relics from harm, participants at different levels showed that the campaign against the "four olds" was not simply a one-sided, all-consuming mass movement in which Chinese culture was wholly repudiated, but a series of shifting battlefronts between actors with different agendas. To some Chinese, cultural relics were imbued with palpable value that went beyond material worth. "I felt the sky cave in on me," recalled a former core group member of the Communist Youth League, whose house was raided by red guards in August 1966. "Those priceless works of art . . . had all been burnt into a pile of ashes. Do you know what it feels like to be completely deprived of your life?"[128] James Scott's work on resistance has alluded to "a set of minimal cultural decencies that serve to define what full citizenship in that local society means." To fall below the minimum level of decency, Scott writes, "is not merely to be that much poorer materially; it is to fall short of what is locally defined as a fully human existence."[129] The people who sacrificed their time, energy, and even personal safety to save a few ancient artifacts must have felt them somehow essential to a meaningful life itself.

Red guard Ken Ling was a self-avowed foe of "old culture," but he too found himself pondering the meaning of the Destroy the Four Olds campaign. What did the movement propose to accomplish through destruction, and was there to be construction? Ling wracked his brain in search of answers but was finally forced to admit: "I was so busy and few of my comrades were farsighted; when I asked them what would be the next step after destroying the old world, they either answered with an empty phrase 'Foster a new world' or not at all." He was deeply disturbed when someone accused him: "All you people know is how to make rebellion against the dead. You don't do a thing for the living!" What are we to make of the seven incidents Ling recounts of old people rushing into the bonfires to save a few relics? Or of an elderly lady who even wanted to burn herself to death with the idols? The fires of iconoclasm, it seems, were not the only ardors ignited by the Cultural Revolution. Ling confessed, "The stubbornness of these people angered me, but it also moved me."[130]

Instead of slaying the old world, the Cultural Revolution hoisted cultural relics out of limbo and into the melee of modernity. Cultural relics suddenly assumed a living significance to both destroyers and would-be protectors. On the one hand, the symbols of old culture were regarded as a counterrevolutionary threat, critical targets of red guard search-and-destroy missions; on the other, they were precious objects for which individuals at various levels in Chinese society walked the rickety path of resistance. No longer were they merely "safe" or "museumified" traces of a dead past. As the late Joseph Levenson wrote, "old books, once assumed to have been sterilized by history of the power to harm, slipped into obscurity, if not into the flames. All kinds of relics were treated as ominously significant for the here and now; they seemed no longer safely dead, or simply historically significant."[131] During the Cultural Revolution, the ghosts of the past were declared alive and well after years of hibernation, and had to be ritually dragged out and killed once more.

In studying resistance to the "four olds" campaign, we ultimately confront the weightiness of the past in modern China. This concern with the fate of "old culture" was as pressing on the eve of the Cultural Revolution in 1966 as it had been in the May Fourth movement beginning in 1919. Surely a nagging sense of déjà vu on the occasion of May Fourth's fiftieth anniversary was what prompted Maurice Meisner to ask: "Is there something inherently peculiar about modern Chinese history, or about Chinese culture in the post-Confucian age, that demands 'cultural revolutions'?"[132] We might also recall that Taiwan's so-called Cultural Renaissance movement (*wenhua fuxing yundong*)—with the avowed purpose of saving Chinese culture—began on November 12, 1966, almost exactly the same day that the Confucius Temple complex fell to the red guards. In 1970, referring to the violence of the Cultural Revolution and the stagnation of the Cultural Renaissance, Warren Tozer wrote provocatively: "Traditional Chinese culture may be facing extinction."[133] Modern Chinese history has in many ways been a struggle to come to terms with China's historical and cultural legacy. Smaller versions of this struggle are still visible today in the defense of Beijing alleys (*hutong*) and courtyard homes (*siheyuan*) against the demands of modern city planning, and in grassroots efforts like author Feng Jicai's campaign for cultural protection in Tianjin.

Far from bowing to the Maoist battle cry of youth over age, new over old, some stood for their own ideas of human continuity. Robert Jay Lifton once wrote: "One can even say that every expression of resistance to the excesses of the Cultural Revolution involves a reassertion of some such alternative to the prevailing blueprint for revolutionary immortality."[134] In the case of protecting cultural relics, such an alternative image might have revolved around pride in one's local or national culture, or simply the selfish desire to keep valuable relics to oneself. This chapter is by no means an inquiry into the individual motives of each and every protector of cultural relics. Yet it is fruitful to ponder, as Lifton does, issues of longevity that transcend the biological. Preserving and transmitting cultural objects to future generations may well have been a kind of social and cultural raison d'être that was more meaningful to some Chinese than the revolutionary vision of smashing the "old world." If we think of the Cultural Revolution as fundamentally a struggle to deal with a nation's "ineradicable historical legacy" in a time of great uncertainty about the future, then cultural revolutions are not limited to China.[135]

And lest we imagine that issues of cultural destruction and protection are relevant only to China's "turbulent decade," the aftermath of the recent war in Iraq serves as a poignant reminder of something more universal. In April 2003 the National Museum in Baghdad, one of the Middle East's most important archaeological repositories, was ransacked by an Iraqi mob taking advantage of the general chaos.[136] A foreign reporter declared, "5,000 years of history, the most complete timeline of civilization that existed in any museum in the world . . . is shattered, it is smashed."[137] Iraq's principal historical archive, the House of Wisdom, also suffered severe damage. Museum workers tried desperately to call troops for help, but their efforts were to no avail; many items, however, were saved through the foresight of curators who managed to secrete them in underground vaults.[138] Still, as cultural workers sifted through the ruins, the profound sense of loss that saturated the air was deeply connected with the feeling that some larger cultural longevity had been irreparably violated. "A country's identity, its value and civilization resides in its history," said an Iraqi archaeologist. "If a country's civilization is looted, as ours has been here, its history ends. . . . This is not a liberation. This is a humiliation."[139] Though the time, place, and scale of these recent events differ greatly, with attentive ears we can hear the echoes sounding down through the decades since China's Cultural Revolution.

FOUR

Mass Killings in the Cultural Revolution: A Study of Three Provinces

Yang Su

Students of the Cultural Revolution are familiar with its violence, including the ubiquitous beating and torture of teachers, intellectuals, and government officials,[1] and the casualties during street battles among warring mass factions.[2] Less familiar are scattered reports of mass killings, a qualitatively different phenomenon in which a large number of unarmed civilians were massacred in a systematic fashion. These reports include a memoir by a former cadre on perhaps the earliest event of this sort, in Daxing, a suburban county of Beijing. In the five days between August 27 and September 1, 1966, 325 members of "class enemy" households, whose ages ranged from thirty-eight days to eighty years, were executed.[3] The best-known case, and perhaps the most tragic, was in Daoxian County, Hunan Province. An article published in a Hong Kong magazine reports that a series of pogroms spread across the county in late 1967; within two months, 4,950 were killed.[4] Zheng Yi's controversial book on massacres in Guangxi Province may be the best known to the western world thanks to its English translation and its tales about cannibalism.[5] A recent volume edited by Song Yongyi adds cases from Yunnan, Qinghai, Inner Mongolia, and Beijing to this list of atrocities.[6]

Such reports are troubling, but how widespread were such incidents? I had this question in mind when I embarked on my research project on the Chinese Cultural Revolution, using published county gazetteers (*xian zhi*). I found that while the cases cited above may be particularly severe, similar mass killings were relatively common in some rural regions from late 1967 to 1969. As I will show, the evidence is overwhelming. Bear in mind that these gazetteers are publications compiled by local governments. There is little reason to believe such county gazetteers would exaggerate political violence. If anything, we should suspect underreporting.[7] This chapter will document mass killings based on the county gazetteers of three provinces, two of which (Guangxi and Guangdong) report widespread mass killings, and one of which (Hubei) reports relatively few.

In order to understand the extensive violence reported here, I will also discuss the political context of the time. Most mass killings took place when the party-state began to form new local governments and to demobilize mass organizations. By the time Mao and the party center called for a "revolutionary great alliance" in late 1967, the mass movements of the Cultural Revolution had been underway for more than one year. Local governments had been dismantled; the masses had been let loose to form organizations and alliances to contest for power. Mass organizations fought armed street battles. It was an all-but-impossible task to form revolutionary committees (the new organs of power), to have them command obedience, and most of all, to disband and disarm mass organizations. Social and administrative problems were attacked through a time-honored method, "class struggle"— a shorthand term for destroying overt defiance and searching for hidden "enemies." An important difference was that this time local representatives of the state turned "class struggle" into a reign of terror. Mass killings ensued.

Documenting Mass Killings with County Gazetteers

In 1978, the Third Plenum of the Eleventh Central Committee called for rehabilitation of victims in "false," "innocent," and "wrongful" cases in the Cultural Revolution.[8] The policy generated valuable information regarding the scope and severity of tragic events during the Cultural Revolution at the local level, most of which were later documented and published in county gazetteers (xian zhi). The new xian zhi, with few exceptions, have a "Major Events" section that records, among other historic events in the county, key events during the Cultural Revolution. These records also include death and injury statistics for the Cultural Revolution as well as population, party membership, and county leaders' background.

There were about 2,250 such jurisdictions in 1966.[9] For this study, I chose the three provinces of Guangdong, Guangxi, and Hubei, which contain

TABLE 4.1
The Sample Counties, by Province

	Guangxi	Guangdong	Hubei
Counties in sample	65	57	65
Total counties in province, 1966	83	80	72
Percent of counties in sample	78.3	71.3	90.2

some 235 counties, for in-depth examination.[10] Table 4.1 shows the percentage of counties for which I was able to collect county gazetteer information about the Cultural Revolution.

The extent of published detail in accounts of the Cultural Revolution varies greatly due to possible self-censorship or inadequate information gathering. I will report numbers of deaths *as reported* in the county gazetteers. The statistics based on this approach hence should be considered as minimum figures.[11] This conservative coding is a deliberate strategy I have adopted to unambiguously establish the fact of mass killings.

Following Benjamin Valentino, I define mass killing as "the intentional killing of a significant number of the members of any group (as a group and its membership is defined by the perpetrator) of non-combatants."[12] A few elements of this definition are worth further discussion. First, identification of the victim is based on "membership" in some group, as opposed to one that is based on immediate threat to the perpetrator. In the case of the Cultural Revolution, the membership was based on alleged political crimes or unfavorable family background. Second, the intent to kill can be imputed in the perpetrator's action. This separates mass killing from other causes of death in the Cultural Revolution, such as beating during a public struggle session (when the initial intent is more symbolic humiliation than physical killing), or torture during the course of interrogation (when obtaining a confession is the main purpose). Third, the event must not occur during armed combat between mass factions. However, if the victims were disarmed captives taken prisoner after armed combat, I consider them as noncombatants since they no longer posed a threat to the perpetrators. Hence mass killing differs from casualties in armed battles, a widespread phenomenon in the earlier stages of the Cultural Revolution. Finally, the criterion of "a significant number" indicates some concentration in terms of time and space. To decide whether an event constituted a *mass* killing, I use ten deaths as a cut-off point.

A record from Quanzhou County, Guangxi, is typical among the gazetteers that use unequivocal language to describe mass killings:

> October 3, [1967]. In Sanjiang Brigade, Dongshan Commune, the militia commander Huang Tianhui led [the brigade militia] to engage in a massacre. They pushed off a cliff and killed seventy-six individuals of the brigade—former landlords, rich peasants, and their children—in snake-shaped Huanggua'an canyon. . . . From July to October, [another] 850 individuals [in the county]—the four-type elements (landlords, rich peasants, counterrevolutionaries, and bad elements) and their children—were executed with firearms.[13]

This presents one of most devastating cases of mass killings. Quanzhou was otherwise a typical county in terms of demography, governing structure, and recent history. In 1966, about 93 percent of its population of 485,000 was rural, organized into three levels of government: county, commune (township), and brigade (village). In the land reform of the early 1950s, 10,110 families were classified as landlords, and 3,279 as rich peasants.[14] In subsequent political campaigns the ranks of these "class enemies" were enlarged by others who were labeled "counterrevolutionaries" or "bad elements." Together, this segment of the population, including their family members, was known as "four-types" (*silei fenzi*). Whenever "class struggle" rhetoric was whipped up, they were an instant target for harassment and persecution. Their tragedy reached a climax in the Cultural Revolution. By 1971, when the most violent period of the Cultural Revolution had ended, 2,156 men, women, and children of Quanzhou County had died "unnatural deaths," like those in the example quoted above.[15]

An account like this provides information on the timing, location, identities of the victims and the perpetrators, and the way in which the deaths occurred. These accounts represent one of the major types of mass killings, which I call *pogrom against the "four-types."* Other county gazetteers provide less explicit information about the manner of killing. But based on the time period specified in the record and the large number of deaths, mass killings clearly occurred. In the following example from another county, Lingui, Guangxi, the "four-types" comprised the majority of victims, indicating a possible pogrom like that in Quanzhou County, but the victims also include those who were newly labeled as members of an alleged conspiracy. This suggests a second type, which I call *killings in a political witch-hunt.*

> In the name of "cleansing the class ranks" and "mass dictatorship," indiscrimi-nate killings took place across the county. Between mid-June and August [of 1968], 1,991 people were killed as members of "Assassination Squads," "Anti-communist Army of Patriots," and other "black groups." Among them were 326 cadres, 79 workers, 53 students, 68 ordinary urban residents, 547 peasants, and 918 four-type elements and their children. Among the 161 brigades [of the county], only Wenquan in Huixian and Dongjiang in Wantian did not indis-criminately detain and kill.[16]

Unlike in a pogrom against the "four-types," the identity of victims in a political witch-hunt was constructed more recently, based on the accused's association with alleged conspiratorial groups such as the "Assassination Squad" and the "Anti-communist Army of Patriots." While 918 victims were family members of the "four-types," a significant number of individu-als were apparently not in this category—those described as cadres, workers, ordinary peasants, and urban residents.

A third type of mass killing is the *summary execution of captives.* These victims were disarmed after a factional battle and were no longer armed combatants. Killings of this type occurred after one alliance (or faction) already had defeated another. The following example vividly illustrates the nature of this type of event. After a joint meeting attended by public secu-rity officers of a few counties on August 18, 1968,

> the People's Armed Forces Department (Renmin wuzhuangbu) in each county went ahead and carried out the "order." About 4,400 (a number that exceeded what had been stipulated in the meeting) armed individuals of the "United Headquarters" (Lianzhi)[17] besieged the members of "7.29" [a dissenting mass organization] who had fled to Nanshan and Beishan in Fengshan County. More than 10,000 were detained (the county population was then 103,138). During the siege and the subsequent detentions, 1,016 were shot to death, making up more than 70 percent of the total Cultural Revolution deaths of the county. . . . After the violence swept across the county, the establishment of the Revolutionary Committee of Fengshan County was finally [announced] on the twenty-fifth [of August, 1968].[18]

I should also say a few words about those counties for which I am not able to establish that mass killings occurred. If the reported number of deaths is fewer than ten, I do not count the event as a mass killing. Even for those counties whose gazetteers mention a substantial number of deaths, I do not regard the county as experiencing mass killings, if

(1) substantial numbers of deaths are implied rather than explicitly recorded;
(2) recorded deaths were due to armed battles, not imposed upon unarmed civilians; or,
(3) the recorded number of deaths is an aggregated number for the entire period of the Cultural Revolution and the manner in which the deaths occurred cannot be determined.

Quotations from three counties illustrate, respectively, these three scenarios:

> On the evening of March 20 [1968], the militia of Huangqiao Brigade, Xinlian Commune, indiscriminately killed people on the pretext of quelling the "Pingmin Party." Afterwards indiscriminate killings *frequently* occurred across the county and were particularly severe in Youping and other places.[19]
>
> March 3, [1968]. The two [mass] factions engaged in armed battles in Liantang, resulting in 144 deaths.[20]
>
> During the ten-year Cultural Revolution, 2,053 cadres and members of the masses were struggled against; 206 were beaten to death or otherwise caused to die; 541 were injured or permanently disabled during beatings.[21]

The first quotation, from the Mengshan County gazetteer, reports "indiscriminate killings" on March 20, 1968, and afterwards. From the text, we can discern that the number of deaths must be very substantial. But because no specific number is provided, I do not count those events as mass killings. In the second quotation, from Hengxian, 144 deaths are recorded on March 3, 1968, alone; but since these deaths were a result of armed conflict, I do not count this as a mass killing. The third quotation, from Tianlin County, reports 206 deaths, but because the manner of killing is not clear, I do not count this as a mass killing.

Mass Killings in Three Provinces

SCALE

The most severe mass killings were in Guangxi Province. Of sixty-five counties for which I have gazetteers, forty-three, or 66 percent, experienced mass killings (see Table 4.2). Among the most severe cases were fifteen counties that reported more than 1,000 deaths.[22] Wuming County had the highest death toll of all, 2,463. In one campaign alone, 1,546 were killed between mid-June and early July of 1968.[23] Guangxi Province exhibited all three types of mass killing I described above: pogroms against the "four-types," killings in political witch-hunts, and summary executions of captives.

Guangdong Province exhibited a similar pattern. Twenty-eight out of fifty-seven counties, or 49 percent, experienced mass killings. In six counties the number of deaths exceeded 1,000.[24] The most severe case was Yangchun County, with 2,600 deaths between August and October 1968. The mass killings in Guangdong belong to two categories: pogroms against the "four-types" and political witch-hunts. No summary executions of captives, the third type, were reported.

In contrast, mass killings were rarely reported in Hubei Province—only four out of sixty-one counties. These four cases, however, all involved large numbers of deaths due to beatings in waves of political witch-hunts. No pogroms or summary executions were reported.

It is clear from Table 4.2 that mass killings were a widespread phenomenon in Guangxi and Guangdong. At the same time, Hubei seems to stand as a negative case, if the statistics from the county gazetteers of this province reflect the true historical picture.[25]

At about the same time that mass killings occurred widely in Guangxi and Guangdong, counties in Hubei were by no means quiet. On the contrary, this was also a high time of persecution of previously and newly designated "class enemies." Thirty-eight counties, or 60 percent of my Hubei sample, report that more than 1,000 people were beaten in the persecutions, many suffering permanent injuries. Unlike Guangxi and Guangdong, however, large-scale beatings in most cases stopped short of mass killings. Here is an example:

> September 6, [1967]. The county seat witnessed the September 6 "Violent Event." A group of "Rebels" paraded twenty-two "capitalist roaders" and "stubborn conservatives" during the daytime, and injured thirty-two individuals (eight permanently) during the night. These activities quickly spread to communes and villages, where 1,015 were severely beaten. Among them forty-four suffered permanent disabilities, one was killed, and nine others died of causes related to the beatings.[26]

Most counties that experienced similar large-scale beatings report fewer than ten total deaths. In the particular case quoted here, although the death toll

TABLE 4.2
Frequencies of Reported Mass Killings, by Province

	Guangxi	Guangdong	Hubei
Total counties in sample	65	57	65
Counties with mass killings	43	28	4
Percent with mass killings	66.2	49.1	6.2
Counties with at least 500 deaths	27	10	0
Percent with at least 500 deaths	41.5	17.5	0
Average number of deaths	526	278	46.5
Highest overall county death toll	2,463	2,600	115

in a concentrated period reached my cut-off point of ten, I do not count it as a case of mass killing, because nine of these deaths were not explicitly intentional (the intention to harm and injure notwithstanding). Among the sixty-five counties of Hubei, I decided that four had experienced mass killings due to the number of deaths from the epidemic of beatings at the time. They are Yichang (10 killed, 105 driven to suicide, 60 permanently injured), Enshi (2,350 beaten, 51 killed, 314 permanently injured), Zigui (2,500 beaten, 40 killed, 440 severely injured, 35 permanently) and Yunxi (32 killed in Hejiaqu Commune, with 512 beaten and 276 "killed or disabled" in the county as a whole).

TIMING

Although the earliest known episode of mass killings occurred in August 1966 in the Beijing suburban county of Daxing,[27] in the three provinces in this study, mass killings did not occur until late 1967 or 1968, shortly before or after the establishment of the revolutionary committees there. Figure 4.1 compares the dates of the founding of the county-level committee with the dates of mass killings in Guangxi, Guangdong, and Hubei respectively. The data clearly show that the peaks of mass killings closely followed the founding of the revolutionary committee.

As shown in Figure 4.1, both in Guangxi and Guangdong, mass killings peaked in July 1968, just after most counties established their revolutionary committees. This was the month when the center issued two well publicized directives to ban armed battles and to disband mass organizations.[28] In Guangxi, the provincial revolutionary committee was not yet established, and the opposition mass alliance, known as April Twenty-second, led insurgencies in all the major cities. The provincial authorities therefore implemented the two directives to crack down on the opposing faction, forcing some of its members to flee to rural counties. At the same time, the newly established governments at the lower levels were called on to "preemptively attack class enemies."[29] Some local governments, particularly communes, seemed to respond to this call with great zeal, whether or not there was significant organized resistance in the jurisdiction. In Guangdong, although the provincial government had been established since February, organized defiance represented by the Red Flag faction persisted, just as did the resistance of the April Twenty-second faction in Guangxi. The Guangdong provincial government also used the two directives from the center as a weapon in its face-off with Red Flag. As in Guangxi, policy pronouncements from Beijing and the provincial capital that targeted organized resistance translated into a climate of terror in lower-level jurisdictions (counties, communes, and brigades), whether or not organized resistance was widespread. Mass killings took place in such a climate.

In contrast to Guangdong and Guangxi, the few cases of mass killings in Hubei occurred not in July but about two months earlier (Figure 4.1). Beijing's two directives against mass organizations seemed to have affected Hubei very differently from the way they affected the other two provinces. This may indicate that mass factional alignments in this period help to explain provincial differences in mass killings. In Hubei, unlike Guangxi and Guangdong, the rebel faction had been included in the new government (to be discussed further below).

Figure 4.1 shows that the mass killings in all three provinces were concentrated in a few months. This is important because it ties the mass killings to the establishment of revolutionary committees and the demobilization of mass organizations. It is known that most killings occurred in the wake of the formation of revolutionary committees, but we do not know the specific mechanism that produced them. Some scholars attribute them to a series of later campaigns, especially the Cleansing of the Class Ranks (*qingli jieji duiwu*) and One-Strike, Three-Anti (*yida sanfan*).[30]

Our data show that in fact these national campaigns did not always lead to severe persecutions at the local level. Gazetteers suggest that counties selectively chose the rhetoric of some, but not all national campaigns. Just as important, the timing of adoption varied greatly across provinces and coun-

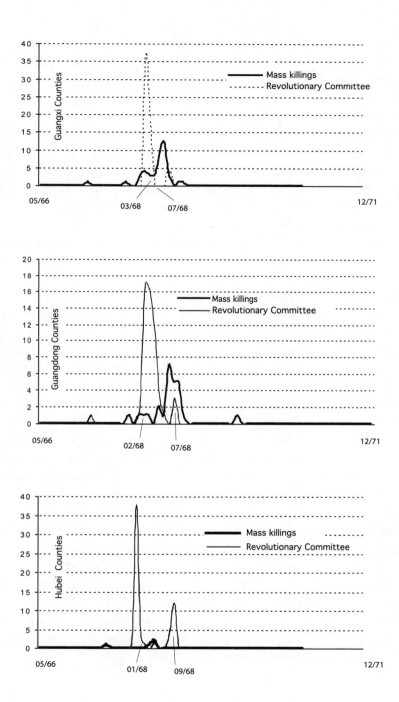

FIGURE 4.1   The Timing of Mass Killings in Relation to the Founding of Revolutionary Committees

ties. Each of our three provinces, in fact, generated its own campaign waves, which respectively affected persecutions in its counties.

LOCATION

Mass killings tended to occur in jurisdictions below the county level, usually in the commune (township) or in the brigade (village). If we recall the quotations above, specific names of communes or villages are mentioned in relation to mass killings. For example, Sanjiang *Brigade* is specified in the well-known Quanzhou (Guangxi) pogrom in which seventy-six family members of the "four-types" were pushed into a canyon. In the Lingui County case (Guangxi), the report specified that only two out of 161 brigades did not have mass killings. Among the twenty-eight Guangdong counties where mass killings were reported, six gazetteers contain detailed information regarding names of the related jurisdictions. For example, *Qujiang xian zhi* states: "In January [1968] serious incidents of illegal killings occurred in Zhangzhi *Commune*. Thirteen *brigades* of the commune indiscriminately arrested and killed; 149 were killed."[31] Other examples include the following: "Large number of beatings and killings occurred in the three *communes* of Chitong, Zhenglong, and Beijie, resulting in twenty-nine people being killed"; "Mass dictatorship was carried out by the security office of *various communes*"; "Litong *Brigade*, Xin'an *Commune* buried alive fifty-six 'four-types' and their family members."[32] The contrast between the lack of mass killings in the urban settings and their abundance in rural villages may reflect a *disconnect* between lower-level jurisdictions and the upper-level authorities, indicating the weakness of state control at the lower level.

The observation that mass killings were more likely to occur where state control was weakest is supported by another consideration with regard to geography: the variation in incidence across counties. In Table 4.3, I compare counties with mass killings and those without.[33] The table shows that more mass killings occurred in lower-level rural jurisdictions. The average distance of counties with mass killings from the provincial capital is 212 kilometers, while that of counties without mass killings is 179 kilometers. Counties with mass killings also were more sparsely populated and had lower per capita government revenue (see Table 4.3).

VICTIM IDENTITIES

Most county gazetteers do not provide detailed information regarding the

TABLE 4.3

County Characteristics and Mass Killings in Guangxi and Guangdong

	Counties with mass killings	Counties without mass killings
Average distance from provincial capital (kilometers)	212	179
Population per square kilometer	139.7	219.1
Government per capita revenue (yuan)	15.1	20.8

identities of the victims. Where such information is available, the most frequently mentioned category of the population is the so-called four-types, those previously classified as "class enemies." A detailed breakdown of victims is available in some counties, such as one cited above from Lingui County, Guangxi. As shown in Table 4.4, among the 1,991 victims, 918—almost half—were "four-types" or their children.

A few points can be summarized from the profiles of victims presented in Table 4.4. First, as noted, the largest group of victims was the "four-types." This shows clearly that mass killings targeted the weak rather than those who constituted a real threat to the authorities (alleged conspiracy notwithstanding). Second, the majority of victims were rural residents—that is, mass killings mostly occurred outside the county seat. This is also important, because it shows that mass killings occurred in the lower reaches of the government hierarchy where state control was particularly weak. Third, in some places, a significant number of non–four-types and non-rural individuals were killed. This may reflect mass killings in the form of a political witch-hunt or summary execution of captives. When mass killings were used to eliminate rival faction members, victims other than those of the "four-types" account for a very significant proportion. For example, in the case of Fengshan County described above, among the 1,331 victims killed in the wake of a siege, 246 were cadres or workers (both being urban residents).[34]

A remarkable fact about the victims was the large number of children in "four-type" households. Some report that the perpetrators' rationale was that they may grow up to seek revenge.[35] In some cases, it seemed to be an afterthought. In Daoxian, after killing the adult "four-types," the perpetrators came back to drag out the children, killed them, and finally looted the victims' residences.[36] But in other cases, the children were guilty by association and were killed along with their parents. The former landlord Liu

Xiangyuan and his wife, who came from a poor-peasant background, had two children. One was one year old and the other three. Before Liu was ordered to jump to his death in the Quanzhou County incident, Liu pleaded with the militia head Huang Tianhui: "Tianhui, I have two kids. Could the government decide that one of them belongs to my wife? How about I jump with one child but you spare the other one for my wife?" Huang said: "No!"[37]

THE PERPETRATORS

The mass killings were by no means committed by misguided and spontaneous crowds. Where information is available, we find that the perpetrators were invariably organized by governmental authorities, usually militia members, members of mass organizations, or new volunteers. Without exception, available detailed accounts (about Daxing, Quanzhou, Daoxian, and Fengshan) report painstaking organizational meetings before the killings. In Zhang Cheng's account about Daoxian, meeting participants voted to decide who would be killed. One by one, the potential victims' names were read and votes were tallied. The process lasted for hours.[38] In another district in the county, Zhang reports: "From district to communes, mobilization took place through every level, involving the district party secretary, deputy secretary, commander of the 'Honglian' [a mass factional organization], the public security head and district chief accountants."[39] The killings were committed in a highly organized manner. The victims usually were rounded up and killed in a location away from public view. There were also cases in which a mass rally was held and a large number were killed, the so-called execution meetings.[40]

Interviews with the perpetrators many years later indicate that most of them carried out the killing as a political duty.[41] There is evidence that such acts were politically rewarded. In late 1968 and early 1969, provinces and counties began a campaign to rectify and rebuild the party organization. A large number of activists were recruited. Some official statistics show a chilling connection between violent zeal and political reward. According to a document published by the Guangxi government, during the Cultural Revolution in Guangxi, more than nine thousand people who had killed were recruited as new party members; another twenty thousand who had joined the party earlier in the Cultural Revolution through "fast-track" recruitment later committed murders. Another seventeen thousand party members were responsible for killings in one way or another.[42]

TABLE 4.4
Profiles of Victims of Mass Killings, Selected Jurisdictions

Jurisdiction	Identity of Victims	Number	Percent
Linggui County	Four-types and their children	918	46.1
	Peasants	547	27.5
	Cadres	326	16.4
	Urban residents	68	3.4
	Workers	79	4.0
	Students	53	2.7
	Total	1,991	100
Binyang County	Rural residents	3,441	88.7
	Cadres	51	1.4
	Teachers	87	2.5
	Workers	102	3.0
	Total	3,681	100
Lingling Special District	Four-types	3,576	39.3
	Children of four-types	4,057	44.6
	Poor and middle peasants	1,049	11.5
	Other backgrounds	411	4.5
	Total	9,093	100

SOURCES: *Lingui xian zhi* (Beijing: Fangzhi chubanshe, 1996), 492; *Guangxi wen'ge dashi nianbiao* (Nanning: Guangxi renmin chubanshe, 1990), 111; and Zhang Cheng, "Daoxian da tusha," *Kaifang zazhi* (July, Aug., Sept., Dec. 2001).

Provincial Variations

The difference in the scale of mass killings between Hubei and the other two provinces in this study is very large. It suggests that the level of violence was a function of both national politics and local conditions. What accounts for this difference? I propose some tentative hypotheses.

The baseline hypothesis is that the provincial difference documented here is not a historical fact but an artifact of editorial policies in compiling xian zhi. The compilation and publication of county gazetteers was organized by a hierarchy of government agencies. Counties in one province may have followed a set of policy guidelines different in another. Among those guidelines was the principle known as "recording in broad strokes, not in detail" on the history of the Cultural Revolution.[43] It is possible that the compilers in Hubei Province were more conservative and left out more information than their counterparts in the other two provinces. Indeed the average length of accounts of the Cultural Revolution in the Hubei gazetteers—2,361 words—is barely half that devoted to the subject in the gazetteers for Guangdong (5,198 words) and Guangxi (5,117).[44]

On the other hand, although the Hubei gazetteers rarely report mass killings, they do not shy away from reporting large numbers of people who were beaten and injured. In fact they report many more injuries than the gazetteers of Guangdong (see Table 4.6). There are therefore reasons to suspect that the differences in the reported number of killings may actually indicate real differences in the course of political events across provinces.

Differences in death tolls could plausibly be linked to the divergent paths of prior conflict leading to the founding of revolutionary committees in these three provinces. According to Xu Youyu's summary of provincial-level conflicts nationwide, Hubei and our other two provinces represented two different paths.[45] Prior to the founding of their revolutionary committees, all provincial capitals experienced mass mobilization by factions and numerous government reorganizations. Two opposed alliances emerged. Typically, one of them sought to overthrow the pre–Cultural Revolution government, while the other made more moderate demands or in fact fought to defend the government. Power often shifted back and forth between the two sides after the January Storm of 1967, but after the Wuhan incident in July of that year, the balance of power shifted in Hubei, and in many other provinces. With the tacit support or explicit approval of the center, the more militant faction was designated as the revolutionary side. The government was thoroughly reorganized, and the moderate alliance discredited. Members of the more militant alliance were incorporated into the new government in large numbers.[46]

But there were exceptions to this scenario, including both Guangdong and Guangxi. According to Xu, the center's policy was different for border regions—Inner Mongolia, Xinjiang, Tibet, Guangdong, and Guangxi—due to considerations of national security.[47] In this group of provinces the faction that was more supportive of the incumbent government was designated as "revolutionary" and assumed a major role in the revolutionary committee. The revolutionary committee, in turn, cracked down on the more militant rebel faction.

TABLE 4.5
County Death Tolls in Two Types of Provinces

	Deaths per county	Number of counties
Type 1 Provinces	45.2	1,271
Type 2 Provinces	451	259
Type 2 Provinces, excluding Guangdong and Guangxi	70.3	135

In both types of provinces, mass conflict was severe. Superficially, the fault line was between pro- and anti-government factions. However, in provinces like Hubei—which I will call type 1 provinces—the government incorporated many who had stridently opposed the pre–Cultural Revolution government. A new fault line developed between opposition rebels who were included in the revolutionary committee and their former allies, who were excluded. On the other hand, in provinces like Guangdong and Guangxi—type 2 provinces—the revolutionary committee united officials from the former government with leaders of the more moderate faction and then used their power to crush the rebel opposition.

Following Xu's analysis, I classify provinces into two types. Type 1 provinces are those whose political experience was similar to Hubei's; type 2 provinces are those whose experience was similar to Guangdong's and Guangxi's. Table 4.5 summarizes information for a national sample of 1,530 counties. The table makes clear that the death toll in the 259 counties located in type 2 provinces far outstripped that in the type 1 provinces. The average number of deaths per county in type 1 provinces was 451, but in type 2 provinces it was only 45, a ten-fold difference. Even if we exclude Guangxi and Guangdong, two provinces with particularly severe violence, the average number of deaths per county in type 2 provinces is still 50 percent higher. Therefore, we may conclude that the difference between Hubei and the other two provinces may represent a nationwide phenomenon.

It is unclear what mechanisms produced these differences. Some suggest that the severe violence in Guangdong and Guangxi can be attributed to retaliation by "conservatives" operating as government-backed militias against the opposition faction. There is some evidence to support this explanation. For example, the mass execution of captives in Guangxi seemed to be an instance of retaliation. Also, in Guangxi the opposition April Twenty-sec-

TABLE 4.6
Deaths, Injuries, and Numbers Persecuted per County in Three Provinces

	Deaths per county	Injuries per county	Numbers persecuted per county
Guangxi	574.0	266.4	12,616
Guangdong	311.6	28.1	6,788
Hubei	10.8	44.5	2,317
All provinces	80	68	5,397

ond faction repeatedly organized protests against mass killings.[48] But, as we have shown, the majority of the victims were four-types, and we have no evidence that they joined the rebel faction in disproportionate numbers. In the remote villages and communes where mass killings were most extensive, it is not clear whether there was factional mobilization prior to mass killings at all.

In light of the literature on genocide, one may propose a different hypothesis from a policy angle. The fact that the victims were mostly from four-types families suggests the mass killing was an extreme version—extermination—of the party's long-standing class-elimination policy. Theorists of genocide and mass killing in comparative perspective suggest that a more representative polity provides a deterrent.[49] It is suggestive that the Hubei government was more representative of the oppositional elements than the Guangdong and Guangxi governments.

What can these findings tell us about the scale of mass killings in China's other provinces? Guangxi and Guangdong may represent provinces with particularly severe mass killings and Hubei may represent those provinces at the mild end. Most provinces may be in between, but were closer to Guangxi and Guangdong than to Hubei. This conclusion can be reached by comparing the total number of rural deaths during the Cultural Revolution. Based on the 1,530 collected county gazetteers, the national average of deaths per county is 80. The averages in Guangxi and Guangdong are far above the national average (574 and 311 respectively), while Hubei (10.8) is far below. The numbers injured and targeted for persecution show a similar pattern (see Table 4.6).

The Political Context

Extreme violence such as mass killing and genocide challenges both our conscience and intellect. One would be remiss not to attempt an explanation. The pattern of mass killings in fact provides some clues. They appear to be political in nature: the timing, the perpetrators, and the identification of victims were all tied to the consolidation of power by newly established local governments. The killings do not seem to be random and unfocused. If this premise can be established, an explanation needs to address two issues. The first is about the political environment surrounding the events. What are the political and legal conditions under which a perpetrator believes that killing will not result in punishment? A second has to do with the psychology of the perpetrator. Even if there is everything to gain (political or otherwise), why does he or she willingly commit such a repulsive act?

I will focus primarily on the first issue. What motivates my discussion of the causes of mass killings is this question: did state policy makers *intentionally* kill in this manner, or were the mass killings largely an *unintended* consequence? This question may seem simplistic at first glance, but it is nonetheless a useful starting point that will lead us to explore the state policies and structures related to the mass killings. In the following discussion, a distinction is made between the central authorities and local governments. On paper, central policy pronouncements time and again admonished against violent excess, but they were taken to heart only by some local leaders. This distinction will prove to be crucial as the discussion unfolds.

DEMOBILIZING MASS MOVEMENTS AND FORMING
NEW GOVERNMENTS

The Cultural Revolution began in May 1966 and subsided in 1971. Two waves of events divided the movement into three periods: the power seizure campaign in January 1967 and the formation of new local governments (revolutionary committees) in late 1967 and 1968.[50] Participants at first only included students and intellectuals, but later involved people from all walks of life, including workers, peasants, and bureaucrats. For more than one year, citizens were permitted to form their own political groups. The freedom and "great democracy" (*da minzhu*), however, did not produce the new order that Mao may have had in mind. Instead, citizens everywhere split into factions and fought street battles.

By late 1967 mass factions were to be demobilized. Mao called for "great revolutionary unity" of a divided and militant population. He envisioned new forms of government—revolutionary committees—in every jurisdiction by February 1968, the Chinese New Year.[51] For local bureaucrats at the provincial, county, commune, and brigade levels, however, this was no easy task. In fact, Mao's plan failed. The last provincial revolutionary committee was not set up until September of 1968 (in Xinjiang). Some revolutionary committees at lower levels were not established until September 1969.[52] In Hubei, the provincial revolutionary committee was established on February 1, 1968, and most new county governments were formed in the spring of that year. In Guangdong, the provincial revolutionary committee was founded on February 20, 1968; most county-level committees were founded in the months of January, February, and March. Guangxi's provincial committee was set up August 20, 1968, although most county governments were formed in the months of February, March, and April of the year (see Figure 4.1).

Establishing a new order involved two related tasks: installing an effective local government and cracking down on dissenting mass opposition. The new revolutionary committees were to consist of army officers, selected leaders from the former government, and selected leaders of mass factions. Which officials from the former government and which leaders of mass factions would be appointed to the revolutionary committee was often hotly contested, and leaders of mass factions who were shut out of the revolutionary committee could become vehement opponents of the new order. In Guangdong and Guangxi, oppositional alliances continued to wage armed battles against those who supported the new government. In Guangxi, armed battles plagued Nanning, the provincial capital, and delayed the formation of the revolutionary committee until August 1968, and even then it occurred only after the center's concerted intervention.[53] In Guangdong, Premier Zhou Enlai called for the formation of a revolutionary committee within a month and a half in early November 1967, but the task was not accomplished until February 20, 1968.[54] Nor did order ensue immediately. The dissenting mass alliance, Red Flag, remained openly defiant and engaged in numerous street battles, known as "great armed struggles" (*da wudou*), for the next three months.[55] In Hubei, the provincial revolutionary committee was an outcome of mass factional struggle that culminated in the well-known Wuhan incident of July 20, 1967, in which the former government and its mass allies fell in disgrace. The opposition emerged victorious, thanks to the center's backing. Armed battles peaked that summer. The new government was formed on February 5, 1968, with the former opposition faction dominating the seats for mass representatives.[56]

Persistent disorder in the provinces concerned the party center, which urged the new revolutionary committees to defend their power and to treat opposition in "class struggle" terms. The revolutionary committees took up the suggestion, and often played up the class rhetoric, which in turn influenced the behavior of officials in counties and other lower-level jurisdictions. Many responded with terror campaigns, whether the political threat was real or imagined.

DEFINING VICTIMS AND MANUFACTURING THREATS

The central party leaders' call for a political solution to establish the new order was unequivocal. A typical passage regarding such policies was the 1968 New Year editorial that appeared jointly in the party's three flagship publications:

> Chairman Mao says: "All reactionary forces will fight to the last gasp at their pending doom." A handful of traitors, spies and capitalist power-holders in the party, the demons and ghosts (that is, those landlords, rich peasants, counterrevolutionaries, bad elements, and rightists who have not yet been well reformed) in society, and the running dogs of the American imperialists and Soviet Revisionists are bound to continue their sabotage and instigation with all possible means, including spreading rumors and planting divisions.[57]

Hitler's Nazi state promoted a racial theory that portrayed Jews as subhuman. Stalin's communist state created a category of "enemies of the people" who were subject to extermination. As such, early in the process, mass killings often involved the state propaganda machine dehumanizing a segment of the population. The Chinese equivalent of the subhuman category was "class enemy." What was unique during the demobilization of the Cultural Revolution is that the defining characteristics were based not so much on ascriptive traits (race, ethnicity, or religion) as a political standard: a class enemy was whomever the local government deemed to be standing in the way of the new social order. "Whether or not one is willing to overcome factionalism," asserted the same editorial, "is the most important sign of whether or not one is willing to be a real revolutionary under the present circumstances."[58]

As at other times, party policy was general rather than specific. While it stressed the existence of "class enemies" and their potential threat, it did not provide criteria for identifying them. Local governments could define "class enemy" as they saw fit. To compensate for the deficiency in general pronouncements, the party promoted a series of examples of local practice. For example, four days after the above editorial, the center issued a directive praising the work of "deeply digging out traitors" by Heilongjiang Province.[59] At mid-year, a report on a Beijing factory's experience of "fighting enemies" was distributed nationwide with great fanfare.[60] Local governments emulated these examples to comply with the national policy.

The rhetoric of "class struggle" was not new, nor was its effect unprecedented in dehumanizing certain categories of the population. For violence as extreme as mass killing to occur, there was an additional process at work: manufacturing threat. As commonly seen in other cases of mass killing in which the state not only creates a category of the subhuman but also manufactures a pending danger of inaction, the provincial and the lower-level governments manufactured tangible threats to justify terror.

In this case, local governments rushed to concoct stories of organized activities by so-called conspiratorial groups. Local governments called for "preemptive attacks against class enemies," often in a manner of "launching a force-12 typhoon." In Hubei Province, a moderate period came to an end in late March 1968 when Beijing suddenly stopped the anti–ultra-leftist campaign and switched to a so-called counterattack on rightist trends. In the provincial capital the self-styled mass dictatorship group turned the Wuhan Gymnasium into a large prison. Many were beaten.[61] The anti-rightist attack also swept counties, as April and May that year witnessed a reign of terror across the province, under the banner of a campaign to "oppose three, smash one" (*sanfan yi fensui*), against the so-called class enemy's ferocious attack (*jieji diren de changkuang jingong*).[62]

In Guangxi and Guangdong, a large-scale conspiratorial network—"Patriots against the Communists" (PAC)—was reportedly unmasked on June 17, 1968. It was alleged that the Guangxi part of the network was only a "division," and that the headquarters was in Guangzhou, the provincial capital of Guangdong. One of the two warring mass factions—the United Headquarters (Lianzhi)—soon attacked its rival in these terms: "The PACs are deeply rooted in the April Twenty-second Organization. The leaders of

April Twenty-second are the PACs. Let's act immediately. Whoever resists arrest should be executed on the spot."[63]

There is evidence that the mobilization of terror was directly facilitated by the diagnosis of the situation by a few key central leaders. In a meeting with Guangxi mass representatives on July 25, 1968, Zhou Enlai and Kang Sheng sanctioned this theory of a large-scale conspiracy. They agreed that the PAC headquarters was based in Guangzhou and there were branches in Guangxi. More significantly, both leaders specifically linked the PACs to two mass alliances (April Twenty-second in Guangxi and Red Flag in Guangdong).[64]

The general climate encouraged rumors of conspiracy and threat in communes and villages. Not only were those labels handed down from above used to signify danger, but allegations about tangible threats abounded—"assassination squads" and "action manifestos" were reported to have been uncovered. In the cliff-killing case of Quanzhou County, Guangxi, cited above, the commune militia head came back from a meeting in a nearby county and instructed his subordinates that the "four-types" were about to act, and that the first groups of victims would be cadres and party members, followed by poor peasants.[65] Information is limited in the county gazetteers of the three provinces, but a speech by the county leader in Zhang Cheng's detailed account of Daoxian (Hunan Province) may illuminate the typical rhetoric of manufacturing an imminent threat before a mass killing:

> At this time the class struggle is complicated. A few days ago, there appeared reactionary posters in the No. 6 district.[66] The class enemies spread rumors that Chiang Kai-shek and his gang will attack mainland China soon and the American imperialists will launch a new world war. Once the war breaks out, they [class enemies] will first kill party members, then probationary party members. In the No. 1 district, a [former] puppet colonel [who had served in the puppet army during the Anti-Japanese War, that is World War II] sought out the brigade [party] secretary and the peasant's association chair and demanded re-instatement.[67]

ADMONISHING AGAINST EXCESS

Understanding the role of the state in mass killings will not be complete without noting the other side of the story: the central and provincial officials constantly warned against excessive violence. No explicit endorsement of mass killings can be found in any party document or speech. To the extent that information about mass killings was passed upward and treated as credible, the upper-level authorities reacted with condemnation and in some cases sent in the army to restore order.

As early as November 20, 1966, the party Central Committee distributed a Beijing municipal policy directive to all local governments nationwide, prohibiting "unauthorized detention stations, unauthorized trial courts, and unauthorized arrests and beatings." It warned that those behaviors were a "violation of state law and party discipline."[68] Thereafter, the spirit of "struggle through reason, not violence" was reiterated again and again by the center through a series of major policy pronouncements (for instance, on December 15, 1966, January 28, 1967, April 6, 1967, June 6, 1967, May 15, 1968, July 3, 24, and 28, 1968, December 26, 1968).[69]

Although it is debatable whether a provincial government such as Guangxi was serious when it warned against excessive violence, it did so at least on paper. In December 1967, about one month after a new wave of mass killings spread across the province, the provincial authorities issued a ten-point order including this statement: "Mass organizations should not randomly arrest, beat, or kill. All the current detainees should be released immediately." From this point on, a new term was coined, "indiscriminate beatings and killings" (*luanda luansha*) to label the widespread violence as a violation of social and political order.[70] For example, on December 18, 1967, the provincial authorities issued a report on luanda luansha in Li Village, Rong County; on May 3, 1968, issued an order to stop luanda luansha after an investigation in nine counties; on June 24, 1968, issued the document "Instructions about Prohibiting Luanda Luansha"; on September 19, 1968, confiscated firearms from mass organizations; and finally, on September 23, 1968, issued a "Notice about Stopping Luanda Luansha."[71]

The most compelling evidence of official opposition to excessive violence is that in many locations, when the information about such incidents could be passed upward, the authorities sent in leaders or the army to intervene. For example, in the earliest incident of mass killings in the suburb of Beijing, a county leader went to Macun Village five times to stop the killings. His effort involved high-ranking leaders of the Beijing city government.[72] In the case of the most severe mass killings in Daoxian, Hunan, an army division was sent in to end it.[73] Although no detailed information is available in the county annals as to how the mass killings came to an end, the data show that they were usually concentrated in a certain period of time, and in most counties the upsurge in killings occurred only once, indicating that some sort of external constraints were imposed from above.

It is reasonable to conclude that such official policies from both the center and the provincial authorities served to prevent mass violence from escalating even further. But these efforts were relatively ineffective for two reasons. First, the official policy did not carry any real punishment. The admonition was usually meant to serve only as a guide for the future. In fact, there is no evidence of any punishment during or immediately after any mass killing. The following quote from a speech by Minister of Public Security Xie Fuzhi on May 15, 1968, is a telling example of the leniency toward the perpetrators of violence. In this speech, which was supposed to admonish against violence, he seemed to suggest that no violence would be punished:

> Even counterrevolutionaries should not be killed, as long as they are willing to accept reeducation. It is doubly wrong to beat people to death. *Nonetheless, these things [killings] happened because of lack of experience; so there is no need to investigate who is responsible.* What is important is to gain experience so as to carry out in earnest Chairman Mao's instructions to struggle not with violence but with reason.[74]

The prosecution of perpetrators did not happen until the late 1970s, some ten years after the fact.

Second, it is not clear whether provincial and lower governments meant business in their warnings against extreme violence. For example, the above list of Guangxi actions regarding mass killings coincided with another long list of policies persecuting "class enemies." Although the province may have seen the luanda luansha in communes and villages as unwarranted, its incentive to play up violence against the oppositional mass organizations in the cities undercut its role as guardian of social order.

STATE CONTROL CRIPPLED

The very nature of the Cultural Revolution—dismantling and rebuilding local governments—had severely damaged the vertical bureaucratic hierarchy. This included the overhaul of the public security system and the legal systems. By August 1967, the attack on these systems had been called for by no less than the minister of the Public Security, Xie Fuzhi:

> From the beginning of the Cultural Revolution last year until the January Storm this year, the majority of apparatuses of public security, prosecution,

and the court were protecting capitalist roaders and repressing revolutionary masses. . . . The situation is hard to change, unless the whole system of public security is overhauled. The old machine must be entirely smashed.[75]

In 1967, according to county gazetteers, the agencies of these systems ceased to function in local counties, communes, and villages. Detentions and prosecutions were carried out not according to any sense of law but according to the political standards of the moment.

Another result of the Cultural Revolution was the clogged channels of information flow both from top down and bottom up. Particularly germane to our discussion was the failure of the bottom-up information flow, such that when bad things happened at the lower reaches of the state, the upper authorities usually did not know until it was too late. When local leaders publicized their "achievements" in the movement, violence was covered up. For example, in January 1967 the Beijing municipal government submitted to the center a report about how the new administration of Qinghua University faithfully carried out the center's policy. This report painstakingly described how the people who had committed "bad deeds" were well treated and given opportunities to reform themselves. The report drew Mao's attention and he instructed it to be distributed across the nation as a model for emulation.[76] Not until 1978, ten years later, would another report, issued in an entirely different political climate, rebut the initial account, detailing the real fate of the struggle targets at this university. According to the new report, within only two months of the class cleansing campaign, more than ten people were killed in one way or the other.[77] Similarly, in local counties, due to the failure of information to flow from the bottom up, the upper-level authorities intervened only after large numbers of people had been killed.

Conclusion

We have uncovered four prominent features of the pattern of mass killings. First, they varied greatly across the three provinces, while within each province there appears to have been a great degree of uniformity. This pattern indicates that the occurrence of mass killings was more a function of province-specific political conditions than national politics as a whole. I tentatively attribute the provincial difference to the provincial pattern of mass factional alignment vis-à-vis the governmental authorities. In Hubei, the opposition faction, having prevailed in the previous conflict with the central government's support, was incorporated into the new government. In contrast, in Guangxi and Guangdong, the opposition was excluded from power, and revolutionary committees in these two provinces were more prone to use violence against the insurgents.

Second, mass killings were concentrated in the months after most counties established revolutionary committees but at a time when the provincial capitals were still entangled in mass factionalism. The peaks of mass killings coincided with two directives from the party center in July 1968 banning factional armed battles and disbanding mass organizations. This finding helps us understand the nature and source of mass killings. The fact that most of them occurred after the new revolutionary committees were put in place indicates that mass killings were the result of the repression by the local state rather than the result of conflicts between independent mass groups. The fact that they coincided with the crackdown on the oppositional mass organizations in the provincial capitals indicates that the provincial authorities promoted the rhetoric of violence, although extreme violence in local communes and villages may not be what they intended.

Third, mass killings were primarily a rural phenomenon. In other words, they occurred not in provincial capitals or county seats, but in communes and villages. This is in stark contrast to earlier mass movements of the Cultural Revolution such as campaigns against intellectuals and government officials and the factional street battles, which mostly occurred in urban settings. The image of top-down diffusion does not apply to the mass killings. This suggests that the class struggle rhetoric disseminated from urban centers found an expression in extreme violence in rural townships and villages, possibly due to the failure of the state to hold the lowest bureaucrats accountable for their actions. This explanation is supported by another piece of evidence—the poorer and more remote counties were more likely to have mass killings.

Fourth, the perpetrators were local leaders and their mass followers (for example, militia members). This speaks to the political nature of the mass killings in the Cultural Revolution.

What can we make of these patterns? What do they say about the role of the state in the mass killings? In order to answer these questions, let me explicate my conception of the Chinese state that has implicitly guided my discussion thus far. I differentiate the state into three levels—the center, the province, and the local governments (county, commune, and brigade).

The central authorities in Beijing played up the class struggle rhetoric as their time-honored method of solving the problem of the moment—how to set up local governments and demobilize mass movements. In this sense, they had a sponsoring role in the mass killings. However, as evidenced in the policy pronouncements, the center also saw extreme violence at the local level as an indication of unwarranted disorder. In this sense, the fact that mass killings nonetheless occurred represented a failure of the state to influence local actors' behavior.

The provincial authorities, particularly in Guangxi and Guangdong, had an incentive to promote class struggle rhetoric in dealing with mass opposition in the cities. They may have had more tolerance for violence than the center due to the particularly severe challenges they faced. In this sense, the state was the sponsor of mass killings. In fact, the high point of mass killings was exactly when the provinces used the two July central directives to crack down on mass opposition. However, it is unclear whether the large number of killings in local communes and villages, mostly against unorganized "four-types," helped the crackdown on the opposition in the cities. It may be reasonable to believe that it was not instrumentally useful except that it may have helped generate a climate of fear. In other words, the provincial authorities would also see the mass killings in villages as unwarranted, an indication of state failure at the provincial level.

In comparison, local governments (at county, commune, and village levels) were clearly the direct sponsors of the mass killings, although their motives are not clear. They may have misinterpreted the policies disseminated from above and showed their compliance with an extreme level of zealotry; or, they may have seen terror as a convenient way to solidify their grip on power in the local community. For whatever reason, it was the local bureaucrats and their followers who committed the violence. At a time when the formal public security and court systems had ceased to function and in an era when the justification for violence seemed to be palpable, local leaders, particularly those at the grassroots level and in remote areas, were unaccountable.

As such, when the state is considered not as a unitary whole but as a collection of actors at various levels, mass killings were created not by state sponsorship or state failure alone, but by a combination of both. The tragedy of mass killings in the later part of the Cultural Revolution was rooted in this paradox of state sponsorship and state failure.

A generation of research on the Cultural Revolution mass movement has been dominated by works that search for the underlying interest-group base of "rebellion."[78] Missing from these studies are two important features of the Cultural Revolution: violence and state sponsorship. The violence was rooted in the Stalinist doctrine of unmasking hidden enemies. Earlier scholars often bypass this doctrine and the violence it entailed. Their research is more about the interests and idealism of actors behind their violent actions. However, "as experienced by participants, bystanders, and victims alike, it [the Cultural Revolution] is now commonly understood not as a pursuit of abstract ideals," Walder once reminded us, "but for what it turned out to be: an unprecedented wave of state-instigated persecution, torture, gang warfare, and mindless violence."[79] The Stalinist doctrine in Mao's China was taken to heart by all actors in the political system. It matters little whether they were for or against the status quo. Seen in this light, the recent discussion by a group of Chinese scholars about the "democratic" elements in the Cultural Revolution is misguided.[80] The political witch-hunt approach and the bloody treatment of opponents did more to damage any semblance of democracy in social life than to advance it.

> If the CR [Cultural Revolution] was "really" an idealistic quest for equality and democracy or a dispute over national policy, why did it take the form of a search for hidden traitors and enemies? If CR radicalism was a rhetorical mask for rational interest-group activity, why did these rational actors appear to take their rhetoric so seriously and routinely kidnap, humiliate, and fight wars of annihilation against other radical workers and students?[81]

In this study I confront the disturbing feature of violence head on. I do so by searching for an explanation in state institutions and state actors.

This leads us to the second defining feature of the Cultural Revolution: state sponsorship. Previous research often focused on preexisting social divisions that allegedly motivated mass movements. But as I have shown above, not only did the state lead the movement through policy pronouncements, but also local state actors took the interpretations of these pronouncements into their own hands. One of the consequences was the large-scale violence examined here. A switch of analytical focus to state institutions and state actors is necessary to do justice to this important feature of the Cultural Revolution.

FIVE

The Death of a Landlord: Moral Predicament in Rural China, 1968–1969

Jiangsui He

To the villagers of Yangjiagou, in northeastern Shaanxi Province, April is the best month of the year. After a long and harsh winter, the weather becomes warmer and the land revives. It is a time to prepare for the beginning of a new year. It is a time for the peasants to plant their hopes in the soil. Yet for Ma Zhongtai, April 1969 was the end, not the beginning. On the evening of April 28, after being tortured in a struggle session, Zhongtai was dumped at the foot of a hill. The next morning he was found dead in the spring wind.

Ma Zhongtai was a member of the eminent Ma landlord family that dominated the social hierarchy of Yangjiagou in Mizhi County from the 1700s to the 1940s. In early 1969, during the Cleansing of the Class Ranks (*qingli jieji duiwu*) campaign, Ma Zhongtai and his wife, He Hongfan, were sent back to the village from their work unit in Lintong, a city near the provincial capital in Xi'an and three hundred miles from Yangjiagou, the village they had left twenty years earlier. In early April, soldiers stationed in Yangjiagou found some old account books and sheaths of swords and pistol holsters in Zhongtai's old house. Immediately, Zhongtai and Hongfan became the targets of cruel struggle meetings. Allegedly representatives of the "evil landlords" who were dreaming of returning to exploit others, Zhongtai and Hongfan were beaten. Ten days after the old account books were found, Zhongtai died. Three days later, Hongfan committed suicide in their home. Incredibly, Zhongtai and Hongfan were the only two members of the large Ma landlord family who died as victims of popular violence after land reform in the 1940s. The deaths of Zhongtai and Hongfan traumatized the village and have become a symbol of the fortunes and mishaps of the Ma landlords.

On May 18, 1998, twenty-nine years after Ma Zhongtai's death, I visited Yangjiagou, where Zhongtai and his wife were buried. In my preparation for the first trip, I had gotten used to hearing about the tragedy of Zhongtai from previous interview tapes. On the fifth day of my trip, I visited the couple's gravesite. Their tomb was simple but dignified, standing alone on the top of a hill east of the village. The previous day, I had visited the Ma family cemetery, which stands at the top of another hill. Although the family cemetery was dilapidated, I could still appreciate, from the broken tablets and the well-laid-out tombs, the family's past glory. Moreover, on the way I also saw several splendid new family graves, which belonged to the new elites who rose after land reform.[1] In contrast, Zhongtai and Hongfan rested in solitude. They were not buried with Zhongtai's forefathers; and there was no other tomb around their burial place.

On our way to the tomb, my colleagues and I were lost until we ran into an old woman, Liu Zhangshi, who later introduced herself as the daughter of Zhongtai's wet nurse. I noted that she called Zhongtai "milking elder brother" (*nai gege*). Having led us to Zhongtai and Hongfan's tomb, Liu Zhangshi began to talk about the death of her "elder brother." She was still upset about how her good will had unintentionally facilitated Hongfan's suicide. After Zhongtai died, Liu Zhangshi asked her own brother to help out Hongfan by filling her water vat. Yet Hongfan later unexpectedly drowned herself in that water. Listening to Liu Zhangshi's confession at the tomb, I became aware that Zhongtai's tragedy was still painful for the villagers. That was why many people mentioned Zhongtai's death in interviews, though few talked about it in detail. It also explained the silence around Zhongtai's graveyard. It dawned on me at that moment that Zhongtai's death could serve as a window on the moral suffering of peasants in socialist China.

According to the communist blueprint for a new and modern country, moral transformation was central to the reconstruction of Chinese society.[2] Before the Communist Party controlled the village, peasant views of their world were mainly based on local norms, which came from the experiences of everyday life.[3] Such customary morality sustained order in the village by emphasizing harmonious relationships among people. Most important, the relationships among villagers were based on everyday life interactions, not simply on the ownership of the means of production as the Communist Party suggested. Therefore, although they paid a substantial rent to their landlords each year, many ordinary peasants regarded a landlord as a rich villager, a family member, a friend, or a partner in agricultural production.[4] Compared to customary morality, communist morality is derived not from daily life but from abstract theoretical doctrine. Unlike customary morality, which held that "one's moral obligations to another depended on the precise nature of one's relationship to the other," communist morality emphasizes that "one's moral obligations toward another are defined by general norms equally applicable to all persons of a particular category"—specifically, a class category.[5] After the communists entered the village, they began to use class discourse to reshape relationships among villagers. Class labels that did not necessarily coincide with villager experiences were used to stratify people. For example, a landlord who had helped villagers in a time of famine was now held accountable for the misery the peasants suffered. Instead of emphasizing harmony, struggles with "enemies" were advocated in communist morality to create a new moral order.

To establish a new order, the party attacked customary morality. The communists launched a series of campaigns to facilitate moral transformation.[6] It seems that people's behavior was inevitably shaped to some extent by the new communist morality advanced in waves of campaigns. However, the customary morality rooted in people's everyday experiences was not easy to eradicate. Therefore, due to the tension between the customary moral ideals of the peasantry and the dictates of the official ideology, Chinese peasants constantly found themselves caught in moral predicaments, and were at a loss about how to conduct themselves.[7]

By tracing the life course of a single landlord, Ma Zhongtai, this chapter tries to demonstrate the changes Zhongtai, his family, and Yangjiagou villagers experienced during this moral transformation. The goal of the chapter is to shed light on the characteristics of the communist morality and the moral predicaments Chinese peasants faced. How did the communists initiate moral transformation? What caused changes in Yangjiagou and pushed Zhongtai to his death? In what moral predicaments were peasants caught in the Cultural Revolution? How did the villagers deal with these predicaments?

Yangjiagou was not a typical village. Before the communist revolution, the Ma landlord family owned about 14,000 *shang* (7,000 acres) of land. Their prosperity made Yangjiagou a special place. To what extent can the case of Yangjiagou be used to illustrate a broader pattern in peasant life? Researchers doing case studies normally find that in rural China "there was, and is, no typical village."[8] Every village is different with regard to income, economic and cultural activities, lineage relations, and ties to the state. It is impossible to imagine that changes in Yangjiagou were exactly the same as changes in other villages. However, as some researchers indicate, throughout rural China, "the social forces in conflict, the basic problems, the goals and the final outcome of the Revolution were the same."[9] If the research "works with given general concepts and laws about states, economies, legal orders, and the like to understand how those micro situations are shaped by wider structures," it can go beyond the specific micro case, and help explore the macro structures.[10] Therefore, the experiences of residents of Yangjiagou can reasonably offer glimpses into the fates of other peasants. Studying Zhongtai's death and its meaning for Yangjiagou villagers will contribute to an understanding of the moral predicaments of Chinese peasants in general.

All data about the Cultural Revolution in this chapter originate from oral history interviews with Yangjiagou villagers conducted during six periods of fieldwork between 1997 and 2001 by the Beijing University Research Center for Oral History of Social Life.[11] It is impossible to observe what happened at the time of Zhongtai's death. Moreover, it is not easy to find detailed records regarding Zhongtai, who was not an influential figure at all. No written materials concerning his death have been found in the county or prefectural archives. Illiterate villagers were important witnesses to Zhongtai's death, but they could not write down what they saw and experienced. Therefore, the oral history testimonies from Yangjiagou villagers are the only available sources to study this tragedy.

The Cultural Revolution was one among many long-term efforts of the party to enforce communist morality. Against this background, Zhongtai's death can help us explore the social changes initiated by moral transformation as well as the inner world of Chinese peasants involved in such transformation. This chapter begins with a delineation of the history of Zhongtai's family and the initial efforts at moral transformation during land reform. It then proceeds to focus on the village in the Cultural Revolution, Zhongtai's tragedy, and the moral predicament Yangjiagou villagers experienced. Finally, based on the representation of Zhongtai's death at present, the chapter discusses moral issues that arose in the post–Cultural Revolution period.

The Advent of Communist Morality

The eldest son in his family, Zhongtai was born in 1908. At that time, Zhongtai's lineage had lived in Yangjiagou for about two hundred years. Yangjiagou is a village in the loess hills of northeastern Shaanxi Province. It is about seven hundred miles from Beijing, and fifteen miles from the county seat, Mizhi. Many Yangjiagou villagers believe, "As Ma landlords brought great fame to Yangjiagou, people outside may not recognize Mizhi, but they know Yangjiagou."

A VILLAGE OF THE MA LANDLORDS

In the early eighteenth century, Ma Zhongtai's eighth generation ancestor moved to Yangjiagou.[12] Although Ma is a typical surname among northwestern Muslims, Zhongtai's family was not Islamic. By transporting merchandise from Shaanxi to north China for the famous traders of Shanxi, Zhongtai's ancestors were able to earn the money to purchase land from the residents of Yangjiagou. The old residents in the village either moved out or became tenants of the Ma family. Thus, Zhongtai's lineage became the masters of Yangjiagou.

One hundred years later, the great-great-grandfather of Zhongtai became a famous member of the local gentry in Mizhi County. At that time, Zhongtai's ancestors owned lands not only in Yangjiagou and surrounding villages, but also outside the county. Moreover, Zhongtai's forefathers studied for and passed the imperial examinations, and some were selected to be officials.

In 1908, the year of Zhongtai's birth, the Ma lineage functioned as the lords of Yangjiagou and benefactors of all the villagers. In a 1942 survey of Yangjiagou, Zhang Wentian, a senior leader of the Communist Party, found that among the 220 ordinary village households, all but four were tenants, sharecroppers, or servants of the Ma landlords.[13] The prosperity of the Ma landlords attracted peasant households from other villages to move into Yangjiagou to look for jobs. Ma landlords provided the peasants not only with tools and cattle, but also houses. Yangjiagou was a community that tied the Ma landlords to all other peasants. In particular, as the Mas gradually came to own more and more land outside the village, Yangjiagou villagers assisted them in managing their business with people in other villages, including the collection of land rents. Moreover, most villagers' wives worked as servants or wet nurses for the Ma landlords. Close personal ties thus grew between landlords and peasants.[14]

Under these circumstances, the Ma landlords seldom hesitated to be cordial with and supportive of villagers. In 1867, facing threats from Muslim rebels, the cousins of Zhongtai's grandfather built a fortress to protect all residents in Yangjiagou. During famines, the Ma landlord family usually set up a relief station, serving free food to the villagers of Yangjiagou and surrounding villages.[15] Additionally, the Ma landlords bestowed small favors on their neighbors such as lending them grain or helping them find wives.

As a result of cooperation in production and noteworthy charitable deeds, the Ma landlord family established decent relationships with their tenants and servants. Villagers' images of the Ma landlords were drawn from life experience. The Ma landlords were partners in production, neighbors, relatives, and friends whom they could ask for help in life's everyday crises.[16] The relationship between the Ma landlords and other residents of Yangjiagou reveals a pattern of customary social ethics in action, which placed a sacred value on loyalty generated by kinship, friendship, and charity.[17]

Of course, Yangjiagou was not free from resentments and conflicts. However, public conflicts were exceptions rather than the rule. The village appeared to be a lively and relatively harmonious community, which is fundamentally different from the Communist Party's image of village life under landlord rule.

A PREVIEW OF THE NEW MORALITY

Due to the tumult of the late Qing, Ma Zhongtai's father, born in 1883, only studied in the family school. After the 1930s, he sold some land to his cousins and sent his children to prestigious schools in China's major cities. His eldest son, Zhongtai, was sent to Beijing University, where he majored in biology.[18] In this he was typical of many Ma offspring. Under the new educational system that started during the New Policy period of the late Qing, young Ma students, both male and female, got a chance to study in such new-style institutions as normal schools. Many went to college in Beijing, Tianjin, Xi'an, and even abroad. The new generation of Mas was exposed to many new ideas, including Marxism. Some became the earliest Communist

Party members in the county.[19] "The underground party organization was first established in schools," said Liu Chengyun, who joined the party in 1942 and worked as a leader in the township (*xiang*). "There were children of the Ma landlords in these schools. They were the earliest members of the party."[20] However, these revolutionary forerunners devoted themselves to the revolutionary cause outside Yangjiagou, while other people initiated the revolution that challenged the authority of the Ma landlord family in Yangjiagou itself.[21]

Zhongtai did not join his revolutionary cousins. Instead of becoming a Communist or working for the Nationalist Party, in 1935–36 Zhongtai chose to abandon his studies to return to Yangjiagou.[22] At that time, Yangjiagou was already affected by the tide of revolution. In 1934, communist guerrillas appeared in the surrounding areas. The Ma family had to call in a company of Nationalist soldiers for protection. It became increasingly difficult for the Ma landlords to collect rents, not to mention retain their power. Zhongtai was thus destined to witness dramatic changes in his village.

Just one hundred and fifty miles south of Yangjiagou, Mao Zedong and his comrades established the headquarters of their famous base in Yan'an in the mid-1930s. Following the outbreak of the war against Japan in July 1937, Yan'an began to attract patriotic youth from all over China. A new moral order, not only for the Ma landlords, but for all Yangjiagou villagers, was emerging in the communist base.[23] In the view of the communists, harmony between landlords and peasants was a mere illusion. Instead, the new communist morality paid great attention to conflict and dissent, which was attributed to the inequality in ownership of the means of production, especially land. The party aimed to wipe out the inequality between landlords and peasants. A new code of ethics was promoted. According to the communists, the Ma landlords were morally "evil." Their monopolization of land meant that they were the exploiters, not the benefactors, of Yangjiagou's villagers.

Because of the war against Japan, the Ma fall from power, although drawing closer and closer, was postponed. In July 1937, the communists joined a united front with the Nationalist Party. Mizhi County was subsequently included within the garrison area of the communist forces. A people's political regime (*renmin zhengquan*) led by the communists was gradually established in Mizhi County in 1941.[24] The Ma fortress in Yangjiagou was soon penetrated by the new communist regime.

At that time, the Ma family largely retained its privileges. In order to solidify the wartime multiclass united front, the party treated the Ma landlords as a potentially cooperative partner.[25] The Mas soon found positions throughout the different levels of the people's government. One was even elected head of Yangjiagou district. Zhongtai also got a job in the new local government.[26] However, the communist rent and interest reduction (*jianzu jianxi*) policies, accompanied by heavy taxes (*aiguo gongliang*), severely weakened the economic power of the Ma landlords. As a report from the township of Yangjiagou states, "These years, several Ma landlords sold their land . . . [and] several mortgaged their land out."[27] Moreover, to the party, cooperation with the "evil" landlords was just a temporary tactic. In less than a year after the end of the war against Japan, the Communist Party changed its policy toward the landlords. In particular, the May Fourth Directive (*wusi zhishi*) of 1946 initiated land reform. The directive focused on both land redistribution and an attempt to establish a new social order based on communist morality.

AFTER LAND REFORM

According to the party's conception of rural life, the village was dominated by landlords and rich peasants who exploited and oppressed the rest of the villagers. The evil landlord was the root of peasant misery. Only after poor peasants struggled with their landlords, under the direction of the party, could a new social order be established. During land reform, the antagonism between peasants and "evil" landlords was highlighted. The party tried to overturn the old social order by mobilizing peasants to struggle against landlords.[28] In Yangjiagou, during land reform, the Ma landlords became the targets of struggle meetings. Although the head of his family, Zhongtai's father did not attract public attention. In contrast to his eminent cousins, who owned over 500 acres, Zhongtai's father held only 50 acres of land under his own name. Further, the personality of Zhongtai's father was very mild.[29] All these factors helped Zhongtai and his family escape struggle sessions during land reform. However, the more successful cousins of Zhongtai's father were not as fortunate.

An uncle of Zhongtai, Ma Xingmin, was an eminent figure in both Yangjiagou and in the whole base area. After studying architecture in Shanghai and Japan, Xingmin went back to the village and worked as a leader of the Ma family. During the famine of 1929, he hired Yangjiagou villagers to construct a splendid cave house. In the view of Liu Chenggao, a former Ma tenant, Xingmin's project was designed to provide the villagers with food during that famine. "That guy," he said, "was a benevolent landlord" (*ende dizhu*). Xingmin's fame made him the first target in land reform. In the struggle meeting, the benevolent Ma Xingmin was condemned as immoral. The work team members taught the villagers a song, in which Xingmin was criticized for being "rapacious as a wolf and savage as a cur" (*lang xin gou fei*).

However, the Yangjiagou villagers did not really accept this criticism. In our interviews, almost every person who talked about this struggle meeting praised Xingmin as a good person. Conversely, many villagers regarded those who criticized Xingmin as ingrates. In 1934–35, when Nationalist troops were stationed in Yangjiagou, they detained many people from the surrounding areas and accused them of being communist sympathizers. "Xingmin always went to ask the Nationalist army head to set these people free after beating them instead of killing them." The villagers preserve vivid memories of Xingmin's benevolence to this day. However, in the struggle meeting, one of the persons saved by Xingmin came forward to beat his savior. A villager described the scene in an interview: "This old guy [Xingmin] said, 'I do not feel injustice if others beat me; but now that you beat me, I feel bitterness.'" In my interviews, most of the villagers who recalled this scene deplored this injustice toward Xingmin.

The struggle meeting was a public confrontation between communist morality and customary morality. According to customary village ethics, it is unjust for a former beneficiary to beat his benefactor. However, this perfidious behavior was not only legitimate but advocated in communist morality. Regardless of how well landlords had treated the villagers, villagers should now transcend personal relationships to condemn landlords as representatives of the "evil" landlord class. Moreover, speaking out against an acquaintance in a public struggle meeting indicated to the authorities and to one's peers that the critic placed the new ethics over and above old loyalties to his associates.[30]

The party rewarded people who expressed loyalty to the new morality with opportunities for advancement. But Yangjiagou villagers used the label "black skins" (*heipi*) to refer to the brazen persons rewarded by the party for beating a landlord. Nevertheless, the party had already labeled the Ma landlords as "enemies" of the other villagers. After several villagers were criticized as Ma henchmen or backward elements for expressing their disapproval of the accusations against the Mas, no one dared to dissent publicly from communist morality.

When the Ma landlords and the party's supporters were respectively labeled "enemies of the masses" and "revolutionary masses," the villagers caught between these poles were in a torturous situation: according to village tradition and their life experience, the villagers could not accept struggles against their patrons; however, if they still supported the Ma landlords, they would be regarded as accomplices of the "enemies."[31] The discrepancy between customary morality and communist morality definitely threw Yangjiagou villagers into a predicament. Most of the time, the only possible choice for these tortured villagers was to do nothing.

Compared with landlords in other villages, the Ma landlords did not suffer a great deal. In the first phase of land reform (1946–47), during which Ma Xingmin was struggled against, corrupt local cadres who confiscated the property of the Ma landlords for their own use soon became targets. The Ma landlords, meanwhile, were almost forgotten. By the second phase of land reform (1947–48), Mao Zedong was residing in Yangjiagou, hiding from the Nationalist armies then advancing into northern Shaanxi. Thus, the struggle session during the second phase lasted only a single day in February 1948 before it was stopped by Mao. The good fortune of the Ma landlords was also the luck of the Yangjiagou villagers. The Ma landlords escaped physical torment, and the villagers were saved from psychological suffering.

After land reform, the Ma landlords who escaped persecution soon left Yangjiagou. Their superior educational background and revolutionary relatives helped them to find good jobs in the cities. After his father died in 1948, Zhongtai moved with his family to Yan'an. By 1949, only two or three Ma landlords remained in Yangjiagou. Everyone recognized that Yangjiagou was no longer a Ma family stronghold. Nobody, not even Zhongtai, foresaw that Yangjiagou would become a place of suffering for the Ma landlords in the distant future.

THE CONFRONTATION BETWEEN TWO MORALITIES

Twenty years after Zhongtai's family moved out of Yangjiagou, Zhongtai and his wife were sent back to his old home. In the two decades he spent outside Yangjiagou, he had worked successively as head of the Yan'an Sugar Refinery and as an office clerk for the Heavy Industry Department of Shaanxi. Later on, Zhongtai was demoted to be a research fellow at a research institute of the Ministry of Chemical Industry in Lintong, a satellite town of Xi'an. In fact, the ups and downs of Zhongtai's career were directly due to his family relations.

The landlord class label that Zhongtai inherited from his family made him vulnerable to the various campaigns launched after 1949. However, in the new state, one's relationships with one's relatives and close friends (*shehui guanxi*) were also considered a measure of one's political inclinations, a measure almost as important as class origin.[32] Thus, since several of Zhongtai's family members were high cadres of the party, he was sheltered from attack.

Marriage was an important method that the Ma landlord family used to expand and strengthen its social networks. Before the rise of the communists, Ma landlords married their daughters to other local gentry families and took wives from these families. For example, Zhongtai's mother was from a famous intellectual family in the county seat. After the Communist Party rose to power in the 1940s, personal connections with the new regime were established through marriages. Numerous Ma family daughters, including Zhongtai's youngest sister, Shuliang, married party cadres.[33] Shuliang's husband, Ma Mingfang, was a high-ranking communist who had joined the party in 1925. After the new state was established, Mingfang was the PRC's first governor and first party secretary of Shaanxi Province, a major player in the Northwest Bureau, and later, a minister in the central government.[34] Such an influential brother-in-law greatly benefited Zhongtai.

Moreover, Zhongtai's eldest daughter, Ma Li, was also a high official in the party. Before 1949, Li worked for the Department of Civil Affairs in the Shaan-Gan-Ning border region. After 1949, she worked in the General Office of the State Council.[35] Li's husband, Zhong Ling, was both a famous artist and an important state official. Zhong Ling went to Yan'an in 1938 at the age of seventeen and studied at the Lu Xun Art Academy. It is said that during the Anti-Japanese War most of the slogans in Yan'an city were written by him. Zhong Ling was also one of the designers of the state emblem and a major organizer of the founding ceremony of the People's Republic on October 1, 1949. Furthermore, Zhong Ling was responsible for writing the two slogans hung on Tiananmen after 1949.[36]

Zhongtai's powerful relatives built a safe shelter for him in the various political campaigns that followed 1949. During these campaigns, he was never considered a class enemy and was in a safe position even during the 1957 Anti-rightist campaign. Zhongtai's special connection with party officials was common in the Ma landlord family as a whole. Every Ma landlord could list several remote or close relatives who were eminent revolutionaries. In the seventeen years from 1949 to the start of the Cultural Revolution, only one Ma landlord was attacked during the Anti-rightist campaign and two were victimized during the 1962 Return to the Village movement. Personal relationships were an important aspect of customary morality, one that sustained the social order. Although the communist regime targeted the old social system for destruction, personal relationships were still important in the PRC.

Since the Mas became city residents after the new state was established and only periodically visited Yangjiagou, they were regarded as remote relatives of the villagers. Though few Ma landlords lived in Yangjiagou after 1949, many still regarded Yangjiagou as their home. In 1963, for example, the eldest cousin of Zhongtai's generation, Zhonglin, was buried in Yangjiagou after his death in Xi'an.[37] Moreover, in the 1950s, almost every spring at the Qingming Festival, some Ma landlords returned to sweep the graves of their ancestors.

At the same time, despite the absence of the Ma landlords from village life, Yangjiagou was continuously labeled a "landlords' nest" (*dizhu wo*). In the views of county leaders and the peasants in surrounding areas, Yangjiagou villagers still maintained close relations with the absent Ma landlords. They even believed that it was Yangjiagou villagers who had helped the Ma landlords escape punishment during land reform.[38]

During the 1963 Socialist Education movement, the county selected Yangjiagou as a model site for intensive study and struggle, due to its fame as a "landlords' nest." A work team led by a county vice-magistrate stayed in Yangjiagou for three months. The work team was disappointed to find that the villagers were still reluctant to criticize the Ma landlords.[39] Ma Hanshu, one of Zhongtai's nephews, who had returned to Yangjiagou from a bank in the city during the 1957 Anti-rightist campaign and then worked as a temporary accountant in Yangjiagou for about a year, became the scapegoat in the team's search for corruption in the village. The village leaders were also criticized for "sitting in the midst of landlords" (*zuo zai dizhu huaili*). The Socialist Education movement was an attempt by the communist state to push class discourse in villages once again, and it was a prelude to the Cultural Revolution.[40]

Chaos and Persistence

During the Great Leap Forward, a broadcast system was installed in every household in Yangjiagou. Several years later, on June 1, 1966, Yangjiagou villagers heard the broadcast of the *People's Daily* editorial "Sweep Away All Monsters." Through their reading of other editorials and documents, the villagers became familiar with the thrust of the discourse found in the editorial. "Class struggle has not ceased in China," it stated, thus it was time to "demolish all the old ideology and culture and all the old customs and habits [the 'four olds'], which, fostered by the exploiting classes, have poisoned the minds of people for thousands of years," and to "create and foster among the masses an entirely new ideology and culture and entirely new customs and habits."[41] The antagonism between the old and the new was the central topic of this editorial. As the masses were still deeply influenced by the old cultural system, a Great Proletarian Cultural Revolution was necessary to enlighten the backward elements with communist morality. From this editorial, we see that one aim of the Cultural Revolution was to demolish the old customary morality and foster the new communist morality.

It was impossible for ordinary peasants in Yangjiagou to foresee what was going to happen in this new revolution. Were great changes going to take place, or was it just the usual propaganda? No one knew at the time. Yet it was not long before the villagers witnessed a great upheaval. Three months later, in September 1966, the Destroy the Four Olds (*po sijiu*) campaign carried out by young students brought the first stage of the Cultural Revolution to the village.

The middle schools were the starting place of the Cultural Revolution in Mizhi County.[42] In June 1966, red guard organizations were established in these middle schools. Students were extremely enthusiastic about the call of the Cultural Revolution, and by September 1966 the students of Mizhi County were fervently participating in the Destroy the Four Olds campaign.

The red guards did not overlook Yangjiagou, the famous nest of landlords. The prosperous Ma landlord family had left behind numerous relics of their illustrious past. During land reform, few of these relics had been destroyed.[43] The glorious gates of the Ma fortress, their ancestral halls, and the two stone tablets remained important parts of Yangjiagou until September 1966.[44] Moreover, the well-decorated homes of the Ma landlords, in which more than one-third of the villagers lived at that time, suggested to outsiders the village's splendid past. While Yangjiagou villagers enjoyed the structures left by the Ma landlords, militant revolutionary youths did not appreciate these remnants of the old society.

"The two well-built memorial arches (*pailou*), the Buddhist temple, the temple of the Goddess of Fertility, and one ancestral hall of the landlords were all smashed by the red guards," said Li Huaishan, whose uncle, a famous mason, had directed the construction of one arch standing at the entrance to the Ma landlord fortress. This memorial arch was built in honor of a Ma landlord's widow. Many villagers, like Huaishan, sang high praise for this pailou: "It was the best one in the whole Shaanbei area." In an effort to sweep away this symbol of the old culture, "the red guards tried to smash the pailou, but they failed. Neither could they pull it down." Zhongyi, one of the two landlords who returned in 1962, recounted the sad destruction of this pailou: "Then they drilled several holes at the bottom, buried some dynamite, and blew up the memorial arch." The explosion shocked the villagers, and they reacted docilely in the face of the radical youth from the county seat.[45] A villager, Guo Chengde, explained: "They went to my house, and searched for the 'four olds.' An incense burner and several traditional New Year pictures were found. They shattered these. I was there, but what could I do? I just sat there and ate."

However, the red guards did not sweep away all the "four olds" in Yangjiagou. The whole Ma fortress was preserved, partly due to Mao's stay there during land reform. Along with the compound in which Mao lived, placards inscribed with landlords' calligraphy were preserved. In the center of the village a pavilion and a temple were destroyed, but the two stone tablets recording the good deeds of Ma landlords, though not connected in any way with Mao, were also preserved. In village memory, the preservation of these two tablets was extremely dramatic. "The red guards wanted to smash the tablets," Ma Zhihui, a village youth at that time, said, "but we villagers did not permit it." Rather than risk a public confrontation with red guards who used dynamite to destroy the "four olds," the villagers hid the two tablets. The night before the red guards came, someone plastered mud over the tablets. Later, as Zhihui recalled, "Bricks were used to seal these tablets, and they were turned into a propaganda board. An image of Chairman Mao wearing a military uniform was later painted on that wall."[46] To the villagers, these two tablets were relics of former community life. "The tablets represented help given to us in time of distress (*jiu ming*)," said Li Huaishan, whose sentiment was quietly shared by many Yangjiagou villagers. Although the demolition of the cultural monuments of the Ma landlords was accompanied by startling violence, the villagers still appreciated the relics of the village past more than the new communist morality.

During the early stages of the Cultural Revolution, Zhongtai's cousin Zhongyi, as a representative of the evil landlords, was paraded through the street with a tall white hat and a humiliating placard placed around his neck. Meanwhile, Zhongtai remained at the research institute near Xi'an. He probably could not have imagined that in Yangjiagou the red guards had already destroyed his grandfather's tomb. But Zhongtai also led a difficult life at that time. His family origins received increased scrutiny, and his revolutionary relatives themselves became targets of the Cultural Revolution. Ma Mingfang, Zhongtai's high-ranking brother-in-law, was publicly criticized for his skepticism of the policies of the Cultural Revolution, and later he became a major target in the attack on the Northeast Bureau, where he worked as the second in command.[47] Instead of gaining shelter from his relatives, Zhongtai was now implicated in the cases of these "counterrevolutionaries." Zhongtai's stay in the city was about to be cut short.

THE RETURN OF THE MA LANDLORDS

The passionately revolutionary students went back to their schools soon after they ran out of "four olds" to destroy, and Yangjiagou was left in a mess. The memorial arch and temples were demolished. The village leaders who rose during land reform were asked to stand aside (*kaobian zhan*). Soon the factional conflicts that engulfed the red guards also spread to Yangjiagou.

The young villagers, most of whom returned to Yangjiagou after finishing middle school, organized themselves into two factions: the Red Rebel Army (Hongse zaofan jun) and the Red Rebel Corps (Hongse zaofan tuan). At the county seat, the two factions not only engaged in armed battles, but also sent special attack teams (*wudou dui*) to besiege the nearby county seat of Jiaxian. By contrast, the red guard factions in Yangjiagou were far more moderate. There were continuous public debates, but only one violent struggle. This occurred during the "power seizure" (*duoquan*) period of February 1967. At that time, the commune government was located in Mao's former Yangjiagou residence.[48] Both the Red Rebel Army and the Red Rebel Corps wanted to control the commune government. Their battle lasted one night. Although no one died, the brutal fight led many youths to reconsider their actions. Ma Rutong, a central figure in the Red Rebel Army, dropped out after experiencing such a terrible night. "No matter what happens," said Rutong, "I will not join again."

On March 8, 1968, the central government issued a special directive for spring planting in rural areas. Agricultural production was emphasized. It urged "all the poor and lower-middle peasants and the proletarian revolutionaries and revolutionary cadres to immediately mobilize to break a new spring cultivation record."[49] In Yangjiagou the old leaders with experience in agriculture were recruited to work with the young revolutionaries and more and more of the younger generation went back to the fields with their fathers. The peasants were very realistic. They knew well that revolution alone could not produce food.

After 1967 Mao began to advocate the establishment of revolutionary committees at all levels to quell the violence in the cities.[50] The revolutionary committee in Mizhi County was established in February 1968, but violent fighting did not cease until June. To strengthen the rule of the new revolutionary committees, the central government released another directive that initiated a new political campaign, the Cleansing of the Class Ranks (*qingli jieji duiwu*). After the Twelfth Plenum of the Eighth Party Congress in October 1968, the cleansing campaign became the major task of the Cultural Revolution. A proclamation of the Twelfth Plenum stated: "We must carry out the Cleansing of Class Ranks campaign well in factories, rural communes, organizations, schools, all enterprises and streets, to dig out the handful of counterrevolutionaries hidden among the masses."[51] The campaign soon spread nationwide.

According to official directives, the campaign had multiple targets. First, the cleansing campaign targeted the leaders of red guard factions considered responsible for the disorder of the past two years. Ma Rutong, who withdrew from the red guards after the "power seizure" episode, witnessed the violent beating of his successor during the cleansing campaign. "He was beaten to the ground, and then someone poured cold water on him. Fortunately, I escaped from this." Rutong's decision to withdraw from the red guards had saved him.

However, others were destined to become targets of the cleansing campaign. This campaign followed the basic aim of the Cultural Revolution—to demolish the old culture and foster a new communist morality. Those with bad class backgrounds were easily identified as potential counterrevolutionaries who should be struck from the ranks of the people. This time the members of the Ma landlord family who worked and lived in cities were inevitably labeled "enemies of the people" because of the wealth of their forefathers. "There had been no class distinctions for a long time. But after that point more landlords were brought forward." As a member of the Ma landlord family, Zhongyi was very dissatisfied with this change, which in his view was completely arbitrary. After the cleansing campaign directives were issued to grassroots units in winter 1968, more and more Ma landlords became targets. Soon some were sent from their work units back to Yangjiagou, where they were subjected to continuous political attacks.

As early as May 1968, when the Liaoning provincial revolutionary committee was established, Zhongtai's brother-in-law, Ma Mingfang, who was once the leader of the provincial government and the Northeast Bureau, was labeled a prominent counterrevolutionary.[52] His relationship to Mingfang made Zhongtai more vulnerable in the cleansing campaign. In January 1969, Zhongtai and his wife, He Hongfan, were sent back to the county seat of Mizhi by Zhongtai's research institute. Several days later, the couple was brought to Yangjiagou, their home village where they had lost their family property twenty years before.

In many ways, Zhongtai was not a likely candidate for struggle. Before land reform, Zhongtai's family was not among the richest households of the Ma lineage. Moreover, throughout his adult life Zhongtai had rarely stayed in Yangjiagou for long periods of time. After his fourteenth birthday, he lived mostly outside of the village, studying or working. Between 1939 and 1948 he worked in the nearby township and later the Mizhi county seat but seems to have frequently returned to Yangjiagou, where his wife and children lived. Even during that time, his father was still the head of the family. Thus, it was not easy to identify Zhongtai's supposedly "bad" deeds. At this point, Zhongtai could only be criticized as a member of the Ma landlord family, a representative of the "evil" landlord class. Zhongtai's other vulnerability was his relationship with his brother-in-law. As Liu Xuezhang, a teacher in the Yangjiagou elementary school during the campaign, commented, "Zhongtai himself did not do anything bad." Therefore, the struggle session marking the couple's return was routine. "The landlord who was the target stood at the center, while other landlords stood to the side," said Liu Xuezhang. That evening, Zhongtai stood at the center of the struggle session. He was asked to confess to his crimes, and was warned to work honestly under the supervision of the poor and lower-middle peasants of Yangjiagou.

Zhongtai met several of his relatives after returning to the village. They had also been sent back from their work units. Zhongbi, Zhongtai's cousin, had worked in the provincial Department of Agriculture. Ma Qian, Zhongtai's distant nephew, was a political commissar in the army. Ma Kai, a distant grandnephew, was a factory worker in a nearby town. Chang Jiexuan, a remote niece-in-law of Zhongtai, was a well-known figure in the surrounding areas. She was two years older than Zhongtai and had retired from the county government.[53] In addition, three Ma landlords had returned to Yangjiagou before the Cultural Revolution. Hanshu, a nephew of Zhongtai, came back as a "rightist" in the 1957 Anti-rightist campaign. Two of Zhongtai's cousins, Zhongyi and Shiqi, returned during the 1962 Return to the Village movement. At that time, in January 1969, there were a total of nearly ten households of the Ma landlord family in Yangjiagou. Zhongtai and his wife joined them in a humiliating parade around the village. A villager, Ma Zhenyin, recalled the scene: "There were eight or nine people altogether," he said, "One person hit a drum; one held small cymbals. All of them wore tall paper hats and recited confessions."

However, it seems that even at that time the Ma landlords were still respected by Yangjiagou villagers. Stories were told about Zhongtai's renowned niece Chang Jiexuan. Ma Rutong remembered that as a revolutionary rebel in 1967, he had publicly debated Chang. "I was twenty-seven or twenty-eight," Rutong said. "This old woman was in her sixties. Her hair was cut into a yin-yang pattern." The debate between Rutong and Chang, the "evil" landlord wife, lasted a whole day in Yangjiagou. Even today, Rutong continues to praise Chang. He stated, "She had high prestige in this village. Her head was very clear." After this public debate, Chang was confined in the village and labored under surveillance. In the view of the Yangjiagou villagers, the Ma landlords were not mere representatives of the "evil" landlord class. They were concrete persons in past and present village life. Even putting the past benevolence of the Ma landlords aside, struggling against the Ma landlords or any other people did not conform to the villagers' conception of a proper life.

THE ARMY'S ARRIVAL

After land reform, Zhongtai's family retained some land and two rooms of their old house on the east hill. When he moved out in 1948, Zhongtai sold the land and permitted a former tenant to live in the two rooms. However, when Zhongtai and his wife returned to Yangjiagou, it was impossible for them to move back to their old home. An army unit was stationed in Yangjiagou just two weeks after Zhongtai's return. Zhongyi was Zhongtai's close cousin and his house was very close to Zhongtai's. Before the army came, Zhongyi had already been asked to move out of his own house. "All the houses on the east hill were requisitioned by the army," he said. "We moved into the old mud-house down the hill."

According to the county gazetteer, "From winter 1968 to April 1970, PLA unit 8321 was stationed in Yangjiagou to prepare for war" (*bei zhan*).[54] Here, "Yangjiagou" refers to the entire Yangjiagou commune. The soldiers lived in several of the commune's villages. One battalion, unit 4785, lived in Yangjiagou. "They came in the first month and left in the tenth month, staying almost one year," Zhongyi remembered. "They were an engineering unit. They came here to excavate some caves in the back hill." The construction in Yangjiagou was ordered by the central government as preparation for a possible war with the Soviet Union.[55]

The coming of the engineer corps changed Yangjiagou. Before, there had been no road connecting Yangjiagou and the county seat. To facilitate its construction project, the army built a road connecting Yangjiagou to the outside world. Because of the size of the army's trucks, Yangjiagou's rear gate, which had been preserved during the Destroy the Four Olds campaign, was pulled down. However, the impact of the troops was more profound than these physical changes. During their stay in Yangjiagou, these engineers were deeply involved in the politics of the local Cultural Revolution. In particular, they led the Cleansing of the Class Ranks campaign in Yangjiagou.

After the chaos of 1966 and 1967, Mao decided to rely on the army to suppress disorder, restore order and authority, and then continue the Cultural Revolution. In a January 1967 directive, the central government made it clear that "the PLA must firmly take the side of the proletarian revolutionaries," and "the demands of all true revolutionaries for support and assistance from the army should be satisfied."[56] From that point on, the army played a significant role in the Cultural Revolution nationwide. Guided by the dual principle of "grasping revolution and promoting production," the engineer corps would not fail to make revolution in Yangjiagou, even while busily working on construction.

In Ma Zhenyin's memory, the soldiers were very cordial. They fed chickens for Zhenyin and repaired his worn shoes. "They came to chat with me almost every day," Zhenyin recalled. On the other hand, it is likely that without the engineer corps, revolution would have been placed on the back burner in Yangjiagou. The army sent some soldiers to work in the fields with the villagers, and there was also a special group of soldiers in charge of assisting the village leaders in carrying out the Cultural Revolution. Guo Chengde, who graduated from the village elementary school, admired the experts in the army. "They drew pictures of Chairman Mao all over the village, in our rooms and on the doors," he reminisced. "Their calligraphy was also great. They left so many slogans."[57]

The soldiers also gave villagers up-to-date information on the larger purpose of the Cultural Revolution. Guo Chengde still remembers these exciting times: "Every time some new central directive was released, they sent us a copy, with much beating of drums and gongs." In contrast to the red guards, the army was made up of complete strangers, whom the villagers viewed as connected to the prosperous outside world. Sometimes, however, the villagers found that they were put in painful situations by these outsiders. In spring 1969, for example, the engineer corps set in motion a series of events that would lead to the death of Zhongtai.

THE DEATH OF ZHONGTAI

After being sent back in January, Zhongtai and his wife, He Hongfan, worked in the collective under surveillance. According to Zhongyi, Zhongtai's close cousin and fellow sufferer, physical labor was not punishment, but a test for people with "bad" class origins: "It is not easy to distinguish black from white. You cannot decide arbitrarily. It is necessary to work under surveillance; people can judge you by your work." Under such circumstance, it is likely that Zhongtai and his landlord relatives had to work hard to demonstrate that they were not "enemies of the people." Farm work was not easy for Zhongtai. He was already sixty-three, and he had never before done any physical labor. The work was not heavy during the winter, but when the spring planting drew near, Zhongtai became busier. Work in the fields exhausted old Zhongtai and Hongfan, but it was still bearable. The routine evening meetings were not very troublesome either. They were seldom beaten, though severe reprimands were unavoidable. Bowing and honest confessions were the correct public gestures. However, this routine life was broken on April 19, 1969, when new "evidence" of Zhongtai's "crimes" was found.

Ma Zhongyi witnessed Zhongtai's whole ordeal: "Some soldiers were living in Zhongtai's old house. They wanted to build a toilet in the storage area. In the process, they dug up some old account books and several sheaths of swords or pistol holsters." Burning the account books of landlords was a special ritual during land reform. In Yangjiagou, after the burning a memorial tablet honoring *fanshen* (overturning the old class hierarchy) was also erected. According to the revolutionaries, an old account book that recorded the land and other properties belonging to a landlord was the symbol of exploitation by the landlord class. Thus, keeping a copy of an account book was regarded as a sign of waiting for "a change of the sky," and then restoring the old system of exploitation. But during land reform, Zhongtai was already working outside the village. "It must have been Zhongtai's father who buried this stuff," Zhongyi deduced. It is not easy to imagine what Zhongtai's father was thinking when he buried the account books. At that time, he was already in his sixties and had lost all his belongings in one night. "The sheaths must have been left by Hu Zongnan's troop," Zhongyi told us. In autumn 1947, Nationalist troops under Hu Zongnan had passed through Yangjiagou after they were defeated by the communist army in Shajiadian, about eighty miles from Yangjiagou. Zhongyi believed that Zhongtai's father did not own a sword. "Probably he wanted to use the sheaths of swords to make a kitchen knife," Zhongyi guessed.

No one knows whether Zhongtai knew about the existence of the account books and sheaths left by his parents. But now he was responsible for these "evil" items. As soon as the account books were found, the soldiers informed the commune government and village leaders. What an excellent negative example for the cleansing campaign! The landlord class never gave up its ambition to restore the "evil" exploitative institution. They were definitely "the enemies of the people." More importantly, in Zhongtai's case, the evil landlord had infiltrated into the revolutionary camp long ago. He was connected to a national target, Ma Mingfang, Zhongtai's brother-in-law who had been jailed as a traitor. The activists were pleased about finding such a villain. Continuous struggle meetings awaited Zhongtai in the following days.

It was the busy season for spring cultivation, so struggle meetings were held in the evening. The theater stage located at the center of the village was used to conduct the struggle meetings. Now Zhongtai and his wife were placed at center stage. Several villagers described the struggle meetings against Zhongtai. As Ma Rutong remembered, in the routine struggles the landlords were only asked to bow, while the struggle of Zhongtai was different: "Zhongtai and his wife stood with hands bound in back." In contrast to the routine struggle sessions, this "evil landlord" was violently beaten. Ma Zhenyin said he had some problems with his eyes, but he was still shocked by the bloody scene. "Someone wrenched Zhongtai's neck, and another used an iron rod to hit him. It was very horrible even to glimpse." Nor was Zhongtai's wife, He Hongfan, able to avoid the brutal treatment. Liu Xuezhang remembered that Hongfan's hair caused her great pain. "The hair of Zhongtai's wife was pulled out. These people were really atrocious." But, who precisely were these atrocious people?

"These struggles were in fact directed by the army," Ma Rutong said. According to directives issued to the army in the Cultural Revolution, the soldiers definitely should have supported the masses in their struggles against all kinds of counterrevolutionaries. In Zhongtai's case, it was the soldiers who found evidence of his "crime." Naturally, the army was fervent about taking part in and even directing the struggle against Zhongtai. But in Ma Zhenyin's view, the soldiers themselves were very moderate. "I remember an army company commander saying, 'Comrades, we are here to figure out his problem. Do not hurt him. We should focus on his crime.'" Ma Zhenyin's memory reflected a general impression of the army in Yangjiagou: they were reasonable.

However, He Zhifu was more precise about the role of the army: "In public, they did not beat Zhongtai, but they supported the local toughs." According to the party's mass line, the soldiers could not run the struggles all by themselves. In fact, the soldiers' task was not to struggle against Zhongtai, but to mobilize the villagers for the struggle. So all villagers were asked to show up during the struggles against Zhongtai. After some villagers joined in the struggle against Zhongtai, the army showed support for these revolutionary masses. Even though violence was used in the struggle, it was inappropriate according to its own regulations for the army to condemn or stop the revolutionary local toughs.

All memories of the local toughs converged on several young men, all of whom were former red guards or revolutionary rebels who worked as low-level leaders in the village. "At that time, the young red guards were really brutal," said Liu Xuezhang, identifying one person by name. "Zhang Ming. He was very fervent in such rebellious activities (*zaofan*)."[58] Zhongyi also named another rebel. "It was Yang Jizhan who made Zhongtai suffer."

Both Zhang Ming and Yang Jizhan had returned to Yangjiagou after studying in the county middle school, and both were rebels at the beginning of the Cultural Revolution. Liu Xuezhang testified that neither of these local toughs personally resented Zhongtai: "Their fathers were not tenants of Zhongtai's family. Based on their ages, when Zhongtai moved out, they must have been kids or infants." Unlike their fathers, whose entire world was their village with its familiar customary moral code, educated youths like Zhang and Yang not only lacked interactions with the Ma landlords, but had also been exposed to communist doctrine since primary school. After years and years of communist education, these youth who were born and grew up under the red flag were very familiar with the class discourse that condemned the Ma landlords as enemies of the village, and more importantly, of the party. At that time, Zhongtai, in the view of the radical youths, was not an old man of blood and flesh, but a representative of the "evil" landlord class, as they learned in school.

The recollection of Ma Rutong, who was a peer of Zhang and Yang but withdrew from the red guards after the "power seizure" of 1967, is helpful to understand these radical youth: "We youths always wanted to show that we were revolutionary and were the eligible successors of the revolution." Moreover, in their school life, the youths, like Zhang Ming and Yang Jizhan, knew well that only when people expressed their loyalty to the party could they get rewards, such as a promotion, from the party.[59] It is not easy to know the precise motivations of Zhang, Yang, and other youths who joined in beating Zhongtai. But it is reasonable to deduce that the possibility of such rewards provided the youths with the incentive to struggle mercilessly against this "enemy of the people." Furthermore, from the rise of the new village elite after land reform, these new rebels knew very well that the struggle against Zhongtai was also a chance to demonstrate their power, and even establish their authority in the village. When Liu Xuezhang tried to guess the motives of Zhang and Yang, he presumed that these young men were very pragmatic: "I am not sure, but probably they were party members, or they wanted to be party members."

In contrast to the young activists, most villagers acted as silent witnesses. Although the villagers had lived under the communist regime for twenty years, it appeared that they still could not heartily accept the antagonism between "the people" and "the enemies of the people" as spelled out in communist morality, and they could not bring themselves to be enthusiastic about the merciless struggle against such "enemies." Furthermore, as Zhongyi pointed out, the peasants were at the bottom level of Chinese society; thus, there were few things that the state could take away: "Could they steal my hoe from me?" In rural areas, on the periphery of the state, the regime was not able to buy widespread compliance from the peasants by giving rewards.[60] Therefore, it was possible for Yangjiagou villagers to stay away from the struggles against Zhongtai. According to Ren Xiulan, an old woman, most villagers just "did not join these struggles."

The predicament that Yangjiagou villagers faced in the case of Zhongtai was similar to their experiences in land reform. Zhongtai had been labeled an "enemy of the people." Only those who supported the struggle against Zhongtai could be counted as "revolutionary masses." Any sympathy toward Zhongtai would be regarded as support for the "enemies of the people" and as "counterrevolutionary" behavior. Thus, to escape their predicament, the villagers' only possible choice was once again to do nothing. They just stood by in the struggle meetings, and did not give a hand to either the local toughs or Zhongtai. As Ma Rutong confessed, most of villagers believed "the less trouble the better," and that this was the only way they could protect themselves.

Although all the villagers were asked to show up, some, especially women, showed their lack of enthusiasm by staying home. Liu Zhangshi did not go to the struggle meeting at all. "My children went, but I did not. One reason is that I know I am a relative of Zhongtai." Liu Zhangshi's mother was the wet nurse of Zhongtai. According to the communists, Liu Zhangshi's mother was exploited by Zhongtai's family. Zhongtai was definitely Liu Zhangshi's enemy. But it seemed that Liu Zhangshi did not think that way. In the villagers' view, a person was related to his or her wet nurse's family. As Liu Zhangshi stated, she was a relative of Zhongtai, just like Zhongyi, who was Zhongtai's close blood cousin.

In fact, during the brutal struggles, it is Liu Zhangshi who took care of the poor couple, as if Zhongtai were her blood brother. In Yangjiagou, water was very scarce. People had to carry water from the well in the gulch to their houses on the hill. Carrying water was not an easy job for Zhongtai. Liu Zhangshi covertly gave a hand to Zhongtai and his wife. "Every ten or more days, my brother or my husband carried some water for them during the night," said Liu Zhangshi.

After the discovery of the old account books and sword sheaths, struggle meetings were held every evening. "Zhongtai was beaten every day. It lasted about ten days, and in the end Zhongtai was beaten to death," Zhongyi told us. On April 28, 1969, Zhongtai's wife, He Hongfan, was sick, and she was therefore exempted from the struggle meetings. Zhongtai was beaten that night. At the end of that struggle meeting, Zhongtai was not able to stand up due to injuries sustained during the ten days. He was dumped at the foot of the east hill. Although his house was very close, Zhongtai could not walk home by himself. That evening, many Yangjiagou villagers heard Zhongtai's moans, but no one gave him a hand. The next morning, April 29, 1969, Zhongtai was found dead.

A well-known local tough in Yangjiagou is believed to have beaten Zhongtai after Zhongtai was left at the foot of the east hill. Ma Rutong testified, "Liu Chengfa was in charge of raising animals at that time. The animal shelter was very close to the place where Zhongtai lay. Zhongtai's groans annoyed Liu Chengfa. So he went to beat Zhongtai again." During land reform, Liu Chengfa was already an infamous local tough. In a struggle meeting during land reform, Liu brutally beat one of Zhongtai's cousins, Zhongyue, and forced Zhongyue's daughter to marry him. After the 1952 marriage law, Zhongtai's niece divorced this brutal local tough, who later rose to a leading position in the village militia. On that fateful night, it is possible that Liu Chengfa wanted to settle old scores with the Ma landlords.

Zhongtai was buried by his cousin Zhongyi. "I was working in the fields. The village leader sent someone to ask me to bury Zhongtai," Zhongyi said. "They said it would be counted as work points. I bought a coffin on credit from a villager, and buried him." However, the tragedy of Zhongtai had not yet ended. His wife, Hongfan, committed suicide three days later. Hongfan was so sick that it was not easy for her to kill herself. "After Zhongtai died, I clandestinely sent some food to his wife. I found there was no water left," said Liu Zhangshi. "I asked my brother to carry some water. Three days later, he filled the whole water vat. The old woman drowned herself in that water vat." Liu Zhangshi was extremely upset about Hongfan's death. On May 1, 1969, Hongfan wrote several sentences just before her death: "I am asked to turn in a rifle. Where is it? Long live the Communist Party! Long live Chairman Mao!"

THE AFTERMATH OF ZHONGTAI'S DEATH

After 1978, the Ma landlords who had been sent back to Yangjiagou during the Cultural Revolution gradually got their jobs back and returned to their homes in the cities. Only Ma Zhongtai and He Hongfan were left behind. In April 1984, Zhongtai's four children returned to Yangjiagou to rebury Zhongtai and Hongfan. A traditional Chinese poem written by Zhong Ling, Zhongtai's son-in-law, was engraved on the back of a gravestone. Zhong Ling, whose handwriting is hanging on Tiananmen, left his script in Yangjiagou.

In spring 1998, twenty-nine years after Zhongtai and Hongfan's death, Liu Zhangshi said at their graveyard: "We wanted to help the old woman, so my brother carried water for her. Why did she use it to kill herself?" Zhongtai's death never faded from village memory. For Liu Zhangshi and others, Zhongtai's death is not merely a story, but a personal moral torture.

After the 1980s the benevolence of the Ma landlords was once again publicly discussed. In 1995 the two stone tablets hidden in a wall saw daylight again. Various Ma offspring have returned to visit their forefathers' village. Researchers, including our group, attracted by the tale of the Ma family, have reminded villagers of the success of the Ma landlord family in Yangjiagou.[61] The existence of the Ma landlord family is again part of Yangjiagou's identity.[62]

It appears that, with the end of the Cultural Revolution, communist morality has collapsed. More specifically, communist morality focusing on class discourse has been discarded. Yangjiagou villagers are no longer asked to condemn the evil landlord class. However, life in Yangjiagou has not been restored to the relatively harmonious balance of the Mas' heyday. Yangjiagou as a community has been destroyed by the struggles of the communist period. The new village elites are not able to shape the villagers into a community. The administrative leaders are powerful, but in the view of the villagers, they are of dubious character. The former cadres have successfully restored some folk religious practices, but few of these former cadres have been broadly accepted by the villagers. Even worse, the village elites themselves are divided by the conflicts that pitted them against one another during the campaigns of the communist period.[63]

Moreover, Yangjiagou today is somewhat anomic. No one has been criticized publicly or punished for the miseries suffered in Yangjiagou during the communist period.[64] The villagers generally do not want to talk about their former miseries. Instead, they prefer to emphasize that, in contrast to other villages, Yangjiagou enjoys unlimited blessings from the gods. Zhongtai's death is merely mentioned as an exception, and no one really wants to talk about the details. Only those who have moved out or are already dead are identified as the ones responsible. Nobody currently living in the village did anything wrong during that miserable period. Each misery, even death itself, is reduced to an absurd joke involving some unknown outside power.

Nevertheless, when speaking with the villagers about Zhongtai's death, we could feel their pain. They spoke in a low voice, as if revealing a secret, and they occasionally stopped. It seems that they wanted to say something, but hesitated to speak out. Discussion of Zhongtai's death has in fact become taboo in the village. It is true that the institutional base of communist morality has broken down. Yet without a full reflection on the communist period, it will not be easy to reestablish moral order in the village.

Conclusion: Moral Predicament in Communist China

Before the communists arrived, Yangjiagou was a cooperative community. Peasants worked for the Ma landlords and, in exchange, the Ma landlords provided the villagers with aid when they needed it. In the face of outside threats, landlords and peasants often worked together to safeguard their community. Moreover, in the everyday world of the village, landlords and tenants were perceived to be neighbors, relatives, and even friends. Close personal ties linked all villagers. Of course Yangjiagou was never free of conflict. The Ma family monopolized village land, and there were always marginalized villagers, such as those who could not rent land from the Ma landlords. Yet such conflicts were the exception rather than the rule. Harmonious human relationships were the norm in Yangjiagou.

Chinese communist activists regarded such village harmony with disdain. They emphasized the conflicts in village life. In their view, in sharp contrast to the ideal of equality in communist society, traditional society was riddled with exploitation, repression, and inequality. According to Marxist doctrine, the ruling class—in the case of Yangjiagou, the Ma landlord family—reproduced its domination not only through exploitive relations of production, but also through hegemonic ideology, such as the "four olds," thus providing an illusory picture of harmony in society. In order to replace the old society with a new one, the revolutionaries had to destroy the old ideology. Customary morality, which helped to sustain social order in village life, was part of their target. First, the communists developed a set of class labels to classify people. Then they emphasized the antagonisms among villagers, which reflected the sharp distinction between "the people" and "the enemies of the people" in communist ideology. The landlords were held responsible for all hardship experienced by the villagers. More important, dismissing the concept of harmony in the old morality, the communists believed that it was only through struggle that a good society could be forged.

After land reform, the communists endeavored to establish a new morality through various political campaigns. In their blueprint for a new China, moral transformation was an important component. They wished to make people "more virtuous in their motivations, commitments, and relationships."[65] The new morality was in conflict with the life experience of villagers, but it soon became the standard for proper behavior. However, the communist regime was not totally successful in replacing the old morality with the desired communist morality. In the case of Yangjiagou, the Ma landlords were an integral part of village identity, even after the Mas moved out. Thus, villagers found that the conflicts between the two contending moralities led to painful moral predicaments.

Zhongtai's death provides a chance to scrutinize the peasants' experience with the two moralities, especially in the Cultural Revolution period, when the new morality was promoted by violent means. In this case, it was the army stationed in Yangjiagou, rather than the revolutionary masses as the party hoped, that was the most critical force in Zhongtai's death. The young generation in Yangjiagou tended to become activists. Some youths, like Zhang Ming and Yang Jizhang, were opportunistic. By demonstrating their loyalty to the party, these youths wanted to win rewards or promotions from the state. For most Yangjiagou villagers, because they lived on the periphery of the communist state, the state's control was relatively weak. Thus, it was possible for villagers to choose nonaction in the struggles against Zhongtai. Nonaction was, in fact, a form of resistance peasants could use to resolve their moral predicament. The old morality was endangered, but nobody served as an all-out apologist for the new morality.

The party tried to destroy the old moral system in the rural areas. The old morality was incessantly denounced. However, in Yangjiagou as in many other villages, the new morality was never fully accepted by the peasants, since it alienated people from village life. Thus, the new, "more virtuous" morality never brought order to village life. It only forced villagers to face all kinds of moral predicaments.

Ironically, instead of fostering a more righteous society, the moral transformation initiated by the communists did not work as they expected. The new system "generates acrimonious political competition, avoidance of activists, retreat into the private world of friends and family, and disaffection from the regime." People are left to be "more rather than less alienated from one another and from the state."[66] Like the Yangjiagou villagers, many other Chinese felt that the efforts to carry out the new morality in the communist period led to the extreme anomie of the post–Cultural Revolution period. The communists' attempt to achieve moral supremacy instead led Chinese peasants to face moral predicaments and moral corruption in their villages. Even today, Chinese peasants, like other Chinese, have difficulty constructing a moral order that can bring together their communities, from village to nation.

SIX

Staging Xiaojinzhuang: The City in the Countryside, 1974–1976

Jeremy Brown

As I stepped out of a minivan and greeted Wang Zuoshan, the sixty-nine-year-old former village party secretary of Xiaojinzhuang, my taxi driver suddenly realized that he recognized the old man. Driver Li had last seen Wang in 1976, when Li was an elementary school student in the Baodi county seat, a town about forty-five miles north of Tianjin and fifty-three miles southeast of Beijing.[1] Li was part of a crowd of ten thousand watching transfixed as Wang, kneeling on an elevated stage in the town's main square, bowed his head and accepted the slaps and insults of his accusers.[2] This was a time of political upheaval in China. Mao Zedong had died, and his wife and the rest of the "Gang of Four" were arrested as the curtain fell on the Cultural Revolution. But in late 1976, Wang Zuoshan was the target of a classic Cultural Revolution ritual, the mass criticism and struggle meeting.

Wang Zuoshan had the misfortune of being the leader of Xiaojinzhuang, a village of 101 households on the Jian'gan River. His village, about a thirty-minute drive east of the Baodi county seat, became a national model for arts and culture after Jiang Qing visited in June 1974 and called it her "spot." Wang and other villagers emerged as the poetry-writing and opera-singing stars of a political drama sponsored by Jiang and staged by her allies in the Tianjin municipal leadership. Xiaojinzhuang's fortune was tied to Jiang Qing and other "radicals" who sought power by affirming the anti-capitalist, collectivist Cultural Revolution policies of constant class struggle and strict artistic standards. The model village became a weapon in the radicals' 1974–76 political battle against "moderate" targets of the Cultural Revolution like Deng Xiaoping, who advocated economic pragmatism, a limited return to private plots in agriculture, and more relaxed arts policies.[3]

Yet Xiaojinzhuang and its residents were more than just bit players in the mid-1970s drama over whether to embrace or repudiate the radical politics of the Cultural Revolution. As a rural model, Xiaojinzhuang was presented to all of China as a cultural utopia worthy of emulation. The fantasy image of Xiaojinzhuang, which included a vibrant night school, prolific poets, skilled singers, and policies encouraging gender equality, was only loosely based on village reality. It was instead the invention of urban politicians who consistently displayed a profound disdain and distrust of rural residents. While the most prominent aspects of Xiaojinzhuang's model utopia changed according to the shifting needs of city authorities—from agricultural advances in the early 1970s to education, culture, and women's equality in 1974, and finally to anti–Deng Xiaoping insults in 1976—villagers' lack of political influence remained constant. Xiaojinzhuang's inferior position allowed city officials to colonize the village and transform it into their cultural theme park. This development sparked discontent from people who lived in and around Xiaojinzhuang. In spite of their political subjugation, villagers asserted their agency in a variety of ways. Some embraced the experience of living in a model village and garnered national fame, while others complained about the urban-imposed changes.

As Wang Zuoshan knelt in front of thousands and winced from stinging slaps, he and his village were double losers. Not only was their political line deemed incorrect after Jiang Qing's arrest, but they were victims of a pervasive anti-rural bias. To be sure, the political use and abuse of staged model units, along with the miserable post-1976 fate of people prominently linked to Jiang Qing, were not limited to the rural sphere. However, like the rest of rural China during the 1970s, Xiaojinzhuang occupied the lowest rung in a political hierarchy dominated by city officials. This fact was just as ruinous as the village's high-flying association with Mao's wife. It is ironic that during the Cultural Revolution, a movement that sought to eliminate the gap between town and country and proclaimed rural China to be the ultimate repository of national and revolutionary virtue, rural residents had scant influence over the political and economic decisions that affected them most.[4]

The dynamics of Xiaojinzhuang's rise and fall combined the subordinate position of China's countryside with the unique political theater of the late Cultural Revolution period. Tension between urban and rural China

certainly transcended Xiaojinzhuang's 1974–76 high point. Since the beginning of the twentieth century, if not earlier, Chinese city dwellers have
idealized rural China as a realm of authenticity and purity, while at the
same time labeling farmers as passive, ignorant objects in need of reform.[5]
However, this disconnect between rhetoric and reality—between celebrating rural innovation and oppressing rural people—reached its apex in the
mid-1970s with the Xiaojinzhuang model. The institutional dimensions of
this oppression, including the restrictive household registration system and
excessive state grain requisition, are well understood.[6] But rural-urban tension in the 1970s remains understudied. Xiaojinzhuang's story illuminates
the social and political consequences of anti-rural discrimination during the
Cultural Revolution.

With fewer than six hundred residents, Xiaojinzhuang is a small village by north China standards. The village was known for growing garlic
but boasted no remarkable achievements during the 1950s and early 1960s,
when it suffered from constant flooding and low-yielding saline-alkaline
soil. During the Great Leap Forward in 1959, villagers labored for a month
removing water from low-lying land near the river. They threw seeds onto
the exposed mud and reported their success to nearby Lintingkou, the commune headquarters and local market town, but a few days later a rainstorm
washed away their hard work. Xiaojinzhuang residents went hungry and
gnawed on raw garlic for sustenance.[7]

Rural Baodi had long enjoyed a rich cultural life. Many villages had their
own opera troupes, and most villagers could sing a few lines of *pingju*, the
local opera of north China.[8] During the Cultural Revolution, old opera
ensembles were dismantled, but some people in Baodi continued to sing
the didactic revolutionary model operas promoted by Jiang Qing. Xiaojinzhuang itself escaped major turbulence during the early stage of the Cultural Revolution. There was no temple to smash, so people burned books
and struggled against a poor soul who was designated a "capitalist roader."[9]
During the power seizures that swept across China in 1967, some Xiaojinzhuang brigade leaders were forced to "step aside" (*kaobian zhan*).[10] Wang
Tinghe, a long-standing leader who had served as village party secretary,
was punished for his "capitalist roader mistakes," but he returned as a vice-
secretary shortly after Xiaojinzhuang's government was reconstituted as a
revolutionary committee.[11] This was a typical pattern in rural north China,
and there appeared to be little about the village's experience in 1966–69 to
foreshadow Xiaojinzhuang's meteoric rise.

Setting the Stage: The City in the Countryside

Without question, it was Jiang Qing's visit in June 1974 that catapulted Xiaojinzhuang to national prominence. In the immediate wake of Jiang's tour, the city headed for the countryside, an event that intimated drastic changes for the village. In effect Xiaojinzhuang would cease to be rural, even though its physical location in China's countryside was never in question. Tianjin-based authorities and work team members occupied the village and packaged it into their utopian vision of rural China. This image was the product of urban officials' imaginations and the political dicta of the time, which required rhetorically supporting the virtues of rural socialist construction. Urban and military models were fine, and Jiang Qing had those too.[12] However, as an ambitious politician and cultural revolutionary, she needed the jewel in the crown of the "worker-peasant-soldier" triumvirate. She needed a rural model, and Tianjin leaders placed it in her lap. For Jiang, it was immaterial that the city's role in staging the Xiaojinzhuang show would shape the village into a repository of urban imaginings of the countryside.

If Jiang Qing was seeking a model village, why did she settle on Xiaojinzhuang? A confluence of village achievements, county-level model-making efforts, city involvement, and national elite politics set the stage for the 1974 occupation. Xiaojinzhuang's rise was neither random nor predetermined. Instead, it was the product of a political environment that pressed local officials into grooming potential rural models so that provincial, municipal, or national officials could draw upon them for symbolic or publicity purposes. Ubiquitous propaganda trumpeted rural achievements, but only partially concealed the contemptuous view many urban elites held of Chinese villagers. As we shall see, the model-making process—coupled with anti-rural contempt—denied local autonomy to affected villages and sparked intravillage friction, even as it led to fame and new opportunities for some residents.

Xiaojinzhuang first appeared as a blip on the radar screens of Baodi county and Tianjin municipal leaders during the early 1970s. Local authorities had learned not to expect much from the small village. With its poor soil and vulnerability to flooding, Xiaojinzhuang was known as a place with serious and long-standing problems (*lao da nan*). Things began to change after 1969, when villagers worked during the winter transporting frozen earth to fill in salty swampland near the river.[13] They also dredged the riverbed, built a dyke, and covered the saline-alkaline soil with river mud.[14] These efforts began to pay off with several seasons of increased agricultural yields that attracted the attention of commune and county officials. By 1973, the year that Baodi County became a part of the newly established Tianjin municipality, Xiaojinzhuang produced 551 catties of grain per *mu* and was recognized for its special achievements by Tianjin authorities.[15] Breaking out of mediocre economic performance was a precondition that had to be met before any village could garner model status.

Crucial to Xiaojinzhuang's local fame was the long-term residency of a Baodi county cadre named Hu Penghua. In April 1972, the county propaganda department dispatched Hu to Xiaojinzhuang for the express purpose of developing the village into a model unit. Hu, a Baodi native who graduated from a local high school in 1964, visited a number of other villages before finally settling on Xiaojinzhuang as a promising site. Xiaojinzhuang caught Hu's eye because of its united leadership, comparatively educated populace, and recent agricultural gains.[16]

One of Hu's main tasks in Xiaojinzhuang was to work with the brigade party branch to establish a political night school (*zhengzhi yexiao*) as part of the national movement to study Dazhai, China's most famous model village. The school met three nights a week and provided basic literacy training for illiterate and semi-illiterate residents, along with courses for young people in current events, politics, and agricultural technology.[17] If energetic youth had time, they sang model opera excerpts and invented lively political jingles.

Hu's work directing the night school would have attracted little attention had he not produced a steady stream of glowing reports for county officials about Xiaojinzhuang's educational and agricultural progress. Two journalists from a local newspaper in Hebei Province caught wind of Hu's reports and decided to visit Xiaojinzhuang. Hu recalled that the propaganda articles he coauthored with the two journalists resulted in several full-page spreads on Xiaojinzhuang. In turn, this publicity led to inspection visits by Hebei provincial propaganda officials and Zheng Sansheng, second party secretary in Hebei and commander of the Tianjin garrison. But in August 1973, administrative reshuffling placed Baodi County under the control of Tianjin municipality. Hebei authorities could not foster the promising village as a potential model anymore, for Xiaojinzhuang was no longer under their jurisdiction. Tianjin officials like Major General Wu Dai, however, could not have been more pleased. The city could now draw upon advanced rural units in Baodi as political resources in upcoming campaigns.

Xiaojinzhuang would have remained a simple local success story had Wu Dai not taken an interest in the village. General Wu, along with his fellow Tianjin party secretaries, particularly cultural leader Wang Mantian and first secretary Xie Xuegong, were perfectly situated to become the producers and stage managers of the Xiaojinzhuang show. The role of municipal authorities in elevating the village to national stardom under Jiang Qing's sponsorship should not be underestimated. They publicized the model in the Tianjin press, invited village representatives to city meetings on agriculture and women's issues, and funneled resources to favored rural units. Just as important, Tianjin leaders' reputations as cultural revolutionaries allowed them to bring the village to Jiang Qing's attention. Whereas Wu Dai was a survivor, a military man who rose in prominence after Lin Biao's death, Xie Xuegong and Mao Zedong's cousin Wang Mantian were politicians whose careers took off during the Cultural Revolution.[18] All three promoted their city as a base from which Mao's wife could bolster herself and her politics. Xiaojinzhuang would be but one part of the package that Tianjin leaders presented to Jiang Qing—the rural part.

Agriculture in Tianjin fell under the purview of General Wu, who was serving concurrently as vice–political commissar of the Beijing military region and Tianjin's second party secretary. Wu's military background made him averse to sitting behind a desk in his city offices. He much preferred driving around the countryside on inspection visits to sitting idle in his city office.[19] Wu enjoyed touring villages, chatting with cadres, and checking up on agricultural production. He visited Xiaojinzhuang and other nearby brigades several times and built up amiable working relations with local officials.[20]

In spite of the good impression Wu Dai had of Xiaojinzhuang, by early 1974 he had not yet settled on the village as a favored spot. In January 1974, Wu Dai sent a ten-person "Spread Dazhai Counties Work Team" (Puji Dazhai xian gongzuo zu) to Baodi County. The work team bypassed Xiaojinzhuang and set up shop instead in Dazhongzhuang, a larger village and commune headquarters that had come to Wu Dai's attention on one of his rural tours.[21] But only a few weeks after the work team's arrival, a new nationwide political movement blew on the scene, confounding the outside cadres in Dazhongzhuang and paving the way for Xiaojinzhuang's rise.

Perhaps Wu Dai viewed Dazhongzhuang as the most appropriate spot for a work team to preach the Dazhai message of self-reliance and innovation in agriculture. Yet the new campaign to criticize Lin Biao and Confucius, initiated by Jiang Qing and her allies with the approval of Mao at the end of 1973, was better suited to Xiaojinzhuang. At the national level, this campaign pitted political beneficiaries of the Cultural Revolution like Jiang Qing against veteran officials linked to Premier Zhou Enlai. Both sides utilized esoteric historical arguments to battle over the significance of the past eight years and who would lead China after Mao.[22] Not surprisingly, in Chinese villages the campaign bore scant resemblance to the epic struggle between Confucianism and Legalism depicted in national magazines and newspapers.

According to the former head of the 1974 work team, farmers in Dazhongzhuang, like their counterparts throughout rural China, were unenthusiastic about the anti-Confucius campaign.[23] The work team struggled to connect with residents who had never read any of Confucius's works. Under pressure from superiors in Tianjin to produce positive reports about the campaign, harried urban cadres called meetings and urged farmers to rail against feudal sayings. Although *Tianjin Daily* featured several vague front-page articles praising Dazhongzhuang's achievements, the unwieldy anti-Confucius movement was threatening to sink the village's utility as a model.[24]

Meanwhile, Tianjin municipal leaders including Wu Dai learned that Jiang Qing wanted to visit their city after she read an internal report about vigorous "Criticize Lin Biao, Criticize Confucius" activities at the Tianjin railway station. She would be coming to promote the campaign by identifying and publicizing additional models, including an army unit and a village.[25] Wu Dai was well aware of his work team's troubles in Dazhongzhuang. He realized that smaller Xiaojinzhuang, with its night school and more lively cultural activities, might be just what Jiang Qing was looking for. On the eve of Jiang's visit, Wu Dai began to elevate Xiaojinzhuang in the context of criticizing Confucius. First, Wu ordered his work team to quit Dazhongzhuang and return to Tianjin.[26] Then on June 11, 1974, *Tianjin Daily* published "Sights and Sounds of Criticizing Lin and Confucius in Baodi's Xiaojinzhuang," the first article on Xiaojinzhuang to appear in the paper since January.[27]

By the time this article was published, Wu Dai and other city officials were busy preparing for Jiang Qing's upcoming visit to Tianjin, which was only a week away. Xiaojinzhuang's prominent appearance in the city's main newspaper was a signal that big changes were in store for the village, but villagers remained in the dark. Even people in Jiang Qing's entourage were unaware that they would be accompanying her to Tianjin, let alone Xiao-jinzhuang, until just before departing Beijing. Fan Daren, a member of the Liang Xiao writing group (a team of professors from Qinghua University and Beijing University who were the rhetorical brain trust behind a series of historical articles linking Lin Biao's "revisionism" to Confucius), recalled that he was given ten minutes to prepare a change of clothes and toiletries for an "important activity."[28] Fan reckoned that he was going to meet Chairman Mao as a car whisked six excited Liang Xiao writers to an unknown destination. Only when he boarded a special train filled with such luminaries as Minister of Culture Yu Huiyong, singer and cultural official Hao Liang, dancer Liu Qingtang, table tennis star and sports official Zhuang Zedong, and Qinghua leaders Chi Qun and Xie Jingyi, did Fan realize that he would be accompanying Jiang Qing and Politburo member Ji Dengkui to Tianjin.[29]

On June 19, 1974, Jiang Qing spoke in Tianjin at a large meeting about the historical struggle between Confucianism and Legalism.[30] Jiang shared the speaker's platform with Wang Mantian, Wu Dai, Ji Dengkui, and a senior Liang Xiao scholar.[31] After 1976, Jiang's speech was remembered for her remark that during the Han dynasty, "women were fairly free, they could have 'kept men' (*mianshou*). Do you know what a 'kept man' is? It's a boyfriend aside from the husband. They could have male concubines."[32] This comment later became fodder for attacks alleging that Jiang cavorted with young boyfriends and sought to become China's "empress." Jiang's motives for promoting women's power may not have been pure, but her point that Confucian morality oppressed women was consistent with the wide-ranging anti-Confucian tone of the speech. She drove home the message that to oppose the campaign against Confucianism was anti-Chinese. "Whatever is Legalist is patriotic," she said, "whatever is respectful of Confucianism . . . is traitorous."[33]

After her speech, Tianjin leaders puffed up the package they were offering to Jiang Qing. At a Tianjin hotel, municipal officials reported to Jiang on a number of advanced villages in the region. None especially interested Jiang until Wu Dai mentioned an exciting village that boasted a successful night school and lively cultural activities.³⁴ Tianjin authorities carefully stressed that Xiaojinzhuang's night school not only excelled at political study, but also featured revolutionary model opera singing and poetry readings.³⁵ The mention of singing got Jiang Qing's attention. As the promoter of officially sanctioned model dramas during the Cultural Revolution, it was pleasing to hear that villagers in rural China were singing "her" songs.³⁶ "I want to go to Xiaojinzhuang," Jiang said, and after perfunctory protestations that the road to the village was too rough, her Tianjin allies assented to the visit.³⁷

Propaganda about Xiaojinzhuang ramped up. On the morning of June 21, 1974, a report about the village's night school appeared on the front page of *Tianjin Daily*.³⁸ Wu Dai also summoned Baodi county leaders and Xiaojinzhuang's party secretary Wang Zuoshan to a meeting in Tianjin.³⁹ Wang called back to the village and told his colleagues in the party branch to expect an inspection visit from a central leader. Municipal authorities informed villagers of their scripts, instructing them to prepare a meeting to criticize reactionary sayings and to be ready to sing excerpts from revolutionary model operas. Baodi cadre Hu Penghua scrambled to coach seventeen handpicked villagers on their lines.⁴⁰

To many villagers, a visit from Mao's wife was an honor and an exciting diversion. But Xiaojinzhuang residents had no say in the matter, scant advance warning, and little idea of how drastically Jiang's interest in their home would change their lives. The village had fallen victim to a model-making process that kept political control out of villagers' hands. Xiaojinzhuang had already become a tool of urban politicians eager to earn points in an environment that required rhetorical celebration of rural achievements.

By encouraging Mao's wife to visit Xiaojinzhuang, Tianjin leaders had placed the village on a national stage. The urban invasion of Xiaojinzhuang began in earnest when Jiang Qing stepped out of a sedan in the center of the village on the morning of June 22, 1974. She was wearing a skirt and white sandals, and she was not alone. Her entourage totaled around forty people, including opera singers, cultural officials, Tianjin leaders, and Liang Xiao writers. Also on hand were Xing Yanzi and Hou Jun, Baodi County's two famous "iron girls" (*tie guniang*) who had been celebrated as models since the early 1960s for volunteering to return to their villages instead of pursuing city jobs or university educations.⁴¹ Thanks to Jiang's visit to Xiaojinzhuang, several village residents would soon join Xing and Hou in the pantheon of Baodi villagers turned national celebrities.

Jiang Qing toured the village and nearby fields, and then the preselected Xiaojinzhuang villagers joined Jiang and her entourage for a meeting.[42] Young women sang excerpts from revolutionary operas, which pleased Jiang. In an anti-Confucian mood, Jiang also took it upon herself to suggest name changes for villagers whose names she deemed "too feudal" (*tai fengjian*). Thus Wang Xiaoxian, an instructor in Xiaojinzhuang's political night school, became Wang Miekong (Wang "Exterminate Confucius").[43] After over an hour of reports, singing, poetry reading, and name changing, the meeting broke up.[44]

Xiaojinzhuang would do, Jiang Qing decided. As she was preparing to leave, she turned to the Tianjin leaders at her side. "Comrade Xie Xuegong, you must come here often," she told the municipal first secretary. "This is my spot (*wo de dian*), and if you don't run it well you'll be prodded." She asked to be given status reports on Xiaojinzhuang in the future, "because I don't know how often I'll come around to my spot."[45] Jiang would only make it back to the village twice, once with Imelda Marcos in September 1974 and again in August 1976, when she was embroiled in a struggle over who would succeed the ailing Mao as China's leader. But Jiang's loud claim during her first visit that she was representing the party center and Chairman Mao, plus her instructions to Xie Xuegong, were enough to change everything for the village. A few days after Jiang Qing's visit, a joint Tianjin-Baodi work team, along with Beijing-based writers, teachers, and coaches, moved into Xiaojinzhuang and the commune guesthouse down the road.[46] They plunged into producing and staging the model village.

Two leading journalists from the national Xinhua News Agency traveled to Xiaojinzhuang and wrote a confidential article that was distributed to party center and provincial leaders throughout China. The piece alerted officials to prepare large-scale nationwide propaganda on the Xiaojinzhuang model.[47] A separate article by the Liang Xiao writing group about Xiaojinzhuang's night school garnered Jiang Qing's approval for nationwide dissemination and appeared in *People's Daily* and *Tianjin Daily* on September 8. By fall 1974, without the benefit of any official party directives, extensive publicity had enshrined Xiaojinzhuang as a national model and visitors began to flow into the village to view opera performances and poetry readings.[48]

If the new work team, Xinhua journalists, and Liang Xiao writers produced these performances, then what was the script that villagers were expected to follow? In 1970s China, urban politicians did not share a uniform vision of the countryside. The image of Xiaojinzhuang presented to the nation reflected one specific use of rural China by such leaders as Jiang Qing and her Tianjin allies whose political careers depended on celebrating, defending, and continuing the Cultural Revolution. In the face of challenges from moderates like Deng Xiaoping who emphasized production, Xiaojinzhuang had to serve as proof of the benefits the Cultural Revolution had brought to villages. This vision mandated that cultural advances and attention to political movements could not be sacrificed to the details of agricultural work.

A pro–Cultural Revolution script emphasizing transformation in culture and consciousness guided Xiaojinzhuang as it ballooned from a modest local advanced unit to a national model during the summer and fall of 1974. On August 4, a front page *People's Daily* article about "Xiaojinzhuang's ten new things" (*Xiaojinzhuang shi jian xinshi*) conveyed the essence of radical urban elites' utopian vision of the countryside.[49] This article was reprinted in at least seven books about Xiaojinzhuang and also appeared in provincial newspapers all across China. The "ten new things" script, penned by Xinhua and *Tianjin Daily* journalists, along with Baodi propaganda cadre Hu Penghua, wildly exaggerated the village's achievements.[50] Xiaojinzhuang's ten innovations included starting a political night school, building up a team of "poor and lower-middle peasants" (*pin xiazhong nong*) versed in Marxist theory and anti-Confucian history, singing revolutionary model operas, establishing an art propaganda team, writing poems, opening a library, telling revolutionary stories, developing sports activities, and "transforming social traditions, destroying the old and establishing the new" (*yifeng yisu, pojiu lixin*). This last item, number ten on the list, focused mostly on women's issues, including encouraging newly engaged women to return betrothal gifts and delay their wedding dates. The article applauded married women for drawing up birth control plans and convincing their husbands to share in household chores.

Missing from the roster of ten new things was agriculture, one of the advances that attracted county officials to Xiaojinzhuang in the first place. The script instead emphasized the village's "revolution in the superstructural sphere" (*shangceng jianzhu lingyu geming*), a key message for culture-first politicians during the mid-1970s.[51] The cultural bent of the ten new things comprised the main theme of the Xiaojinzhuang show, and subsequent publicity, as well as the physical appearance of the village itself, had to reflect this script. Resources, advisers, coaches, journalists, and tourists poured into the village, in effect creating a cultural theme park. In addition to funds spent on fixing the road into Xiaojinzhuang, the village received 100,781 yuan in grants, 51,800 yuan in loans, 370,000 bricks and tiles, 135.99 cubic meters of wood, 155 tons of fertilizer, and 92 kilograms of steel products. Around 9,000 yuan were spent to improve toilet facilities.[52]

The money and material represented a windfall for the village. However, such expenditures were required if Xiaojinzhuang was to adequately perform the "ten new things" script and create the infrastructure to receive thousands of tourists every day. Thus, Deng Xiaoping's 1975 criticism that Xiaojinzhuang had gotten fat on state funds was valid, but such was the case for any model unit.[53] What must have really annoyed Deng was the culture first, production second image that Xiaojinzhuang's producers and scriptwriters had created. When Deng took control of government and party tasks in January 1975, he moved to quash the Xiaojinzhuang model. He ordered the withdrawal of a choreographed placard display containing the characters "Xiaojinzhuang" from the national games' opening ceremony and the village virtually disappeared from the pages of *People's Daily* during the second half of 1975.[54]

As the political battle between Jiang Qing and Deng Xiaoping heated up, Xiaojinzhuang's script shifted. The "ten new things" were too innocuous after Jiang Qing and her allies regained the upper hand at the beginning of 1976 and attacked Deng. The village's image as a rural cultural haven gave way to a message full of anti-Deng invective proclaiming that the advances of the Cultural Revolution could never be rolled back. In early 1976, Beijing-based Liang Xiao leaders Chi Qun and Xie Jingyi allegedly visited Xiaojinzhuang three times, on one occasion accompanied by other members of the writing group.[55] These visits meant that scriptwriters had edited lines and were prompting villagers with updated cues.

Overall, how did Xiaojinzhuang residents handle their roles in the political drama that had overtaken the village since June 1974? Although urban politicians had taken control of the village for their own purposes, villagers still had room to maneuver and assert their own agency. Some enjoyed the privilege of living in a model village newly rich from state resources, while others rejected and deviated from the city-imposed script. A few, like village leader Wang Zuoshan, rose to become stars of the show. But life in the spotlight was not easy.

Stars and Show Stealers: Model Villagers
Scripted and Unscripted

These days, just about everyone in Baodi has an opinion about Wang Zuoshan. "Zuoshan is pitiful," said a county resident. "He really wanted to work for the people and for a while he got along well with Jiang Qing, but when he became county leader he lacked confidence in himself."[56] But just how pitiful was this local cadre turned national star? Wang, village party secretary since 1969, received the most national exposure of anyone from Xiaojinzhuang. For the producers pushing the Xiaojinzhuang message, this hardworking young cadre was an ideal leading man. According to their script, Wang Zuoshan was undeniable proof of the success of the Cultural Revolution in rural China. Yet Wang would later self-effacingly describe himself to visitors as an "ignorant farmer," a "donkey in a stable await-ing orders," and a "dung beetle on an airplane, stinking to high heaven."[57] There is no question that Wang Zuoshan soared like an airplane from 1974 to 1976. He threw himself wholeheartedly into his prominent role as a rural promoter of the Cultural Revolution. But urban politicians distrusted Wang and treated him as if he *were* just an ignorant dung beetle, betraying their pervasive anti-rural bias. Wang had been handed an unworkable script. His impossible struggle to please his superiors, glorify Mao Zedong, and serve his local constituents transformed him into the pitiful figure kneeling on stage in front of young driver Li and thousands of other onlookers in late 1976, the subject of insults and slaps.[58]

Wang Zuoshan was a young man of "poor peasant" background whose family, fleeing famine conditions elsewhere, settled in Xiaojinzhuang ear-lier in the twentieth century.[59] His status as a relative outsider may have helped him rise in the village's leadership ranks during the Cultural Revolu-tion. He became Xiaojinzhuang's party secretary in 1969, when the village's party branch was reconstituted after the Ninth Party Congress.[60] Wang was twenty-six years old at the time. After taking charge, he promoted the agri-cultural improvements that led to three straight bumper harvests and local recognition for the village. Along with sent-down Baodi cadre Hu Penghua, Wang supported the village's political night school. He enjoyed particu-larly good relationships with the sent-down and returned educated youth in Xiaojinzhuang and encouraged them to teach in the school.[61] These were young Wang Zuoshan's considerable achievements, and until Jiang Qing visited the village on June 22, 1974, he had managed to successfully balance the competing demands of rural residents and his superiors. Sometimes farmers complained about the night classes and attendance was spotty, but a corps of activists remained committed to promoting movements like the campaign to criticize Lin Biao and Confucius.[62] The village was doing fairly well.

Jiang Qing's first visit was also going smoothly for Wang Zuoshan until he unwittingly offended Mao's thin-skinned wife. After deferentially reporting on village achievements to Jiang, the young secretary accompanied her and Tianjin city leaders to a wheat field, where Jiang wanted to stage photos harvesting with a sickle.[63] Jiang took a few awkward whacks at the wheat stalks, and a concerned Wang urged her to stop, fearing that she would get tired. She exploded at the well-intentioned cadre. "Leave me alone! What the hell are you doing?" (*Ni bu yong guan wo, ni shi gan shenme de?*) she yelled.[64] After this incident, Tianjin officials decided to keep Wang away from Jiang Qing for the time being. He was not allowed to leave his home when Jiang accompanied Imelda Marcos to Xiaojinzhuang in September 1974. He had a cold, he said, and city leaders were afraid he might be contagious.[65]

Wang Zuoshan's run-in with Jiang Qing may have diminished Tianjin leaders' confidence in him, but he continued to host visitors to Xiaojinzhuang, including the writer Hao Ran, who wrote glowingly of the party branch secretary as a "heroic grassroots cadre."[66] Wang still carried symbolic power as a new kind of villager, a creative achiever who could combine agricultural success with cultural advances. He remained the public face of Xiaojinzhuang and was honored as a representative and Standing Committee member of the Fourth National People's Congress in January 1975. Wang Zuoshan attempted to patch up his relationship with Jiang Qing by sending her positive reports. For Wang, as for so many other people in China during the Cultural Revolution, Jiang's proximity to her divine husband made her a representative, if not an incarnation, of Mao himself.[67] Wang had journalists stationed in the village write to Jiang to affirm his loyalty to her and Mao—and to their Cultural Revolution, which after all had transformed him into one of China's most famous villagers.[68]

Jiang Qing appreciated Wang's enthusiasm and reportedly scribbled a note that said, "Wang Zuoshan is a good cadre."[69] After this, Tianjin leaders could not touch him, even if they still thought he was "uneducated and clueless" (*mei wenhua, ye mei tounao*).[70] Under Jiang Qing's sponsorship,

Wang attended the Central Party Academy in Beijing for six months in 1975, was promoted to Baodi county secretary in 1976, and reportedly received internal approval for a promotion to head a state-level ministry.[71] Wang appeared to relish his prominence and threw himself into the project of defending the Cultural Revolution. For anyone reading the *People's Daily* in 1976, this appeared to be the case. After Mao turned against Deng Xiaoping's production-first policies in late 1975, Wang Zuoshan and Xiaojinzhuang were repeatedly associated with the campaign to criticize Deng. In the aftermath of the devastating Tangshan earthquake in late July 1976, Wang was quoted on the front page of *People's Daily*, saying, "We're in the middle of earthquake relief right now, but we can't forget to criticize Deng. We've got to make criticizing Deng a top priority."[72]

Did Wang Zuoshan truly let forth the torrent of invective attributed to him in the Gang of Four–controlled press? He certainly praised Jiang Qing effusively during his remarks at a summer 1976 army conference in Liaoning.[73] Even if journalists invented some of his supposed utterances, Wang was too deeply intertwined with Jiang Qing—and, as a rural cadre, too powerless to withstand the continued disrespect of city officials—to survive her arrest in October 1976. His promotion to county leader had been based on her support, and for Tianjin leaders he represented a perfect symbol in the new campaign against the Gang of Four. Whereas Xie Xuegong, the Tianjin first secretary who welcomed Jiang Qing so attentively in 1974, held on to power until 1978, whipping boy Wang Zuoshan was paraded around for struggle meetings and languished in jail in Baodi for a year. City officials used Wang's achievements in order to gain favor with Jiang Qing, then were the first to blame him when things turned sour. Xiaojinzhuang and Wang Zuoshan were political resources for Jiang Qing and other city leaders, more symbols than real people. Once again, China's rural residents suffered as the city extracted resources from the countryside.

Wang Zuoshan stuck to his script, perhaps too closely, but was trying to make the most out of his village's model status. Xiaojinzhuang's real achievements before 1974—bumper harvests, the night school, and youthful energy—plus its exaggerated triumphs after becoming a national model made it impossible for the village's political leader to shy away from the Cultural Revolution's embrace. Yet although only Wang Zuoshan was publicly pilloried after his patron fell, other prominent village stars also felt let down by the end of their show's run. For the energetic young women whose very identities were shaped by Jiang Qing, the model village's script was perhaps a more natural fit. In fact, Xiaojinzhuang's leading ladies Zhou Kezhou, Yu Fang, and Wang Xian accepted a script that may have seemed empowering.

Recent memoirs and scholarly works have highlighted the pride and excitement many young, unmarried women felt during the Cultural Revolution as they emulated the stars of revolutionary model operas and assumed local leadership and activist roles.[74] In Xiaojinzhuang, Zhou Fulan, Yu Ruifang, and Wang Shuxian belonged to this group. When Jiang Qing first visited the village, she bestowed new revolutionary names on the three women. Jiang's magic touch made the women's new identities even more entwined with promoting revolutionary culture. Zhou Fulan, the head of the brigade's women's association, became Zhou Kezhou (Zhou "Overcome Zhou").[75] Yu Ruifang, the women's leader of a village production team, became Yu Fang after Jiang eliminated the offending character *rui*, which means "auspicious." Wang Shuxian (*shuxian* means "gentle and virtuous"), a militia and youth league member, was now Wang Xian (Wang "First").[76] The young women activists were some of the busiest stars in Xiaojinzhuang, performing opera excerpts and giving poetry readings daily for the thousands of visitors to the village.

In publicity photos, Xiaojinzhuang's young women struck poses evocative of model opera heroines. These photos, along with the concrete policies the women advanced in the village—including equal pay for equal work, returning or refusing betrothal gifts, and matrilocal marriage—suggest that although the poses and policies may have been choreographed, the women had, like many of their counterparts across China, internalized their scripts and embraced revolutionary identities.[77] Images including Yu Fang's clenched fist and erect posture at a poetry reading, the stylized pose of a Xiaojinzhuang woman singing model opera, and a floral Wang Xian in the role of the *Red Lantern*'s Li Tiemei, tutoring a Granny Li–like older woman, all indicate the extent to which the women of Xiaojinzhuang embodied the theatricality of the Cultural Revolution.[78]

Zhou Kezhou, Wang Xian, and Yu Fang embraced their leading roles as revolutionary young women.[79] But their own assumption of the mannerisms and ideals of revolutionary models was eclipsed by the platitudes of male writers, who had their own agendas. When the writer Hao Ran, touring Xiaojinzhuang with Wang Zuoshan, gazed admiringly at the nineteen-

FIGURE 6.1.   Jiang Qing assists in rebuilding a damaged building in Xiaojinzhuang in August 1976, following the devastating Tangshan earthquake. To her immediate left is Wang Xian, a village militia and youth league member. Two years earlier Jiang had changed Wang's name from Wang Shuxian (*shuxian* means "gentle and virtuous") to Wang Xian (Wang "First").

year-old Yu Fang loading sorghum onto a cart, he was jolted with an almost erotic charge. Only half listening as Wang explained that she represented "a new generation of woman who completely came of age in the wind and rain of the Cultural Revolution," Hao Ran gushed, "this young woman was extremely healthy. Her red, red face simply merged together with the tassels of sorghum all around."[80] The proud bearing and physical beauty of the young women of Xiaojinzhuang aroused not so revolutionary desires in urban male spectators, who depicted the countryside as a ripe, virginal female realm.

Although Xiaojinzhuang was a model for equal pay for women and fighting what Zhou Kezhou called "the buying and selling of women" in marriage, entrenched views about proper gender roles limited the scope of change, particularly outside of the confines of the model village.[81] Even within Xiaojinzhuang, published images reveal the limits of efforts for gender equality in rural China. Wang Xian, the captain of the village's celebrated women's volleyball team, said that the team was formed at the behest of local leaders. They feared that Jiang Qing would lodge accusations of male chauvinism if the only sport played in the village was men's basketball.[82] Interestingly, no one thought to form a women's basketball team or a coed team. Basketball was for men, volleyball for women.[83] And in publicity photos of the village's party branch, Zhou Kezhou sits quietly as Wang Zuoshan and four other men lead the discussion.[84] The proper place for the young woman heroes of Xiaojinzhuang was in the propaganda team and women's groups. The party branch belonged to men.

Of the men in the village's party branch, Wang Du was the most politically savvy. A Xiaojinzhuang native, he graduated from the commune high school in 1972 at the age of twenty-one and rapidly integrated himself into village politics, becoming a teacher in the night school, head of the village militia, and vice-secretary of the party branch by 1973.[85] Sent-down cadre Hu Penghua lived in Wang Du's family's home for the full three years he was stationed in Xiaojinzhuang. Hu took Wang Du under his wing and the two collaborated closely, planning the night school's curriculum and writing propaganda together. Unlike Wang Zuoshan, Wang Du quickly gained the trust of Tianjin leaders and Jiang Qing. He met with Jiang four times and regularly worked with visiting journalists.[86] Wang Du was more aware than any other villager that Xiaojinzhuang's model experience was highly scripted and he participated actively in creating and modifying the script. He was able to let his writing talents and philosophical acumen shine, but ended up frustrated by the limits of his rural status. For Wang Du, being a star within the confines of the model village was not enough.

Wang Du was the best poet in Xiaojinzhuang, a village full of farmer bards. Although residents of rural Baodi County were renowned for their singing, humorous banter, jingles, and doggerel, Wang Du took these rhymes to a new level and reshaped his neighbors' poems into publishable form.[87] Seven of his poems were included in the 1974 *Xiaojinzhuang Poetry Anthology*, and he still considers reciting his "My First Visit to Beijing" at a study meeting in the capital to be one of the proudest moments of his life.[88] Wang Du was a product of the forgotten educational successes in China's countryside during the 1970s, when more rural youth attended elementary and middle school than at any other time in China's history.[89] His training allowed him to return home and teach farmers the basics of Marxist philosophy and to become a prolific writer and editor.

The problem was that Wang Du did not especially want to return to Xiaojinzhuang. He hoped to go to college. During the Cultural Revolution, however, rural primary and middle schools expanded while universities were sacrificed. University entrance examinations were abolished and the only route to college was for students classified as "workers, peasants, and soldiers" to rely on personal relations. Wang Du knew full well how this worked. At a meeting in Beijing, he established a good relationship with Liu Zehua, director of the history department at Tianjin's Nankai University. Liu recognized Wang Du's academic potential and sent university representatives to Xiaojinzhuang with an official admission letter. The next step was securing approval from county and Tianjin authorities, which should not have been a problem, considering Wang Du's regular interaction with Tianjin leaders and Jiang Qing. The architects of the Xiaojinzhuang model, however, had different plans. They needed Wang Du right where he was, pumping out poetry and reports on the village's achievements.

When Tianjin cultural leader Wang Mantian heard of Wang Du's wishes, she approached him in the village and shook her head. "So, you want to go to college?" she asked. "Isn't Xiaojinzhuang one of the best universities in the country?" His hopes were dashed. "She was a city party secretary, a real big shot," he said. "She had spoken, what could I do?"[90] City elites had their own uses for the countryside and its inhabitants. Regardless of how effective the Cultural Revolution's educational reforms had been in rural areas, increased schooling bred resentment and frustration when young educated villagers were not allowed to use their education to advance their careers in the cities.

Unable to attend college, Wang Du continued contributing to the Xiaojinzhuang script. When the village was at the forefront of the 1976 campaign to criticize Deng Xiaoping, he was quoted in *People's Daily* excoriating Deng's "nonsense and lies" (*pianren de guihua*), and wrote poetry blasting the anti–Gang of Four April Fifth Tiananmen incident as "noxious winds and evil waves" (*yaofeng, e'lang*).[91] Wang Du, like village leader Wang Zuoshan, was deeply implicated in the criticism of Deng, but much better attuned to the changing political winds. He egged Jiang Qing on when she lashed out at Deng during her August 1976 visit to Xiaojinzhuang, yet after her arrest he was quickly in print criticizing her as a "scheming double-dealing counterrevolutionary."[92] Always a master at adhering to and elaborating upon the scripts of the Cultural Revolution's political drama, Wang Du knew that his old lines were passé and adopted new ones.

Whether they were collaborating in producing their roles or internalizing them, the celebrities of Xiaojinzhuang like Wang Du, Zhou Kezhou, and Wang Zuoshan could not escape from the model village's political script. But other, less prominent villagers scorned it, especially when Xiaojinzhuang's stardom led to tension between opera-singing stars and laboring farmers. In late 1974, politically correct outsiders reportedly criticized discontented villagers for circulating subversive doggerel (*shunkouliu*). A sarcastic rhyme about the "ten ranks of people" (*shi deng ren*) described how Xiaojinzhuang's rise to national fame had privileged cultural performers and tour guides over laboring farmers.[93] As Perry Link and Kate Zhou have shown, shunkouliu provide a vivid glimpse of otherwise hidden popular sentiment.[94]

The "ten ranks" jingle began with the "first rank," people engaging in diplomacy, living in hotels, eating bread, lavishing gifts, and getting reimbursed. It ended with those in the lowly tenth rank, the "old black class," who had to walk on the side of the road and engage in compulsory labor without earning work points. Also near the top were the broadcasters who read reports over the loudspeakers (second rank), the party secretary and militia leader (third rank), who were almost impossible to find, and propaganda team members (fifth rank), who could receive a full day's worth of work points just by "singing a few lines of opera." Those in the bottom half of the status ratings included cart drivers (sixth rank), livestock raisers (eighth rank), and lowly tillers and farmers (ninth rank), who "wield a hoe and gasp for air."

Perhaps unaccustomed to the biting doggerel of rural north China, outsiders chastised villagers for reciting lines so at odds with the public image of Xiaojinzhuang as an idyllic farmer's utopia. But for the circulators of the jingle, developments in Xiaojinzhuang since Jiang Qing's visit seemed upside-down and patently unfair. Divisions within villages had always existed, and the miserable lot of those unlucky enough to be classified as landlords and counterrevolutionaries (the "old blacks") had been a constant since the 1950s.[95] Yet the village's rise to national fame heralded a disturbing new development. Not only had life been disrupted by an endless stream of urban cadres and tourists; villagers whose main talent was farming, not opera singing or poetry recitation, felt denigrated and excluded.

While thousands of tourists visited Xiaojinzhuang daily during the model's high point, some outsiders stayed on for longer periods. At one point, sixty or seventy outside cadres, over one hundred journalists, and more than one hundred volleyball coaches, poetry tutors, and opera teachers lived in the village.[96] Some stayed for as long as six months, earning daily wages and food rations, and eating in a newly established cafeteria.[97] The tillers of the land who called themselves "ninth rank" villagers only marginally benefited from this colonization and occupation of their home. Tianjin authorities installed experimental drip irrigation systems on 170 acres of surrounding land and lavished fertilizer on the village, but when it came time to harvest, many young villagers were too busy receiving guests and could not work in the fields.[98] The brigade decreed that members of the propaganda team were exempt from agricultural labor (*tuochan*), and an army unit was ordered in to help collect the harvest.[99]

If the farmers who circulated the "ten ranks" jingle heard about the front page *People's Daily* article celebrating how Xiaojinzhuang's campaign to criticize Lin Biao and Confucius had spurred agricultural production and led to a bumper harvest, they must have found fodder for more subversive verses. The October 1974 piece trumpeted the notion that cultural advances supposedly lead to improvement in material life, but everyone in the village knew that the harvest required outside assistance in order to take place at all.[100] Songs and poetry were supreme, but the details of agricultural production were an afterthought, not a natural consequence of Xiaojinzhuang's "advanced superstructure." As a model village, Xiaojinzhuang was required to have yearly bumper harvests and the appearance of agricultural abundance. But a model village featuring only sweating farmers toiling around the clock would have been boring and at odds with the point Jiang Qing and her Tianjin allies wanted to make. In their vision, villagers had to be portrayed as the source of creativity and positive knowledge. No matter that farm work required real investments of time and energy. Why not just call in the troops to take care of it?

Some residents of the village felt that stars like women's leaders Zhou Kezhou and Wang Xian had let their suddenly acquired fame go to their heads. A sent-down youth from Tianjin who moved into the village with seven of her high school classmates in October 1974 remembered that Wang Xian's imperious and tough manner of speaking scared other villagers.[101] Baodi cadre Hu Penghua was horrified at how arrogant certain village cadres had become, ordering others around and seeking personal benefits. "I was behind the scenes," Hu said. "I wrote the articles but who got the credit? They did! They weren't mentally prepared to be big stars. It was like they'd drunk half a *jin* of liquor."[102] At a meeting Hu publicly criticized Zhou Ke-zhou for circumventing proper channels to obtain specially rationed wood for a new house. Shortly thereafter he requested to be transferred out of the village. The friction that arose after his carefully groomed test point became a national model had become too painful for Hu to bear.

It may not have been the intent of the Tianjin-based managers of the Xiaojinzhuang model to sow discord among rural residents and to devalue farm work, but that was the end result of their show. Disgruntled villagers accustomed to being looked down upon by urbanites made light of their plight by circulating wry jingles, but the irony of being nationally celebrated as an advanced model village while suffering new humiliations must have stung. The officially sanctioned cultural achievements seemed ridiculous and exclusive to those who witnessed the occupation of their village, so they made up their own lines and made the best of the situation. Those dissatisfied with the state of affairs must have known that it could not last forever. Indeed, payback time came after Jiang Qing's arrest, when humbled former members of the propaganda team returned to the fields. Even into the early 1980s, farmers who had classified themselves into the "ninth rank" made a gleeful show of carefully supervising the ex-stars' every swing of the hoe.[103]

Neighboring villagers also relished Xiaojinzhuang's downfall. While being stars of the show was a rush for Wang Zuoshan, Zhou Kezhou, and Wang Du, surviving next to the noisy playhouse meant headaches. A man who lived near Xiaojinzhuang remembered that his village had to start a political night school after Jiang Qing's visit. There, farmers memorized and recited Mao's quotations at night after toiling in the fields, not as fortunate as Xiaojinzhuang's agriculture-exempt propagandists.[104] In fact, more than 3,400 political night schools were established in the Tianjin suburbs after Xiaojinzhuang made it big.[105] These night schools served as safety valves for local officials required to follow their neighbor's example. If superiors asked, village cadres could report on the glorious achievements of their own political night school, but after Xiaojinzhuang fell the schools quickly disappeared. In 1977, when Xiaojinzhuang residents like former party vice-secretary Wang Tinghe ventured outside the village, they faced snide comments from put-upon neighbors: "Oh, you're from Xiaojinzhuang? Why don't you sing or read some poetry?"[106]

When Xiaojinzhuang was riding high, rural Baodi residents felt a mixture of envy and fear about their neighbors' soaring stature. A woman who had a chance to meet Jiang Qing during her third trip to Xiaojinzhuang in August 1976 ran away in fright. Her story exemplifies how neighboring villagers deviated from Xiaojinzhuang's harmonious official image. Ms. Zeng married a young leading member of Xiaojinzhuang's party branch in 1976. She confessed that when a matchmaker arranged the marriage, her fiancé's ascendant political status made him an especially attractive prospect, even though he was a little too short for her liking.[107] Xiaojinzhuang was supposed to be a model for matrilocal marriages, where new nonnative grooms, not brides, would settle, but Zeng moved there from her home village. She said that like many neighboring villagers, she felt envious of the special treatment Xiaojinzhuang received and was happy to marry into the village. When the newlyweds heard that Jiang Qing would be visiting after the Tangshan earthquake, Zeng's new husband made preparations to welcome Mao's wife. Zeng, however, was not a poet or a singer, and she was mortified that Jiang might single her out to perform. She packed her bags, fled back to her home village, and lay low until she was sure that Jiang Qing had come and gone.[108]

For Zeng, marrying into Xiaojinzhuang seemed like a positive move, but becoming part of the show was out of the question. She was not well rehearsed and knew that a misstep in front of Jiang Qing could mean trouble. Yet other outsiders were more than willing to take advantage of association with the Xiaojinzhuang brand name and to put on a show of their own. Before Xiaojinzhuang became a model, the main access to the village was by boat across the Jian'gan river. With the huge influx of tourists in 1974, the state allocated funds for a new bridge linking the village to a nearby road. Laborers from around the Tianjin region came to build the bridge and after completing the job each worker received a commemorative shirt. The top half of the shirt displayed "Xiaojinzhuang" in three large characters, while the bottom half read "bridge-building souvenir" (*xiuqiao liunian*) in smaller script. These flashy shirts were a coveted prize for some workers. The bridge builders tucked their new shirts deeply into their pants, concealing the part identifying the shirt as a souvenir. They then went to Tianjin, where they swaggered and blustered behind the Xiaojinzhuang brand name, acting so intimidating that others dared not question them.[109]

For the workers who built the bridge to Xiaojinzhuang, the three Chinese characters making up the village's name connoted power and status. By wearing new costumes and acting tough back in the city, the workers

THOMPSON-NICOLA REGIONAL DISTRICT LIBRARY SYSTEM

enacted roles quite at odds with the official script lauding Xiaojinzhuang as a happy pantheon of advanced culture and gender equality. Yet at the same time, the tucked-in wannabes were unintentionally engaged in a wholly accurate form of model emulation. In fact, the bridge builders had leapt beyond the showy froth of model propaganda and grasped its essence—Xiaojinzhuang meant power in the city. Far from emulating Wang Zuoshan or other model villagers, the workers proudly strutting their association with Xiaojinzhuang back in the city were excellent copies of Jiang Qing, Wu Dai, Wang Mantian, and Xie Xuegong. Urban political elites had constructed a rural paradise; Tianjin workers had built a bridge. But both groups used their ties to an idealized, concocted rural China in order to strengthen their own agendas—and egos—in Tianjin.

Xiaojinzhuang's Audience: Consumers, Tourists, and Copycats

The Tianjin bridge builders actively utilized Xiaojinzhuang's reputation for their own purposes, but most people who read or heard about the village were more passive cultural consumers. Their concern was figuring out the message behind the model. What, then, did Xiaojinzhuang mean to its audience throughout China? How aware was the public of the model's concocted nature? The reactions of cultural consumers, revolutionary tourists, and potential emulators varied according to their vantage points and the prevailing political winds. Although the producers of the drama were primarily based in large cities and the model's stars hailed from the countryside, the show's intended audience was both rural and urban. Media coverage urged rural cadres to learn from Xiaojinzhuang's opera and poetry. Propaganda also provided clues to city dwellers about the relative influence of Jiang Qing and her allies. The majority of Xiaojinzhuang's audience never set foot in the village, but read about it from afar or viewed it on television.[110] People familiar with the political use of model units knew not to accept at face value articles celebrating miraculous achievements.

Daily newspapers were the best source for decoding shifting messages about Xiaojinzhuang and its links to national politics. After Jiang Qing's first visit, a trickle of reports on the village gave way to a cascade of references. Thirty articles mentioning Xiaojinzhuang appeared in *People's Daily* in late 1974, including eight front-page pieces exclusively dedicated to village achievements in political education, poetry, women's equality, and opera singing. In 1975, Xiaojinzhuang's media prominence first soared but then dropped off entirely. Newspaper readers could have correctly concluded that the model and its sponsors had fallen into political disfavor. Sixty-two *People's Daily* pieces referring to Xiaojinzhuang appeared before June, but as the year progressed, Deng Xiaoping took control of government tasks, Mao criticized his wife for her political activities, and Xiaojinzhuang's national exposure dwindled to zero. During the four-month period between August 26 and December 26, the village vanished completely from the pages of China's main newspaper. Xiaojinzhuang residents wondered what had happened to so thoroughly stifle their village's year-old fame. At the time they had no idea that Deng Xiaoping's distaste for Jiang Qing's rural model was behind the silence.[111] Had the curtain fallen for good on the Xiaojinzhuang show, or was the media silence simply a long intermission?

The answer partly depended on the outcome of the political battle between radicals like Jiang Qing and moderates represented by Deng Xiaoping. However, the ailing Mao Zedong played a decisive role in creating the political atmosphere necessary for Xiaojinzhuang's return to national prominence. Mao's comments about art and literature, along with the general trend of moderation in mid-1975, helped banish Xiaojinzhuang to temporary obscurity. In July, Mao complained to Deng Xiaoping about the paucity of artistic offerings. "There are too few model dramas, and if people make even small mistakes they are struggled against," he said. "There are no novels or poetry."[112] Mao probably never read Wang Du's verses, or perhaps he saw the poetry and dismissed it. Regardless, Xiaojinzhuang stayed invisible until Mao decided that Deng's policies, including his proposals on industrial rationalization, developing science and technology through borrowing from abroad, and reviving higher education, had gone too far in rolling back the Cultural Revolution.[113] Mao approved a new campaign attacking Deng in late 1975, and the curtain rose on Xiaojinzhuang's strident second act. Thanks to shifting elite politics, the rural cultural utopia morphed into an anti–Deng Xiaoping model.

People's Daily readers who had forgotten Xiaojinzhuang received a blunt reminder with their morning paper on December 27, 1975. A front page article declared, "Everyone's familiar with Xiaojinzhuang, an advanced model. Many concerned people are asking, 'What new changes have occurred in Xiaojinzhuang?'"[114] The model was back with a vengeance and recovered its position as a mainstay in the pages of *People's Daily* during 1976, the final period of primacy for Jiang Qing and her allies. Three of the year's total of eighty-two articles that referred to the village were front-page screeds dedicated to Xiaojinzhuang residents' criticism of Deng Xiaoping. Twenty-four other references to Xiaojinzhuang in 1976 mentioned the village in the context of larger articles attacking Deng and proclaiming the triumph of the Cultural Revolution over its purported enemies. Readers who may have been somewhat confused about how to react to the initial 1974 coverage of Xiaojinzhuang (Should we just write poetry? Sing more often?) could make no mistake about the model's message in 1976: criticize Deng, squash any kind of market activity or agricultural sideline, and defend the glorious fruits of the Cultural Revolution from all doubters. By this time, it was clearer than ever that Xiaojinzhuang was a political tool.[115]

The publicity blitz elicited both positive and negative reactions. Some consumers were moved to write to the village. People from Anhui, Henan, Jiangsu, Jilin, and Liaoning wrote letters to Xiaojinzhuang accusing local cadres in their provinces of various infractions.[116] What kind of criticism did writers include in their correspondence to Xiaojinzhuang? They probably wrote to lament the inadequate emulation efforts of local officials back at home. This was likely a tactic to gain leverage in local power struggles by supporting what seemed to be a "Maoist" project. How better to challenge local cadres than to appeal to the mecca of rural cultural transformation itself?

It is unknown whether such fan letters to Xiaojinzhuang led to repercussions for the accused cadres, but a separate case of hate mail spurred a harsh response. The story of Han Aimin, who became a model in his own right during the post-1976 onslaught of accusations against the Gang of Four, suggests that some consumers recognized the concocted nature of the Xiaojinzhuang model and reacted angrily. During 1975, Han, an ex-sailor based in Qingdao, allegedly bought a copy of the *Xiaojinzhuang Poetry Anthology* in a Beijing bookstore.[117] He noticed that several poems referred to a "dear person" (*qinren*) who had visited the village, realized that this unnamed visitor was Jiang Qing, and became upset.[118]

A 1978 report claims that in July 1975, just when press coverage of the model village began to taper off, Han wrote a letter warning the people of Xiaojinzhuang. The veracity of his hyperbolic attack may be dubious, but is still worth quoting here at length:

In your *Xiaojinzhuang Poetry Anthology* you extol a "dear person" and a "comrade leader." May I ask, what kind of leader or dear person is she? She is not a leader, but is a traitor and running dog of the imperialists, revisionists, and reactionaries. She is not dear but is a newborn capitalist. I hope that the poor and lower-middle peasants of Xiaojinzhuang can rub their eyes clear, swing round and catch her off guard (*caliang yanjing, sha ta de huimaqiang*). A battle to pay back Jiang Qing's blood debts has already started. The people are great; all antiparty, anti-socialist, anti–Mao Zedong Thought scoundrels must be destroyed, must be destroyed! Must be destroyed!![119]

Later accounts about Han note that this correspondence, along with criticism letters to other government ministries, landed him in jail for nearly a year.[120] Clearly, the effort to publicize Xiaojinzhuang through newspapers and books motivated cultural consumers to voice their opinions. The variety of responses to the model reflects the uncertain, anxious mood in China during the 1970s. As the relative influence of opposing factions waxed or waned, constantly shifting messages in the official media induced readers to either rejoice or despair. While the people who wrote notes in support of Xiaojinzhuang placed their bets on Jiang Qing, others like Han Aimin hitched their hopes to a train moving in a different direction.

Letter writing was one of the only methods for people in China to raise complaints or accuse cadres of wrongdoing during the 1970s. Similarly, an inspection tour of a model unit was one of the few chances Chinese people had to travel during the final years of the Cultural Revolution. Around one hundred thousand sightseers toured Xiaojinzhuang during 1975, and for many visitors the opportunity to leave home and view a rural theme park was refreshing.[121] Xiaojinzhuang residents working in the village's new reception office ascertained the rank and origin of each visiting group, and arranged tours accordingly.[122] Leading cadres at the county level or higher enjoyed special treatment, including meetings with the Xiaojinzhuang party branch and opera and poetry performances. Average tourists were treated to a simpler program: look around, watch a film, and hear a villager report on the model's achievements.[123] Even this abbreviated itinerary excited city visitors, including a young Tianjin student who toured Xiaojinzhuang on an elementary school field trip. After inspecting a farmer's home and attempting to plant wheat in a nearby field, the student left the village impressed by its "advanced" (*xianjin*) design and exhilarated by the opportunity to see real farm fields.[124] For him, the rural utopia invented by Tianjin politicians was magnificent.

Other tourists approved of Xiaojinzhuang's physical appearance. The village had become a cleaner, brighter place since Jiang Qing's visit, when one writer accompanying her remembered it as "average" (*yiban*) and "nothing special" (*meiyou shenme liaobuqi de*).[125] Since then, material improvements had transformed the village. A visiting soldier marveled at sparkling streets and whitewashed buildings during fall 1974.[126] A Liang Xiao member who visited Xiaojinzhuang after it became a model recalled that the village lacked the "messy" qualities he expected to see in the countryside (*meiyou luan de*), and he found the poetry performance "very simple and sincere" (*hen pushi*).[127] The Xiaojinzhuang theme park's combination of rural simplicity and cleanliness catered to the tastes of city visitors. They could maintain a sense of superiority over the village's "simple farmers," without dealing with the odors or messiness that were part of agricultural life.

Rural visitors to Xiaojinzhuang who knew what life was really like back on the farm had a different experience. They knew that the whitewashed buildings, inevitable bumper crops, and hours of free time for cultural activities were impossible to attain without massive infusions of state resources. Going on a trip was still an adventure, but figuring out how to copy the model was vexing. A young woman from Wugong Village in Hebei Province visited Xiaojinzhuang as part of a cultural delegation in September 1974. Wang Zuoshan was "too busy" to receive her group, but as she listened to Wang Du's report on Xiaojinzhuang's poetry and singing, she fretted about how to explain its significance to her village party branch. Wugong, like other villages near Tianjin, ended up copying what it could. Political night school classes commenced, villagers wrote verses, and farmers took breaks from agricultural work to sing and listen to arias.[128]

Local models began to earn praise for studying Xiaojinzhuang during fall 1974. Villages relatively close to Xiaojinzhuang and Tianjin were the first to receive national recognition for opening night schools, forming political theory teams, and singing opera tunes.[129] Later, units far from Tianjin became advanced "study Xiaojinzhuang" models.[130] Often the villages singled out for successfully studying Xiaojinzhuang had already received recognition for copying China's most famous rural model, Dazhai. It bears reminding that Xiaojinzhuang itself started down the road of national fame by becoming a local advanced "study Dazhai" unit. In 1964, Mao called on the nation to emulate Dazhai's collective agriculture and self-reliance.[131] Mao's elevation of Dazhai, a brigade in Shanxi's Xiyang County, gave the model a magic aura and it remained prominent throughout the Cultural Revolution, only to be briefly eclipsed by Xiaojinzhuang in late 1974 and again in early 1976. Was there enough room in China for two rural mega-models?

Tension between Dazhai and Xiaojinzhuang was unavoidable. After coverage of Xiaojinzhuang began to surpass that of the ballyhooed Shanxi model in the national press, a group of eight delegates from Xiaojinzhuang traveled to Dazhai. By that time, Dazhai's famous leader Chen Yonggui was in Beijing, serving as a vice-premier. Yonggui's son Chen Mingzhu chaired a meeting with the Xiaojinzhuang delegation and introduced Wang Du, politely asking for Wang's "instructions" (*zhishi*). As Chen Mingzhu waited to see if the upstart cultural model would dare to give lessons to Dazhai, Wang Du stood up and started for the front of the room with his speaking notes. Halfway to the podium a Baodi county cadre who had accompanied the Xiaojinzhuang group pulled Wang Du aside and told him, "you can't speak." Wang Du quickly opted for modesty. He strode on stage, shook Chen Mingzhu's hand, and then returned to his seat without saying a word. Chen Mingzhu interpreted Wang Du's silence as a snub and became livid after the meeting, complaining that Wang Du looked down on Dazhai. Yet lecturing Dazhai about Xiaojinzhuang's achievements would have made Chen even angrier.[132]

The fallout from Wang Du's silent handshake exposed the strains between the two models. Dazhai and Xiaojinzhuang were not natural antagonists, but national politics placed them in opposition. As Edward Friedman notes, both rural models were political tools.[133] The bigger a national model got, the less control villagers had over their own destiny. Many of Xiaojinzhuang's poems lavishly praised its model predecessor, even after Wang Du's tense moment. However, Xiaojinzhuang's rapid rise caused friction. It was irrevocably linked to Jiang Qing, while Dazhai's message had gone through so many contortions that everyone tried to claim it as a badge of legitimacy. In 1975, Deng Xiaoping contributed to the perception that the two model villages were combatants. When Deng criticized Xiaojinzhuang for getting rich from state funds, a charge that would have been equally valid against Dazhai, he also complained, "now it's study 'small' (*Xiao*), not 'big' (*Da*). . . . Xiaojinzhuang does not study Dazhai."[134] Deng, in favor of private plots and agricultural modernization, appealed to his own pro-mechanization version of Dazhai to attack Jiang Qing and belittle her "spot." All of China's leaders paid lip service to Dazhai, regardless of where they fell on the political spectrum.[135] Jiang and Deng both spoke at the national conference to study Dazhai in September and October 1975. Jiang warned of the threat of a capitalist comeback in the countryside, while Deng again advocated mechanization and national development.[136]

In the end, there was room for both Dazhai and Xiaojinzhuang only while the latter's patron was politically strong enough to bolster her utopia. Dazhai lingered on as a catch-all rural model until 1980, but soon after Jiang Qing was arrested Xiaojinzhuang became an anti-model. Even after Xiaojinzhuang's final fall from grace, urban politicians and propagandists refused to let go of the village and its potent symbolism. Xiaojinzhuang's night school, once lauded as a creative fountainhead, was condemned as an institution that stifled technological innovation.[137] Rural opera singing and poetry writing no longer shone as cultural beacons, but were presented as hindrances to agriculture and scientific education.[138] Even after the tourists, journalists, and poetry coaches departed, Xiaojinzhuang remained on stage as a negative example until gradually fading from public view. This was a welcome development for many residents who resented the consequences of the village's model stardom. For them, the only thing worse than being denigrated during the model's high point may have been the humiliation of living in an anti-model.

However, the blessed media silence after 1978 did not signal a return to normalcy for Xiaojinzhuang's ex-stars. Former leading man Wang Zuoshan struggled to adapt to a changed script. After October 1976, Wang languished in detention in Baodi for almost a full year, only leaving his cell to make appearances at criticism meetings. Festering conflict in Xiaojinzhuang contributed to Wang's woes. Because his family was relatively new in the village, he lacked the long-standing lineage ties that could have softened his fall. Leaders from the dominant lineage group reportedly heaped blame on him and protected themselves.[139] Wang's party membership was suspended until 1984, when a Tianjin committee restored his status. One factor the committee cited in its decision was that "he is a farmer, after all, and is uneducated" (*ta bijing shi ge nongmin, you meiyou wenhua*).[140] Even as the relieved Wang Zuoshan celebrated this long-awaited good news, the insults continued. Wang's humbling experience with confession and self-criticism made him an adept spinner of the last official word on Jiang Qing and

Xiaojinzhuang.[141] "Jiang Qing was plucking peaches" (*zhai taozi*), he often says, meaning that Jiang stole rural innovations and used them for her own political purposes.[142]

There is truth to this version of the story, but the Xiaojinzhuang model's rise and fall is too complicated to fit into a simple "plucking peaches" trope. The village was doomed by its subordinate position in a political system dominated by urban politicians. Yet villagers' adoption or rejection of the model script confirms that local agency endured. In 1999, Wang Zuoshan defended himself to a local visitor, saying that he had simply followed orders. "What they made me do, I did," he claimed; "What they made me say, I said."[143] Granted, Wang's position as a rural cadre pressured by Tianjin officials, coupled with his understanding of Jiang Qing as a representative of the divine Mao, put him in a difficult bind. But Wang enjoyed some tasty "peaches" too. He followed his orders with flair and was honored by appointments to the National People's Conference and Central Party Academy. Similarly, Wang Du, who now runs a chemical fertilizer factory in Baodi, retains fond memories of his stardom, and Wang Xian's 1975 trip to Japan as a representative of Xiaojinzhuang was a rare chance for a rural woman to travel outside of China.[144]

Tianjin leaders criticized and abandoned Xiaojinzhuang soon after Jiang Qing fell, but the decollectivization and money making of the reform era also left the village behind. In October 1991, Wang Zuoshan took a bus to Daqiuzhuang, a village near Tianjin that gained fame in the late 1980s and early 1990s as a model of reform. The new model's enterprises had transformed it into China's richest village, and Wang took his pilgrimage in order to ask Daqiuzhuang's leader, Yu Zuomin, for financial support. One wonders what Wang, who was more aware than anyone of the shaky stilts on which China's model villages were built, could have been thinking as he made his appeal. Xiaojinzhuang's one small metal processing factory had failed, Wang Zuoshan explained as Yu Zuomin listened sympathetically. Yu cut Wang a check for 60,000 yuan, treated him to a banquet, and sent him home in a limousine.[145] Yet when Wang Zuoshan reported this development to the Baodi county party secretary, the county official, fearful of the implications of horizontal ties between individual villages, ordered that Wang return the money. Wang continued to negotiate with Daqiuzhuang and eventually succeeded in garnering financial support.

Daqiuzhuang was totally discredited in 1993, when a court sentenced Yu

Zuomin to twenty years in prison for stealing state secrets, hiding criminals, and obstructing justice. Xiaojinzhuang was tainted again because of its connection to its disgraced neighbor. Today, Xiaojinzhuang seems lackluster, with no industry and many young people away in the cities laboring as second-class citizens. In some ways, Xiaojinzhuang's current situation is worse than when Tianjin leaders shaped it into a model during the mid-1970s. In the Cultural Revolution, urban politicians shielded their anti-rural bias behind paeans to village progress, but in the new millennium overtly discriminating against and insulting China's villagers are in vogue among city dwellers.[146] Today, someone like Wang Zuoshan could never rise to become a county secretary or attend the Central Party Academy. Politics and national leaders have changed, but rural China's subordination persists.

SEVEN

Labor Created Humanity: Cultural Revolution Science on Its Own Terms

Sigrid Schmalzer

Historical accounts of science in twentieth-century China typically have little good to say of the Cultural Revolution—and often little at all. Perhaps even more than in other fields, the Cultural Revolution in science is seen as a ten-year gap, a time when political struggles interfered with or even put a stop entirely to scientific work. I would suggest, however, that the history books themselves contribute to this gap: they give the Cultural Revolution scant coverage because they do not recognize its priorities. If we broaden our understanding of science to include popular science, a key Cultural Revolution concern, the gap can be closed considerably. This, then, is a case study of popular science in the Cultural Revolution, focusing on the very popular science of paleoanthropology—the study of human origins. Paleoanthropology was "popular" in two senses: it was strongly represented in science books, exhibits, magazines, films, and other materials produced for general audiences; and as a field science it lent itself to the promotion of cooperation between scientists and local people.

The approach taken here thus differs significantly from that found in existing literature on science in the Cultural Revolution. It is in some ways most similar to accounts published during the late Cultural Revolution by western visitors to China, in that it takes seriously the stated goals and methods of Cultural Revolution–era "mass science." Foreigners invited to China during this period often had positive views of science as it was then being conducted. The discovery of the Mawangdui archaeological site, the delivery of primary healthcare, the development of integrated techniques for controlling insect pests, and advances in earthquake prediction were among the touted examples of recent Chinese scientific achievements. Many of these new accomplishments, moreover, were explicitly linked to contemporary Chinese ideas about mass participation in science.[1] American paleoanthropologists were no exception to this trend. They took advantage of an invitation in 1975 to visit the Institute of Vertebrate Paleontology and Paleoanthropology (IVPP) in Beijing and expressed their positive impressions in their lengthy report, which included a full chapter on the importance of "Public Archaeology in China" by Kwang-chih Chang.[2] Political circumstances, however, prevented the authors of such studies from seeing more than what their hosts wished (or dared) to show them. Their accounts thus lack a critical perspective on the negative effects of the Cultural Revolution on science.[3]

The fall of the Gang of Four in 1976 and the implementation of the Four Modernizations under Deng Xiaoping in 1978 opened the floodgates on criticisms of Cultural Revolution policy toward science and scientists.[4] Chinese as well as foreign accounts began to see the story as one of scientists persecuted and science stultified, making it almost impossible for scholars and journalists to return to the previous, rosier view. Scientists and other intellectuals were common protagonists in what became known as "scar literature"—personal stories of people psychologically oppressed, physically tortured, and not infrequently, killed during the Cultural Revolution.[5] Western scholars have picked up their stories and written about their experiences undergoing forced agricultural labor and becoming targets for political criticism and violence.[6] These and other narratives, both foreign and Chinese, have also recast the Cultural Revolution as a period in which political campaigns and censorship made scientific achievement virtually impossible.[7] Such writings all move away from the view, dominant in the Cultural Revolution, that science is or should be a socialist enterprise in which the means (including mass participation and revolutionary spirit) are as important as the ends. Rather, they focus on science as a professional endeavor in which economic development and scientific truth (in that order) are virtually the only clear priorities. While there are many good reasons to hold Cultural Revolution science to the same standards as science in other regional and historical contexts, it is sometimes helpful to put these standards temporarily aside in order to gain a better understanding of the historical period on its own terms. This study, then, will reexamine science in the Cultural Revolution by taking one of the stated goals of the time seriously—that is, the promotion of popular science. At the same time, however, it will benefit from access to information and oppositional perspectives unavailable to writers during the Cultural Revolution itself.

A Favorable Time for Popular Science

Popular science in Mao-era China consisted of two disparate spheres: participation and dissemination. Slogans and policies aimed at improving popular participation emphasized the class politics of science and promoted "mass science" (*qunzhongxing kexue* or *qunzhong ban kexue*) by refiguring science as an activity characterized by labor and dependent on the laboring classes. "Mass science" meant facilitating laborers' participation in science and publicly acknowledging their contributions. Science dissemination (*kexue puji* or *kepu*), on the other hand, served the conjoined purposes of stamping out superstition (*po mixin*) and spreading a materialist view of the world. In the case of paleoanthropology (the study of human origins), the goal was specifically to eliminate the Christian notion that "God created humanity" (*Shangdi chuangzao le ren*) and the similar Chinese story of the legendary Nüwa creating humanity, and to establish in their stead Frederick Engels' theory that "labor created humanity." Engels had theorized in his 1876 treatise *The Part Played by Labor in the Transition from Ape to Human* that it was the "first labor" of constructing tools that had transformed our ape ancestors' hands, stimulated the growth and development of their brains, and precipitated the emergence of language and complex forms of social organization.[8] Science dissemination materials produced on human origins in socialist China invariably focused on Engels' conclusion that "labor created humanity itself" (*laodong chuangzao le ren benshen*) as a means of eradicating superstition.

Between these two spheres of participation and dissemination lay both a profound contradiction and a possibility for resonance. The contradiction was general to popular science in the People's Republic. How could scientists be expected to "rely on the masses" (*kao qunzhong*) when the masses were officially held to be superstitious and ignorant? To look at it in the other direction, how could the project of science dissemination—which followed a top-down model of bringing knowledge from the experts to the masses—be expected to function when the very notion of expert knowledge repeatedly came under attack?[9] For the period before the Cultural Revolution, the answer to this paradox was that—with the notable exception of agricultural and industrial technology, particularly during the Great Leap Forward—educating the masses took precedence over "relying on the masses." The far more radical politics of the Cultural Revolution, however, offered new opportunities for "mass science" to flourish.

The resonance, on the other hand, was specific to paleoanthropology, although similar points of connection may well be found in other scientific fields. Both the content of popular science materials on human origins and the philosophy undergirding popular participation in paleoanthropology centered on labor. Popular science materials proclaimed that labor created humanity, that labor was the fundamental driving force in human evolution and social development, that labor continued to define what it meant to be human and not animal, and that the laboring masses thus carried the torch of humanity. Rhetoric accompanying calls to promote class struggle in science similarly trumpeted that labor had created science, and that science was best practiced under the guidance of the laboring masses of "workers, peasants, and soldiers" (*gong nong bing*). Paleoanthropology was especially easy to portray as a science based on labor, since it included so much dusty work in the field where shovels, picks, and wheelbarrows figured as prominent tools of the trade.

The late Cultural Revolution (1971–78) was the time most likely to see this resonance produce interesting and productive combinations.[10] The chaos and violence of the early years of the Cultural Revolution, beginning in 1966, had subsided. The spectacular demise of Mao's chosen successor Lin Biao in 1971 and the rapprochement with the United States in 1971 and 1972 signaled a shift in party policy and "touched off an unheralded movement of intellectual liberation at the height of the Cultural Revolution."[11] Classes had already resumed in most schools in 1968, and after 1971 museums reopened and publishing presses recommenced operation. In 1972, Zhou Enlai began working toward a new scientific initiative, with the urging and support of scientists, that would place more emphasis on basic science and scientific theory, a direct challenge to the radicals' conviction that "scientific knowledge could be acquired only through practice" and only applied science (technology) was of use to society.[12] Although it was an uphill battle until Mao's death and the fall of the "Gang of Four" in 1976, Zhou's efforts, along with those of Deng Xiaoping, Hu Yaobang, and others, offered new hope to scientists.

These years also saw an explosion of renewed activity specifically in disseminating scientific knowledge of human evolution. In 1971, at the urging of Yao Wenyuan (arrested in 1976 as a member of the Gang of Four), Mao authorized the retranslation and republishing of Thomas Huxley's *Man's Place in Nature* (1863) and *Evolution and Ethics* (1893).[13] The Mao quotations chosen for the frontispiece of *Evolution and Ethics* both related to the theme of learning from the past and from the west, a significant break from the early years of the Cultural Revolution.[14] Nineteen seventy-one also saw the opening of new and colorful exhibits on the theme "labor created humanity" in museums across China, and in 1972 the Institute for Vertebrate Paleontology and Paleoanthropology (IVPP) launched the popular magazine *Fossils* (Huashi).

Nonetheless, radical politics still held sway: scientific and educational institutions remained under the control of "worker propaganda teams," and political campaigns continued to focus the country's attention on class struggle. Even more than in previous decades, labor became the central focus of both science dissemination and scientific research in paleoanthropology. Moreover, the two were more closely integrated. Popular science materials more explicitly emphasized the class politics of scientific research and dissemination; and research practices more often included a dissemination component to facilitate the participation of nonscientists. Thus, the late Cultural Revolution produced what appears to have been the most likely climate in which the two previously separate spheres of science dissemination and "mass science" could be brought together. The analysis that follows is meant both to appreciate the radical character of popular science activities in the Cultural Revolution and to acknowledge where and why they failed to realize their potential.

Dissemination: Fossils *Magazine Strikes a Blow for Popular Science*

In 1972, IVPP published a trial issue of a new popular magazine, entitled *Fossils*, that began semiannual publication the following year and quarterly publication in 1976. The magazine, still published today, reached its height of about three hundred thousand subscribers in its earliest years during the Cultural Revolution when it had little competition from other popular science magazines.[15] Based on article submissions and letters to the editor, distribution appears to have been widespread throughout China. Museum workers, employees of cultural centers (*wenhuaguan*), and teachers were likely best represented, but readers also included factory workers, students, and others. The trial issue and subsequent issues solicited articles written by "the broad masses of workers, peasants, and soldiers, revolutionary cadres, and revolutionary intellectuals."[16] The readership was imagined to consist of "the broad masses of workers, peasants, and soldiers, revolutionary cadres, stratigraphy workers, museum workers, and youth," and writers were thus urged to use clear, lively language that was "popular and easy to read."[17]

Considering the special focus of the magazine, its offerings were diverse. The covers sported colorful photographs and paintings of science workers in the field, exhibits, and reconstructions of prehistoric animals. Inside, readers found poems on evolution, explanations of current research, debates on theoretical issues, and of course criticisms of creationism using Engels' theory that "labor created humanity." In keeping with the time, quotations from Marx, Engels, and Mao often peppered the articles in bold print. Many of the authors were scientists and other workers from IVPP, but famous popular science writers like Gao Shiqi, scientists and museum workers from other institutions, and lay readers also contributed materials.

From the beginning, IVPP recognized that publishing a popular magazine required more than just scientific expertise, and the institute staffed *Fossils* with people possessing substantial writing and editing experience. The first general editor of *Fossils*, Liu Houyi, had worked for the translation and editing department of the Academy of Sciences and for the Science Press before becoming a graduate student at IVPP in 1957. By the time he began work on *Fossils*, Liu had also written many short essays on science for newspapers and a widely popular book entitled *Quick Calculation* (Suan de kuai).[18] Liu soon brought in an outsider to help with the magazine, someone he knew from the Science Press named Zhang Feng.[19]

Although Zhang's colleagues at IVPP respected his writing and editing abilities, he quickly crossed swords with them over the institute's handling of the magazine. Zhang was frustrated by what he saw to be IVPP's unwillingness to devote significant resources to *Fossils* magazine in comparison with its professional journal, *Vertebrata PalAsiatica* (Gu jizhui dongwu yu gu renlei) and other publications.[20] He considered this representative of a larger problem: China's scientific institutes did not pay enough attention to popular science, a situation that betrayed their elitist character. Failing to reach a satisfactory resolution within the institute, on September 6, 1975, Zhang Feng took his grievance to the highest authority by writing a letter to Chairman Mao, then a very old man whose word was nonetheless sacrosanct. Mao, who had already favored the magazine by requesting a large-print copy for his nearsighted review, appeared to take the issue seriously.[21] He personally read Zhang's letter, appended his own comment, and wrote a note to Deng Xiaoping and Yao Wenyuan, dated September 16, 1975, asking them to review it and consider circulating it to Central Committee members. Unfortunately, his comment, consisting only of the phrase "a speak-bitterness letter" (*yi feng suku de xin*) was ambiguous to say the least.[22] Did he mean that the letter was only a common sort of complaint? Or did he mean that Zhang's grievance was worthy of the same kind of respect and attention that poor peasants were granted when they "spoke bitterness" about their oppression at the hands of landlords?[23]

While people then were hard put to decide how to implement Mao's wishes on the issue, people today have difficulties remembering what was actually done in the end. My interview data on this subject illustrate both the uncertainties of the time and the fragmented character of institutional memories of the Cultural Revolution. One person remembers hearing that Mao called a mass meeting at Workers' Stadium that tens of thousands of people attended.[24] Another rejects this story and says instead that Hu Yaobang, then director of the Chinese Academy of Sciences and thus ultimately responsible for IVPP itself, was forced to come to IVPP to be criticized.[25] A third person agrees that Hu Yaobang came to IVPP in response to Zhang Feng's letter, but does not remember him being criticized. Rather, she recalls that he gave a carefully worded speech intended to encourage the beleaguered scientists, saying that as vertebrate paleontologists they should all have "strong backbones" to withstand the trials they were undergoing.[26] Although the stories contradict one another, taken together they document a serious political response from the highest levels to the charges that IVPP was not paying enough attention to popular science.

The last of these accounts is likely the most accurate. The teller attended Hu Yaobang's talk at IVPP, and the story tallies with tangential documentary evidence. In late 1975, Hu Yaobang gave speeches at a number of scientific institutes in which he made comments supporting intellectuals and warning against excessive populism in scientific research.[27] It would not have been surprising for him to have given a similar speech at IVPP.

Moreover, shortly after Mao circulated Zhang Feng's letter, Deng Xiao-ping mentioned *Fossils* at least twice in ways that suggest he consciously sought to use this episode to promote professional science. On September 19, Deng referred to *Fossils* in a conversation with Hu Qiaomu, then in charge of the State Council's Office of Political Research (Zhengzhi yanjiu shi). A week later, he mentioned the magazine while commenting on a re-port Hu Yaobang made to the State Council about scientific issues. In each case, Deng interpreted Mao's interest in *Fossils* as evidence of the Chairman's support for two of Deng's own priorities. First, he encouraged both Hu Yaobang and Hu Qiaomu to step up their involvement in more theoreti-cal periodicals. If Mao was concerned "even about periodicals like *Fossils*," how much more would he be concerned about other science periodicals like *Laws of Natural Dialectics* (Ziran bianzheng fa) or a general-interest periodical published by the Ministry of Education?[28] Second, he suggested that Mao highlighted the *Fossils* letter to demonstrate his support for the development of scientific research, and even his "high regard for basic theo-retical science" (*jichu lilun kexue de zhongshi*).[29] This position reflected the interests of research scientists over Cultural Revolution radicals who favored applied science along with popular science. Whatever Mao's intent, Deng's interpretation thus flew in the face of Zhang Feng's populist stance.

While Deng and Hu were attempting to steer science back onto a pro-fessional track, the attention from above nonetheless encouraged IVPP to put more energy into popular science. In preparation for increasing *Fossils'* publication frequency from two to four issues per year and for sending the magazine to foreign as well as domestic audiences, the editors drafted a detailed plan for the 1976 issues and circulated it along with a cover let-ter to other work units for feedback.[30] The editors suggested a number of areas ripe for criticism, including "excusing 'exceptionalism' in science and technology," "denying that workers, peasants, and soldiers were the main forces in the army of scientific research," and "opposing the policy of mak-ing scientific research serve proletarian politics and the workers, peasants, and soldiers and [making scientific research] unite with productive labor." Such criticisms were all aimed at eliminating the privileged status of science as intellectual work and that of intellectuals within science.

The issues for 1976 were to include first and foremost materials in cel-ebration of the hundredth anniversary of Engels' treatise *The Part Played by Labor in the Transition from Ape to Human*. The editors also proposed a range of other topics to satisfy the requirements of being a popular science magazine in a politically charged period: everything from natural history in the service of stamping out superstition, to strategies in science dissemination, to such Cultural Revolution staples as "In agriculture, learn from Dazhai."[31] Many of the topics—for example, the "struggle" between natural science and theology—had been core themes at least since 1949.

What was new, however, was the amount of explicit attention given to the class politics of knowledge. For example, under the category "introductions to scientists" (meaning, biographies of scientists), the editors recommended focusing on "the contributions of laboring people and 'small characters' in paleontology and paleoanthropology," explaining that "science originates in practice and comes from the people," and highlighting the "great truth that 'the lowliest are the smartest'" (*beijian zhe zui congming*).[32] Similarly, when discussing Engels' theory that "labor created humanity," the editors suggested authors use this opportunity to criticize the ideas that "intellectual education is most important" and that "in conducting scientific research, one cannot open the doors [to the masses]." While not all the topics had such an explicitly political focus, the editors evinced an awareness that class and education issues were applicable even in the most technical of articles. For example, they emphasized that articles on fossil identification should be clearly written and devoid of overelaboration to facilitate their use by workers, peasants, and soldiers.

There was much in *Fossils* that people who had encountered popular materials on human evolution from the 1950s would find familiar. The difference lay in the higher intensity of the political rhetoric and the greater emphasis on class politics of knowledge. Although many books and other materials had been published in earlier years for popular audiences, *Fossils* was a medium that sought to bring people from wide-ranging backgrounds together between the same covers. Articles were written by and for everyone from the "broad masses" to "revolutionary intellectuals." The magazine further sought to portray science as an endeavor in which all classes participated, and articles sometimes even foregrounded the contributions of workers. Finally, with its vibrant covers and variety of content, *Fossils* was an effective emblem of the importance attributed to popular science during the Cultural Revolution.

Dissemination: Dinosaurs and the Masses at Zhoukoudian

Fossils was not the only venue for such new emphases: exhibits at the Peking Man site at Zhoukoudian (thirty miles southwest of Beijing) and elsewhere were part of the same trend in popular paleoanthropology.[33] The new exhibits created in the early 1970s added color and energy to the familiar slogan "labor created humanity," and emphasized more than ever before the "popular" in popular science. The new public exhibit at Zhoukoudian had its origins in efforts beginning in late 1968 or early 1969 to honor the twentieth anniversary of the People's Republic and the fortieth anniversary of the discovery of the first Peking Man skullcap. IVPP sent a team of scientists, political advisors, and artists to tourist sites around Beijing and as far away as Hangzhou and Kunming in order to learn how to create better exhibits for popular audiences.[34] The team then put together a small exhibit (not open to the public) on evolution in the reception hall at Zhoukoudian in late 1969. Guo Moruo, the famous archaeologist and then president of the Chinese Academy of Sciences, visited the exhibit and recommended that it receive funding for expansion, replacing the existing exhibition hall that had been established in 1953 and had remained relatively unchanged since 1959.

Preparations for the new exhibit at Zhoukoudian coincided with preparations for similar exhibits all around the country, for example in Shanghai, Hangzhou, Xi'an, Tianjin, Liuzhou, and Guilin. In 1976 IVPP took a traveling exhibit, based on the one at Zhoukoudian, to Tibet. This mission held particular political importance: Engels' lesson that "labor created humanity" would help assault the stronghold of "superstition" that the Tibetan religion represented.[35] Two hundred thousand people reportedly viewed this exhibit.[36]

As in so many other areas during the Cultural Revolution, youth played a central role in the new exhibits. Both IVPP and the Xi'an Banpo Museum (and likely other institutions) brought in youths to serve as guides.[37] In 1971, ten graduating students (six women and four men) from a secondary school near Zhoukoudian began assisting with the creation of the new exhibit and taking classes from IVPP scientists to prepare for their work as guides when the exhibit opened. They were fortunate: serving as guides was pleasant work, particularly compared with the hard agricultural labor many of their peers experienced when they were sent down to serve in the countryside.[38] Moreover, for some this was just the first step in what were to become fruitful careers in these scientific institutions.

The content of the Zhoukoudian exhibit was decided on by a "renovation small group" led by the party branch secretary, several scientists, an artist, and the "military representative" (*jun daibiao*) obligatory in all revolutionary committees at that time. With support from Guo Moruo, they were able to expand the exhibit to 1,000 square meters—three times its previous size. They also greatly enlarged its scope. Whereas it had been a "site museum" dedicated specifically to preserving and presenting the relics of Peking Man and the related fauna, the politics of the Cultural Revolution demanded its transformation into something akin to a natural history museum with broader popular appeal and greater instrumentality as a vehicle for the dissemination of a materialist view of biological and human evolution. Rather than limiting the content to the site itself or even to the story "from ape to human," the small group sought to convey the whole of biological evolution from a materialist perspective. They even decided to include dinosaurs in the new exhibit despite the lack of dinosaur fossils at Zhoukoudian, a clear sign that popular rather than professional interests had come to the fore. Looking back, renovation small group member Lu Qingwu calls the dinosaurs "presumptuous guests who usurped the hosts" (a Chinese saying, *xuan bin duo zhu*), the "hosts" being Peking Man and the other true Zhoukoudian fossils.[39] Scientists at the time may also have seen the masses themselves as "presumptuous guests" whose low-brow interests had usurped the rightful position of paleoanthropologists and paleontologists at the scientific site of Zhoukoudian.

Even at the time, the transformation of the exhibit's focus was not without its detractors. One was Jia Lanpo, the influential paleoanthropologist and author of many popular materials on human evolution. The previous year (1970) had been different, Jia said, since at that time all other museums were closed. Now that the museums were opening again, however, an exhibit at Zhoukoudian seeking to encompass all evolutionary history risked redundancy. To avoid this, Jia suggested that the prehuman part be kept to the minimum necessary to illustrate Mao's theories, from his famous 1937 essay "On Contradiction," of internal and external causes and of the "new superseding the old." With this exception, Jia said, the emphasis should remain on the Zhoukoudian site and its distinctive fossil discoveries. On the other hand, Jia agreed that the "pre–Cultural Revolution exhibit" was sadly deficient in that "workers, peasants, and soldiers" could not understand it. Not only was it "academic for the sake of being academic," but it failed to present even the basic story of evolution. The solution, according to Jia, was for the exhibit to provide a clear explanation of human origins and development based on the political thought of Chairman Mao. In this, at least, he was in accord with the final decision.[40] Zhoukoudian was on the road to becoming a site explicitly oriented to popular interests and political propaganda.

Dissemination: Learning about Humanity at Zhoukoudian and Beyond

The new exhibit at Zhoukoudian opened to the public on October 1, 1972, the twenty-third anniversary of the People's Republic. The exhibit encompassed three parts.[41] The first was titled "The Gestation of Humanity" (*renlei de yunyu*) and sought to demonstrate that humans were the product of a long process of unceasing development from the simplest organisms through the stages of fish, amphibians, reptiles, and mammals. The last presented the achievements of Chinese paleoanthropology since 1949. In between was the core of the exhibit: "Labor Created Humanity." Here visitors learned that a century earlier Darwin had "demonstrated that humans had evolved from apes and refuted the fallacy that God had created humanity." But Darwin had suffered from the influence of idealist philosophy, and had not fully comprehended the difference between humans and other animals. This was left to Engels, who explained how humans had evolved their special characteristics through engaging in labor.[42] This account was consistent with the story of human origins told by science disseminators throughout China since 1949, and especially during the Cultural Revolution. The notion that God had created humanity represented a kind of "religious superstition" that the "oppressor classes" used as "opiates" to "paralyze the laboring people."[43] Thanks to the combined forces of Darwin and Engels, however, a materialist and scientific understanding of human evolution was now possible.

Not only the content but the format of the Zhoukoudian exhibit was greatly elaborated and made to serve mass audiences. The original exhibit had been very simple. Fossils had lain exposed on stands without even any glass to protect them.[44] Signs had provided little interpretation beyond identification of the species displayed.[45] A previous renovation completed in 1959 had added only a few pieces of interpretive art.[46] The Cultural Revolution renovation, on the other hand, used IVPP resident artists and visiting artists from other institutions to create reconstructions of the society and environment of Peking Man and Upper Cave Man in the form of large oil paintings and sculptures that brought the old bones to life.[47] For example, Li Rongshan, who came to IVPP with an art degree in 1965, used the Czech artist Zdeněk Burian's depiction of Java Man as the model for a colorful reconstruction of Peking Man.[48] One of the new guides, Zhang Lifen, had greatly enjoyed the small diorama at the site when she had visited as a child; in 1971 she had the opportunity to assist in creating a much larger diorama for the new exhibit.[49] And, in keeping with many other cultural productions of the Cultural Revolution, the exhibit displayed a quotation from Chairman Mao in enormous characters, flanked by a portrait. In this case, as with most books on human evolution, the quotation selected characterized human history as "a continuous development from the realm of necessity to the realm of freedom," and emphasized the unceasing progress and change found in both the social and the natural worlds.[50]

Most visitors came in large groups organized by their schools, army units, and work units.[51] One of the young guides, Zhao Zhongyi, recalls that during the high tide, they had one to two thousand visitors every day, and he once gave a lecture to four hundred visitors in the large lecture hall.[52] Visitors were often passionately interested in the disappearance of the Peking Man fossils in 1941, presumably at the hands of imperialist nations.[53] It is less clear how many felt strongly about the core materialist, antireligion, antisuperstition message that labor, and not God or the Chinese legendary figure Nüwa, had created humanity. Another guide, Duan Shuqin, recollects, "Lots of people didn't know before they visited that people came from apes. After we explained it to them, they believed it. Maybe some people didn't completely believe, but they still saw that this explanation had a definite logic to it."[54] Visitors often had more practical questions for the guides, such as why all these early humans had died in one place (had the cave collapsed on them?), how scientists knew the artifacts were tools and not just rocks, and how they identified which scraps of bone were from males and which from females. For many visitors, what was truly exciting was the prospect of finding fossils themselves. So many visitors dug holes in the floors in search of fossils that IVPP was eventually compelled to lay cement.[55]

A 1976 movie, *China's Ancient Humans* (Zhongguo gudai renlei), captured the spirit of popular science at Zhoukoudian.[56] The director took every opportunity to show crowds of people clustering around a scientist at
a make-shift fossil exhibit or pouring through the Zhoukoudian exhibition
hall and fossil localities. Such sequences highlighted the mass-oriented character of the new exhibit. The movie was also a means to portray the masses
engaged in labor—not, in this case, the ancient labor of stone tool production, but the labor of modern field science. Footage of excavations in progress depicted scores of laborers digging with picks and shovels and moving
dirt in baskets and wheelbarrows, while groups of people who appeared to
be scientists and workers (although the similarity in dress made it difficult
to tell) sat together discussing some of the fossils excavated.

This picture of science harmonized with popular written accounts of
the discovery of Peking Man published during this period, which emphasized the contributions of laborers. For example, a short book by Jia Lanpo
published in 1975 and sold to accompany the Zhoukoudian site exhibition
maintained, "The discovery of this treasure house—the Peking Man site—
cannot be separated from the local limestone-burning workers," whose discoveries of "dragon bones" (fossils' alterego in traditional Chinese medicine)
had helped lead scientists to the site. Jia went on to give the credit for the
1929 skullcap find collectively to "Chinese workers and science workers"
rather than to a single scientist, Pei Wenzhong, as is the norm today.[57] This,
then, was the other side of the popular science coin: at the same time that
Fossils magazine and the new exhibits were seeking to disseminate scientific
knowledge about human evolution to an ever wider audience, science itself
was also ostensibly being transformed into an activity in which workers had
as much of an acknowledged role as scientists did. The increasing number
of popular science materials that emphasized the ideals of "mass science" is
an indication that the two spheres of popular science—dissemination and
participation—were becoming more tightly integrated during the Cultural
Revolution.

Participation: Laborers and Hobbyists

If dinosaurs had been one kind of "presumptuous guest usurping the host"
at Zhoukoudian, the "great masses of workers, peasants, and soldiers" were
a far more serious kind. The Open-door Schooling movement (*kaimen ban*

xue) welcomed workers, peasants, and soldiers into universities and research institutions while compelling students, teachers, and researchers to set up shop in factories and other places of production.[58] In 1976, *Fossils* printed an article that extended this concept to "open-door science" (*kaimen ban keyan*). It reported on a new relationship between the Chongqing Museum in Sichuan Province and IVPP. In previous years, the Chongqing Museum had been required to send newly discovered fossils to IVPP in Beijing, where only a few people studied them for several years in a "cold and sterile" (*leng-leng qingqing*) manner. Now that IVPP was taking the "open-door science road," technicians and researchers from IVPP went to Chongqing to study the new dinosaur finds and help create a public display for the masses. In the meantime, workers and technicians from the Chongqing Museum had several opportunities to visit and study at IVPP.[59]

"Open-door science" was closely related to the concept of "mixing sand" (*chan shazi*).[60] One form of "mixing sand"—in which the work stations of IVPP technicians and scientists were integrated so that every room contained both technicians (for example, engaged in the fossil preparation) and scientists (for example, writing articles)—was very disruptive and seems only to have lasted for one or two years.[61] However, "mixing sand" was also used to refer to the longer-lasting policy of allowing workers, peasants, and soldiers from outside the institute to enter IVPP for work, study, and criticism.[62] In a case related by an IVPP scientist, a soldier came to the institute to work as a technician making casts. During the Cultural Revolution, the soldier-cum-technician was assigned to head an excavation team, following the Cultural Revolution policy of scientists "standing aside" (*kaobian zhan*) to let workers, peasants, and soldiers lead. In actuality, the technician knew too little about fieldwork to offer any direction, and the scientists in the team had to provide guidance in a discreet manner.

There were positive forms of popular participation to be had in the field. However, the members of "the masses" who took part were local peasants, rather than workers and soldiers, and their roles were ones they knew how to play. Fieldwork in the Cultural Revolution often placed great emphasis on engaging with local people. Although scientists had been relying for decades on local people to lead them to sources of "dragon bones," solicitation of local assistance became much more direct and formal during the Cultural Revolution. One of the best examples comes from Yuanmou in the southwestern province of Yunnan, home of China's oldest *Homo erectus* (the species that encompasses Java Man and Peking Man, among other early human fossils). A geologist first discovered a fossilized human tooth in Yuanmou on International Labor Day in 1965, leading IVPP to send a small team to investigate in 1967. Full-scale excavations took place between 1971 and 1973. In a 1974 article in *Yunnan Cultural Relics Bulletin* (Yunnan wenwu jianbao), IVPP scientist and *Fossils* magazine editor Liu Houyi wrote of the "power of the masses." He said that whenever the team uncovered a number of fossils, the county party committee instructed it to hold an exhibition on biological and human history. Team members provided interpretation as to the reason for the investigations, the significance of the discoveries, and the evidence they supplied for historical materialism and the theory that "labor created humanity."[63] Jiang Chu, a member of the county cultural center who later became the director of the Yuanmou Man Exhibit Hall, recalls that each time they held an exhibition, seven or eight thousand people attended. Commune leaders typically mandated their participation, but this was the kind of activity people were happy to stop work to attend.[64]

These exhibits were not only opportunities to teach local people about evolution; they also served to encourage locals to assist in the discovery of fossils. Liu Houyi noted that many people had provided clues leading to new fossil discoveries or even sent fossils they had discovered to the excavation team's field station.[65] Jiang Chu remembers this as one of the important outcomes of the dissemination work. "The people" (peasants and miners) covered a lot of ground in their daily work, whereas the excavation team could only hope to investigate a small area. Once they had learned "a little basic popular science knowledge," they became very dedicated in reporting anything fossil-like they found.[66] The biggest payoff of this kind of integration of dissemination and participation came more than ten years later. In 1986, while cutting grass in the hills, a local girl named Li Zixiu found a fossil. She reported it to her mother, who passed it on to the relevant authorities. Identified as an ancient anthropoid ape, it represented a find of great scientific value.[67]

Similar stories are told about Nihewan, a basin that straddles the border between western Hebei and eastern Shanxi provinces and is home to "the earliest well-documented Paleolithic occurrences containing large artifact assemblages in eastern Asia."[68] During the Cultural Revolution, local peasants like Wang Wenquan (then about twenty years old) made significant contributions to IVPP's field work in the area.[69] These contributions made print in a 1975 *Fossils* article entitled "The Road of Mass Science Gets Broader the More It Is Traveled" and in a 1978 book *Conversations about Fossils*.[70] As at Yuanmou, the encouragement of popular participation in paleontology and paleoanthropology in Nihewan continued to bear fruit in later years. When Wei Qi, one of the scientists who worked in Nihewan in the 1970s, was asked to lead an investigation in the Three Gorges in 1994 as part of a last-chance archaeological effort before the dam flooded the area, he insisted on bringing along Wang Wenquan and several of the other peasants who had actively participated in the 1970s excavations because their experience and diligence far surpassed that of college students.

The 1970s also saw a dramatic increase in the number of letters IVPP received from "workers, peasants, and soldiers" reporting fossil finds. An article in the 1972 trial issue of *Fossils* applauded that in recent years many "workers, peasants, and soldiers" from all over China had sent letters with important clues for researchers, some had sent fossils via post, and a few had been so devoted that they had brought fossils to the capital in person. "Their concern for the scientific work of the ancestral country can teach and inspire us specialists; their love and care for the cultural treasures of the ancestral country is worth studying," the author commented.[71] With the publication of *Fossils* magazine, the number of such letters greatly increased. Of course, the majority of these reports were dead ends—either fossils of little scientific interest or everyday rocks that only appeared to be the remains of some ancient life form. Yan Defa, who for many years was responsible for reviewing and replying to the letters, recalls many letters reporting such geological improbabilities as "fossilized eyes." Nonetheless, in at least a few cases, reports from "the masses" led to important discoveries.[72]

Writing these letters and bringing fossils to IVPP in person represented a radically different kind of participation from that of local people guiding scientists to troves of "dragon bones," being employed as workers on a dig, or even learning about fossils and then reporting subsequent finds to locally stationed researchers. These letters mark the emergence of what may loosely be termed "fossil hobbyists"—people who developed a personal interest in fossils as scientific objects nurtured through such activities as reading *Fossils* magazine and hunting for and reporting fossil discoveries. One hobbyist began fossil hunting in 1973 when in his late thirties, around the same time he started reading *Fossils* magazine. As a pharmacologist, his interest in fossils overlapped with an interest in herbs used in Chinese medicine, and he hunted for both simultaneously.[73] Another such hobbyist was Li Xuwen, a tax collector in Lijiang, Yunnan, who put the peripateticism required by his job to a new use when he began hunting for fossils in 1971. He took an active and critical interest in excavations there in the 1970s, differing with IVPP scientists on issues of methodology and interpretation. At seventy-five in 2002, he remained an avid fossil collector respected for his amateur contributions by local employees of the cultural center and scientists at the provincial capital of Kunming.[74]

It is tempting to see these kinds of popular participation as evidence that paleoanthropology in the Cultural Revolution was open to people of all classes, and to attribute this openness to the socialist political context. Such a conclusion, however, requires several qualifications. First, the most active "hobbyists" were almost undoubtedly relatively well educated, as with the pharmacologist and tax collector just discussed. Second, popular participation and especially cooperation between scientists and local people are characteristics commonly found in paleoanthropology, and field sciences as a whole, around the world. Paleoanthropologists and many other kinds of scientists all rely heavily on local people to provide "expert" knowledge about local environmental and social conditions. Even "mass science" has counterparts outside the communist world. The Audubon Society's Christmas Bird Count, held annually since 1900 in the United States and Canada, is a good example. Amateurs report the numbers and species of birds observed, and their data become the basis for population estimates. Other examples abound. Even if Chinese paleoanthropological finds have involved nonprofessionals either as first finders or as valued assistants more often than those in the West, this is probably due to the relatively small number of scientists in China and the large number of farmers and miners digging over a significant portion of the land.

Whatever the scale and type of actual popular involvement in socialist China compared with that in other social and historical contexts, the meanings ascribed to such participation were nonetheless specific to its socialist context—and meanings are important. The Christmas Bird Count is not celebrated as a victory of the uneducated, working class over the ivory tower. Far from it: bird watching, at least in the cultural imagination, is the hobby of intellectuals or even aristocrats.[75] In contrast, the rhetoric surrounding popular participation in science in China during the Cultural Revolution hailed nonscientists' contributions to science as examples of the great benefits of traveling "the mass-science road."

Mass Participation: Criticism of Scientists

The formal criticism of scientists by the masses, on the other hand, was an area in which not just meanings, but social relations, were different for Cultural Revolution–era China. Inviting "workers, peasants, and soldiers" into scientific institutions was a case in point. Several workers and soldiers—apparently no peasants—took advantage of this opportunity to study and criticize at IVPP, although they did not participate in research.[76] Others did not physically enter the institution, but studied by themselves and published articles in *Fossils* and sometimes in the institute's academic journal *Vertebrata PalAsiatica* and in *Science Bulletin* (Kexue tongbao). In general, scientists then at IVPP remember these people and their actions as disruptive, domineering, ignorant, and generally useless. As a scientist recalls, "There were no good ideas [in what they wrote]. . . . When we work, we look at fossils, compare them with other fossils, and then generate some ideas. They weren't like this. They just invented ideas out of thin air (*kongxiang*)." A few people, however, are more sympathetic. One of the former guides at Zhoukoudian says, "They cared about [evolutionary theory]. Also, I have to say they studied a little and knew a little bit about it." Where these two members of IVPP agree is that the workers and soldiers immersed themselves only in theory—especially the writings of Engels and Mao—and did not engage in empirical research. Nonetheless, their theoretical disputations were sometimes quite lively, and twice provoked extended debates in the popular forum presented by *Fossils* magazine.

An article by IVPP scientist Zhou Guoxing, printed in a 1973 issue of *Fossils*, ignited the first of these debates. His topic was the question "Can Modern Apes Become Human?" The answer was "no." Human evolution had occurred under specific environmental conditions that no longer existed, and modern anthropoid apes had evolved considerably since the times of our common ancestor. Zhou concluded, "History cannot run backward. For modern apes to return to the ancestral state of not yet being specialized, and for them then to become human under a 'specific environment' of your creation is impossible."[77]

The first to take issue with the article was a worker from a low-pressure boiler factory in the Yangtze River city of Wuhan named Yuan Hanxing, who together with a Wuhan secondary school student wrote a letter published in a 1975 issue of *Fossils*.[78] The editors introduced the letter by celebrating this departure from the past practice of debating issues of human evolution only in the "cold and sterile" manner of a small number of researchers addressing a specialist audience. The critics' principal concern was that Zhou had focused too heavily on the question of the "specific environment" in which human evolution had occurred. This interpretation did not "fit scientific facts," they argued. As evidence, they produced a line from Mao's "On Contradiction": Dialectical materialism "holds that external causes are the condition of change and internal causes are the basis of change, and that external causes become operative through internal causes" (bold in original, as with all quotations from Mao, Marx, Engels, Lenin, and Stalin).[79] The "external causes" of human evolution included environmental conditions, while the more important "internal cause" of human evolution was twenty or thirty million years of undergoing labor in a struggle for survival. Moreover, they objected to the term "specific environment" (*teding huanjing*), which in Chinese can also be understood as "specified environment" or "specially designated environment." They contended that the changes in the earth's crust and climate were due "chiefly to the development of the internal contradictions in nature, and not to someone specially arranging it that way."[80]

The next issue of *Fossils* printed two letters from workers defending Zhou Guoxing. The first was a full-page letter from a "young worker," Chen Chun, at a Shanghai casting factory.[81] Chen agreed that an answer to the question of why modern apes cannot become human had to address both internal and external causes. Nonetheless, he defended Zhou Guoxing's use of the term "specific environmental conditions," and said that it referred not to conditions "specially arranged by someone," but rather to "a period of time with special features manifested from out of the long, slow river of history." He further restated Zhou's main points and argued that, far from "obscuring the dialectical relationship between internal and external causes," Zhou had "properly analyzed dialectically the relationship between internal and external causes." The second letter, from a "young worker" at a brick and tile factory in Taian, suggested that Zhou's original article did acknowledge the primary importance of labor in human origins, and that Zhou's critics had failed to acknowledge the importance of the role played by the "specific environment" as the external cause of human evolution.[82]

These letters of support did not, however, prevent Zhou Guoxing from being labeled a "counterrevolutionary" and having to write a self-criticism. Nor did Zhou's rocky relationship with Yuan Hanxing end with the publishing of the letter. Yuan was one of the "workers, peasants, and soldiers" invited to come to IVPP to help "lead" the institute. Yuan spent his time at IVPP reading and writing, and he published other articles in *Fossils* and in *Vertebrata PalAsiatica*.[83] Zhou Guoxing remembers helping Yuan become Jia Lanpo's graduate student, go to Zhoukoudian, and later go to Shanghai's Fudan University (famous for its anthropology department). He also remembers Yuan coming to his house to eat and discuss his ideas about paleoanthropology, at which time Zhou told Yuan that, as Mao had said, knowledge required practice, and Yuan was short on practice. Yuan then allegedly reported that Zhou had used food and capitalist ideology against him. When the tables turned after the fall of the Gang of Four in 1976, however, Yuan still hoped to make a career in paleoanthropology. He wrote letters to Zhou asking to become his student, an honor Zhou refused.[84] In the end, then, it was the worker and not the academic whose intellectual ambitions suffered the more crushing defeat, a reversal that was undoubtedly far more common than has been conveyed by the literature on suffering in the Cultural Revolution.

On the other hand, for one of the workers who came to Zhou's defense, Chen Chun, the *Fossils* magazine debate served as a launching pad to fulfill scientific dreams. Zhou was impressed by Chen's self-taught knowledge of paleoanthropology. He was also undoubtedly moved to help a stranger who had supported him in a difficult situation. Although Chen had no college degree, Zhou convinced Jia Lanpo to take him on as a graduate student at IVPP. Chen proved a deserving student and went on to study in Canada before taking a position at Fudan University in Shanghai where he remains active in archaeological research.[85]

Zhou Guoxing was not the only IVPP scientist to be criticized in the pages of *Fossils*. From 1975 to 1977, *Fossils* published articles and letters debating IVPP scientist Wu Rukang's attempts to deal with the paradox of *Australopithecus*: was it ape or human? This issue had originally arisen in the early 1960s and had been resurrected in *Vertebrata PalAsiatica* in 1974 before spilling over into the more popular arena of *Fossils* the following year. In all, *Fossils* published eleven letters and articles on the subject (seven criticizing Wu, four defending), and these were only a few of the many submissions the editors received.[86] The debate centered on Wu Rukang's use, in a 1974 article published in *Vertebrata PalAsiatica*, of Engels' concept of "both this and that" from *Dialectics of Nature*.[87] Engels had deemed "hard and fast lines" of "either/or" characteristic of a metaphysical outlook insufficient for understanding the process of biological evolution. He suggested instead a dialectical "outlook on nature where all differences become merged in intermediate steps, and all opposites pass into one another through intermediate links," thus replacing "either/or" with "both this and that." The quintessential example for Engels was the transition between the bird-like reptile *Compsognathus* and the reptile-like bird *Archaeopteryx*.[88] To Wu, it seemed logical to extend the theoretical concept of "both this and that" to address the problem of *Australopithecus*, who appeared to represent an intermediate stage that was "both ape and human."

Unfortunately for Wu, not everyone agreed. The lengthiest criticism came from a soldier, Lai Jinliang, in the rear service department of the People's Liberation Army in Nanjing. Even before his polemic was published in the fall 1976 issue of *Fossils*, Lai had already sent it to *People's Daily*, which printed an article summarizing his points and celebrating Lai's work as evidence against "Deng Xiaoping's reactionary fallacy that workers, peasants, and soldiers do not understand science."[89] Lai particularly focused on the way Wu allegedly downplayed the chief difference between ape and human, namely labor. Making *Australopithecus* a midway point between ape and human, contended Lai, split the qualitative change of ape to human into two parts, leading to the preposterous conclusion that "the long period of struggle with the natural world and the long period of labor had only created half a human!"[90] At the end of the article, Lai somewhat feebly made a link to the pressing political issues of the day: criticizing capitalism, revisionism, and eclecticism (*zhezhongzhuyi*)—and, of course, the *People's Daily* article took this link as its focus. In September, an expanded version of Lai's article appeared in *Science Bulletin*, which had already published several articles on the debate over the previous year and a half.[91]

Wu Rukang rode the waves fairly successfully, despite all this negative attention. He continued to publish: for example, he had the honor of authoring the chief article commemorating the hundredth anniversary of Engels' "labor created humanity" in the spring 1976 issue of *Fossils*.[92] And in 1977, *Fossils* published both a new article in which Wu defended himself on the subject of "both ape and human" and an article by a worker and a shop employee asserting that although Wu's notion of "both ape and human" was "not complete enough," it was "basically tenable."[93]

What, then, do we make of these passionate debates on human origins?

First, *Fossils* (and to some extent professional journals as well) certainly succeeded in creating a forum for nonspecialists to sink their teeth into important scientific questions. It is true, as a scientist quoted above noted, that the workers, soldiers, students, teachers, and others who contributed to this forum had no empirical evidence with which to anchor their theories. However, the original articles whose positions they debated were largely theoretical themselves, and what empirical data they presented were well within the grasp of many nonspecialist readers. Second, these were "real" debates in the sense that both positions were given space, and the editors did not explicitly endorse either side. Given the fervor of political campaigns then under way, the letters were also remarkably polite: even when using political rhetoric to criticize scientists' theories, they fell significantly short of labeling the scientists themselves as revisionists or capitalists. Third, the debates did serve as a way for one worker—Chen Chun—to "enter science" in a meaningful and lasting way; if this had been a more common outcome, the judgment on "mass science" might be more positive than it is today.

On the other hand, this kind of mass participation constrained scientists by compelling them to debate in terms readily accessible to nonspecialists. Moreover, it was an ugly experience for the scientists whose work became the target of criticism. It is very possible that some of those who made the criticisms—particularly those like Yuan Hanxing who were resident at IVPP—were coached by others at the institute who bore grudges against the targeted scientists. To be criticized by lay people was a particularly difficult burden to bear: the intellectual authority scientists wielded had to bow before the political authority of the "workers, peasants, and soldiers." Their only hope was that some of these privileged members of "the masses" would come to their defense, and fortunately for them, some did.

The Missing Link

In 1978, Deng Xiaoping moved into position to become China's next leader. One of the key stepping stones in this process was the National Conference on Science and Technology held in March 1978. There Deng gave a speech in which he asserted his commitment to the Four Modernizations (agriculture, industry, science and technology, and national defense). He further promoted science and technology as a "primary productive force," rather than part of the "superstructure" as had been the case during the Cultural

Revolution. This in turn signified that scientists' intellectual work could again be acknowledged as labor, and thus scientists could be considered members of the working class rather than people fundamentally divorced from the proletariat.[94] The same year, IVPP assigned Huang Weiwen to overhaul the Peking Man site exhibit again, and the exhibit reopened in 1979 on the fiftieth anniversary of the discovery of the first Peking Man skull cap. No longer did the exhibit display dinosaurs or other fossils not present at Zhoukoudian. Neither did it take on the whole of biological evolution in order to educate the masses about materialism. Zhoukoudian once again became a place that celebrated scientific research, past and present, rather than popular science.[95] Professional interests had risen again over popular ones: the hosts had returned to expel the "presumptuous guests."

I began by suggesting that we could help close the "ten-year gap" in the history of modern Chinese science through an investigation of Cultural Revolution science on its own terms. To what extent, then, was the project to "popularize" science successful? The late Cultural Revolution (1971–78) was the closest China came to a productive union between the top-down model of science dissemination and the bottom-up model of "mass science." New, colorful popular media like the "labor created humanity" exhibits and *Fossils* magazine emphasized the role of "the masses" in paleoanthropological research. Dissemination in the field encouraged local people to become active participants in the location and protection of fossil sites. *Fossils* magazine also encouraged the emergence of a new kind of participation: that of "hobbyists" who hunted for fossils out of an interest in their scientific value, as opposed to their medicinal and commercial value as "dragon bones." Moreover, *Fossils* provided a forum for debates on issues of human evolution in which nonprofessionals participated.

Nonetheless, the union of science dissemination and mass science fell far short of its radical potential. The notion that "labor created humanity" was central to all dissemination materials. At the same time, laborers were entering scientific institutions, leading paleontological digs, and challenging scientists on their theories of human evolution. These two kinds of labor—that which defined humanity and that which provided the backbone of contemporary science and society—were closely related. They were both understood specifically as physical labor: labor preceded the development of the brain in Engels' account of human evolution, and intellectual work was excluded from the definition of "labor" during the Cultural Revolution. With the two spheres of dissemination and participation becoming more integrated, and the concept of labor being foundational to both, it would seem to have been an easy jump to say, "Because labor created humanity, laborers are uniquely qualified to interpret evidence of human origins." Indeed, Paleolithic archaeologists in China and elsewhere have often engaged in "experimental archaeology," producing primitive stone tools in their attempts to understand Paleolithic technologies. In the West, archaeologists have also turned to modern flint knappers to learn these skills and gain insight into early tool manufacture.

And yet, it appears no one ever made this link. One might well expect to find materials—even if they were only the most flagrant propaganda—suggesting that those who worked with their hands had important insight into the first labor, the production of tools. One might expect there to be an explicit connection made between knowledge about human origins on one hand and the people who produced that knowledge and the practices through which they produced it on the other. The lack of such an explicit connection indicates the absence of a serious, class-based reappraisal of the structure of scientific knowledge.

An example of what such a reappraisal could have looked like in popular paleoanthropology of the Cultural Revolution can be found among a few Marxist geologists in postwar Japan. Nakayama Shigeru has written on the philosophy of science and "grass-roots geology" that geologist Ijiri Shōji proposed and implemented in the early decades after World War II.[96] Ijiri was the leader of the Society for Corporate Research in Earth Science, a part of the Association of Democratic Scientists. Through the society, he helped organize amateur geologists around Japan whose fieldwork genuinely contributed to ongoing geological research. The society's "bible" was Ijiri's *On Science—Centering On Paleontology* (Kagaku ron—koseibutusgaku o chūshin to shite), in which Ijiri described (geological) science as based on personal experience, hypothesis venturing, and fieldwork—all equally accessible to amateurs as to professional scientists. Indeed, Ijiri saw hypothesis venturing in particular as dependent on a "denying or dissenting spirit" identified with "class-consciousness itself."[97] With respect to fieldwork, as Nakayama interprets Ijiri, "those whose labors involve endless walking and exhaustive observations, whether amateurs or semi-professional geologists, know more and know it better than an established top-notch geologist settled in Tokyo."[98]

In contrast, the *Fossils* article that in 1975 celebrated the "road of mass science" as "traveled" in Nihewan said nothing about what "the masses" as "the masses" brought to science. Rather, it was only "after the masses had grasped science and understood science" that they became useful to science by "hunting for, reporting, and protecting fossils."[99] In short, despite ostensibly being about "mass science," the article paid much greater homage to "science dissemination." It even suggested that as a result of participating in "mass science" the local people had begun to have "preliminary knowledge" about the "natural geographical features of their own village." Specifically, local people had learned from scientists that the area, dry today, was home to a large lake two million years ago. This account conflicts strangely with IVPP scientist Wei Qi's memory of working with local people for whom the lake's past existence was old news: local legend said the same.[100] Had the authors of the article been serious about "mass science" in the sense of a class-based claim to knowledge and knowledge production, the local legend come true would have been an easy way to discuss what local peasants knew by virtue of their being peasants—that is, by virtue of their connection to the land and their inheritance of knowledge in the form of legends—as opposed to what they knew only after being taught by scientists.

Rhetoric and policy on popular science in the People's Republic of China contained a deep-seated and unresolved contradiction between reverence of the masses on the one hand and concern about their lack of scientific knowledge on the other. Science dissemination throughout the 1950s, 1960s, and 1970s was almost synonymous with "stamping out superstition." What has become evident through an examination of the Cultural Revolution is that even in the most radical period, the notion that the masses were "superstitious" outweighed any idea that they might have had special access to knowledge. While propaganda asserted time and again the emptiness of "the fallacy that workers, peasants, and soldiers do not understand science," their understanding was seen only as the outcome of successful science dissemination rather than the result of knowledge forms or mental orientations they possessed by virtue of their class position. It is possible that such a rigorous, class-based philosophy of science—a Marxist standpoint epistemology—was more explicitly elucidated in other scientific fields, for example industry, agriculture, or seismology.[101] Paleoanthropology represents a "harder case" since its connection to popular forms of knowledge is less conspicuous. However, since apparently no one made the obvious connection that, because "labor created humanity," laborers were uniquely suited to study human evolution, such a philosophy of science could not have been well entrenched in the natural sciences as a whole.

EIGHT

To Be Somebody: Li Qinglin, Run-of-the-Mill Cultural Revolution Showstopper

Elya J. Zhang

On April 25, 1973, Chairman Mao Zedong sent the whopping sum of 300 yuan out of his own pocket to a humble primary school teacher in Fujian Province. At the time, this was roughly an entire year's salary for an average worker, or about double the monthly salary of a Politburo member like Mao himself. Attached to this considerable sum of money was the only known letter Mao himself wrote to an ordinary citizen during the ten years of the Cultural Revolution.[1] Mao's pithy note, beginning with the words "Comrade Li Qinglin . . . " was circulated nationwide and memorized by an entire generation of Chinese. To this day, most former sent-down youth can still recite the thirty characters verbatim.[2] Thus, seemingly overnight, Li Qinglin was transformed from a nobody into a household name. In schools and work units across China, people must have been wondering the same thing: who in the world is Li Qinglin?

Now, more than three decades after the fact, this simple question remains a tough puzzle to crack. Accounts about Li Qinglin seem wildly incompatible. To some, Li is remembered as a little man who wrote a letter to China's supreme leader and miraculously received a reply. Former sent-down youth laud Li as their savior, a man who boldly spoke out for their livelihood at a time when they were most desperate. Others may recall Li as the infamous mouthpiece and "black hand" of the Gang of Four. If memory seems to present us with a foggy picture, the historical record is no less murky. On July 2, 1973, Li stood center stage in the Fujian provincial gymnasium and gave a speech to an excited audience of sixty thousand who had gathered to celebrate Mao's famous reply to him.[3] Four years later, he stood in the very same place surrounded by six thousand people shouting: "Down with Li Qinglin!" For three hours Li suffered through insults and condemnations that were broadcast to over five million listeners, after which his official arrest was hailed by a thunderous "hurrah!"[4]

Whether Li was a hero or villain, a remarkable opportunist or just an ordinary individual swept up in extraordinary circumstances is largely a matter of perspective. But the real question is: what, if anything, did Li *do* to deserve any of these titles? Were such assessments thrust on him, or did he intentionally or unwittingly invite them on himself? How did Li react to the experience of suddenly being in the limelight, and how did people respond to this newcomer on the political stage? What choices did he make to shape his role, and how did his role in turn mold him? In the only English account of Li, Mobo Gao presents Li as a typical example of a helpless figure tossed around in the severe factional politics of the Cultural Revolution. His research, although instructive on issues such as the policy implications of factionalism, informalism, and authoritarianism in Maoist China, draws primarily on central documents and published secondary sources.[5] When I visited Li's hometown in the summer of 2003, I was fortunate to get access to local archives that were on the verge of being destroyed.[6] Extensive personal interviews with Li, his family, and his former colleagues provided a human portrait that goes beyond the standard cardboard-cutout hagiographies and demonizations of the Cultural Revolution period and after.[7]

As we unearth answers to the many questions surrounding Li Qinglin, his story becomes more than the tale of a man who went on a political helicopter ride from obscurity to national fame and down again in Maoist China. Li's personal experience provides an alternate window to view the Cultural Revolution period beyond red guards, Mao, the Gang of Four, party bureaucrats, and sent-down youth. Li's version of the Cultural Revolution was interlaced with many of the above but seems to fit none of the standard categories. As a primary school teacher struggling to make ends meet, Li was among the most ordinary of people. But as the man who desperately appealed to Mao and got a reply, he was virtually touched by a god. Was Li truly one of a kind? Or does his story tell us something meaningful about the Cultural Revolution itself, as it was experienced by common people with chances to be important for a few days, weeks, or even years? Whether it describes an individual, a group, a generation, or a saga of "ten years of madness," Li's life story should be allowed to speak for itself.

The Day God Replied

Nothing in Li Qinglin's previous forty-six years of life could have prepared him for becoming a celebrity. Before 1973, Li Qinglin had lived a calm and relatively uneventful life. Born into a poor family in Putian, a small county in Fujian, in July 1927, Li grew up struggling for a living like millions of other have-nots in China. His grandfather was a hapless scholar who failed the civil service examination and died prematurely at the age of forty-two. His father was once a beggar and later made a living at various temporary jobs. Li Qinglin spent his childhood in extreme poverty and was suspended from school three times because his family could not afford the tuition. He finally graduated from normal school in 1948 thanks to the collective financial support of relatives and neighbors and soon became a primary school teacher. The 1949 Liberation seemed to have little effect on his life, and Li continued to teach, married a peasant girl in 1952, and had two sons in four years.[8]

The only ripple was a rightist label incident in 1958. The 1957 Anti-rightist campaign involved the repression of Chinese intellectuals who disagreed with the party. It brought on numerous tragedies in big and middle-sized cities but sometimes resulted in farces in small counties and towns. Li Qinglin was a typical case. He was labeled a rightist at Qiankeng Primary School in 1958 because the school needed to fill the officially allotted rightist quota (*youpai ming'e*). He was singled out for two reasons. First, having been transferred to the school less than one year earlier, Li was still a newcomer (and thus vulnerable) compared with other teachers. Second, all the students in his class failed the entrance exam to middle school that year. Thus, instead of criticizing the quality of his teaching, school officials handed Li a "rightist hat" (*youpai maozi*) in 1958, only to take it off (*zhaimao*) in 1960 when the party began to rehabilitate some rightists. During his two years as a rightist, Li's monthly wage was reduced from 40 to 32 yuan, but school officials canceled the reduction after he was rehabilitated.[9] Because Li was labeled a rightist for such absurd reasons, people later considered his brush with rightism more of a joke than as a serious political failing. Li lived quietly through the Great Leap Forward and the Socialist Education movement, feeding his six-member family (consisting of himself, and his seventy-year-old mother, wife, two sons, and one daughter) with his meager income.[10]

Even the outbreak of the Cultural Revolution had caused Li few political troubles. Red guards in Putian hardly took notice of Li's existence. Li was not a "valuable" target worth attacking since he neither came from a so-called bad family background nor held power in his school. Few people even bothered mentioning his former rightist label because that incident was known to all as a comic episode.[11] But from 1970 onward Li was bothered by the miserable condition of his eldest son, Li Liangmo, a sent-down youth in Shuiban Brigade, Qiulu Commune, fifty miles from Li's home. Li Liangmo, like other youth in the village, could barely get enough to eat, received no wages to cover daily expenses, and had no fixed place to live. Every month Li Qinglin had to pay a significant amount of money to buy food, clothes, and other basic things on the black market and send them to his son. It was a heavy financial burden because Li earned only 40 yuan a month and had a big family to feed.[12] Since the Up to the Mountains, Down to the Countryside (*shangshan xiaxiang*) movement was promoted and praised by the government, Li was shocked to find that neither urban officials nor rural leaders really cared about or assumed responsibility for the plight of the rusticated youth.[13]

Li's appeals to the Fujian authorities on this issue were frustrated from beginning to end. He started at the commune where his son worked. The party secretary of the commune ignored Li and quickly referred him to the vice-secretary before Li could even finish his statement. The vice-secretary sent Li off in search of the cadre in charge of sent-down youth. The cadre gave Li the runaround and told him that the commune actually did have money and food, but it could not distribute them to sent-down youth since the county government had not issued any such orders. So Li took his case to the county government. The answer he got there was that the commune, not the county government, was responsible for rusticated youth issues. However, when Li returned to the commune, the cadre shouted at him impatiently: "I've already told you that we can do nothing until we get orders from our superiors! Go and ask for them."[14] Throughout 1971 Li Qinglin was kicked back and forth between commune and county like a soccer ball. He began to raise his complaints at the municipal and provincial levels in 1972, but still got cold shoulders and no answers.[15]

After two years of failure, the desperate Li finally decided to appeal directly to such top leaders as Zhou Enlai and Mao Zedong. Li had no idea how to ensure that his letters would reach the leaders, so he tried the simplest method. He addressed his letters "To Chairman Mao" or "To Premier Zhou" and dropped them in the mailbox, hoping they would reach their destination. The first two letters to Mao disappeared completely, likely intercepted and discarded by cadres en route. Finally, Li decided he had to try a different tack. He noticed that whenever Mao appeared on television he was accompanied by a young lady named Wang Hairong. Wang, a distant relative of Mao and reputedly one of the Chairman's favorites, was acting special assistant to the Foreign Affairs Ministry in 1973. It was to her that Li addressed his third and final letter on December 26, 1972, sealing his pleas to Mao in a separate little envelope inside. It seems that Wang was suitably impressed by Li's distress call and forwarded the letter to Mao. Later on, as the legend grew, tall tales about swimming pools, volleyballs, and Mao randomly picking up Li's letter were spread by word of mouth. But according to Li Qinglin himself, addressing the envelope to Wang was the stroke that finally got him in touch with the Chairman in April 1973.[16]

Li's letter was outspoken and full of small details and emotional pleas. He gave an exhaustive account of the daily problems his son encountered in the village, revealed the corruption and nepotism surrounding sent-down youth, and begged Chairman Mao for help. In all, the letter contained more than 1,700 words. After briefly introducing himself and his son, Li stated the problem straightforwardly: "Since the beginning of 1971, when the central government cut off the food supply and living subsidy for sent-down youth and delegated responsibility to local governments, there have been all kinds of problems." Li described three major difficulties, the first being the food shortage. "The youth labor all year without enough grain rations," he said, and "until now the most my son has ever gotten in one year is two hundred pounds of millet, ten pounds of wheat, and three pounds of sweet potatoes—this is obviously not enough for a teenage boy who works in the field all day!" Thus, Li had to admit: "For six months or more of every year my son has to subsist on the food I buy on the black market." Another problem was the lack of wages. According to Li, "The boy isn't paid a single penny for a year's work. If he feels sick, he doesn't have money to find a doctor and can only try to get through by himself. . . . This sounds ridiculous but it's the truth," Li protested. "All the daily living expenses of my son since 1969 have been supplied by my family."

Li's third area of grievance was housing. "Since there are no sent-down youth dormitories," Li said, "my son and several other youth have to live temporarily with a poor peasant family in the village." The situation soon got worse when Li Liangmo was evicted because the peasant needed the room for his son's wedding. Li complained: "The youth work like peasants but don't have a fixed place to live!" Li was most frustrated by the fact that "the relevant cadres totally turn their backs on the problems of youth, leaving it to be solved by parents." He protested angrily, "How can things be so appalling! If I suddenly died one day and my son lost his family support, how on earth could he make a living?"

Besides these practical problems, Li also revealed agonizing injustices in the processing of back-to-the-city opportunities. "Cadres' children or those who have connections with high officials have all been transferred out of rural areas to meet the 'requirements of socialist construction,'" Li said. "For those people who left the village quickly through the 'back door,'" Li pointed out, "having served as a 'rusticated youth' is little more than a vogue and useful political capital. Ordinary people's children, like my son, seldom get this kind of opportunity no matter how hard they work. So their only fate is to spend the rest of their lives in rural areas, devoting themselves to the great revolution." Li boldly pointed out that favoritism and corruption were still major facts of life, despite the Cultural Revolution's Spartan rhetoric.

Li's long-repressed grievance was fully expressed in the last sentence of the letter. "Chairman Mao," Li pleaded, "I am now helpless with nowhere to turn (*jiaotian tian buying, jiaodi di buling*), so I have to take the liberty of 'appealing to the emperor' (*gaoyuzhuang*)."[17] Although the party had made great efforts to propagate Marxist ideology for more than twenty years, ordinary people like Li still retained some of their old habits. Thus, when he encountered a serious problem, Li easily adopted the traditional expression *gaoyuzhuang* and regarded the top leader, Mao, as an old-style emperor with ultimate jurisdiction over litigation and social problems.

Cadres monitoring the official channels would have had good reason to stop Li's letter from reaching Mao. Since the beginning of the Up to the Mountains, Down to the Countryside movement, official propaganda had lauded the policy, and major media such as *People's Daily* were filled with positive accounts of the exciting experiences of sent-down youth. The awful truth that Li lamented was discordant with the official symphony and would annoy officials. Li's use of the traditional Chinese expression "appealing to the emperor" also contradicted the revolutionary theme of the Great Proletarian Cultural Revolution. But Mao saw this unusual letter and reacted in an unanticipated manner. On April 25, 1973, he sent Li three hundred yuan from his own pocket and a thirty-character reply.

"Comrade Li Qinglin," Mao wrote, "The issue you wrote about seems ubiquitous around the country and needs to be solved as a whole. Please accept this 300 yuan. I hope it can help you to some degree. Mao Zedong."[18]

This was the only known letter Mao himself wrote to an ordinary citizen during the ten years of the Cultural Revolution. Furthermore, in accordance with Mao's instructions, the original correspondence between Mao and Li was copied and distributed to the Politburo for discussion.[19] Mao's reaction to Li's letter was unique. Generally he only made such short comments on letters as "Noted" or "Please transfer this to Comrade Wang Dongxing" (Wang was the director of the party Central Office during the Cultural Revolution).[20] The reason for this special treatment might lie in the sensitive sent-down youth problem raised by Li in his letter. Since the Up to the Mountains, Down to the Countryside movement was directly initiated by Mao's famous December 28, 1968, directive, "Educated youth should go down to work in the rural area, to be reeducated by poor and lower-middle peasants," Mao had reason to be concerned about the youth who were once his red guards, the vanguard of the Cultural Revolution. Moreover, Li's outspokenness distinguished it from other, formalized and euphemistic missives. Mao received two major types of letters during the Cultural Revolution. One type concerned individual problems, including victims appealing for political reevaluations and exonerations. The other was expressions of loyalty, filled with sentences like "the current revolutionary situation is amazing" or "I myself ardently support the Great Cultural Revolution."[21] Letters reflecting social problems or mentioning problematic state policies did exist, but were usually circumspect. In contrast, Li's letter not only referred to a major social problem, but also treated the issue with startling bluntness. By addressing Mao like an emperor, Li may have appealed to the Chairman's vanity. He certainly got Mao's attention.

Mao's interest and the distribution of the correspondence to the Politburo led to an April 29, 1973, Zhongnanhai emergency meeting chaired by Zhou Enlai. The participants included Zhang Chunqiao, Wang Hongwen, Li Xiannian, and Ye Jianying. Zhou opened the meeting by saying, "We must be responsible for the sent-down youth. We should not let these problems bother Chairman Mao." The meeting was thus entirely focused on the problems of sent-down youth raised in Li's letter. The Finance Ministry was ordered to supply 300 yuan to every sent-down youth who was in the countryside at that time.[22] After the meeting, twelve investigation teams including representatives from the party center, provincial governments, and the army were sent to twelve provinces to investigate the sent-down youth issue. When the teams reported back, the State Council reproduced the Li-Mao correspondence in Central Document 21 (1973) on June 10 and ordered it disseminated at every level. Li's "appeal to the emperor" and Mao's regal reply became part of the official record.[23]

The party Central Office also issued a directive regarding the distribution of Document 21. Every province and military region was required to spare one day to study Document 21, and notices were to be delivered to all cities, urban districts, counties, and communes, letting it "reach all sent-down youth and the masses."[24] The wide circulation of Document 21 led to a series of policy shifts and measures that improved the lives of sent-down youth. First, there was a systematic reorganization of the administrative units handling the sent-down youth issue. Before that, the State Council had only a small "sent-down youth supervisory group" with as few as five members. Each local county government had a temporary sent-down youth unit whose task was completed once youths were sent to the villages. But beginning in June 1973 a special office for sent-down youth affairs was set up in every provincial, city, and county government under the orders of the State Council. Each office was staffed with a high-level official and a number of full-time cadres and was responsible for resolving problems as well as negotiating with other organizations. This kind of office, regardless of its actual effectiveness, at least gave sent-down youth a measure of psychological comfort; it was a political organization directly concerned with their livelihood and a nearby place where they could make appeals to cadres.[25]

The living conditions of sent-down youth improved in both psychological and material terms. Most of them, it appears, got the 300 yuan subsidy distributed by the Finance Ministry. Many villages built separate housing for sent-down youth, and newly assembled urban medical teams traveled around the rural areas once a month. Youth started to get paid based on work points and their grain ration was increased to the same level as that of local peasants.[26] As one youth later recalled, "After Chairman Mao replied to Li Qinglin, we got a piece of meat every week!"[27]

Intensive criminal investigations and strict punishments helped to address issues of personal security for rusticated youth. In the nationwide investigation, numerous crimes of assault, illegal imprisonment, and rape of rusticated youth who had no local connections surfaced and shocked the central leaders. In June 1973 a report on the first-round of national investigations showed that from 1969 to 1973 there were more than 3,400 cases of assault or rape of rusticated youth in Liaoning Province alone. Zhou Enlai was enraged when he heard the news: "Public Security should act! Don't be softhearted!" Li Xiannian said more bluntly: "Kill the bastards, otherwise we can't appease the people."[28] In June 1973 the party Central Office and Central Military Commission jointly issued Document 104 (1973), which publicized the death sentence of Huang Yantian and Li Yaodong, the leaders of a Heilongjiang military construction brigade, because they had colluded to rape more than thirty young sent-down females. Three months later, the rapists Jiang Xiaoshan and Zhang Guoliang, officials in a Yunnan military construction brigade, were also executed. In 1973 many leaders in similar positions were harshly punished for their physical mistreatment of rusticated youth.[29]

Although Li's letter had been a self-centered plea for his own son, not an idealistic appeal for the whole population of sent-down youth, Mao's reply and the circulation of Document 21 made Li Qinglin seem like a national spokesman.[30] Since the living conditions of sent-down youth improved markedly after the circulation of Document 21, the masses, especially sent-down youth and their parents, naturally attributed the changes to Li's magic touch.[31] Li could not have expected that airing his private grievances to China's supreme leader would earn him the adulation of millions of parents who likewise worried about their children and applauded Li for expressing what they dared not say. A Fuzhou resident exclaimed: "Since Chairman Mao has replied to Li Qinglin and sent him money, it is just as if he has replied to all of us. . . . Now our hearts are at ease about sending our children up to the mountains."[32] The erstwhile unknown schoolteacher was now a household name.

Suppressing a Superstar

If Maoism was a religion, with Mao as its god—as is often claimed—the case of Li Qinglin reveals that sometimes even the commands of supreme deities have to contend with local bureaucratic foot-dragging. One of the first things Chairman Mao did after replying to Li's letter was to ask Premier Zhou Enlai if Li was already a party member. If so, Li was to be allowed to attend the Tenth Plenum of the Communist Party, which was to be held in four months. If not, Mao wanted Li to be admitted to the party and then invited to the Tenth Plenum. Mao specified that Li should attend the Fourth People's Congress as a representative even if he had no aspirations for party membership, and then the Chairman expressed an interest in seeing Li's letter added to textbooks as required reading.[33] At a time when a vague word or nod of approval from Mao could be (and was often) interpreted as the greatest political capital and imprimatur for any action, one could hardly have asked for a more glowing endorsement.

In Putian, however, county officials were masters of their own universe, and many tried to prevent Li from getting any big ideas. Although Mao's reply caused a sensation and made Li nationally famous, Li continued to be stifled in his own county and made no official public appearance for the next two months. The Chairman's wish that Li be inducted into the party was documented in the Fujian provincial records. Even so, Li did not attend the Tenth Plenum at all and was denied party membership for nearly a year before local officials grudgingly gave way. So much for any neat picture of local functionaries tripping over themselves in complete subservience to show their obedience to Mao.

When Mao's letter and the enclosed funds finally reached Putian in the first week of May 1973, Li Qinglin was required to hand the letter over to Liu Gong, the party secretary of Putian County. Liu Gong read through the correspondence and showed some displeasure about the things Li had written in his letter, especially the part about "back-door" favoritism. When Li asked if Liu could arrange a temporary job for his wife, Liu retorted: "You already got 300 yuan from the Chairman, didn't you? Won't that be enough?"[34] After the conversation Li went home disgruntled, and Liu started thinking of ways to deal with this new troublemaker.

Meanwhile, an article entitled "Congratulations on the Big Harvest in Putian" appeared on the front page of *Fujian Daily* on May 7. The article had special praise for the Qiulu Commune, where Li's son worked, but not a word about Li's letter.[35] Three days later, two investigation teams were sent by the Putian county government to Qiulu Commune with the purpose of gathering evidence to refute Li's complaints about the miserable conditions of youth in the villages.[36] On May 15, Lin Yujin, a Putian cadre in charge of mass appeals (*xinfang*) castigated Li Qinglin's eldest son, Li Liangmo. "You bastard!" he shouted. "Without devoting yourself to labor in the village, you dared to lie to Chairman Mao. How can you say you were not paid a single penny? My investigation shows that you got at least 80 yuan every month."[37] The cadre also tried to intimidate Li Liangmo by emphasizing that he was speaking on behalf of the whole Putian party committee.[38] Not long afterwards, Li Qinglin's primary school started receiving demands for detailed reports on Li's "historical problems" (*lishi wenti*).[39] The two investigation groups returned from the commune, and county secretary Liu Gong triumphantly declared: "The actual situation [for sent-down youth] differs from Li's account."[40] Li Liangmo registered for the college entrance competition at the end of May, but the brigade cadres claimed he was unqualified and forbade him to even take the exam.[41]

Liu Gong and the Putian cadres were hardly the only ones trying to hamstring Li. Up until May 17, Han Xianchu, the party secretary of Fujian, refused to mention a single word about the Li-Mao correspondence in any of his provincial meetings.[42] Even after the nationwide dissemination of Central Document 21 in mid-June, Han Xianchu vetoed all attempts by *Fujian Daily* to invite Li to write an article. "Don't give him any publicity," Han ordered.[43] Days, weeks, and then months went by without any mention of Li Qinglin in *Fujian Daily*. Under these circumstances, when Li received the 300 yuan from Mao through the post office, he dared not accept the money for some time and even contemplated returning it.[44] Phone calls, letters, and visitors were barging their way to Li Qinglin's door, but for the first two months after Mao's reply, Li Qinglin was more victim than celebrity. He certainly was not an active political figure. He just went on teaching his classes. While his name was being lauded all around China, in his home province and county Li was forced to keep his head down for fear of local harassment. In Putian, even a letter from Chairman Mao was not an instant ticket to political stardom.

The blanket of silence that local cadres had wrapped around Li Qinglin might well have continued indefinitely despite the "magical touch" he had gotten from Mao. Li himself did not seem to have much (if any) confidence in his newly acquired fame, which apparently translated into little in the way of real political power. He did not even attempt to apply for party membership at this time.

Pressure from the central government altered the playing field during the National Sent-Down Youth Work Conference in June 1973. Zhou Mantian, the head of Fujian's sent-down youth office, attended the conference and made three emergency calls to the Fujian provincial government between June 21 and June 30.[45] Zhou was alarmed by the central government's request for a report on Li's current situation. Fujian's handling of the sent-down youth issue, propagation of Central Document 21, and even "learning from Comrade Li Qinglin" had clearly fallen far behind other provinces. At the conference top officials like Li Xiannian and Hua Guofeng criticized Putian County's suppression of Li Qinglin and exclaimed that "a person's attitude toward Chairman Mao's reply to Li reflects his attitude toward the grand revolutionary course."[46] The city of Hangzhou had already organized a twenty-thousand-member rally to celebrate Mao's reply to Li. Fujian needed to have one too.[47]

Thus, on June 29 provincial party secretary Han Xianchu finally stopped stonewalling and invited Li to Fuzhou for a meeting. Two days later, the Putian county government submitted an apologetic review of the mistakes it had made in dealing with the Li.[48] On July 2, it seemed that Li's big day had finally come. He had a chance to give a public speech in front of a crowd of sixty thousand. After being grounded for a couple of months, the helicopter bearing Li's political career seemed finally about to rise.

As it turned out, however, this was not the end of Li's tangles in Fujian. The Fuzhou rally of sixty thousand had been merely an appeasement measure. Fujian officials promptly trumpeted the news to central bureaucrats at the ongoing National Sent-Down Youth Work Conference, then left it at that. Once the Fuzhou rally had served its purpose, Han Xianchu and his colleague Xia Renjing (head of the Fujian Propaganda Department) ordered that Li's speech and photos were not to be distributed in newsprint or radio broadcast.[49] Nor was Li to be honored at any more special public appearances. In provincial-level meetings Xia continued to dismiss Li with such cursory assessments as "Li is not a bad man, but he's not a good one either."[50]

Still, Li Qinglin seems to have let the Fuzhou rally go to his head. Elated by his first major public appearance, Li began to show more confidence in the newfound opportunities for improving his political status. On July 9, one week after the speech, Li applied for party membership for the first time in his life.[51] When Putian secretary Liu Gong reported Li's first tentative stab at political life to the provincial authorities, his superior Han Xianchu snorted that Li had a mind only for economic needs and not one whit of political consciousness.[52] Apparently this was not just Han's spur-of-the-moment reaction. Three weeks later, he gave Liu Gong an even clearer order: "Don't be in a hurry about the question of Li's party membership. Take time. Think more."[53]

This sort of foot-dragging suggests that in the provincial and county are-
nas, widespread name recognition and Mao's imprimatur were not enough
to enable a political nobody like Li to break into the circle of power. Mao
had not ordered anyone to transform Li into a famous public speaker, provincial official, or anything of that magnitude. But he had explicitly stated
that Li was to be given party membership and allowed to attend the Tenth
Plenum. On this count, the provincial and county officials in Fujian could
not claim ignorance. In early July 1973, Mao's instructions regarding Li
Qinglin were repeated at the National Sent-Down Youth Work Conference.
The staff of the party Central Office then called the Putian County office
and asked if Li was party member. The Putian party committee gave them
the following answer: "Li is not a party member. He was once with the
Guomindang."[54]

Thus, local party officials procrastinated and decided to shelve Li's application on the pretext of a "historical investigation" into his pre-Liberation
political activities. The Putian party committee claimed that somebody in
the county had accused Li of being a former member of the Guomindang
Youth League (Sanqingtuan). Li's application could not even begin to be
considered until the alleged sordid activities of his past were fully exposed.
Local cadres organized a special investigation team and dredged up a class
roster from Li's days as a schoolboy. On it were around thirty circled names,
including Li Qinglin's. It could have meant anything: outstanding student,
poor grades, tardy for roll call, and so on. But in order to "make sure" that
the circle was not a special mark of the Guomindang Youth League, the
cadres claimed that they needed to do extensive background checks on all of
the students whose names were circled.[55]

The "research" dragged on for around eight months, and Li completely
missed the Tenth Plenum. That was almost certainly what authorities like
Liu Gong and Han Xianchu had intended. Early in August 1973, before the
nomination of Fujian's representative to the Tenth Plenum, some people
had suggested that Li be allowed to join the party immediately. To this, Han
had replied: "Li's background still has unresolved problems. We need to be
cautious."[56]

In the meantime, Mao had not completely forgotten about Li Qinglin.
In December 1973, Mao mentioned Li's name again at a conference with
the generals of the eight military districts. "The letter from Comrade Li
Qinglin of Fujian is a very good one—I read it through three times before I

replied to him," Mao declared. "Some people think that his letter is just full of thorns. I say that we need exactly this kind of 'thorny' letter."[57]

The Chairman's continuing favorable comments likely contributed to Li being invited by the People's Central Broadcast Station to give a speech on January 31, 1974. In Fujian, however, Mao's words somehow remained in time lag. In December 1973 Li managed to get an article published in *Red Flag*, the party's authoritative theoretical journal. Li had submitted exactly the same article to *Fujian Daily*, but the newspaper refused to publish anything by or about Li.[58] At the turn of 1974, the Fujian Education Bureau proposed adding Li's letter to middle school textbooks as Mao had wished. Another four months slipped by without approval from the Fujian provincial government.[59]

Emboldened by his first national publication in *Red Flag*, but still struggling for political recognition at home, Li raised the party membership issue again in February 1974. The net that had been keeping Li down suddenly burst open. At long last, Li received his much-coveted party membership on March 18.[60] In April, Li gave a public speech to a huge audience on the anniversary of Mao's reply. And finally, after a full year of media silence in his home province, articles about Li appeared on the front page of *Fujian Daily* two days in a row.[61]

How was it that Li's political career suddenly took off after being restrained for a whole year? It is not as if provincial bigwigs like Han Xianchu and Xia Renjin abruptly had a change of heart. Here we must turn to the clique politics and campaigns of the late Cultural Revolution period. The campaign to Criticize Lin Biao and Confucius (*pi Lin pi Kong*), a leftist movement targeting Zhou Enlai and his allies at the party center, gathered momentum in early 1974. In the provinces, as the campaign was twisted to suit local purposes, it fueled infighting among local political cliques and helped to turn the situation around for Li. In this period of struggle, the so-called rebels in provincial and county governments seized the opportunity to challenge their former supervisors. Power-holders like Han and Xia suddenly faced a barrage of criticism from their subordinates. And what were their alleged crimes? Their suppression of Li Qinglin in Fujian "proved" that they were opposing Chairman Mao, which by the logic of the day meant that they were open to attack as counterrevolutionaries or henchmen of Lin Biao. Once the power-holders came under attack, Li could get his party membership, gain prominence in the pages of *Fujian Daily*, and be praised all around for stalwartly following Chairman Mao and resisting the suppression campaigns leveled against him by Han, Xia, and their local cronies like Liu Gong. This could not have happened without the support of local cliques who appropriated him as prime—but as we shall see, certainly not passive—political real estate. Now that the obstacles above him were gone, Li's political career seemed to soar unimpeded to new heights. The real question in this next phase was, would Li be in the driver's seat, or would he be taken for a ride?

Attack Dog on the Loose

On April 23, with the opening of the Symposium for the Anniversary of Chairman Mao's Reply to Comrade Li Qinglin, two thousand sent-down youth representatives from around the province assembled in Fuzhou.[62] This commemorative event was organized by the provincial sent-down youth office and the Communist Youth League. During these four days, Li Qinglin was king of the hill. He welcomed the representatives to meeting after meeting, listened to their reports, and issued instructions; his rapt audiences scribbled furiously to record his every word. *Fujian Daily* even published a special issue devoted solely to this grand occasion, with Li's name generously heaped on every page. In the numerous photographs, Li was always the central figure—gesturing broadly while giving speeches, sitting center stage and flanked by provincial leaders on both sides, or surrounded by cheerful sent-down youth who gazed up at him with adoration. Li appeared high-spirited and vigorous, with a complacent smile on his face.[63]

Li's swelling confidence was apparent in his keynote speech, in which he depicted himself as a brave revolutionary fighter and his enemies as insidious reactionaries. First of all, he began to puff up his letter to Mao—which had originally been motivated by purely personal concerns—as a selfless act of social justice. "While my son, who had been honestly and diligently working for years, could not even be sure of basic daily meals," Li stated, "cadres' children, who had just briefly 'visited' the rural areas, were enjoying comfortable lives." As Li claimed, the sight of this unfair gap not only stirred his heart to righteous anger, but had more importantly become a serious social problem in Putian. If not solved, it would surely have endangered the dictatorship of the proletariat. "In order to ward off this crisis," Li went on gravely, "I began to have the idea of writing to Chairman Mao."[64]

Even the simple act of dropping the letter into the mailbox was developed into a full-fledged drama of inner reflection and outer inspiration. The first phase of the drama might be called Vacillation. "As I stood before the mailbox, gripping the letter tightly in hand, I was so nervous that I was soaked with cold sweat," Li told his audience. He speculated on the possible consequences of his actions: "I knew that terrible disaster could befall me if the letter were returned by the party center and the local officials found out about it. I wandered around and just didn't know what to do." The next phase was Inspiration. "At that moment, I suddenly caught a glimpse of the movie poster for *Red Lantern* (Hongdengji) in the shop window across the street." The valiant image of protagonist Li Yuhe infused him with courage: "I saw the hero Li Yuhe standing there composed and fearless in front of the Japanese enemy. His bravery greatly inspired me. 'How can you be such a coward?' I asked myself." The final phase was Determination. "I sat down on a chair nearby, recalled Chairman Mao's instructions, and carefully considered my behavior. Finally I made up my mind. I stood up abruptly and rushed to the mailbox, dropping in the letter."[65] This account sounds like a minor version of a revolutionary model opera, with Li himself as the protagonist.

Li's head just kept getting bigger and bigger as the speech went on. Once he was done exalting himself, Li shifted into attack mode and spent more than two thousand words criticizing by name almost all of those cadres who had once suppressed him. He claimed that a group of incumbent officials in Putian had shamelessly opposed the revolutionary course set by Chairman Mao. Included on Li's list were the official in charge of mass appeals who had inveighed against his son, some investigative cadres who had tried to discredit Li by fabricating false reports, a chief justice who had suggested that Li be relabeled a "rightist," and a primary school principal in Hanjiang County surnamed Chen, who had threatened to reveal Li's "notorious past" to Chairman Mao. Li also recounted the county officials' foot-dragging on his party membership in exhaustive detail, including the contents of many phone calls. In closing, he bluntly blamed the chief instigators behind these misdeeds, Liu Gong and Han Xianchu.[66]

Although Li gave his keynote speech on the pretext of celebrating the anniversary of Chairman Mao's reply and "defending Chairman Mao's revolutionary course," he clearly used the occasion to carry on his own personal grudge. As Li stood at the podium and vented his past frustrations, most of the named county officials had already been dismissed or demoted. Fujian propaganda chief Xia Renjing was under investigation for conspiring to deny Li media coverage, while Liu Gong and Han Xianchu had been transferred out of Fujian. Furthermore, by this time Li had already gotten his party membership and his name in the papers. In other words, Li did not need to keep verbally drubbing his old opponents and harping on their past mistreatment of his case. He could have given an inspirational message to commemorate Mao's care for the masses or congratulated everyone for working so hard to improve the sent-down youth movement. However, he refused to let go of the past and insisted on grinding out the sordid details of his already defeated enemies in front of two thousand sent-down youth.

Li's personal grudge perfectly suited the agenda of those "rebel" officials who tried to get ahead by trampling on their superiors. On April 28, 1974, two articles simultaneously appeared on the front page of *Fujian Daily*. One was an editorial titled "Exposing the Crimes of the Former Provincial Leaders against Chairman Mao's Reply to Comrade Li Qinglin." The other was a short essay published under Li Qinglin's name and entitled "Bravely Go against the Tide and Stick to the Right Course."[67] The editorial stated that former provincial party secretary Han Xianchu and his colleagues represented the "wrong tide." By suppressing comrade Li Qinglin, they had done the unthinkable: opposed Chairman Mao. Then on the lower part of page, the essay under Li's name echoed, "We should be brave and go against the wrong tide."[68] As these articles show, the 1974 national campaign to Criticize Lin Biao and Confucius (*pi Lin pi Kong*) was localized in Fujian as a campaign to criticize Han Xianchu and his followers. "Rebels" at every level seized this chance to denounce their enemies as Han's cronies and opponents of Li Qinglin. Big character posters and mass struggle sessions, long the staple of Cultural Revolution politics, were once more the order of the day.[69]

By the middle of 1974, Li had become an untouchable figure in Fujian Province. Most of his former enemies were out of power, and since he was both the legendary individual touched by Mao and the national "Go against the Tide" hero, any new critics risked being accused of opposing Chairman Mao. In June 1974, Li acquired a slew of political offices, including vice-directorship of both the Putian sent-down youth office and the provincial college admission office.[70]

However, Li did not become just another ordinary bureaucrat dealing with daily issues. Instead, his valuable time was occupied with all kinds of meetings. Organizers of mass movements were always happy to invite this legendary figure, whose name recognition could guarantee public attention. Li Qinglin was a must-have showstopper at any event related to sent-down youth issues. Sometimes, even if the content of the meeting or event had nothing to do with Li, the speakers or policy makers would still invite Li to "supervise" the meeting so that his special connection with Chairman Mao would add an aura of legitimacy.[71] It seemed that everybody wanted a piece of Li.

Thirty years have passed, but Putian residents still remember the hectic scene outside Li's door. Almost every day an official car would come and pick up Li for a meeting or convention. Sometimes cars were sent by units within the county, at times from neighboring areas, and occasionally even from the provincial capital. Fujian residents and parents of rusticated youth also crowded into Li's home. They sobbed out their grievances, pleaded with Li to solve their problems, and sometimes even asked Li to forward their letters to Chairman Mao.[72]

Meanwhile, Li began to receive numerous letters (up to a hundred each day) from within and without Fujian. The number of visitors and letters was so overwhelming that the Putian county government later allocated a special cadre to help Li read, categorize, and reply to letters as well as handle visitors.[73]

It seems that Li Qinglin enjoyed being this kind of needed person. As his son recalled, Li had an office in the county government, but not once did his son ever see him go there to do mundane business. Instead, Li happily jumped into the cars parked outside his home and sometimes even waited at the doorway to see if a car would come that day. He was rarely disappointed.[74]

Outspokenness had always been a part of Li's character. His blunt and wordy letter to Mao was a classic example. At this point, when Li came to the realization that he was untouchable, he fully embraced outspokenness as the core of his identity. As the "Go against the Tide" hero, Li believed that he was endowed with the right and personal mission to challenge all kinds of "wrong tides" that conflicted with the revolutionary course, including corruption, power abuse, and any deeds he felt to be inappropriate. He saw himself as Mao's finger of justice, attuned to inequity and ready to raise a firestorm at any moment.

Li's enthusiasm for public display and his conviction that he was the people's champion made him an ideal attack dog. The unscrupulous could make use of his talents just as well as the fair minded. Most of the time Li did not even need to be handed a script. Virtually anyone could feed him some information and Li would go off on a rampage on his own volition. Soon a saying about Li went around: "If there's a meeting, he'll definitely show up. Once he appears, he'll definitely speak up. Once he opens his mouth, he'll definitely blow up" (*you hui bi dao, you dao bi jiang, you jiang bi ma*).[75] This saying was widely known as the "Three Definites" (*san bi*). Li's own son reluctantly admitted that the saying was not far off the mark.[76]

Being an attack dog did not mean that Li simply accused innocent people. Sometimes Li pointed out actual instances of unfairness. As soon as Li was promoted to vice-director of the provincial college admissions committee in June 1974, he vetoed admission for a group of applicants who tried to use their parents' high military status to sneak in through the back door.[77] In doing so, Li was racking up powerful enemies, but he blithely carried on with his activities. At one point, he even blared out some ugly words about a well-established government policy. During the high tide of the Learn from Dazhai (*nongye xue Dazhai*) campaign, thousands of cadres and party members in Fujian were sent by the government to visit the model brigade of Dazhai with all expenses paid. But most travelers just enjoyed the free trip and did not learn anything useful. Li publicly criticized this phenomenon and called the government's "learning from Dazhai" trips a "waste of manpower and money" (*laomin shangcai*).[78]

Li took great pains to cultivate a reputation for incorruptibility. This might have been an innate characteristic, but most likely he also realized that living up to an ideal image was crucial political capital, especially in light of his attacks on others for favoritism. Being incorruptible allowed him to show that he was more than just a poor schoolteacher and desperate father who had written to Mao with only selfish complaints and his own family's livelihood in mind. Thus, once he gained more power and prestige than anyone in his position could have dreamed of, he saw to it that his own family would not benefit one bit. Li stashed away the 300 yuan and refused to spend it. His wife was a common laborer and belonged to the category of temporary worker (*linshi gong*). Li did not use his power to promote her to the category of formal worker (*zhengshi gong*), even when he was in charge of the provincial education system and could have done so with a wave of his hand. He also twice rejected a local commune leader's plan to recommend his eldest son, Li Liangmo, for college. Furthermore, he sent his younger son, Li Liangxiong, to the countryside in December 1974. At that time Li Liangxiong had not yet graduated from high school and according to official policy could have stayed in the city.[79]

Honest though he tried to be, Li made bad decisions and sometimes abused his power for dubious causes. In one case, he received a letter from a sent-down youth in Zhejiang Province, in which the youth reported that he was bullied by his brigade leader. Li immediately lashed out with a furious letter to the Zhejiang provincial government, believing the charges without doing any investigation. Consequently, the accused brigade cadre was beaten and crippled for life. It was only later that the charges were found to be spurious.[80]

Sometimes Li did not know how to mind his own business. On April 29, 1975, two *Fujian Daily* reporters tried to interview Liu Bingren, the party secretary of the town of Hanjiang. Unfortunately for them, Li just happened to be in Liu's office. Instead of simply excusing himself or leaving the business to Liu, Li rudely butted in and dominated the conversation. As always, Li was full of complaints. He immediately started haranguing them for not including enough news about Putian in *Fujian Daily*. When the reporters asked him for specifics on what was wrong with their newspaper, Li exploded: "You are totally shameless! You've done something wrong, yet you pretend to know nothing about it! Now I have to be ashamed for you— shameless, shameless!" Li continued his insults: "*Fujian Daily's* quality and credibility are so pitiful, I don't trust it one bit!" Throughout the conversation, Li barely allowed the reporters to get in two words edgewise—in the end, they had to make a hurried retreat without even talking to Liu Bingren.[81]

Li could keep getting away with outrageous activities as an attack dog so long as he was on the rise. When the Fourth National People's Congress was held in January 1975 in Beijing, Li was one of the twenty representatives for Fujian Province. He reached the pinnacle of his career when he was selected as a member of the congress's Standing Committee.[82] On July 9, 1976, at a provincial meeting where all party committee members were present, Li grabbed the microphone from the presenter and launched into another of his trademark verbal attacks. His target was the incumbent Fujian party secretary, Liao Zhigao, whom he accused of being a follower of the recently disgraced national leader Deng Xiaoping.[83] This proved to be Li's last major act, but it was by no means the end of his political drama. Li could not have expected that his "emperor," Chairman Mao, the fount of his magical rise, would pass away in two months. The sudden change in winds meant payback time for all the people he had offended over the past few years. Li Qinglin, the man who had risen like a helicopter, would finally be shot down.

End of the Flight

Li Qinglin's fall was much faster than his rise. On October 9, 1976, one month after the death of Chairman Mao, Mao's successor Hua Guofeng, along with other veteran central leaders like Ye Jianying and Li Xiannian, ordered the arrest of the Gang of Four. A vilification campaign against the gang was carried out at all levels as long-repressed discontent with the Cultural Revolution and leftism was vented. Within a week, big character posters saying "Down with the Black Hand of the Gang of Four—Li Qinglin" appeared on the streets of Putian. By the end of October, Li was dismissed from all his positions and thrown into a temporary jail—located on an army base—euphemistically referred to as a "study class" (*xuexi ban*).[84]

When the day of reckoning came after three years of sailing above the clouds, Li had no parachute. Having bypassed the usual channels for promotion during his helicopter-like ascent to power, Li's position as a high official was based on arbitrary criteria like the personal approval of Chairman Mao and the support of radical local cliques who were linked to the Gang of Four, rather than the length and quality of his service or any notable achievements. Thus, in the confused power shuffle after Mao's death, Li became highly vulnerable. He had annoyed too many people during his time as an attack dog, and his few allies among the "rebel" faction, such as Xu Jimei and Xu Huoqing, were disgraced and kicked out of office at this time.[85]

Standard accounts of the fall of the Gang of Four have often portrayed this period as a watershed, a liberation from the arbitrary politics and vilifications of the Cultural Revolution. But for many people, the campaign against the Gang of Four was just another chance to settle scores and grab power. Hundreds of local government positions suddenly opened up as the incumbents—who had risen to office by stepping on other people's backs—were now dragged down as objects of struggle. Under the circumstances, squelching and spitting on the Gang of Four and its so-called allies became the most fashionable and practical way to prove one's political credibility. What better target was there than someone who no longer had any powerful friends, someone whose big mouth had produced plenty of incriminating "black material" and who was now strictly forbidden to speak out in his own defense?

Thus, Li did not simply disappear from the political scene. He became a perfect scapegoat, and once again everyone wanted a piece of him. The new provincial authorities identified Li as the second most important ally of the Gang of Four in Fujian and created a special six-person team to investigate his case.[86] The team's first assignment was to collect evidence of Li's "criminal" involvement with the Gang of Four and use his case to collect materials for attack on other "rebels." Throughout November 1976 Li was repeatedly forced to confess his faults and write down names, dates, and events in excruciating detail. His first forty-page draft, mainly concerned with his own experiences, was immediately rejected and criticized as "insufficiently frank and penetrating" (*bugou tanbai shenke*). The members of the special team were not satisfied until Li began to write more details and add information about other people he knew. In mid-December, Li finally completed his forty-thousand-word confession, an exhaustive account of his supposed ties with the Gang of Four and his connection to other rebels in Fujian. Li's confession was hailed as definitive proof of his heinous crimes and was used to incriminate the Gang of Four and its allies in Fujian.[87]

Li was made into a "living exhibition" of struggle in Fujian. Since the struggle session was a vital part of the Denounce the Gang of Four movement, provincial leaders were delighted to parade Li around like a circus animal. Local cadres also recognized that active involvement in the anti–Gang of Four movement, especially successful organization of public struggle sessions, was important for future promotion. Just as Li had once been a celebrity at meetings in previous years, he was now a welcome sight at these struggle sessions since a public attack on the former nationwide "Go against the Tide" fighter enlarged the scale and importance of the meeting. During the first quarter of 1977 Li was "invited" to be the main target for struggle sessions in almost every commune and unit in Putian and Fuzhou. Altogether the authorities hauled Li out to more than three hundred such events and saw to it that he was constantly insulted and beaten up.[88] Li later recalled that at a meeting in Xianyou County (next to Putian), in order to ridicule Li as a "black hand" planted by the Gang of Four in Fujian, the organizer smeared Li's hands with ink and forced him to hold his jet-black hands high throughout the four-hour meeting.[89]

The public attack on Li climaxed on November 14, 1977, in the province-wide "condemn the monstrous crimes of three Gang of Four allies in Fujian Province" broadcast meeting, in which Li and two other well-known figures were the primary targets.[90] Almost all the top leaders of the provincial government, the party, and the army turned out for the spectacle. More than six thousand workers, peasants, soldiers, intellectuals, and residents gathered at the central meeting place—the provincial gymnasium—and five million people listened to the proceedings on the radio.[91] Zheng Huopai, director of the Fujian office for "exposing and criticizing the Gang of Four," gave an exhaustive report on Li Qinglin's crimes on behalf of the provincial government and party committee. In this report Li was painted as a demon who typified the sins of the Cultural Revolution and deserved large-scale public condemnation.[92]

This event has gone down in official history as a brilliant act of justice and the dramatic end of the Cultural Revolution in Fujian.[93] In actuality, the political tactics and distortions of truth made this meeting seem just like any other Cultural Revolution struggle session. Many of the accusations against Li were simply absurd. For instance, the presiding judges accused Li of "mustering counterrevolutionaries to virulently attack Chairman Hua Guofeng and the party center." Since Li owed his entire political existence to Mao's famous reply, it is hard to believe that Li would attack Hua Guofeng, Mao's legitimate successor and the executor of Mao's will. An insidious traitor who embezzled money and weapons and planned to flee to the remote mountains to fight against the government after the fall of the Gang of Four? An incorrigible fomenter of chaos, guilty of "abetting criminals in beating, smashing, and robbing in the Putian area"? Not one shred of evidence was provided in the report to support these ridiculous accusations.

Another fictitious charge leveled against Li was that he had abused his power to arrange urban work for his two sons. The fact was that Li's two sons were still in the village when this charge was read out in the broadcast meeting. Li Liangmo, the elder son and the one Li had mentioned in his letter to Mao, had even been twice denied the opportunity of going to college when his father was in charge of provincial sent-down youth affairs. Li

Liangxiong, the younger son, was sent to a village by his father in December 1974 before he had even graduated from high school. Any legitimate research would have shown that Li had denied special privileges to his own two sons. Afterward, because of Li's fall, the boys were among the last group of youths to leave the village, in May 1981.[94] Li's wife lost everything, even her low-paying temporary job, after her husband's arrest.

The skeletons in Li's closet, which had been cleared out when he was in power, came back to haunt him. Once more county investigators "revealed" that Li was a long-time potential class enemy who had joined the Guomindang Youth League in 1944. The little circles around his name on the class roster, which had been such spurious pretexts for procrastination in Li's 1974 bid for party membership, were gravely described to the radio audience of five million as serious crimes. The speakers also triumphantly waved around the farce of his 1958 "rightist hat" as ironclad proof of his "anti-party, anti-socialist" behavior. Ironically, to signal the official end of the Cultural Revolution, Li's prosecutors were happy to condemn him in the classic Cultural Revolution style: exaggeration, fabrication, displacement of all crimes onto a single person, and digging up arbitrary historical blemishes.

"We should hate the Gang of Four and their allies as we hated the Japanese invaders and the Guomindang reactionaries," thundered Fujian party secretary Jiang Liyin to an audience of five million at the end of the broadcast meeting.[95] The meeting concluded the year-long Denounce the Gang of Four movement in Fujian. It was also the curtain call for Li on the political stage, for better or for worse. Li Qinglin was detained for another year and a half before he was sentenced to life imprisonment and permanent deprivation of political rights. On the morning of June 15, 1979, Li received notice of the ruling from the Putian Intermediate Court. Three days later, the provincial Supreme Court slammed down its final verdict. Li had even been stripped of the right to defend himself.[96] Ten long years would pass before the court finally decided to reduce Li's term of imprisonment to fifteen years for good conduct. Li Qinglin was finally released on August 16, 1994, at the age of sixty-seven.[97]

Waiting for the End (after it is already over)

Some old fellows just never seem to fade away. Many sent-down youth continued to remember Li Qinglin as the man who had saved their lives. When several former sent-down youth discovered Li being bullied by a tough prisoner in jail, they stood up and protected him. They addressed him as "Teacher Li" (*Li laoshi*) and thanked him for his outspokenness about their miserable conditions in the early 1970s. In the early 1980s, a group of Shanghai sent-down youth traveled to Mount Wuyi in Fujian. When they heard that Li Qinglin was in jail on a nearby mountain, they bought fruit and cakes and walked more than twenty miles to visit him, expressing their gratitude for his letter to Mao.[98]

Many continue to resent Li Qinglin to this day. Li's two sons suffered directly because of their father's imprisonment and unsavory reputation. By late 1981, all the other sent-down youth had left the village, but Li's sons had nowhere to go—not a single unit in the city wanted to touch them. The rural brigade leader grew impatient and asked them to leave. Shunned on all sides, the two straggled over to a mountainous neighboring county, where a new road was being built and some stone carriers were needed. They stayed in the mountains for three years, hauling stones every day. Finally, in 1984, a middle school in Putian County accepted Li Liangmo as a gatekeeper; Li Liangxiong had to wait another half year before he found a similar temporary job in another county. Every month, they set aside some of their puny salary for their mother, who never regained her job after Li's arrest and had to depend on her two sons.[99] After his release from prison, Li kept appealing to the county and provincial government in hopes that his case could be reinvestigated and some of the false accusations lifted. His pleas were denied again and again.[100] In 2003, Weng Zhijun, a young *Fujian Daily* reporter interviewed Li and published an article about his recent life in a provincial journal for elderly people. Within a week, the editor and author received dozens of phone calls from old provincial and local cadres excoriating them for giving Li publicity. "What are you trying to do? Are you going to reverse Li's verdict? Don't even think about it!" one of them rebuked Weng Zhijun.[101]

The most recent dramatic change in Li's life was his conversion to Catholicism after his release.[102] In our conversation, Li did not specify his reasons for turning to religion. His son Liangmo pointed out that Li's wife came from a family of devout Catholics. She attended church regularly, and Li might have accompanied her to comfort her in her old age.[103] It is also possible, however, that religion satisfied his inner need to comprehend the powers that kept the world turning after Mao's death. In the 1970s he had briefly been touched by forces beyond his ken. He had willingly left his quiet life and thrown himself into the maelstrom. After rising to an incredible height and then being hurled into an abyss, perhaps Li came to believe that only by placing his faith in a god could he explain his fate. As I left his home, I noticed that he kept a portrait of Chairman Mao prominently displayed in his living room. Li Liangmo had argued constantly with his dad about his past "misdeeds," but Li stubbornly insisted that "Chairman Mao would approve of all my actions."[104] In the end, it seemed that he never quite gave up his old faith.

Li Qinglin died on February 21, 2004. His two sons, already in their fifties, still do not have fixed jobs. Their lives have been ruined, their only inheritance the stigma of being Li Qinglin's children. One of the few things they still care about is the possibility that their father's reputation can be rehabilitated during their lifetimes. Could this hope be realized? At our last conversation, they sighed and lowered their heads.

It would be neat and tidy to claim that Li fell prey to the injustices of the Cultural Revolution, just as in millions of standard victim accounts. But Li's story presents us with a different picture of the so-called years of madness, one that centers on political agency and choices. One of the most basic questions we can ask of the period is this: how could the Cultural Revolution have lasted so long?

The deification of Mao and his personality cult surely had something to do with it. But Mao's power was not supreme as it has been made out to be, and Mao was not the only player sitting before the chessboard. Most local struggles and skirmishes were not even carried out on Mao's orders. Was the trouble all because of red guards and passionate young men and women who tried to topple the old order with their fiery rebel zeal? The red guards wreaked their fair share of havoc, to be sure, but they were only at the forefront for two or three years of the Cultural Revolution, after which the government forcibly removed them to the countryside. As sent-down youth, they were such a forgotten and powerless group that many of them struggled just to get enough to eat and avoid being abused by villagers and cadres. To a certain extent, even an ordinary primary school teacher like Li Qinglin could be their "savior."

The official and most popular explanation sings the same tune as the majority of post–Cultural Revolution "scar literature," in which people invariably claim to be victims of the Gang of Four and their cronies. But how

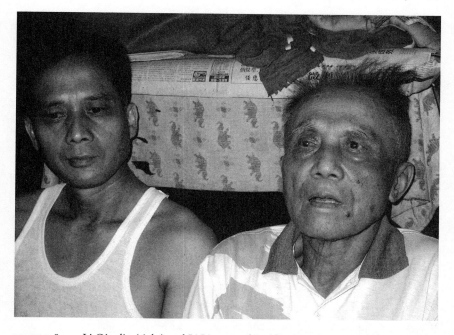

FIGURE 8.1.   Li Qinglin (right) and Li Liangmo, his eldest son, August 12, 2003 (photo by author)

credible is this myth of a nation terrorized by a four-person political clique (with Mao as a kind of ringleader) and a handful of their favorites? Are we to accept the explanation that tens, if not hundreds of millions fell into a mass hysteria of victims with no real victimizers?

In truth, we must admit that the Cultural Revolution could only persist because ordinary people like Li Qinglin actively took to the stage and transformed themselves in the process. On reflection this may seem self-evident, but many still find it difficult to admit that they consciously chose to jump on the political helicopter that later cast them down. The Cultural Revolution disrupted the ordinary workings of the bureaucracy and the fixed system of promotion and evaluation. In such an atmosphere of political turmoil, many have-nots discovered what must have seemed like a once-in-a-lifetime opportunity to get ahead. During extraordinary circumstances like this a nobody suddenly had a chance to become somebody. In two to three years Li Qinglin was able to reach positions that might have taken others twenty to thirty years of hard work to attain.

When he first wrote to Mao as a desperate father full of complaints, perhaps Li was not actively seeking this out. Up to that point, the Cultural Revolution had largely passed him by. But once Li realized that he was touched by the great leader, that some saw his potential and were willing to ally with him against his opponents, and that his big mouth could be an asset, he placed a bet on his newfangled political capital and took the leap. As an attack dog on the loose, Li made many of his own enemies, and they would pay him back in kind as soon as they got the chance. The Cultural Revolution was not simply a decade of madness. There was a kind of brutal calculation to it all, especially in the political methods of the early 1970s that we can see in the Li Qinglin case.

Hence, we may need to redefine the Cultural Revolution as not just a time period, 1966–76, but also as an underlying style of mass politics. Intense campaigns, arbitrary criteria, and sometimes just pure accidents mushed together in a way that seems to make little sense now, but was practical reality then. Promotions were not based on seniority or ability, but on building one's reputation on somebody else's back. Entire careers were founded on attacking people, during and after the Cultural Revolution. When Li Qinglin went down, there was no void—other people gladly rose up to beat him and compete for his position. That was considered a natural way to show one's credentials during a regime change.

In this sense, the spirit of the Cultural Revolution continued after 1976. People still used blanket political labeling, demonization and denunciation, struggle sessions, and forced confessions. They still fabricated facts and made absurd charges. The language of attack did not change, old grudges were not forgiven, and people still rose at the expense of others. Such an earthquake of history as the Cultural Revolution does not simply cease with a nice clean watershed declaration. It only ends when arbitrary standards are replaced by objective criteria.

What are we to make of the case of Li Qinglin? On one hand, Li had the most dramatic of experiences starting from the day his letter got an answer from the god-emperor of the nation. On the other, Li was among the most ordinary of people. He was like countless unknowns who would grasp the chance to be somebody if offered it, even for just a moment. Ready or not, many were given that chance, and the ones who took it ran as far as they could. Their narratives remain untold. No one else had exactly the same story as Li, but at least thousands of people had this much in common. The Cultural Revolution could not have carried on so long without them.

Thus, Li's helicopter ride is an exceptional case, but it is also a window onto the rules of the game. His story reveals something about the experience of the Cultural Revolution from the point of view of an ordinary person trying to fly in extraordinary winds. The ultimate peril of Cultural Revolution mass politics was that it gave people an illusion of power. People with little or no real qualifications and no safety net chose to ascend quickly, thinking they were safe in the pilot seat, but they just as easily put themselves into a tailspin. Oftentimes they were shot down by others coveting the same airspace. The helicopter effect worked both ways.

Almost three decades have passed since the official end of the Cultural Revolution, and a conventional mechanism of promotion has been restored in China, but for Li Qinglin and ordinary people with varying degrees of similar experience, the lingering effects cannot easily be shaken off. The Cultural Revolution was not just a bad dream from which millions suddenly awoke as they patted each other on the back and celebrated their liberation from insanity. Li Qinglin languished in prison for more than fifteen years. For him, the close of the Cultural Revolution was not a liberation. Even the notorious former red guard leader Kuai Dafu, who victimized so many opponents in his heyday (see Chapter 2), was eventually able to return to a normal life as a middling businessman. But a person like Li suffered until the day he died. Li's sons continue to live with the consequences of their father's choices and keep their heads down in the face of their father's old enemies, many of whom are still in power. It is doubtful that their lives can ever get back to "normal."

When will the aftershocks of the Cultural Revolution finally cease? When there is one day that we can look at ordinary cases like Li Qinglin's in an objective manner, with neither personal grudges nor unfair praise. When former adversaries can move on beyond the politics of a generation. There may yet be a day when Li Qinglin's granddaughters and children like them will not be discriminated against for decades-old stigmas.

NINE

The Sublime and the Profane: A Comparative Analysis of Two Fictional Narratives about Sent-down Youth

Liyan Qin

In 1979, Pei Xiaoyun, the heroine in *Snowstorm Tonight* (Jinye you baofengxue) by Liang Xiaosheng, becomes a martyr on her twenty-seventh birthday. She is a sent-down youth in Heilongjiang Province. To her delight, she is given a rifle that day, and is assigned the sacred task of standing sentry at night. No mission is carried out more faithfully. She stands fast at her post in a blizzard, and is frozen to death. Standing upright atop a snowy mount, facing the river that separates China from the Soviet Union, rifle in hand, eyes open and face smiling, her figure is projected by the moonlight onto the "silver-white negative of the vast border land."[1] Thus she is transformed into a holy human monument of heroism and loyalty, her posture reminiscent of the sculptures in front of the Memorial Hall on Tiananmen Square in honor of Chairman Mao. Like them, her figure is devised to evoke a sense of the sublime, and for millions, it succeeded in doing so.

A sharp contrast to this elevating scene is provided by the twenty-first birthday of the protagonist Wang-er in *Golden Age* (Huangjin shidai). In this novella by Wang Xiaobo, Wang-er is a sent-down youth in Yunnan. Lying on the bank of a river and bathing in the glaring tropical sunshine, he becomes acutely aware of his manhood, and is determined to put it to a practical test that day. He decides to guilelessly "seduce" Chen Qingyang, a doctor in the hillside village. He offers Chen unreserved friendship and asks, in return, for sexual rights to her body. Chen, after some hesitation, accepts the deal. Thus, on the night of his birthday, Wang Xiaobo's protagonist receives his first sexual experience, and is initiated into adulthood.

It may come as a surprise to see two such drastically different literary versions of the life of sent-down youth. Both *Snowstorm Tonight* and *Golden Age* are novellas produced by writers from the sent-down youth generation. Bearing the brunt of the impact of the Cultural Revolution, this generation is surely unique in modern Chinese history. Roughly the same age as the PRC itself, this generation has experienced a life trajectory marked by sharp ups and downs closely tied to the vicissitudes of Chinese politics. Many of this generation became enthusiastic red guards during the initial stage of the Cultural Revolution. Then, generally from 1968 on, in response to Mao's call, they rushed to settle in China's countryside and be reeducated. The majority of them did not return to the cities until the late 1970s and early 1980s, when they had lost their youth, and had to cope with an urban life with which they had become unfamiliar.

This generation boasted many writers who dominated the literary scene of the 1980s, many of whom are still active. Life in the countryside proved to be a productive experience to which they turn repeatedly. Yet, their literary representations and interpretations of that life are very different, ranging from the heroic, the violent, the peaceful, to the absurd. Among this galaxy of fictional narratives, *Snowstorm Tonight* and *Golden Age*, standing on the opposite poles of the spectrum, form a near-perfect contrast with each other, both thematically and structurally. Thus, a comparative reading of the two may yield some insights into the scope of literature on the rural experiences of sent-down youth during the Cultural Revolution.

The two novellas are significant not only because of their contrast, but because of their great popularity. As the most widely known fictional works on sent-down youth during the 1980s and 1990s respectively, it is not an exaggeration to call them important cultural phenomena. In the 1980s *Snowstorm Tonight* not only won an official award, but penetrated people's minds so deeply that it helped shape the public image of sent-down youth as heroes. Following the sudden and unexpected death of its author in 1997, *Golden Age* swept the book market and Wang Xiaobo became a god-like figure to another, younger generation of readers. A comparison of the two works may thus offer insights into both the sent-down youth experience and changes in the intellectual and cultural atmosphere from the 1980s to the 1990s. A surprising discovery emerging from this comparison is that the Cultural Revolution mentality, long believed dead, persistently haunted the cultural landscape of the post–Cultural Revolution period. *Snowstorm Tonight* is a disguised celebration of that mentality, whereas *Golden Age* serves to dissolve that mentality.

Published in 1983, *Snowstorm Tonight* unfolds on a critical day in 1979, when thousands and thousands of sent-down youth in Heilongjiang Province rushed back to the cities. Focusing on a construction brigade (*jianshe bingtuan*) in the northernmost part of the province, the story develops in two intertwined lines, one told from a largely public perspective, the other from a private perspective. Pei Xiaoyun, a sent-down girl in the brigade, stands alone on guard. In this pleasant solitude, she reminisces about her experiences in the brigade during the last ten years, and her love for Cao Tieqiang, a model sent-down youth. At the same time, most other sent-down youth in the brigade are engaged in a just struggle to return to the cities, although the "do-gooders" among them choose to stay. Out of malice, the brigade leader tries to hinder the youth from leaving the brigade. The eight hundred sent-down youth besiege the brigade headquarters to protest. Leaders and led finally reach a compromise, following a scene that involves the rescue of state property during the snowstorm, a fire, and an encounter with evildoers. At last, those who want to return to the cities get permission to do so.

The story line in *Golden Age* is not so easy to grasp, due in great part to its loose structure. This novella was first published in mainland China in 1994, but did not gain great popularity until 1997. Wang-er, a sent-down youth who comes to Yunnan from Beijing, develops an intimate affair with Chen Qingyang, and the novella abounds with detailed scenes of their love-making. They escape twice into the surrounding mountains, but are forced to come back each time. Later, their "illicit" relationship is exposed in a campaign. The two then regularly go to struggle meetings as targets, and are busy drafting and redrafting detailed confessions of their sexual sins. Twenty years later, the two meet unexpectedly in Beijing and spend some time together in a hotel, where they reminisce about their experience in Yunnan.

The two birthday celebrations described at the beginning of this chapter may give us a glimpse into the sublime and the profane worlds represented in the two narratives. Wang Ban, in *The Sublime Figure of History*, employs Thomas Weiskel's definition of the sublime. Weiskel argues that "the essential claim of the sublime is that man can, in speech and in feeling, transcend the human."[2] This definition seems an apt description of the content and style of *Snowstorm Tonight*, whose characters are obsessed with transcending the human not only "in speech and in feeling," but in actions. Yet, after further analysis, the sublime ideals prove contradictory. *Golden Age*, however, not only deconstructs such sacred ideals with black humor, but, with abundant erotic scenes, puts sex in the place of heroic ideals.[3] How are the sublime and the profane manifested in each novella's themes and forms? What can we learn, both about sent-down youth in the Cultural Revolution and about the 1980s and 1990s, by studying the difference?

Hero Versus Hooligan: a Thematic Comparison

Snowstorm Tonight is a relentless glorification of those who adhere to the political ideals dominant among sent-down youth, although upon closer examination, the nature of these ideals becomes highly problematic. In *Golden Age*, however, not only are such politically defined ideals absent, but the novella moves away from the political sphere toward the creation of an expansive private realm.

One cannot help being struck by the grand scale and the heroic scenes in *Snowstorm Tonight*, a fictional recounting of the period during which sent-down youth returned to the cities. Wang Meng, an important intellectual figure in post–Cultural Revolution China, admired this novella for its "force and power."[4] Another writer, Jiang Zilong, concluded that, "with a responsible attitude toward history and toward the fate of a whole generation, the novella sheds an uplifting and idealistic light upon the characters," which reminded him of "great epics."[5] Even a writer highly critical of Liang Xiaosheng admitted that *Snowstorm Tonight*, together with Liang's other works, created a moving narrative, and "made readers shed copious tears."[6]

Yet, with all its sublimity, what the novella reveals is an urge to justify the historical role played by sent-down youth. As if to preempt possible accusations from outsiders, or, perhaps more important, to preempt possible feelings of regret among sent-down youth themselves, Liang's novella repeatedly pronounces judgment on the sent-down-youth generation. Its verdict is highly favorable: they belong to a heroic generation, and they should treasure their heroism. The hero of the novella, a company commander (*lianzhang*) named Cao Tieqiang, confronts the sent-down youth in his company (*lian*) who, like almost everyone else in the brigade, are on their way to the brigade headquarters to vent their anger on leaders whose lies prevent the young people from returning to the cities. Cao, both a model sent-down youth and a member of the brigade leadership, stops the protesters and succeeds in appeasing them by evoking their shared sense of historical purpose: "Tonight is perhaps the last page in the history of the brigade!" He also appeals to their identity as brigade soldiers: "The title of a brigade soldier implies our contribution to the country, and this title must not be tarnished!"[7] He is reminding the youth of their responsibility to history, and asking them to play their scripted parts to the end. Because of his appeals, Cao's people, unlike the mob from other companies, line up and march toward the brigade headquarters without any threat of disorder.

Himself a sent-down youth, Cao Tieqiang enjoys great authority, which comes not the least from his official position as a leader. Yet, perhaps fearing that Cao's voice might lack final authority, the novella adds to these judgments the voice of Sun, the brigade's political commissar (*zhengwei*). In keeping with the classic qualities attributed to political commissars in cultural productions in socialist China, Sun embodies the hard core of order, rationality, and political conscience of the party. Despite setbacks and difficulties encountered during the Cultural Revolution, the political commissar, like the party he represents, is reborn like a phoenix from the ashes, and regains his political and moral authority. He is the deus ex machina who descends from out of the blue and resolves all conflicts. Thus he passionately addresses the sent-down youth:

> My brigade soldiers! . . . I believe that in many years to come and on many occasions, this title of brigade soldier will be repeatedly mentioned by yourselves and by others. It is a title you should be proud of, and a title worthy of respect from your contemporaries who do not boast such experience, and from posterity. . . . I, on behalf of the Wild North, thank you, my brigade soldiers, because you leave on the northern land your pioneering footsteps![8]

Here, he is speaking in the name of the party and of the Wild North. With his promise, the sent-down youth can return to the cities with peaceful and even proud minds, reassured by this ultimate affirmation of their sublime historical role.

Or can they? These compulsive judgments and justifications implicitly betray anxiety over the possibility of unfavorable assessment of sent-down youth in the future. Hence the necessity to defend and to explain. If the sent-down youth in this novella manage to salvage a favorable self-image from the ruins of history, who is to bear the burden of guilt for their suffering? The novella cleverly displaces this burden onto a convenient character: the brigade leader, Ma. It is he who cheats the youth into leaving the cities during the Cultural Revolution, and it is he who now tries to detain them when they want to return. The conflicts between Ma the brigade leader, and Sun the political commissar, are presented as conflicts between two political lines, one right and the other wrong. What is right simply stands for the perceived interests of sent-down youth, and in the end right prevails. By employing such a binary, the novella manages to avoid squarely addressing deeper issues of politics and history—such as complicity, responsibility, and guilt.

In *Golden Age*, however, this right/wrong binary collapses. At first sight, the focus of Wang Xiaobo's novella seems to be purely personal, yet it is fallacious to presume that it is devoid of politics as a result. Two characters in charge of the sent-down youth, the team leader (*duizhang*) and the military representative (*jun daibiao*) are depicted in an unfavorable light. Yet, unlike *Snowstorm Tonight*, which presents the brigade leader Ma as committing the almost unforgivable sin of selfishly moving against the historical current, the leaders in *Golden Age*, although nasty and annoying, are not demonized.

What is perhaps more significant is that the protagonist himself is no less nasty and annoying. He asserts without qualms that he is by nature of the same ilk as "hooligans and bandits."[9] He professes no political ambitions or ideals, and does not care at all what record he will leave in national or local history. The reasons for his conflicts with the team leader and the military representative are purely personal and trivial. Unlike the sent-down youth in *Snowstorm Tonight*, the protagonist's methods of dealing with these leaders are far from unimpeachable. To get revenge on the team leader who falsely accuses Wang-er of shooting out one eye of his dog, Wang-er shoots out the other eye of the dog, just as a true hooligan would do. As for the military representative, Wang-er curses him, pretends to be dumb when addressed by him, cuts a gourd in two to scare him away, or simply runs into the mountains. Thus, neither of the two sides is right or wrong, and the moral demarcation between them is blurred.

Similarly, many other individuals vulnerable to potential demonization are in this novella restored to an ambiguous equilibrium. Yet all these people find themselves caught in an absurd Catch-22. It is as if they are playing a game whose unpredictable rules originate from a mysterious source totally beyond their control. They are aware of the absurdity of the rules, yet they must stick to their parts. This sense of absurdity is presented in the novella with good humor rather than bitterness. When Wang-er and Chen are caught, they are asked to confess to their illicit liaison. When this charge is denied by Wang-er, the accusers say, "In that case, confess your crime of economic speculation." Again Wang-er denies any guilt. The accusers say: "Then confess your treason. Anyway, just confess. As to what to confess, figure it out between you two."[10] One is ultimately guilty, no matter what one says. Wang-er and Chen choose to confess their illicit sexual relationship, which entails the least punishment among all the options. After their confession, the illogical logic demands that because they have made a satisfactory confession, they will receive approval to marry, although they have never asked for it, and then they must marry, no matter how much they protest. Finally, they marry in the morning and divorce in the afternoon.

This refusal to marry brings us to the question of sex in *Golden Age*. Sex is the most important theme for the protagonist Wang-er, and the most revealing aspect of his self-styled hooligan nature. Sex, not love, is the bedrock of his identity, and the irrefutable proof of his existence. Although the novella's obsession with sexual details may be highly offensive to readers, what may be more offensive is its insistence on not elevating sex to the level of love. The author takes great pains to convince us that Wang-er does not love Chen at all, and Chen does not love him until the last page. Sex is purely a technical issue. It is true that they are close friends, and their sexual relationship is based on the agreement that as committed friends, they should do anything for each other. Thus Wang-er reasons that "if she wants to use my body as a target for bayonet practice, I will not begrudge her; so if I want to use her body, she should not refuse me either."[11] This hooligan Wang-er repeatedly tells the readers not to mistake his sexual relation with Chen for love. In other words, he refuses to be sublimated.

Wang-er in *Golden Age* believes that everyone is "lustful" by nature, and whoever pretends to be sexually "pure" commits the sin of "hypocrisy," which, according to him, is a more serious of sin than lechery.[12] By contrast, the repeated gesture made by the hero and heroine in *Snowstorm Tonight* is their refusal to be vulgarized, in other words, to be seen as involved in vulgar love. Compared with the shockingly frank sexual language in *Golden Age*, sexuality in *Snowstorm Tonight* is revealed only through many repressions and twists. Thus the heroine Pei Xiaoyun is made as physically thin as possible to minimize her sexual appeal. On one occasion, she joins an emergency muster drill wearing a pair of thin shoes, and her feet are nearly frozen. The hero Cao Tieqiang carries her home, and places her feet on his chest to warm them. When other girls return and tease Cao, he accuses them of vulgarity. On another occasion, Cao and Pei have an opportunity to spend a night sharing a tent on a mountain, and of course nothing significant happens between them. When accused of a possible illicit relationship the next day, Pei admonishes the accuser with the words "Shame on you!"[13] These words imply that whoever thinks of accusing them of sexual sin is himself guilty of impurity, while the hero and heroine remain unmistakably pure and innocent.

To escape the absurd political situation of Cultural Revolution China, the protagonist Wang-er in *Golden Age* not only turns to the forbidden realm of sex, but repeatedly escapes into the mountains, a pre-political or apolitical place characterized by primitive innocence and freedom. He invariably makes this escape after having some trouble with the local leaders. The first time he disappears into the mountains, he builds himself a hut, in which he contemplates the universe and his own being. On a later occasion, he disappears for half a year with his sexual partner, Chen. They settle in a leper's hut in the remote mountains, and cultivate the surrounding virgin land, on which Chen roams naked except for a knife and a pair of boots. The leper's hut, deserted and shunned by civilization yet blessed with extraordinarily fertile land, becomes a utopia for them. On both occasions, Wang-er has to return to civilization reluctantly. Yet later, whenever something unpleasant arises, he wants to return to the mountains. He is so enamored of this escape that on descending from the mountains, he even leaves his treasured tools there, so that he can go back anytime.

The wild mountains and wild nature are thus for Wang-er an asylum from all annoyances. The Wild North of *Snowstorm Tonight*, however, has a drastically different function. Mysterious and sublime, the Wild North represents a place of conquest, which confers a sublime stature on the conquerors. It is also a unifying space upon which the ideals of sent-down youth are inscribed. The denouement of Liang Xiaosheng's novella depends heavily upon this trope. The novella's plot culminates in reconciliation between the brigade leader Ma and the political commissar Sun, and between the brigade headquarters and the sent-down youth. Despite their previous disagreements, they are united by the land, since they are all pioneers within it. This land is at once an enemy to be conquered, a mother embracing her children, and an irresistible force drawing all marginalized figures into its lap.

The marginalized figures in the two novellas are heading in opposite directions. The protagonist Wang-er in *Golden Age* is not content with being on the margin. He desires to leap beyond the margin into a space totally beyond the control of the center. The mountains provide such a space, in that they are inhabited by all kinds of people wandering on the edge of political society, especially ethnic minority groups, such as the Dai, Jingpo, and Acang people. Wang-er likes socializing with these people who, according to him, live a happy and unpolluted life. He finds himself comfortable and popular among them, whereas on the farm, his only friends are literally pigs. However, whether he can truly become one of the noble savages remains in doubt. He is proud of his knife-carving skills, and believes he can make a successful artisan among the Acang people, who are ironsmiths by profession. Yet this dream does not materialize. During their stay as recluses in the mountains, he and Chen on one occasion disguise themselves as Dai people. Yet they are instantly recognized. Thus, not born a "savage," Wang-er cannot become a "savage." Nonpolitical ways of life are not available to him. He must remain within the Han civilization, which, if read between the lines of the novella, is revealed as the result of a slow and inexorable process of domestication and castration.

Wang-er, already on the margin of politics, tries to further marginalize himself by escaping into an apolitical sphere. The marginalized figures in *Snowstorm Tonight*, by contrast, are heading toward the center and the mainstream. They finally adapt themselves to predetermined ideals and heroic roles, and the novella celebrates their success. Pei Xiaoyun, before her martyrdom, is in no way adequate to mainstream standards for revolutionary female soldiers. Her mother was a singer, her father a lecturer of philosophy in some university; both are dead. Thus, hers is a "disgraceful" family background. As far as personality is concerned, she is weak and timid, falling short of the masculine ideal for women popularized during the Cultural Revolution. Her outer appearance could not be plainer. In sum, she has almost nothing to recommend herself.

Yet unlike Wang-er in *Golden Age*, this girl worships mainstream norms, and cherishes these ideals all the more feverishly because of her dissatisfaction with her marginalized position. For example, every sent-down youth in her brigade is assigned a rifle. As she is deemed to be substandard, she is not worthy of one. In reaction, she writes a note with her blood (a common practice among sent-down youth), which reads: "GIVE ME A RIFLE."

Her demand, according to the novella, is sublimely eloquent.[14] The political commissar is struck by her eagerness and Pei is given a rifle, a gesture symbolic of her acceptance into the mainstream. No longer marginalized, she devotes herself to mainstream ideals with zealotry and loyalty. Her death is depicted as heroic and uplifting, because she "consecrates the title of a brigade soldier."[15] Following her death by freezing, she receives the awards and titles of martyr and Youth League member. Once an ugly duckling among the brood, she is finally transformed into a swan.

Yet, the text just refuses to acknowledge the emptiness of these titles, and the pointlessness of Pei's death. Her death can be seen as an unintentional "suicide." She could have easily lived by availing herself of the fire close by. Precisely because she has been marginalized for so long, the norms and ideals of the Cultural Revolution are internalized within her, so she refuses to budge. No one is directly supervising her. It is her internalized ideals and political "conscience" that supervise her behavior with unrelenting severity. This rigid conformity to the demands of the political superego is celebrated in the novella as her ultimate triumph and coming of age.

Pei dies at her post, but what is she guarding against? Perhaps she is standing guard against the revisionist Soviets, who are supposedly conspiring to invade China. However, her death might be more reasonably understood as a symbolic sacrifice to the impossible ideals cherished by the sent-down youth, which are difficult to adhere to, yet equally difficult to abandon. Only ideals can justify their multiyear exile to the countryside. To fulfill these ideals, they should remain there, which most of them cannot afford to do. Of the eight hundred sent-down youth in the brigade, only forty-one will stay, including the two dead martyrs.[16] At the point when most youth leave the country for the cities, it is symbolically significant to displace the burden of staying there onto the most marginalized figures. After this ritual, each has symbolically made his or her share of the sacrifice, and thus can return to the cities without any pangs of remorse.

Liang Xiaosheng's insistence on the sanctity of ideals produces not only the superficially tragic death of Pei, but other irresolvable contradictions. While the sent-down youth protest outside their brigade's headquarters, a fire breaks out, and state property is endangered. The sent-down youth, suddenly forgetting their own concerns, engage in collective efforts to put out the fire. After the crisis of their protest is resolved peacefully by political commissar Sun, the brigade leadership promises that each one who wants to return to the cities will be able to do so. They are to receive the necessary documents and stamps. However, the officer divides the sent-down youth into two lines, and gives one line the privilege of receiving their files first. The other line protests, and demands an explanation. The officer answers by asking them to look at those in the privileged line: each is disheveled because each was in the fire rescuing state property. The unprivileged line withdraws its protest out of shame, while the privileged line, proud of its moral superiority, gets the necessary papers. Here, the fire functions as a test of the sent-down youth's loyalty to their ideals. Yet, the irony is that those loyal to their ideals will be the first permitted to leave, in other words, the first to abandon their ideals.

This hidden paradox can be accounted for only in light of the problematic nature of the ideals shared by sent-down youth. Within the context of the Cultural Revolution, such ideals are easy to understand: they are the ideals for the sent-down youth to perform great acts in the countryside, so that they can become worthier followers of Chairman Mao. Within a post–Cultural Revolution context, this Maoist essence is not quite proper to mention. Thus, the political ambitions of sent-down youth are, in *Snowstorm Tonight*, transformed into the ambition to reclaim virgin land along China's frontier. The former red guards are thus transformed into pioneers, and political struggles displaced by campaigns against nature.

Cathedral and Puzzle: A Formal Comparison

Reading *Snowstorm Tonight* and *Golden Age* provides two entirely different experiences. *Snowstorm Tonight* is like an imposing cathedral. On the altar are two consecrated martyrs. Everywhere else, visitors will encounter larger-than-life human statues with noble and passionate gestures, some standing by themselves, others in small or large groups. In addition, throughout the readers' tour in this grand building, they will hear their guide's persistent voice, not only telling them the stories of each statue or group of statues, but also teaching them how to understand their significance. It is a cathedral for one to wander about, to admire and to learn from, where every effect is designed to "shock and awe." On leaving the cathedral, one is supposed to be purified and morally elevated.

Reading *Golden Age*, however, is like assembling a jigsaw puzzle. Readers are given a box of interesting fragments. They must piece them together, which may take some time and calculation, but which also may be enjoyable and rewarding. And there is more than one way to play the game. After the pieces are put together, previously ignored details may take on new meaning. Some unexpected shapes may begin to emerge. If the cathedral serves to teach, the puzzle serves to entertain and to provoke thought. Of course, acute readers can gain moral edification even from a jigsaw puzzle.

The different methods by which the two novellas unfold are apparent from the very beginning. Both novellas open with the time and the place of the stories, yet the effects are drastically different. *Snowstorm Tonight* begins by stating: "1979 AD. After the Spring Festival. The Song Nen plain in the Northeast is still frozen. Miles and miles of ice, and miles and miles of snow."[17] These epic sentences situate the story in a critical time (1979, when four hundred thousand sent-down youth in Heilongjiang Province were rushing back to the cities) and at a critical place (northernmost China). The novella thus begins in the narrative style of history.[18] The choices of time and place aim at evoking a sublime effect, suggesting that something of great magnitude is happening. Seen through this unique combination of time and place, episodes and characters also achieve an unusual significance.

Golden Age begins by using a humbler, yet perhaps more provocative, tone: "When I was twenty-one, I was a sent-down youth in Yunnan. Chen Qingyang was twenty-six at that time. . . . One day, she came downhill to talk to me about whether she was a slut."[19] The event surely happens during the Cultural Revolution, but Wang Xiaobo's novella refuses to pinpoint the exact time. By specifying the age of the protagonist but not the specific year, the story foregrounds the individual, whose story remains distant from official history. Furthermore, the novella brings up the "profane" issue of sex at the outset, and thus establishes that this story is not only individual, but, against any expectation that it is a kind of spiritual history of one man, it is only about a moment in his sexual history.

Unlike *Golden Age*, which seeks only to capture one aspect of one person's life, *Snowstorm Tonight* attempts a collective narration. The persons to whom Liang Xiaosheng devotes considerable space number almost a dozen, and they only exist as representations of the bigger picture of the brigade, which in turn represents the reality of the Wild North, or even of the whole country. A telling example of this contrast between the two works is located in the authors' depictions of conflict. In *Snowstorm Tonight*, the confrontation between the sent-down youth and the brigade leadership is stunning in its grandeur. Eight hundred torch-bearing sent-down youth besiege the brigade headquarters at night, while at the same time, as if to accompany this spectacular human scene, a fierce blizzard sweeps across the Wild North. Confrontation in *Golden Age*, by contrast, is reduced to the personal conflicts between individuals. Beside the well or on the riverbank (insignificant backdrops compared to the headquarters of *Snowstorm Tonight*), the protagonist Wang-er encounters the military representative, who begins his harangue. Impatient and annoyed, Wang-er feigns to be dumb, or attempts to get away. Here, neither Wang-er nor the military representative represents any larger group.

Both novellas remain true to the tone established by their introductions. In *Snowstorm Tonight*, Liang Xiaosheng's ambitious narrative structure is sustained throughout, with a grand opening, a building-up of conflicts, a majestic progression toward the climax and the denouement. To capture the life of the sent-down youth in its totality, the novella includes representations of both the public and the private, the external and the internal. The structure of *Golden Age*, on the other hand, is far from neat and clear-cut. It seems to play on several themes—by far the most important of which is sex—with some variation each time. Instead of one continuous story line stringing the parts together, the narrative is a collection of loose ends. Not adhering to a strictly chronological order, the story goes back and forth, drops one episode for another, and later picks up the abandoned episode in another light. Additionally, the episodes are often not thematically related. The different structures of the two novellas point to different ambitions of the two authors. While Liang Xiaosheng is confident (or arrogant) enough to frame history in a totalizing structure, Wang Xiaobo can only provide this reality in fragments, and illogical ones at that.

The differing structures are inextricably linked with the differences in narrative points of view. *Snowstorm Tonight* adopts a third-person perspective, which is both omniscient and omnipresent. The author is in the position of not only knowing everything, but also judging everything, and his is the "official" judgment. He often points out the "moral" of the story. While some morals concern specific situations, others attempt to probe the meaning of life itself. Thus, regarding the predicament of sent-down youth, he comments that "if you fail to analyze objectively the contradiction of that bygone era, and to reach a correct conclusion, you can never understand their mixed feelings and their reluctance to leave."[20] These epigrams embedded in the text are supposed to add to the author's already great authority.

The author's comments not only point out meanings of general significance, but also attach interpretations to the characters. In fact, the voices of Cao Tieqiang and political commissar Sun are almost indistinguishable from the voice of the author, since their actions and thoughts are fully approved by the author. Where someone or some episode is not commented upon by these spokesmen, the author supplies his own comments, which are often politically charged. For instance, in a past conflict among the sent-down youth, Cao Tieqiang's group, "motivated by a blind heroism fostered in the Attack by Words, Defend by Force (*wengong wuwei*) movement," resorts to the use of weapons and hastens to the scene of the conflict.[21] Such comments pin down the characters and the episodes, explicitly pointing out their meaning, and leave almost no room for reader interpretation.[22]

Golden Age is told from the first person perspective of Wang-er. What the reader sees and hears, we see and hear through Wang-er's eyes and ears. Unlike a god who knowingly presides over everything that unfolds before his eyes, the narrator of *Golden Age* has much narrower access to his world. Knowledge is often withheld from him. Even Wang-er's internal world, which the first-person perspective is fully entitled to enter, is largely screened from the readers. Most of the time, the narration is focused on external appearance, actions, and words. It is as if Wang Xiaobo, although writing the protagonist's story, is purposely avoiding making too much of his protagonist.

More important, we can hear another voice in *Golden Age*, which sometimes complements, yet more often dilutes and even counteracts the male narrator's narcissistic perspective. This is the voice of Chen Qingyang. Although her voice is heard mainly through her conversation with Wang-er, this female voice preserves much of its autonomy. It often offers another version of the episodes. When Wang-er sits naked in his hut in the mountains, Chen comes to visit him, and later she tells him that on her way to the hut she has dreamed of a beautiful vision, yet the sight of him sitting there naked (a sight too ugly to appear in any dream) ruins all of her expectations. In another scene, Chen tells Wang-er that after one of their episodes of lovemaking, she desires to cry out, yet she restrains herself, because "no man can make her cry out," and because "she is alienated from everyone else."[23] For the male narrator who is proud of his sexual potency and victory, this female voice is devastating. Thus, the first-person narration of the novella is not only limited in its authority; it is intentionally juxtaposed with a female voice that often contradicts that authority. No certainty emerges from this narration, and significant room is left open for readers to draw their own conclusions.

The formal difference between the two novellas is also apparent at the level of diction and episodes. *Snowstorm Tonight* often depicts actions and conversations dramatically, featuring death, blood, tears, confessions, and remorse. The characters swoon, kneel on the ground, or are transported into rapture. Their extravagant words sometimes read more like political slogans than everyday dialogues. Similarly, their exaggerated gestures and expressions, as reflections of the sublime, are often overdone. To enhance the force of each episode of the narration, the author often employs paragraphs of single sentences. Exclamation points abound, not only in the characters' conversations, but in the author's comments as well.

The adjectives and adverbs in *Snowstorm Tonight* are also often morally charged. With them, it is easy to understand which characters are intended as positive models, and which as negative. Good words are monopolized by good people, and bad ones reserved for bad guys. While political commissar Sun can speak out "loud and clear," can walk "in steady steps," and can look at others with "a deep look," the negative figure, brigade leader Ma, can only be "embarrassed," or show a face "with an imperceptible smile" on it.[24] Good people will never suffer embarrassment, and are too candid and sincere to smile slyly. Even Ma's face, with "its features too far away from one another," carries the obvious mark of moral deficiency, reminding us of films made before or during the Cultural Revolution, in which the moral quality of the characters is reflected in their appearances.[25]

The restraint and economy of *Golden Age* provides a sharp contrast to this excess. Wang Xiaobo seldom resorts to adjectives and adverbs. Exaggerations abound in this novella as well, but, interestingly, by foreclosing sentimental interpretations, they often lead to humorous understatements of potentially troubling situations. Thus, Wang-er goes to the infirmary for help with his backache, and receives so many injections that his back is riddled with gaping holes. Then Wang-er turns to physician Chen Qingyang for help, because Chen at least "may know the difference between a syringe and a crochet hook."[26] By use of hyperbole, the pain is turned into humor, and bitterness is averted.

Similarly, the frequent parody in *Golden Age* of seemingly "logical" reasoning often serves to work against logic and reason, and thus gives rise to absurdity. As noted earlier, the team leader blames Wang-er for shooting out the left eye of his dog. Wang-er then reasons that, to prove his innocence, he has to prove:

1. The team leader does not have a dog; or
2. The dog does not have a left eye; or
3. I have no hands, and thus cannot shoot.[27]

Since none of the above can be proved, Wang-er cannot be innocent. The humorous parody of logic only heightens the illogicality of the situation.

As far as formal elements are concerned, the grand and sublime cathedral in *Snowstorm Tonight*, though imposing, is uneasily sustained by strenuous exaggeration, exclamation, and sentimentality. Upon closer examination, readers may detect fissures not well patched up on the walls, and may find the statues unconvincing. The puzzle of *Golden Age*, with its multiple voices and its restrained and often humorous style, presents a much more ordinary yet far richer story.

Windows Opening to the Past and the Present

Snowstorm Tonight and *Golden Age* were the single most popular fictional narratives featuring sent-down youth published during the 1980s and 1990s. *Snowstorm Tonight* appeared in 1983 and was awarded the National Novella Prize that year, before subsequently being broadcast on national radio, adapted into a TV miniseries, and anthologized in high school textbooks as a model of thematic correctness and artistic perfection. Supported by the award-distributing and educational systems and circulated through multiple media, it helped, together with similar works produced by former sent-down youth, construct a dominant sent-down youth image, so much so that the term "Wild North" or even "sent-down youth" (*zhiqing*) might conjure up in people's minds the figure of Pei Xiaoyun in *Snowstorm Tonight*: a heroic soldier in silhouette, rifle in hand, faithfully guarding the motherland. Pei Xiaoyun became a canonized hero much like previous classical revolutionaries, such as Sister Jiang in *Red Crag* (Hong yan).

Wang Xiaobo and his acknowledged masterpiece *Golden Age* experienced an even more dramatic turn of fate. Ten years after *Snowstorm Tonight* won the national novella prize, Wang Xiaobo's *Golden Age* won a different prize in Taiwan, though it brought him little fame in the mainland. In 1982 Wang had already made a silent debut in the literary arena, publishing *Auld Lange Syne* (Dijiu tianchang), a novella that went largely unnoticed. He began writing *Golden Age* while studying in the United States from 1984 to 1988. In 1992 *Golden Age* was published in Taiwan, winning the thirteenth *United News* (Lianhe bao) prize for novellas. However, due to the supposedly ob-scene nature of his work, Wang had great difficulty publishing it on the mainland. It was only after painstaking efforts on both his and his editors' part that *Golden Age* was published in 1994, again receiving little attention. After 1992 Wang worked in multiple roles as a novelist, a columnist, and a sociological scholar collaborating with his wife in research on homosexuality in China. However, in spite of these titles, he lived a largely obscure life.

Everything changed on April 11, 1997. What would Wang Xiaobo's liter-ary fate have been if he had not died unexpectedly of a heart attack that day? No one is able to tell. The irony of his life is that the recognition and acclaim largely denied him while he was alive were bestowed upon him lav-ishly, perhaps too lavishly, after his death. This turn of events was attributed by many to the solipsism of Chinese critics, as if nothing less than a death could rouse them out of their stupor and waken them to the talent of a genius.[28] His sudden death ignited an unexpected explosion of laments and memoirs, bringing him to public attention. Everyone wrote on the Wang Xiaobo that they knew or had heard about. Not only were his published works reprinted, but his early or previously uncollected works rediscovered and treasured. A collection of his essays, *My Spiritual Homeland* (Wo de jingshen jiayuan), was first printed in June 1997, and reprinted the next month. Wang Xiaobo was transformed after his death from a man into a phenomenon and a spectacle. In an age when literature was generally be-lieved to have lost its ability to cause a sensation, he became an event in spite of himself.

These events pose the following questions: how can the two narratives about sent-down youth presented in *Snowstorm Tonight* and *Golden Age* reach such differing conclusions? Why were two such different narratives so highly acclaimed? What can be learned about sent-down youth and about the 1980s and 1990s by looking through these two distinct "windows"?

Clearly, *Snowstorm Tonight*, with its sublime heroism and idealism, its grand structure and its omnipresent narrator, celebrates the official values—

unconditional sacrifice, loyalty and collectivity—of the Cultural Revolution. By contrast, *Golden Age*, by focusing on a marginalized figure eager to go beyond the sociopolitical margins, deconstructs the good-versus-evil binary that the Cultural Revolution rhetoric employed so often. Both writers began publishing in the early 1980s. When Liang was trumpeting heroism and idealism, Wang was already turning his eyes away from politics to personal and private life. Wang's earliest published work, *Auld Lange Syne*, already showed such features as the absence of political ideals, loose structure, and a polite distance from mainstream politics, as well as a rudimentary sense of black humor. Newly emergent from the Cultural Revolution, the two writers were treading on different literary paths. Later, although Liang Xiaosheng seemed to drift away from Cultural Revolution ideals as well, he could never go as far as Wang, and his drifting was marked by ambivalence and confusion.

Aside from such factors as personal temperament and educational background, some important reasons that account for the two writers' different attitudes toward the Cultural Revolution are to be found in their different experiences in the Cultural Revolution itself. These factors shaped their commitment to, and investment in, the idealistic causes of sent-down youth during the Cultural Revolution, and subsequently influenced how soon and how far each would go in post-Mao years to break away from the Cultural Revolution rhetoric.

One such shaping factor is family background. Due to different family origins, one writer was located in the mainstream, while the other landed on the margins during the Cultural Revolution. With both parents illiterate, Liang was one of the few writers of the sent-down generation who came from a "good" family. By contrast, born of intellectual parents, it would have been difficult for Wang to become a mainstream political activist during the Cultural Revolution, even if he wanted to. Wang's father, a famous philosopher of logic, was labeled a "class alien" (*jieji yiji fenzi*) and expelled from the party in 1952, the year of Wang Xiaobo's birth. The incident was a disaster for the family.[29] Fortunately, in April 1957, Wang's father was summoned to discuss issues of logic with Mao Zedong. The two even had lunch together. Perhaps protected by this royal patronage, the senior Wang did not suffer much during the Cultural Revolution. Yet his children were still marginalized. Wang Xiaobo's elder brother later complained that as the child of a "class alien," he could never hope to join the red guards.[30]

Liang Xiaosheng had the class credentials to become a red guard. An "enthusiastic supporter of Mao's rustication program," he went to Heilongjiang Province as early as June 1968, six months before Mao's directive officially initiated the movement.[31] Strictly speaking, Liang was not sent down, but went down by himself, like many others at that time. Wang, however, likened the experience of being sent down to being packed on to a train like luggage.[32] Their experiences during the Cultural Revolution were different as well. Liang said later, not without pride, that as a sent-down youth, he was always the keynote speaker in struggle meetings or eulogy meetings, and that his writing career began with writing "struggle drafts" (*pipan gao*) or "experience drafts" (*jiangyong gao*).[33] Liang was recommended to go to Fudan University as early as 1974 as a worker-peasant-soldier (*gong nong bing*) student, showing that by the political and moral standards of the time, he was a "good" sent-down youth. Wang, however, did not enter university until he passed the national examination in 1977.

The family background of the two writers further affected the places to which they were assigned. Heilongjiang and Yunnan meant very different things to sent-down youth. Heilongjiang, on the border with the Soviet Union, was deemed a highly strategic and romantic place, typically assigned only to students from "reliable" family backgrounds. Zhu Lin, a writer of the same generation, said that "places such as Heilongjiang required higher political standards. Even if you wanted to go there, you might not get permission."[34] In fact, thanks to the efforts of such sent-down authors as Liang Xiaosheng, the dry name Heilongjiang was almost replaced in the 1980s and 1990s by the highly suggestive and emotionally charged name "Wild North." To go to the Wild North was evidence of political recognition, and the pride of actually being there reinforced the commitment of youth. Yunnan, although also a border province and a romantic place, had far less military and strategic importance. To use Wang Xiaobo's own words, in less than a month after the sent-down youths arrived there, their revolutionary fervor dampened.[35] Instead, the wild mountains and ethnic minority groups provided space and inspiration for Wang's imagination. Moreover, sent-down youth in Heilongjiang lived in highly militarized regiments, while official discipline in Yunnan was far less effective. That Wang-er in *Golden Age* could live in the mountains for half a year, and return without punishment, is evidence of this lax discipline, which left more room for individual freedom.

Age also played an important role. Perhaps unlike most other generations of writers, even a minor difference in age was crucial to these sent-
down writers, because age determined their likely emotional investment in
Cultural Revolution idealism, and the extent to which this idealism would
shape their most formative years. Liang was born in 1949, and Wang in 1952.
Both became sent-down youth in 1968, when Liang was a senior high school
graduate, and Wang only a junior high school graduate. Commenting on
the difference between herself and such writers as Liang Xiaosheng, Wang
Anyi, another important writer from the sent-down generation, stressed the
importance of age: "If I were only two years older, I might have had different experiences."[36] Liang Xiaosheng was so steeped in Cultural Revolution
education and propaganda during his formative period that it was extremely
difficult, if not impossible, for him to break entirely away from its ideology.
Wang, only sixteen when he went to the countryside, could at least remain
partly indifferent and "unscathed."[37]

These personal histories are helpful in explaining some of the differences between Liang and Wang, and hence between *Snowstorm Tonight* and
Golden Age. Some perhaps more important reasons for the differences between the two novellas and their receptions lie in the respective periods in
which they were written and published. It was impossible for *Golden Age*,
an "obscene" book with a hooligan as its hero, to get published in the early
1980s, let alone to be recognized as a literary feat. Similarly, it was also hard
to imagine a novella like *Snowstorm Tonight* appearing in the late 1990s. It
is true that *Golden Age* was not written specifically for the market, and that
it became the focus of mass media largely through "mistake and misreading."[38] Yet it surely is not a sheer coincidence that readers in the late 1990s
began to appreciate Wang. Written between 1984 and 1988, *Golden Age* can
be said to have anticipated sentiments that became widespread only later.

Wang Meng's praise of both novellas shows that the differences between
the two cannot be attributed only to personal styles. In 1983, responding
quickly to *Snowstorm Tonight*, Wang Meng penned a eulogy titled "A Cou-
rageous and Sublime Monument to Sent-down Youth." Reading the novella
with "profound respect," he commented that Liang Xiaosheng, "more than
any professional novelist, commands our veneration and admiration."[39] Sixteen years later, Wang Meng, joining the chorus eulogizing Wang Xiaobo,
concluded that Wang Xiaobo was first of all "a person of reason," in other
words, a person with sober common sense who never gave himself to fanati-

cism, and who was always on guard against sublime but empty rhetoric.[40] Among the former literary "rightists" of the 1950s, Wang Meng has been the only one to stay at the "cutting-edge" during the post-Mao era. How had his taste changed so much?

Many writers and critics now look back on the early 1980s with nostalgia, since at that time literature was so intertwined with the dominant political ideology that writers sometimes acted as prophets speaking for the age. Artistic endeavor often had something to do with the memory of the Cultural Revolution, and two groups of writers emerged as the most vocal.[41] One was the so-called return-ers (*guilai zhe*), in other words, the "rightist" writers of the 1950s who triumphantly recommenced writing after their persecution had ended in late 1970s. The other group consisted of former sent-down youth. Like the former rightists, these writers angrily denounced the crimes committed by the Gang of Four, and lamented their past sufferings and miseries, which formed the main motifs of the literary movement loosely referred to as "scar literature."

Then the sent-down youth literature underwent an abrupt shift. Disillusioned with post–Cultural Revolution urban life, the site of their previous suffering (rural China) now appeared to former sent-down youth as a paradise. Hence the release of a batch of works projecting a wholesome, peaceful, or uplifting countryside as opposed to the bewildering, corrupting, or empty urban life that sent-down youth subsequently faced. It was at this moment that Liang Xiaosheng appeared on the scene and instantly attracted public attention with his sublime idealism. Compared with the lamentations of the rightist writers, literature produced by the sent-down youth was characterized by its heroism, which was believed to come "at the right time, eliminating the miserable moan and groan from 1977 to 1981" and showing "pride in youth and no regrets."[42]

Due to the public attention many authors were able to command, the early 1980s was seen as a glorious age for literature. Still, literary reflections on the Cultural Revolution crafted in the 1980s had great limitations. Both the former rightist writers and the sent-down youth writers saw themselves as victims of the Cultural Revolution, which was in turn interpreted as resulting from a conspiracy orchestrated by the Gang of Four and implicitly by Mao. Believing themselves cheated and victimized, they emerged morally intact from the Cultural Revolution. Thus, they failed to explore the psychological and social foundations of the Cultural Revolution's mass mobilization in addition to its legacy of persecution. Moreover, in the name of condemning the Cultural Revolution, they sometimes employed the same worldview espoused during the Cultural Revolution period (such as sharply defined binaries), and consistently developed basic thematics in terms of good/bad, sincere/hypocritical, and idealistic/vulgar polarities. Liang's glorification of the heroic past is a case in point of this self-righteousness.

Although such factors as commodification and desublimation that swept the literary landscape during the 1990s were already latent by the mid- and late 1980s, most critics agree that the 1990s was a "new" decade. What they disagree on is what to name this decade, which has resulted in a proliferation of such labels as "postmodern," "post-new era," or "literature of a new state."[43] Such prefixes as "post" or "new" suggest that the decade made a clear break with the previous one. The failure of the 1989 democracy movement and the subsequent establishment of the "socialist market economy" accounted for the sharp break between the two decades. Literature in the 1990s was characterized by diversification, a distancing from politics, the collapse of grand narratives, and increasing commercialization. As a critic puts it, "On the one hand, radicals and idealists of the 1980s, in the face of an unusual and unexpected incident totally beyond their control, had to reflect on themselves and began to doubt themselves; on the other hand, the subsequent economic tide threatened to dissolve literature from outside the literary realm."[44] Literature was believed to be doubly marginalized by both politics and the market. No longer able to speak for the nation and the people, it was left to uneasily face the market. The loss of a moral and political aura among 1980s writers and the presumably corrupt and hooligan-like nature of 1990s intellectuals led to a heated discussion concerning whether the "humanistic spirit" (*renwen jingshen*) of the 1980s had been lost, and if so, what was to be supplied to fill the resulting vacuum.

Yet the break of literature away from politics may have been a blessing in disguise. With the collapse of the all-encompassing political sphere, and released from the burden of providing moral standards for the general public, writers now found new private realms of literary introspection within which the previously forbidden theme of sex was explored with perhaps excessive enthusiasm. Wang Xiaobo's alternative recounting of the events of the Cultural Revolution, focusing on sex and experiences of marginality, appeared precisely at this juncture when the reading public seemed prepared to receive it, although the work itself was written earlier.

However, it was partly due to the mechanisms of the market that Wang's voice became amplified. Here the market functioned as both a curse and a blessing.[45] As a morally indifferent factor, it caters on the one hand to the emotional demands of those who yearn for the pure, revolutionary past. On the other hand, it also promotes elements that serve to deconstruct that past. Although China's cultural atmosphere changed drastically between the two decades, many sublime residues of sent-down youth literature dominant during the 1980s survived into the 1990s. Thus, 1994 witnessed numerous activities, exhibits, and other cultural spectacles honoring sent-down youth, sparking in some cities a craze for the "culture of the sent-down youth," which culminated in a massive gala entitled "Children of the Republic," staged on January 21, 1995, at Capital Stadium in Beijing.[46] This craze was greatly marketable, and to quench the thirst of consumers, books—often in the form of compilations of "true" stories concerning sent-down youth or reprints of the so-called red canon—were rapidly produced. During this revival, Liang Xiaosheng again played an important role. A television miniseries entitled *Nianlun* (The Years) based on his novel was shown at the height of this nostalgic craze. Celebrating a past that many sent-down youth would not and could not regret, these activities and literary events obscured the historical context of sent-down youths' experience, distilling such themes as heroism and the affirmation of "proud youth" (*qingchun wuhui*) from the stories of participants, many of which were but recycled versions of *Snowstorm Tonight*. Thus the image of heroic sent-down youth reasserted itself.

Wang Xiaobo was highly critical of such narcissistic nostalgia. Ridiculing the television miniseries *Nianlun*, he argued that it was a virtue to be able to admit that one had once been a dupe. According to him, many Chinese lacked this virtue, because they "seem to believe that by refusing to admit one's stupidity, one can really become smarter. Moreover, many tended to aestheticize the ugliness of the past."[47] He hated claims made in the name of the sublime. Commenting on a sent-down youth in the 1970s who sacrificed his life to "rescue" a telephone pole and was honored as a martyr, he asserted that "everyone knows that some sublimity is sheer hypocrisy, which is worse than debauchery."[48] The Cultural Revolution was a recurrent theme in Wang's works in which he often teased out the absurdity of that age with black humor and satire. Yet during his time of unpopularity, his profane affirmation that "I admit I was an asshole" (*wo shi shabi*) seemed too feeble compared to the deafening chorus celebrating the sublimity of the sent-down youth experience.[49] Only after, or because of, his death did the market, in spite of itself, come to his rescue. *Golden Age* and his other works were avidly read by the younger generation. He dismantled everything that was deemed holy or sacred during the Cultural Revolution, presenting it instead as an absurd farce, within which "a historical picture resembling a serious drama or a tragedy is broken into pieces."[50]

The Cultural Revolution: A Haunting Ghost

When asked sometime in the 1990s by a German interviewer why the red guards never repented their crimes, Liang Xiaosheng answered indignantly, "Not all red guards were like the German fascists and the Gestapo!" Proceeding to a fierce attack on German fascism, Liang asserted that although the red guards did harm some, "it was largely a harm committed with ink" (referring to the big character posters).[51] Liang seemed to ignore, perhaps unconsciously, the real bloodshed caused by the red guards. His defense of and apology for the red guards may typify the attitude adopted by many former sent-down youth toward their experience in the countryside. They often pictured themselves either as innocent victims of evil cadres, or as heroes acting out their ideals. The heroic version of their experience gained so much currency during the 1980s, and survived so tenaciously into the 1990s, that even the terms "sent-down youth" (*zhiqing*) or the "sent-down high school graduates" (*lao san jie*) now carry heroic connotations. The fact that the 1990 Beijing exhibition honoring sent-down youth, which appeared under the highly emotional title "Souls Tied to the Black Soil" (*hun xi hei tudi*), was staged in the Chinese History Museum may symbolize the manner in which sent-down youth are in the process of emerging as heroes in the nation's official history.[52]

Laifang Leung, in her collection of interviews of writers who were themselves former sent-down youth, calls the sent-down generation the "lost generation." Writers from this generation certainly did lose a lot. Their youth, that best part of one's life, was spent in the countryside doing backbreaking manual labor. When the lucky ones among them entered universities, they were considerably older than other freshmen newly graduated from high school. Yet, perhaps most important, many of them lost the ability to engage in genuine self-reflection.

Another writer of the sent-down generation, Zhang Kangkang, still resents the slogan of "proud youth," and speaks soberly of her generation as people who "have no courage to negate themselves." According to her, sent-down youth only denounced "others' history," while neglecting their own historical responsibilities.[53] Yet to negate oneself is easier said than done. Zhang, urging everyone to truly reflect, shows the difficulty of reflection herself. She had a precious opportunity to go to college in 1977, yet a malicious party secretary thwarted her plan. Zhang then mobilized an acquaintance holding a high political position to intervene and pressure the secretary from above. Remembering this episode, Zhang believes that this action of hers was not a case of "entering by the back door" (*zou houmen*), but rather a right action in a "struggle between good and evil."[54] Again, the moral binary is evoked, and the former sent-down youth who pens this memory is of course squarely in the camp of the good. In fact, in spite of her call for genuine self-reflection, her memoir *The Wild North and the Frozen River* (Dahuang bing he), true to its title, has little such self-reflection, and to a large extent only reaffirms the familiar theme of heroism.

Ah Cheng, an influential writer of the sent-down generation and a vociferous voice within the "root-searching" (*xun gen*) literary movement of the mid-1980s, is also sharply aware of the serious limitations of writers from the sent-down generation. Some believe that due to the dramatic nature of the Cultural Revolution, the sent-down generation is sure to produce great writers and great works. Ah Cheng challenges this assumption, since according to him, "even those who are against the Cultural Revolution are easily trapped by it, and thus end up on the same level as it."[55] His pessimism concerning the sent-down youth generation seems warranted. The sublime spell of the Cultural Revolution still remains long after the Cultural Revolution itself is supposed to have ended.

The case of Wang Xiaobo shows how much it takes for a contemporary writer to lift this spell. What conditions must have existed for such a writer to be able to break away from the Cultural Revolution? First, the writer must come from a "bad" family background, but not so bad as to lead to alienation from the Cultural Revolution experience entirely (hatred often makes the hater no better than the hated). The writer's parents must be intellectuals, so that a private collection of books to read will be at hand in addition to the meager "official" selections. The writer must be quite young at the outset of the Cultural Revolution, otherwise he or she would be too old to escape the Cultural Revolution rhetoric. The writer must not be too successful during the Cultural Revolution, lest he or she develop a too strong identification with its alleged cause. The writer must enter university, preferably after 1977, since the worker-peasant-soldier university students in the Cultural Revolution only got an impoverished education. The writer must go overseas, as Wang Xiaobo did, to see an alternative way of life and a different culture. In the case of Wang Xiaobo, only after the confluence of these factors was he able to speak unabashedly of the absurdity and stupidity of his years in the Cultural Revolution countryside. Although other writers who succeed in breaking away from the Cultural Revolution rhetoric may have their own reasons, these factors are important to consider.

The persistence of sublime and heroic narratives concerning sent-down youth also evokes the issue of the Cultural Revolution's demise. Most believe that with the downfall of the Gang of Four and the institution of "reform and opening" (*gaige kaifang*) policies, China broke away from the Cultural Revolution once and for all. As far as literature is concerned, this is certainly far from the case.[56] The Cultural Revolution good-versus-evil mindset, long believed dead and buried, continues to haunt China like a ghost in the shroud of heroism and idealism. The sublime idealism exemplified in *Snowstorm Tonight* dominant in the 1980s was a case in point. The first real literary break with the Cultural Revolution arrived, perhaps ironically, with the failure of the 1989 student movement and the official establishment of a market economy. No longer allowed to indulge in grand narratives about such topics as the nation, the people, or epic history, writers began to truly turn against the Cultural Revolution and the whitewashing of its history, and to open up other interpretive spaces. It is only then that such writers as Wang Xiaobo began to move from the margin to the center, while writers like Liang Xiaosheng retreated step by step from the center toward the margin.[57] Of course the picture remains complex; heroic sentiments concerning sent-down youth still linger. Some writers, adhering to their sublime ideals, adopt a belligerent stance and vehemently denounce the profane nature of contemporary literature. Yet, in spite of these countercurrents and residues of the former decade, the hold of the Cultural Revolution over people's psyches seems to be in the process of loosening.

Contributors

Jeremy Brown is a Ph.D. candidate in modern Chinese history at the University of California, San Diego. He is currently writing a dissertation on the formation of rural-urban difference during the Mao period. His publications include "From Resisting Communists to Resisting America: Civil War and Korean War in Southwest China, 1950–1951," forthcoming in a volume on the PRC in the early 1950s.

Joseph W. Esherick is professor of history and Hsiu Professor of Chinese Studies at the University of California, San Diego. He is author of *The Origins of the Boxer Uprising* (1987) and *Reform and Revolution in China: The 1911 Revolution in Hunan and Hubei* (1996), coauthor of *Chinese Archives: An Introductory Guide* (1996), coeditor of *Chinese Local Elites and Patterns of Dominance* (1990), and editor of *Lost Chance in China* (1974) and *Remaking the Chinese City* (2000).

Jiangsui He is a Ph.D. candidate in the Department of Sociology at the University of California, San Diego. She is now writing a dissertation on the gap between state-building policies and policy execution in five Chinese villages during land reform, 1946–52.

Dahpon David Ho, currently a graduate student in modern Chinese history at the University of California, San Diego, received his B.A. from Rice University in 2002. His research interests include Tibetan history, Central Asian frontiers, cartography, and the maritime history of the Qing dynasty.

Paul G. Pickowicz is professor of history and Chinese studies at the University of California, San Diego. He is author of *Marxist Literary Thought in China* (1981), coauthor of *Chinese Village, Socialist State* (1991) and *Revolution, Resistance and Reform in Village China* (2005), and coeditor of *Unofficial China* (1989), *New Chinese Cinemas* (1994), and *Popular China* (2002).

Liyan Qin is a Ph.D. student in the Literature Department at the University of California, San Diego. She received her B.A. and M.A. degrees from Beijing University, and has translated several books (published in China) from English into Chinese. Her research interests include Chinese literature from the late Qing to 1949 and American literature between the two world wars.

Sigrid Schmalzer is assistant professor of history at the University of Massachusetts, Amherst, where she teaches modern Chinese history and the history of science. Her publications include "Breeding a Better China" (*Geographical Review*) and "Fishing and Fishers in Penghu, Taiwan" (*East Asian History*). She is currently writing a book based on her dissertation, "The People's Peking Man: Popular Paleoanthropology in Twentieth-Century China."

Yang Su obtained his Ph.D. degree in sociology from Stanford University and now teaches social movements and political violence at the University of California, Irvine. His publications include "The Cultural Revolution in the Countryside" (coauthored with Andrew Walder) in *China Quarterly*, and "Antiwar Protest and Congressional Voting" (coauthored with Doug McAdam) in *American Sociological Review*.

Andrew G. Walder is professor of sociology at Stanford University and Senior Fellow in the Stanford Institute for International Studies. He is the author of *Chang Ch'un-ch'iao and Shanghai's January Revolution* (1978) and *Communist Neo-Traditionalism: Work and Authority in Chinese Industry* (1986), editor of *The Waning of the Communist State* (1995), *China's Transitional Economy* (1996), and *Zouping in Transition* (1998), and coeditor of *Property Rights and Economic Reform in China* (1999).

Elya J. Zhang, a graduate student in the Department of History at the University of California, San Diego, received her B.A. from Renmin University of China in 2001. Her research interests include Manchu-Han relations, and the history of journalism and communications technology. She is writing a dissertation on the construction of Chinese national identity through social networks in the first two decades of the twentieth century.

Xiaowei Zheng, a graduate student in modern Chinese history at the University of California, San Diego, received her B.A. from Beijing University in 2000 and her M.A. from Yale in 2002. Her research interests include local history of the Qing dynasty and political culture of early republican China. She is currently writing a dissertation on "Political Culture, Protest Repertoires and Mass Nationalism in the 1911 Revolution in Sichuan, China."

Character List

Acang 阿伧

aiguo gongliang 爱国公粮

Baima Temple 白马寺

Baiyunguan Temple 白云观寺

Bandan Zhaxi 班丹扎西

banji 班级

Banpo 半坡

baodao 报道

Baodi 宝坻

baogao wenxue 报告文学

baolu huo sixiang 暴露活思想

bei zhan 备战

bei zhuanzheng 被专政

Beidaihe 北戴河

beijian zhe zui congming
    卑贱者最聪明

bendiren 本地人

Bingling Temple 炳灵寺

bugou tanbai shenke
    不够坦白深刻

Cai Tianxin 蔡天新

Canyihui 参议会

Cao Tieqiang 曹铁强

chan shazi 掺沙子

Chang Jiexuan 常洁萱

chedi zalan jiu Qinghua
    彻底砸烂旧清华

Chen Chun 陈淳

Chen Jiazhong 陈佳忠

Chen Mingzhu 陈明珠

Chen Qingyang 陈清扬

Chen Sihe 陈思和

Chen Yonggui 陈永贵

Chen Yuyan 陈育延

Chen Zaidao 陈再道

chi laoben 吃老本

Chi Qun 迟群

Cui Xuyi   崔绪贻

da chuanlian   大串联

da fan'ge   大翻个

da gong wu si   大公无私

da minzhu   大民主

da wudou   大武斗

Dahuang bing he   大荒冰河

Dai   傣

Dai Jinhua   戴锦华

daohui Kongjia dian   捣毁孔家店

Daoxian   道县

Daqiuzhuang   大邱庄

dashiji   大事记

Daxing   大兴

Dazhai   大寨

Dazhongzhuang   大钟庄

difang zhi   地方志

Dijiu tianchang   地久天长

Ding Dong   丁冬

dizhu wo   地主窝

Dongfang shengdi   东方圣地

Du Fu caotang   杜甫草堂

dui   队

duizhang   队长

dundian ganbu   蹲点干部

duoquan   夺权

ende dizhu   恩德地主

Enshi   恩施

fan xiu fang xiu   反修防修

fan youqing   反右倾

fandong xueshu quanwei
　　反动学术权威

fan'geming baoluan   反革命暴乱

fanshen   翻身

fanyou   反右

feipin shougouzhan   废品收购站

Fengshan   凤山

gaige kaifang   改革开放

Gao Yimin   高益民

gaoyuzhuang   告御状

gong nong bing   工农兵

Gu guantai   古观台

gu wei jin yong   古为今用

Gugong   故宫

gui gong   归公

guilai zhe   归来者

Guiyuan Temple   归元寺

guojia caichan   国家财产

Han Aimin   韩爱民

Han Xianchu   韩先楚

Hanjiang   涵江

Hao Ran   浩然

He Hongfan   贺鸿范

He Pengfei   贺鹏飞

hei zhaoya   黑爪牙

heipi   黑皮

Hengxian   横县

hong haiyang   红海洋

Hong yan   红岩

Hongdengji   红灯记

Honglian   红联

Hongse zaofan dui 红色造反队

Hongse zaofan jun 红色造反军

Hongse zaofan tuan 红色造反团

Hou Jun 侯隽

hou xinshiqi 后新时期

Huang Jiwei 黄集伟

Huang Tianhui 黄天辉

Huang Weiwen 黄慰文

Huang Yantian 黄砚田

Huang Yongsheng 黄永胜

Huashi 化石

hun xi hei tudi 魂系黑土地

Ji Dengkui 纪登奎

Ji Peng 汲鹏

jia geming, zhen baohu
　　假革命，真保护

Jia Lanpo 贾兰坡

Jiang Liyin 江礼银

Jiang Nanxiang 蒋南翔

Jiang Wen 姜文

Jiang Xiaoshan 江小山

Jiang Zilong 蒋子龙

Jian'gan 箭杆

jiangyong gao 讲用稿

jianshe bingtuan 建设兵团

jianzu jianxi 减租减息

jiaotian tian buying, jiaodi di buling
　　叫天天不应, 叫地地不灵

Jiaxian 佳县

jichu lilun kexue de zhongshi
　　基础理论科学的重视

jieji yiji fenzi 阶级异己分子

jieji diren de changkuang jingong
　　阶级敌人的猖狂进攻

Jing Po 景颇

Jinggangshan 井冈山

jiu jundui yi xiaocuo
　　揪军队一小撮

jiu ming 救命

jiu ming bei 救命碑

Juela Temple 觉拉寺

jun daibiao 军代表

kai wanren dingfeng chuan
　　开万人顶风船

kaimen ban keyan 开门办科研

kaimen ban xue 开门办学

kao qunzhong 靠群众

kaobian zhan 靠边站

Ke La 坷拉

kexue puji 科学普及

Kongfu 孔府

Konglin 孔林

Kongmiao 孔庙

Kuai Dafu 蒯大富

Kuaishi renwu 蒯氏人物

Lai Jinliang 赖金良

lang xin gou fei 狼心狗肺

lao da nan 老大难

lao san jie 老三届

laodong chuangzao le ren benshen
　　劳动创造了人本身

laomin shangcai 劳民伤财

Li Huaishan　李怀山

Li Liangmo　李良模

Li Liangxiong　李良雄

Li Qinglin　李庆霖

Li Rongshan　李荣山

li song chu jing　礼送出境

Li Xiu　李秀

Li Xuwen　李续文

Li Yaodong　李耀东

Li Yinhe　李银河

Li Yuhe　李玉和

lian　连

Liang Xiao [pen name]　梁效

liang xiao [two schools]　两校

Liang Xiaosheng　梁晓声

Lianhe bao　联合报

lianzhang　连长

Lianzhi　联指

Liao Zhigao　廖志高

Lijiang　丽江

Lin Yujin　林玉金

Lingui　临桂

Lingyin Temple　灵隐寺

linshi gong　临时工

Lintingkou　林亭口

lishi wenti　历史问题

liu　留

Liu Bingren　刘秉仁

Liu Gong　刘功

Liu Houyi　刘后一

Liu Jufen　刘菊芬

Liu Qingtang　刘庆棠

Liu Tao　刘涛

Liu Xiangyuan　刘香元

Liu Xiaomeng　刘小萌

Liu Zehua　刘则华

Liu Zhangshi　刘张氏

Lu Qingwu　陆庆伍

luanda luansha　乱打乱杀

luxian cuowu　路线错误

Ma Li　马利

Ma Mingfang　马明方

Ma Rutong　马汝同

Ma Shuliang　马淑良

Ma Xingmin　马醒民

Ma Zhenyin　马振银

Ma Zhihui　马智慧

Ma Zhongtai　马钟泰

Mancheng Lingshan　满城陵山

Mashan　马山

Mawangdui　马王堆

mianshou　面首

Mimaciren　米玛次仁

Mizhi　米脂

nai gege　奶哥哥

Nan Fan　南帆

Nanguan dadui　南关大队

Nanputuo Temple　南普陀寺

Nianlun　年轮

nianpu　年谱

Nie Yuanzi　聂元梓

Nihewan　泥河湾

nongye xue Dazhai　农业学大寨

pailou　牌楼

Pei Xiaoyun　裴晓芸

pi Lin pi Kong　批林批孔

pin xiazhong nong　贫下中农

pingju　平剧

Pingmin Party　平民党

Pinxie　贫协

pipan gao　批判稿

po mixin　破迷信

po sijiu　破四旧

pojiu lixin　破旧立新

Putian　莆田

Qi Benyu　戚本禹

Qiankeng　前坑

qingchun wuhui　青春无悔

qingli jieji duiwu　清理阶级队伍

qinren　亲人

Qiulu　萩芦

Quanzhou　全州

Qufu　曲阜

Qujiang　曲江

qunzhong ban kexue　群众办科学

qunzhongxing kexue　群众性科学

Renmin wuzhuangbu　人民武装部

renwen jingshen　人文精神

renmin zhengquan　人民政权

San Kong　三孔

sanfan yi fensui　三反一粉碎

Sanqingtuan　三青团

sansan zhi　三三制

Shaan-Gan-Ning　陕甘宁

shang　垧

shangceng jianzhu lingyu geming
　　上层建筑领域革命

Shangdi chuangzao le ren
　　上帝创造了人

shanghen wenxue　伤痕文学

shangshan xiaxiang　上山下乡

shehui guanxi　社会关系

Shen Ruhuai　沈如槐

shi deng ren　十等人

Shouzu yuan　收租院

Shuiban　水办

shunkouliu　顺口溜

Sigou　寺沟

silei fenzi　四类分子

siqing　四清

Song Nen　松嫩

Sun Nutao　孙怒涛

Tan Houlan　谭厚兰

Tang Wei　唐伟

Tao Dejian　陶德坚

Tao Kong lianluozhan
　　讨孔联络站

Tao Kong zhanbao　讨孔战报

teding huanjing　特定环境

Tian Song　田松

Tianlin　田林

tie guniang   铁姑娘

tuochan   脱产

Wang Anyi   王安忆

Wang Dongxing   汪东兴

Wang Du   王杜

Wang Gan   王干

Wang Guangmei   王光美

Wang Hairong   王海容

Wang Hongwen   王洪文

Wang Huatian   王化田

Wang Mantian   王曼恬

Wang Meng   王蒙

Wang Miekong (Wang Xiaoxian)
    王灭孔 (王孝先)

Wang Renzhong   王任重

Wang Shuo   王朔

Wang Tinghe   王廷合

Wang Xian (Wang Shuxian)   王先
    (王淑贤)

Wang Xianghui   王向晖

Wang Xiaobo   王小波

Wang Xiaoping   王小平

Wang Zuoshan   王作山

Wang-er   王二

Wei Qi   卫奇

Weng Zhijun   翁志军

wengong wuwei   文攻武卫

wenhua fuxing yundong
    文化复兴运动

wenhuaguan   文化馆

Wo de jingshen jiayuan
    我的精神家园

wo shi shabi   我是傻 x

Wu Dong   吴栋

Wu Rukang   吴如康

Wu Xinzhi   吴新智

wudou dui   武斗队

Wuming   武鸣

wusi zhishi   五四指示

Wuyi   武夷

Xia Renjin   夏仁锦

xian zhi   县志

xiang   乡

xianjin   先进

Xianyou   仙游

xianzai shi xiaojiang fan cuowu de
    shihou le   现在是小将犯错
    误的时候了

xiao   销

Xiaojinzhuang   小靳庄

Xie Fuzhi   谢富治

Xie Jingyi   谢静宜

Xie Xuegong   解学恭

Xie Yong   谢泳

Xieleigong   血泪宫

xin zhuangtai wenxue   新状态文学

xinfang   信访

Xing Yanzi   邢燕子

Xitiangufo Temple   西天古佛寺

xiuqiao liunian   修桥留念

xiuzhengzhuyi hei miaozi
修正主义黑苗子

Xu Jimei 许集美

Xu Yuqing 许彧青

xuan bin duo zhu 喧宾夺主

xuesheng ganbu 学生干部

xuexi ban 学习班

xun gen 寻根

Yang Jizhan 杨继章

Yangchun 阳春

Yangguang canlan de rizi
阳光灿烂的日子

Yangjiagou 杨家沟

yaofeng, e'lang 妖风恶浪

Ye Lin 叶林

yiban 一般

yida sanfan 一打三反

yifeng yisu 移风易俗

yi feng suku de xin
一封诉苦的信

you hui bi dao, you dao bi jiang, you
jiang bi ma 有会必到,
有到必讲, 有讲必骂

youpai maozi 右派帽子

youpai ming'e 右派名额

Yu Fang (Yu Ruifang)
于芳(于瑞芳)

Yu Huiyong 于会泳

Yu Xiu 余修

Yu Zuomin 禹作民

yuan 元

Yuan Hanxing 袁汉兴

Yuanmingyuan 圆明园

Yuanmou 元谋

Yunxi 郧西

zaofan 造反

zhai taozi 摘桃子

zhaimao 摘帽

Zhalan 栅栏

Zhang Daoying 张道英

Zhang Feng 涨峰

Zhang Fuhai 张福海

Zhang Guoliang 张国梁

Zhang Hongsen 张宏森

Zhang Jianhua 张建华

Zhang Kai 张凯

Zhang Kangkang 张抗抗

Zhang Yongnian 张永年

Zhang Yumei 张玉美

Zheng Huopai 郑火排

zhengshen 政审

zhengshi gong 正式工

zhengwei 政委

zhengzhi fudaoyuan 政治辅导员

zhengzhi yexiao 政治夜校

zhezhongzhuyi 折中主义

zhiqing 知青

Zhong Ling 钟灵

Zhou Guoxing 周国兴

Zhou Kezhou (Zhou Fulan)
周克周 (周福兰)

Zhou Mantian 周曼天

Zhou Quanying　周泉缨

Zhoukoudian　周口店

Zhu Lin　竹林

Zhuan Xihua　传惜华

Zhuang Zedong　庄则栋

Zhuang Zhipeng　庄志鹏

zichan jieji fandong luxian
　　资产阶级反动路线

Zigui　秭归

Ziran bianzheng fa　自然辩证法

zongzhi　总支

zou houmen　走后门

zuo zai dizhu huaili
　　坐在地主怀里

Notes

Chapter 1: The Chinese Cultural Revolution as History

1. Three very important early contributions were John Lewis, *Leadership in Communist China* (Ithaca, NY: Cornell University Press, 1963); Franz Schurmann, *Ideology and Organization in Communist China* (Berkeley: University of California Press, 1966); and A. Doak Barnett and Ezra F. Vogel, *Cadres, Bureaucracy, and Political Power in Communist China* (New York: Columbia University Press, 1967).

2. For descriptions of the continuing upheavals after 1968 to the death of Mao, see, for example, Keith Forster, *Rebellion and Factionalism in a Chinese Province: Zhejiang, 1966–1976* (Armonk, NY: M. E. Sharpe, 1990); Wang Shaoguang, *Failure of Charisma: The Cultural Revolution in Wuhan* (Hong Kong: Oxford University Press, 1995); and Elizabeth J. Perry and Li Xun, *Proletarian Power: Shanghai in the Cultural Revolution* (Boulder, CO: Westview, 1997). For accounts of the events of 1976 up to the early 1980s, see Roger Garside, *Coming Alive: China after Mao* (New York: McGraw-Hill, 1981); David S. G. Goodman, *Beijing Street Voices: The Poetry and Politics of China's Democracy Movement* (London: Marion Boyars, 1981); and Stanley Rosen, "Guangzhou's Democracy Movement in Cultural Revolution Perspective," *China Quarterly* 101 (March 1985): 1–31.

3. Schurmann, *Ideology and Organization in Communist China*, 2d edition, enlarged (Berkeley: University of California Press, 1968), 504.

4. Michel Oksenberg, "Occupational Groups in Chinese Society and the Cultural Revolution," in *The Cultural Revolution: 1967 in Review*, Michigan Papers in Chinese Studies No. 2 (Ann Arbor: Center for Chinese Studies, University of Michigan, 1968), 2.

5. Ezra F. Vogel, *Canton under Communism: Programs and Politics in a Provincial Capital, 1949–1968* (Cambridge, MA: Harvard University Press, 1969). See

also Ezra F. Vogel, "The Structure of Conflict: China in 1967," in *The Cultural Revolution: 1967 in Review*, Michigan Papers in Chinese Studies No. 2 (Ann Arbor: Center for Chinese Studies, University of Michigan, 1968), 97–125.

6. See H. Gordon Skilling, "Interest Groups and Communist Politics," *World Politics* 18 (April 1966): 435–51; Chalmers Johnson, ed., *Change in Communist Systems* (Stanford, CA: Stanford University Press, 1970); H. Gordon Skilling and Franklyn Griffiths, ed., *Interest Groups in Soviet Politics* (Princeton, NJ: Princeton University Press, 1971); and Jerry F. Hough, "The Soviet Experience and the Measurement of Power," *Journal of Politics* 37 (1975): 685–710.

7. See Paul Kecskemeti, *The Unexpected Revolution: Social Forces in the Hungarian Uprising* (Stanford, CA: Stanford University Press, 1961); and H. Gordon Skilling, *Czechoslovakia's Interrupted Revolution* (Princeton, NJ: Princeton University Press, 1971).

8. See John Burns, *Political Participation in Rural China* (Berkeley: University of California Press, 1980); and Victor Falkenheim, ed., *Citizens and Groups in Contemporary China* (Ann Arbor: Center for Chinese Studies, University of Michigan, 1987), which was based on papers originally prepared for a conference in 1977.

9. For example, Oi's discussion of Mao-era village leaders as brokers who negotiated state demands for grain procurement through strategies of evasion toward the higher levels and collusion with fellow villagers: Jean C. Oi, *State and Peasant in Contemporary China* (Berkeley: University of California Press, 1989); and Zweig's discussion of the politics of implementing radical policy innovations in rural China during the Cultural Revolution and its immediate aftermath: David Zweig, *Agrarian Radicalism in China, 1968–1981* (Cambridge, MA: Harvard University Press, 1989).

10. See, for example, Susan L. Shirk, *Competitive Comrades: Career Incentives and Student Strategies in China* (Berkeley: University of California Press, 1982); and Jonathan Unger, *Education under Mao: Class and Competition in Canton Schools, 1960–1980* (New York: Columbia University Press, 1982).

11. See Jean C. Oi, "Communism and Clientelism: Rural Politics in China," *World Politics* 37 (January 1985): 238–66; and Andrew G. Walder, *Communist Neo-Traditionalism: Work and Authority in Chinese Industry* (Berkeley: University of California Press, 1986).

12. See Elizabeth J. Perry, "Rural Violence in Socialist China," *China Quarterly* 103 (September 1985): 414–40; and Elizabeth J. Perry, "Shanghai's Strike Wave of 1957," *China Quarterly* 137 (March 1994): 1–27.

13. Schurmann, *Ideology and Organization*, 2d edition, 504.

14. Gordon White, *The Politics of Class and Class Origin: The Case of the Cul-*

tural Revolution (Canberra: Contemporary China Centre, Australian National University, 1976).

15. Hong Yung Lee, "The Radical Students in Kwangtung during the Cultural Revolution," *China Quarterly* 64 (December 1975): 645–83; Stanley Rosen, "Comments: The Radical Students in Kwangtung during the Cultural Revolution," *China Quarterly* 70 (June 1977): 390–99; and Anita Chan, Stanley Rosen, and Jonathan Unger, "Students and Class Warfare: The Social Roots of the Red Guard Conflict in Guangzhou (Canton)," *China Quarterly* 83 (September 1980): 397–446.

16. One of the earliest statements was Gordon A. Bennett, "Political Labels and Popular Tension," *Current Scene* (February 26, 1969): 1–15. Later explorations of these themes, based on dissertations completed in the 1970s, were Richard Curt Kraus, "Class Conflict and the Vocabulary of Social Analysis in China," *China Quarterly* 69 (March 1977): 54–74; Richard Curt Kraus, *Class Conflict in Chinese Socialism* (New York: Columbia University Press, 1981); and Stanley Rosen, *Red Guard Factionalism and the Cultural Revolution in Guangzhou (Canton)* (Boulder, CO: Westview, 1982).

17. Hong Yung Lee, *The Politics of the Chinese Cultural Revolution* (Berkeley: University of California Press, 1978).

18. Much of this was anticipated in Vogel's brief prescient sketch in the last chapter of his *Canton under Communism*. Another early example of this perspective, inspired by the writings of Vogel and Lee, was Andrew G. Walder, *Chang Ch'un-ch'iao and Shanghai's January Revolution*, Michigan Papers in Chinese Studies No. 32 (Ann Arbor: Center for Chinese Studies, University of Michigan, 1978).

19. Gordon White, "The Politics of Demobilized Soldiers from Liberation to Cultural Revolution," *China Quarterly* 82 (June 1980): 187–213.

20. See Gordon White, "The Politics of *Hsia-hsiang* Youth," *China Quarterly* 59 (July–September 1974): 491–517; Thomas P. Bernstein, *Up to the Mountains and Down to the Village: The Transfer of Youth from Urban to Rural China* (New Haven, CT: Yale University Press, 1977); Lynn T. White III, "The Road to Urumchi: Approved Institutions in Search of Attainable Goals during Pre-1968 Rustication from Shanghai," *China Quarterly* 79 (September 1979): 481–510; and Stanley Rosen, *The Role of Sent-Down Youth in the Chinese Cultural Revolution: The Case of Guangzhou* (Berkeley: Institute of East Asian Studies, University of California, 1981).

21. Lynn T. White III, "Workers Politics in Shanghai," *Journal of Asian Studies* 35 (November 1976): 99–116.

22. See, for example, Merle Goldman, *China's Intellectuals: Advise and Dissent* (Cambridge, MA: Harvard University Press, 1981).

23. A characteristic example of such resourcefulness is an elaborate analysis

based primarily on extended interviews with one informant: Marc J. Blecher and Gordon White, *Micropolitics in Contemporary China: The Cultural Revolution in a Technical Work Unit* (Armonk, NY: M. E. Sharpe, 1979).

24. For example, Roderick MacFarquhar, *The Origins of the Cultural Revolution 1: Contradictions among the People, 1956–1957* (New York: Columbia University Press, 1974).

25. Noteworthy exceptions are Roderick MacFarquhar, *The Origins of the Cultural Revolution 2: The Great Leap Forward, 1958–1960* (New York: Columbia University Press, 1983); Roderick MacFarquhar, *The Origins of the Cultural Revolution 3: The Coming of the Cataclysm, 1961–1966* (New York: Columbia University Press, 1997); and Frederick Teiwes and Warren Sun, *The Tragedy of Lin Biao: Riding the Tiger during the Cultural Revolution* (Honolulu: University of Hawaii Press, 1996).

26. See, for example, Zhonggong zhongyang zuzhibu, *Zhongguo gongchandang zuzhishi ziliao, 1921–1997* [Materials on the organizational history of the Chinese Communist Party, 1921–1997], 19 vols. (Beijing: Zhonggong dangshi chubanshe, 2000). Companion volumes have been published for provinces, municipalities, counties, and city districts.

27. The Harvard-Yenching Library holds more than 300 such titles, the Universities Service Centre Library at the Chinese University of Hong Kong holds more than 150, and the Shanghai Library more than 100.

28. See the sources described in Andrew G. Walder and Yang Su, "The Cultural Revolution in the Countryside: Scope, Timing, and Human Impact," *China Quarterly* 173 (March 2003). The Universities Service Centre Library at the Chinese University of Hong Kong has close to 2,000 such titles in its collection, and the Shanghai Library and Beijing National Library have more extensive holdings. All three libraries have online catalogs. These sources will be discussed in more detail below.

29. For example, Wang Jianying, ed., *Zhongguo gongchandang zuzhishi ziliao huibian: Lingdao jigou yan'ge he chengyuan minglu (zengdingben)* [Collected materials on the organizational history of the Chinese Communist Party: A registry of office-holders and changes in leadership structures (revised and enlarged ed.)] (Beijing: Zhonggong zhongyang dangxiao chubanshe, 1995).

30. See, for example, Shen Xueming and Zheng Jianying, eds., *Zhonggong di yi jie zhi shiwu jie zhongyang weiyuan* [Members of the first through fifteenth Central Committees] (Beijing: Zhongyang wenxian chubanshe, 2001).

31. See, for example, *Liu Shaoqi nianpu* [A chronological biography of Liu Shaoqi] (Beijing: Zhongyang wenxian chubanshe, 1996); *Zhou Enlai nianpu* [A chronological biography of Zhou Enlai] (Beijing: Zhongyang wenxian chubanshe, 1997); Li Lie, ed., *He Long nianpu* [A chronological biography of He Long] (Beijing: Renmin chubanshe, 1996); Liu Shufa, ed., *Chen Yi nianpu* [A chronological

biography of Chen Yi] (Beijing: Renmin chubanshe, 1995); Wang Yang, ed., *Peng Dehuai nianpu* [A chronological biography of Peng Dehuai] (Beijing: Renmin chubanshe, 1998); Xu Zehao, ed., *Wang Jiaxiang nianpu* [A chronological biography of Wang Jiaxiang] (Beijing: Zhongyang wenxian chubanshe, 2001); Zhang Peisen, ed., *Zhang Wentian nianpu* [A chronological biography of Zhang Wentian] (Beijing: Zhongyang wenxian chubanshe, 2000); Zhou Junlun, ed., *Nie Rongzhen nianpu* [A chronological biography of Nie Rongzhen] (Beijing: Renmin chubanshe, 1999); *Chen Pixian nianpu (1916–1995)* [A chronological biography of Chen Pixian, 1916–1995] (Beijing: Zhongyang dangshi chubanshe, 2000). A chronology of Mao Zedong's activities through 1949 has been published, and one for 1949–76 is reportedly in preparation.

32. For example, Zhonggong zhongyang wenxian yanjiushi, ed., *Jianguo yilai Mao Zedong wen'gao, di shi'er ce* [The collected post-Liberation manuscripts of Mao Zedong, vol. 12] (Beijing: Zhongyang wenxian chubanshe, 1995), which covers all of 1966, 1967, and 1968.

33. Wang Li, *Wang Li fansi lu* [Wang Li's memoirs], 2 vols. (Hong Kong: Xianggang beixing chubanshe, 2001); Mu Xin, *Jiehou changyi: Shinian dongluan jishi* [Memories of turmoil: An account of ten years of chaos] (Hong Kong: Xintian chubanshe, 1997); and Liu Zhijian, "Dongluan zhichu de jingli he zaoyu" [My experiences and misfortunes at the beginning of the turmoil], *Zhonggong dangshi ziliao* 74 (June 2000): 23–59.

34. Li Xuefeng, "Wo suo zhidao de 'wen'ge' fadong neiqing" [What I know about the inside story behind the launching of the "Cultural Revolution"], in Zhang Hua and Su Caiqing, eds., *Huishou "wen'ge": Zhongguo shinian "wen'ge" fenxi yu fansi* [The "Cultural Revolution" in retrospect: Analysis and reflections on China's ten-year "Cultural Revolution"], 2 vols. (Beijing: Zhonggong dangshi chubanshe, 1999), 589–604; and Li Xuefeng, "Huiyi 'wenhua da geming' chuqi de 'wushi tian luxian cuowu': Cong '6.18' shijian dao '7.29' dahui" [Recalling the "50-day erroneous line" of the early "Cultural Revolution": From the incident of "June 18" to the "July 29" mass meeting], in ibid., 641–64.

35. Wu De, with Zhu Yuanshi, *Wu De koushu: Shinian fengyu jishi—wo zai Beijing gongzuo de yixie jingli* [Wu De's oral account: Ten years of trial—some of my experiences working in Beijing] (Beijing: Dangdai Zhongguo chubanshe, 2004).

36. Wang Dongxing, *Mao Zedong yu Lin Biao fan'geming jituan de douzheng* [Mao Zedong's struggle with the Lin Biao counterrevolutionary clique] (Beijing: Dangdai Zhongguo chubanshe, 2004).

37. Quan Yanchi, *Yang Chengwu jianzheng wen'ge* [Yang Chengwu's testimony about the Cultural Revolution] (Beijing: Guangming ribao chubanshe, 2004).

38. Zhang Chengxian, "'Wenhua da geming' chuqi de Beida gongzuozu"

[Beijing University's work team in the early stages of the "Cultural Revolution"], *Zhonggong dangshi ziliao* 70 (June 1999): 16–44; and Zhang Chengxian, *Zhang Chengxian huiyilu: Wo qinli de dang de xuanchuan he jiaoyu gongzuo* [Memoirs of Zhang Chengxian: My personal experiences in party propaganda and educational work] (Beijing: Renmin jiaoyu chubanshe, 2002).

39. Guo Yingqiu, with Wang Junyi, "Guo Yingqiu linzhong koushu: 'Wen'ge' qinliji" [Guo Yingqiu's deathbed testimony: A personal account of the "Cultural Revolution"], *Yanhuang chunqiu* 128 (November 2002): 44–53.

40. Xu Jingxian, *Shinian yimeng: Qian Shanghai shiwei shuji Xu Jingxian wen'ge huiyi lu* [Ten years' dream: The Cultural Revolution memoirs of former Shanghai party secretary Xu Jingxian] (Hong Kong: Shidai guoji chuban youxian gongsi, 2004).

41. Liu Zhende, "Jiyao mishu de huiyi" [Reminiscences of a confidential secretary], in Huang Zheng, ed., *Liu Shaoqi de zuihou suiyue, 1966–1969* [Liu Shaoqi's final years] (Beijing: Zhongyang wenxian chubanshe, 1996), 61–125; and Wu Qingtong, *Zhou Enlai zai "wenhua da geming" zhong* [Zhou Enlai in the "Cultural Revolution"], expanded ed. (Beijing: Zhonggong dangshi chubanshe, 2002).

42. For example, Zhejiang Provincial Party Committee Party School, "*Wenhua da geming" shiqi ziliao xuanji* [Selected materials on the "Cultural Revolution" period] (Hangzhou: Zhonggong Zhejiang shengwei dangxiao dangshi jiaoyanshi, 1984).

43. For example, Beijing boli zongchang hongweibing lianluo zhan, ed., *Zhongyang shouzhang jianghua* [Central leaders' speeches], vols. 1–4 (March–May 1967). These four volumes alone contain 1,081 pages of speeches from January 1 to April 30, 1967.

44. Song Yongyi, ed., *Zhongguo wenhua da geming wenku* [Chinese Cultural Revolution database] (Hong Kong: Xianggang Zhongwen daxue Zhongguo yanjiu fuwu zhongxin, 2002).

45. See Andrew G. Walder, "When States Unravel: How China's Cadres Shaped Cultural Revolution Politics," in Kjeld Erik Brødsgaard and Susan Young, eds., *State Capacity in East Asia* (Oxford: Oxford University Press, 2000), 157–84.

46. An example is Schoenhals's study of the operations of the Central Case Examination Group, which shows that red guards worked closely with high level investigation committees and had to petition to get targets out of prison for mass struggle sessions. Michael Schoenhals, "The Central Case Examination Group, 1966–79," *China Quarterly* 145 (March 1996): 87–111.

47. Center for Chinese Research Materials, *Red Guard Publications*, 20 vols. (Washington, D.C.: Association of Research Libraries, 1975). The vast majority of these materials were from Guangzhou and Beijing. Because of the closed nature of China during that period, the materials that found their way overseas either

crossed the border into Hong Kong, or were collected by diplomatic personnel in Beijing and shipped overseas via diplomatic pouch.

48. Center for Chinese Research Materials, *Red Guard Publications, Supplement 1*, 8 vols. (Washington, D.C.: Association of Research Libraries, 1980); and Center for Chinese Research Materials, *Red Guard Publications, Supplement II*, 8 vols. (Oakton, VA: Center for Chinese Research Materials, 1992).

49. Zhou Yuan, ed., *Xinbian hongweibing ziliao*, English title: *A New Collection of Red Guard Publications, Part I, Newspapers*, 20 vols. (Oakton, VA: Center for Chinese Research Materials, 1999).

50. Song Yongyi, ed., *Xinbian hongweibing ziliao*, English title: *A New Collection of Red Guard Publications, Part II: A Special Collection of Newspapers in Beijing Area*, 40 vols. (Oakton, VA: Center for Chinese Research Materials, 2001).

51. The Service Center for Chinese Publications (P.O. Box 24843, Los Angeles, CA 90024-0843) produces reprint editions and has a catalog that includes hundreds of collections of pamphlets, collected wall posters, reference materials, leaders' speeches, and internal party documents.

52. For example, the archive held at Beijing University, which has supported publications by members of the school's party history office. See, for example, Beijing University Party History Office, "Beida shejiao yundong de shishi jingguo" [The course of the Socialist Education movement at Beijing University], *Zhonggong dangshi ziliao* 81 (March 2002): 90–99; and Hao Ping, "Reassessing the Starting Point of the Cultural Revolution," *China Review International* 3 (April 1996): 66–86.

53. See the studies by Anita Chan, Stanley Rosen, and Jonathan Unger cited above; and Gordon A. Bennett and Ronald Montaperto, *Red Guard: The Political Biography of Dai Hsiao-ai* (New York: Doubleday, 1972).

54. For example, Joel Andreas, "Battling over Political and Cultural Power in the Cultural Revolution," *Theory and Society* 31 (August 2002): 463–519, based in part on interviews conducted during a year's residence at Qinghua University.

55. See Bennett and Montaperto, *Red Guard*; Ken Ling, *The Revenge of Heaven: Journal of a Young Chinese* (New York: Putnam, 1972); and Gao Yuan, *Born Red: A Chronicle of the Cultural Revolution* (Stanford, CA: Stanford University Press, 1987).

56. For example, the notorious "conservative" red guard Tan Lifu has published a memoir that detailed his background and experiences during and after the Cultural Revolution: Tan Bin [Tan Lifu], *Chizi baihua* [Empty talk of an innocent] (Beijing: Beijing tushuguan chubanshe, 1996). The memoir of Mei Jianming, a leader of Beijing Geology Institute's East is Red, a key rebel organization, appeared in Xiao Han and Mia Turner, eds., *789 jizhong ying: Zhongguo gaogan zinü zhong yige teshu qunti de gushi* [Concentration camp 789: The story of

a special group of sons and daughters of Chinese high officials] (Ontario, Canada: Mirror Books, 1998). The top leader of the Qinghua University rebel organization that was the factional rival of Kuai Dafu's group has also published a very detailed memoir focused specifically on this two-year struggle: Shen Ruhuai, *Qinghua daxue wen'ge jishi: Yige hongweibing lingdao de zishu* [An account of the Cultural Revolution at Qinghua University: The personal account of a red guard leader] (Hong Kong: Shidai yishu chubanshe, 2004).

57. See Richard Baum, *Burying Mao: Chinese Politics in the Age of Deng Xiaoping* (Princeton, NJ: Princeton University Press, 1994), 58–118; and Lowell Dittmer, "Learning from Trauma: The Cultural Revolution in Post-Mao Politics," in William A. Joseph, Christine P. W. Wong, and David Zweig, eds., *New Perspectives on the Cultural Revolution* (Cambridge, MA: Council on East Asian Studies, Harvard University, 1991), 19–39.

58. See Geremie Barmé and Bennett Lee, eds., *The Wounded: New Stories from the Cultural Revolution* (Hong Kong: Joint Publishing Co., 1979); Perry Link, ed., *Stubborn Weeds: Popular and Controversial Chinese Literature after the Cultural Revolution* (Bloomington: Indiana University Press, 1983); and Perry Link, ed., *Roses and Thorns: The Second Blooming of the Hundred Flowers in Chinese Fiction, 1979–1980* (Berkeley: University of California Press, 1984).

59. See, for example, Perry Link, ed., *People or Monsters? and Other Stories and Reportage from China after Mao* (Bloomington: Indiana University Press, 1983).

60. Some important collections in this genre are "Shangfang tongxun" bianji-shi, *Chunfeng huayu ji* [Spring breezes and rain: A collection] (Beijing: Qunzhong chubanshe, 1981); Feng Jicai, *Yibaige ren de shinian* [One hundred persons' decade] (Nanjing: Jiangsu wenyi chubanshe, 1991); and Xiang Lin and Hong Yu, eds., *Zhongguo xiandai yuanyu jishi* [True accounts of unjust cases in contemporary China] (Hohhot: Nei Menggu renmin chubanshe, 1989). Selected translations were published in Andrew G. Walder and Gong Xiaoxia, eds., "China's Great Terror: New Documentation on the Cultural Revolution," *Chinese Sociology and Anthropology* 26 (Fall 1993): 3–103; and Feng Jicai, *Ten Years of Madness: Oral Histories of China's Cultural Revolution* (San Francisco: China Books and Periodicals, 1996).

61. See the examples cited in Walder and Su, "The Cultural Revolution in the Countryside," 75–77.

62. Zheng Yi, *Hongse jinianbei* [Scarlet memorial] (Taipei: Huashi chubanshe, 1993); and Zheng Yi, *Scarlet Memorial: Tales of Cannibalism in Modern China*, trans. by T. P. Sym (Boulder, CO: Westview, 1996).

63. Zheng Yi's book contains photographs of the cover pages of such reports.

64. Wang Youqin, ed., *Wen'ge shounanzhe: Guanyu pohai, jianjin yu si de xun-fang shilu* [Victims of the Cultural Revolution: An investigative account of persecution, imprisonment, and murder] (Hong Kong: Kaifang zazhi she, 2004).

65. Wang Youqin, "Student Attacks against Teachers: The Revolution of 1966," *Issues and Studies* 37 (March–April 2001): 29–79.

66. For example, *Dangdai Zhongguo de Guangdong* [Contemporary China: Guangdong] (Beijing: Dangdai Zhongguo chubanshe, 1991), 118–19, reports that thirty thousand people were killed in that province during the Cleansing of the Class Ranks campaign in 1968 and 1969.

67. See, for example, Zhou Yixing, ed., *Dangdai Beijing jianshi* [Brief history of contemporary Beijing] (Beijing: Dangdai Zhongguo chubanshe, 1999).

68. See, for example, Zhou Yixing, ed., *Dangdai Beijing dashiji* [Chronology of contemporary Beijing] (Beijing: Dangdai Zhongguo chubanshe, 2003).

69. See, for example, Guangxi wen'ge dashi nianbiao bianxie xiaozu, ed., *Guangxi wen'ge dashi nianbiao* [Chronology of the Cultural Revolution in Guangxi] (Nanning: Guangxi renmin chubanshe, 1990); and Beijing Municipal Party Committee, "Beijing shi 'wenhua da geming' dashiji" [Chronicle of events during the "Cultural Revolution" in Beijing], *Beijing dangshi ziliao tongxun, zengkan* 17 and 18 (May and June) (Zhonggong Beijing shiwei dangshi ziliao zhengji weiyuanhui, 1987).

70. The largest collections in the United States are at the Center for Chinese Studies Library of the University of California, Berkeley, and the Harvard-Yenching Library.

71. The Universities Service Centre Library of the Chinese University of Hong Kong has more than 1,800 titles in open stacks; the Shanghai Municipal Library and the National Library in Beijing have more than 2,000 each. All three libraries have online catalogs that are accessible on the Worldwide Web, although the Beijing Library requires prior registration and a user's card.

72. The accounts of the Cultural Revolution in the county gazetteers from Shaanxi Province average over 10,000 characters, and those from Shanghai just over 7,200. See Walder and Su, "The Cultural Revolution in the Countryside," 81.

73. The county gazetteers from this province reported an average of 581 deaths, by far the highest in the country. See ibid., 91.

74. See, for example, Wang Xuezhen, Wang Xiaoting, Huang Wenyi, and Guo Jianrong, eds., *Beijing daxue jishi (1898–1997)* [A chronology of Beijing University, 1898–1997], 2 vols. (Beijing: Beijing daxue chubanshe, 1998); Fang Huijian and Zhang Sijing, eds., *Qinghua daxue zhi* [Annals of Qinghua University], 2 vols. (Beijing: Qinghua daxue chubanshe, 2001).

75. See, for example, Zhengzhi xueyuan "sixiang zhanxian" bianjishi zhubian, *Chedi fouding "wenhua da geming"* [Thoroughly repudiate the "Cultural Revolution"] (Beijing: Jiefangjun zhengzhi xueyuan chubanshe, 1985); Zhonggong zhongyang wenxian yanjiushi, ed., *Chedi fouding "wenhua da geming"* [Thoroughly repudiate the "Cultural Revolution"] (Beijing: Renmin chubanshe, 1985); Jin

Chunming, *Chedi fouding "wenhua da geming" shi jiang* [Thoroughly repudiate the "Cultural Revolution": Ten lectures] (Beijing: Jiefangjun chubanshe, 1985).

76. "Guanyu jianguo yilai dangde ruogan lishi wenti de jueding" [Resolution on certain questions regarding party history since 1949], June 27, 1981, Sixth Plenum of the Eleventh Central Committee, *Renmin ribao*, July 1, 1981: 1.

77. Wang Nianyi, *Da dongluan de niandai* [Turbulent decade] (Zhengzhou: Henan renmin chubanshe, 1988). Wang also edited an important early collection of Cultural Revolution documents, part of the foundation for his own research: see Wang Nianyi, ed., *"Wenhua da geming" yanjiu ziliao* ["Cultural Revolution" research materials], 3 vols. (Beijing: Zhongguo renmin jiefangjun guofang daxue dangshi dangjian zhenggong jiaoyanshi, 1988).

78. See, for example, Xi Xuan and Jin Chunming, *"Wenhua da geming" jianshi* [Brief history of the "Cultural Revolution"] (Beijing: Zhonggong dangshi chubanshe, 2003).

79. See, for example, He Yuan and Zhang Tuosheng, "Dangde ba jie shiyizhong quanhui pingshu" [A commentary on the Eleventh Plenum of the Eighth Central Committee], in Zhang Hua and Su Caiqing, eds., *Huishou wen'ge*, 665–87; Liu Jianhui, "'Wenhua da geming' chuqi dang zhongyang jiankang liliang zhizhi zuoqing cuowu de sici zhongda douzheng" [Four major struggles in the party center to resist leftist errors in the early stage of the "Cultural Revolution"], *Zhonggong dangshi ziliao* 68 (December 1998): 124–45; Su Caiqing, "'Wen'ge' chuqi sange huihe de douzheng" [Three rounds of political struggle in the early stages of the "Cultural Revolution"], in Zhang Hua and Su Caiqing, eds., *Huishou wen'ge*, 724–57; Wang Nianyi, "Ping 'pipan zichan jieji fandong luxian'" [A commentary on "criticize the bourgeois reactionary line"], in ibid., 758–73.

80. See, for example, Tang Shaojie, *Yiye zhichun: Qinghua daxue 1968 nian "Bairi da wudou"* [An episode in the Cultural Revolution: The 1968 hundred-day war at Qinghua University] (Hong Kong: Zhongwen daxue chubanshe, 2003); Xu Youyu, *Xingxing sese de zaofan: Hongweibing jingshen suzhi de xingcheng ji yanbian* [Rebellion of all hues: The formation and evolution of red guard mentalities] (Hong Kong: Xianggang Zhongwen daxue chubanshe, 1999). See also Yin Hongbiao, "Hongweibing yundong shuping" [An overview of the red guard movement], in Zhang Huan and Su Caiqing, eds., *Huishou wen'ge*, 688–723.

81. See Bu Weihua, "Guanyu 'wen'ge' zhong Beijing de 'tianpai' he 'dipai'" [On the "heaven" and "earth" factions during Beijing's "Cultural Revolution"], *Zhonggong dangshi ziliao* 73 (March 2000): 100–126; Tang Shaojie, "Cong Qinghua daxue de liangpai tan 'wenhua da geming' qunzhong zuzhi jiegou, gongneng" [Structure and function of "Cultural Revolution" mass organizations: The case of the two factions at Qinghua University], *Zhonggong dangshi ziliao* 72 (September 1999): 66–81; Yin Hongbiao, "'Wenhua da geming' zhong de shehuixing maodun"

[Social contradictions in the "Cultural Revolution"], *Zhonggong dangshi yanjiu* 2 (1997): 77–82.

82. See Bu Weihua, "'Huoshao Yingguo daibanchu' shimo" [The story behind "torching the British diplomatic offices"], *Zhonggong dangshi ziliao* 86 (June 2003): 135–40.

83. See Chen Donglin, "'Wenhua da geming' qunzhong zuzhi baokan yanjiu" [A study of the publications of mass organizations during the "Cultural Revolution"], *Zhonggong dangshi ziliao* 76 (December 2000): 137–52.

84. See Bu Weihua, "Qinghua fuzhong hongweibing chengli shimo" [The story behind the founding of the Qinghua High School red guards], *Zhonggong dangshi ziliao* 70 (June 1999): 96–127; Bu Weihua, "Qinghua fuzhong hongweibing chengli hou de yixie qingkuang" [Some circumstances after the establishment of the Qinghua University red guards], *Zhonggong dangshi ziliao* 80 (December 2001): 126–46.

85. See Mu Xin, "'Quanguo di yi zhang dazibao' chulong jingguo" [How the "the nation's first wall poster" was cooked up], *Zhonggong dangshi ziliao* 75 (September 2000): 166–73; He Luo and Meng Jin, "Quanguo 'di yi zhang dazibao' chulong zhenxiang" [The real story behind the nation's "first wall poster"], *Zhonggong dangshi ziliao* 83 (September 2002): 113–27; and Liu Yigao, "Cong quanguo 'di yi zhang dazibao' he Xiaogang 'hongshou yin' tanqi" [About the nation's "first wall poster" and the Xiaogang village "red fingerprint"], *Zhonggong dangshi ziliao* 87 (September 2003): 144–60.

86. See, for example, Zhang Hua and Su Caiqing, eds., *Huishou wen'ge*; and Liu Qingfeng, ed., *Wenhua da geming: Shishi yu yanjiu* [The Cultural Revolution: Evidence and analysis] (Hong Kong: Xianggang Zhongwen daxue chubanshe, 1996).

87. Jin Chunming, Huang Yuchong, and Chang Huimin, eds., *"Wen'ge" shiqi guaishi guaiyu* [Odd episodes and terminology of the "Cultural Revolution" period] (Beijing: Qiushi chubanshe, 1989); Chao Feng, ed., *"Wenhua da geming" cidian* ["Cultural Revolution" dictionary] (Hong Kong: Ganglong chubanshe, 1993).

88. See, for example, *Tianfan difu kaierkang: Wuchan jieji wenhua da geming dashiji (1963.9–1967.10)* [Deep outrage that moved heaven and earth: Chronicle of major Cultural Revolution events (September 1963–October 1967)] (Beijing: Beijing dizhi xueyuan Dongfanghong bianji bu, 1967). This book-length document was also serialized in *Dongfang hong*, the newspaper of the East is Red faction in the Beijing Geology Institute between September 1967 and February 1968.

89. Examples of the last include accounts of the impact of the Cultural Revolution on the careers of professionals, bureaucrats, and sent-down youth. See Andrew G. Walder, Bobai Li, and Donald Treiman, "Politics and Life Chances in a State Socialist Regime: Dual Career Paths into the Urban Chinese Elite, 1949

to 1996," *American Sociological Review* 65 (April 2000): 191–209; and Xueguang Zhou and Liren Hou, "Children of the Cultural Revolution: The State and the Life Course in the People's Republic of China," *American Sociological Review* 64 (February 1999): 12–36.

90. Teiwes and Sun, *The Tragedy of Lin Biao*; and Jin Qiu, *The Culture of Power: The Lin Biao Incident in the Cultural Revolution* (Stanford, CA: Stanford University Press, 1999).

91. Roderick MacFarquhar and Michael Schoenhals, *The Cultural Revolution* (Cambridge, MA: Harvard University Press, forthcoming in 2006).

92. See Notes 15 and 17 above.

93. Andrew G. Walder, "Beijing Red Guard Factionalism: Social Interpretations Reconsidered," *Journal of Asian Studies* 61, no. 2 (2002): 437–71.

94. Wang Youqin has been the most determined chronicler of red guard violence. See the sources cited in notes 64 and 65 above.

95. These terms are borrowed from Ci Jiwei, *Dialectic of the Chinese Revolution: From Utopianism to Hedonism* (Stanford, CA: Stanford University Press, 1994).

96. Richard Baum, "The Cultural Revolution in the Countryside: Anatomy of a Limited Revolution," in Thomas W. Robinson, ed., *The Cultural Revolution in China* (Berkeley: University of California Press, 1971), 367–479.

97. See Notes 60–62 above; and Edward Friedman, Paul G. Pickowicz, and Mark Selden, *Revolution, Resistance and Reform in Village China* (New Haven, CT: Yale University Press, 2005).

98. Dongping Han, *The Unknown Cultural Revolution: Educational Reforms and Their Impact on China's Rural Development, 1966–1976* (New York: Garland, 2000); and Dongping Han, "Impact of the Cultural Revolution on Rural Education and Economic Development in Jimo County," *Modern China* 27, no. 1 (January 2001): 59–90; Mobo Gao, *Gao Village: A Portrait of Rural Life in Modern China* (Honolulu: University of Hawai'i Press, 1999).

Chapter 2: Passion, Reflection, and Survival

INTERVIEWS

Following is basic information on the interviewees (all former students of Qinghua) mentioned in the notes to this chapter: name (when the name has already been made public), gender, year the individual entered Qinghua, family origin, relationship to the Youth League and party.

1. Anonymous. Male. 1963. Revolutionary cadre background. Party member.
2. Anonymous. Male. 1965. Poor peasant background. Youth League member.
3. Anonymous. Female. 1964. White-collar employee background. Party member.

4. Ji Peng. Male. 1965. Revolutionary cadre background. Party member. Leader of the Fourteens.

5. Wang Fan. Male. 1965. White-collar employee (intellectual). Probationary party member.

6. Sun Nutao. Male. 1960. Poor peasant background. Not party member and had withdrawn from the Youth League. Leader of the Fourteens.

7. Anonymous. Male. 1965. Intellectual background. Not Youth League member.

8. Anonymous. Male. 1965. Intellectual background; father had "political problems." Youth League member.

9. Anonymous. Female. 1961. Revolutionary cadre background. Party member.

10. Shen Ruhuai. Male. 1964. Poor peasant background. Party member. Leader of the Fourteens.

11. Anonymous. Male. 1964. Non-party cadre background. Youth League member.

12. Wu Dong. Male. 1963. Revolutionary soldier background. Leader of the Eights.

13. Kuai Dafu. Male. 1963. Lower-middle peasant / commune cadre background. Youth League member. Leader of the Jinggangshan Corps.

I would especially like to thank these thirteen interviewees who, since we first met in December 2002, have patiently answered endless questions, providing over fifty hours of interview records.

1. Wang Fan interview (no. 5). Wang Fan is a pseudonym.

2. Ibid.

3. Kuai Dafu interview (no. 13); Wang Li, *Wang Li fansi lu* [Wang Li's memoirs] (Hong Kong: Beixing chubanshe, 2001), 606.

4. Kuai Dafu interview (no. 13).

5. Anita Chan, Stanley Rosen, and Jonathan Unger, "Students and Class Warfare: The Social Roots of the Red Guard Conflict in Guangzhou (Canton)," *China Quarterly* 83 (September 1980): 397–446; Stanley Rosen, *Red Guard Factionalism and the Cultural Revolution in Guangzhou (Canton)* (Boulder, CO: Westview, 1982).

6. Chan, Rosen, and Unger, "Students and Class Warfare," 397.

7. Andrew G. Walder, "Beijing Red Guard Factionalism: Social Interpretations Reconsidered," *Journal of Asian Studies* 61, no. 2 (2002): 437–71.

8. Ibid., 463.

9. Rosen, *Red Guard Factionalism*, 112.

10. Liu Guokai and Anita Chan, *A Brief Analysis of the Cultural Revolution* (Armonk, NY: M. E. Sharpe, 1987); Gordon A. Bennett and Ronald N. Montap-

erto, *Red Guard: The Political Biography of Dai Hsiao-ai* (Gloucester, MA: Anchor Books, 1980).

11. William Hinton, *Hundred Day War: The Cultural Revolution at Tsinghua University* (New York: Monthly Review Press, 1973).

12. I am inspired by Elizabeth J. Perry and Li Xun's approach in looking at the leaders. Elizabeth J. Perry and Li Xun, *Proletarian Power: Shanghai in the Cultural Revolution* (Boulder, CO: Westview, 1997), 5.

13. Li Chuanxin, ed., *Qinghua renwuzhi* [Eminent people of Qinghua University] (Beijing: Qinghua daxue chubanshe, 1995), 40–41; Mao Zedong, *Mao zhuxi lun jiaoyu geming* [Chairman Mao on revolution in education] (Beijing: Renmin chubanshe, 1966), 11.

14. Mao Zedong, *Mao zhuxi lun jiaoyu geming*, 10–11.

15. Fang Huijian and Zhang Sijing, eds., *Qinghua daxue zhi* [Annals of Qinghua University] (Beijing: Qinghua daxue chubanshe, 2001), 102–3.

16. Ibid., 443.

17. Ibid., 162.

18. Ibid., 11.

19. Li Chuanxin, *Qinghua renwuzhi*, 40–41.

20. Interviews no. 1 and 9. Also, see Fang Huijian and Zhang Sijing, eds., *Qinghua daxue zhi*, 299–300.

21. Interviews no. 1, 2, 3, and 11. Students who felt pressured and excluded were generally of two kinds: disadvantaged students who could not keep up with their studies because of a poor academic foundation (many of whom came from the inland countryside and had trouble learning foreign languages), and those who had allegedly made counterrevolutionary comments about the school leaders or had really "bad" class labels.

22. Fang Huijian and Zhang Sijing, eds., *Qinghua daxue zhi*, 480.

23. Wang Fan interview (no. 5).

24. Fang Huijian and Zhang Sijing, eds., *Qinghua daxue zhi*, 537. By contrast, the average salary for Qinghua workers was only 52 yuan.

25. Ibid., 822.

26. Ibid., 836.

27. Tao Dejian, *Tao Dejian huiyilu: Fengyu rensheng* [Memoirs of Tao Dejian: A life of hardships], www.taosl.net/fy001.htm (April 16, 2003). Tao Dejian was a member of a party branch study group before the Cultural Revolution. In the Cultural Revolution, she cofounded the Red Teachers' Federation (Hong jiao lian), a teachers' organization that supported Kuai Dafu.

28. Fang Huijian and Zhang Sijing, eds., *Qinghua daxue zhi*, 818. At the end of December 1965, Qinghua had 3,287 party members, which was 20.1 percent of the school's entire population (16,378). Of Qinghua's students and staff, 34.7 percent

of professors, 51 percent of lecturers, 53 percent of assistant lecturers, and 12.4 percent of undergraduates were party members.

29. Ibid., 813. This is the number for 1966.

30. Ibid., 229.

31. Ibid., 231. "Student cadres" is a translation of *xuesheng ganbu,* which included the party and Youth League branch secretaries and the chairpersons of each class, and other student organizers at the school, department, or class level. Political counselors were also included in "student cadres" because they were also students. Later, when I use the term "cadres," I do not include student cadres, only teaching and administrative cadres.

32. Wang Fan interview (no. 5).

33. Fang Huijian and Zhang Sijing, eds., *Qinghua daxue zhi,* 231–32.

34. Bo Yibo, *Ruogan zhongda juece yu shijian de huigu* [A review of certain major decisions and incidents] (Beijing: Renmin chubanshe, 1997), vol. 2, 1132–33. On August 5, 6, 9, and again on September 24 of 1962, Mao explicitly emphasized the importance and urgency of conducting class struggle.

35. Li Chuanxin, *Qinghua renwuzhi,* 47. Starting from 1959, Jiang Nanxiang was the vice-minister of Education, and became the minister in 1962. Qinghua was always in a privileged position under his influence.

36. Wang Fan interview (no. 5); Shen Ruhuai interview (no. 10); Interview no. 1.

37. Interview no. 9. The interviewee was a political counselor and knew her students well.

38. Mao Zedong, *Mao zhuxi lun jiaoyu geming,* 16–17.

39. Liu Bing, *Fengyu suiyue* [Years of hardship] (Beijing: Qinghua daxue chubanshe, 1998), 4.

40. Mao Zedong, *Mao zhuxi lun jiaoyu geming,* 27–28.

41. Interview no. 1.

42. Mao Zedong, *Mao zhuxi lun jiaoyu geming,* 18–21. See also Xu Youyu, *Xingxing sese de zaofan: Hongweibing jingshen suzhi de xingcheng ji yanbian* [Rebellion of all hues: The formation and transformation of the red guard mentalities] (Hong Kong: Xianggang Zhongwen daxue chubanshe, 1999), 30–31.

43. Wang Fan interview (no. 5); Ji Peng interview (no. 4); Interviews no. 1 and 2. These four red guards came from divergent social, political, and economic backgrounds. However, on the eve of the Cultural Revolution, politics had captured their attention and they actively applied Mao's principles in judging their school leaders, teachers, and classmates.

44. "Zhongguo gongchandang zhongyang weiyuanhui tongzhi" [The May sixteenth circular from the Chinese Communist Party Central Committee], in Wang Nianyi, ed., *"Wenhua da geming" yanjiu ziliao* ["Cultural Revolution" research

materials] (Beijing: Zhongguo renmin jiefangjun guofang daxue dangshi dangjian zhenggong jiaoyanshi, 1988), vol. 1, 1–4.

45. Liu Bing, *Fengyu suiyue*, 70.

46. "Chuji renmen linghun de da geming" [A revolution to touch the soul], *Renmin ribao*, June 2, 1966.

47. Tang Shaojie and Ji Peng, "Fengyu ru pan: Qinghua daxue Jinggangshan bingtuan de xingshuai" [Stormy times: The rise and fall of the Jinggangshan Corps of Qinghua University], unpublished manuscript, 12. This manuscript is based on Tang Shaojie's interviews with Ji Peng, an important red guard leader at Qinghua University. Special thanks to Tang Shaojie and Ji Peng for giving me their source-filled manuscript.

48. Shen Ruhuai, *Qinghua daxue wen'ge jishi: Yige hongweibing lingxiu de zishu* [The Cultural Revolution at Qinghua University: An autobiography of a red guard leader] (Hong Kong: Shidai yishu chubanshe, 2004), 6. Special thanks to Shen Ruhuai for giving me his detailed new publication.

49. Interview no. 3. As the party secretary of her class, this interviewee received the order to organize students to write posters to protect Jiang Nanxiang.

50. Shen Ruhuai, *Qinghua daxue wen'ge jishi*, 7.

51. Telephone interview with Tang Shaojie on December 13, 2002; information based on his interview with He Pengfei.

52. Interviews no. 7 and 8.

53. Tang Shaojie and Ji Peng, "Fengyu ru pan," 13.

54. Ibid., 17.

55. Kuai Dafu interview (no. 13); Interviews no. 1 and 2.

56. Interview no. 1.

57. Liu Bing, *Fengyu suiyue*, 78.

58. Interview no. 1.

59. Kuai Dafu interview (no. 13).

60. Kuai Dafu, "Gongzuozu wang nali qu?" [Where is the work team going?], in Qinghua daxue Jinggangshan hongweibing xuanchuandui, ed., *Qinghua daxue dazibao xuan (Kuai Dafu tongzhi de dazibao)* [Selected wall posters of Qinghua University (wall posters by Comrade Kuai Dafu)] (Beijing: 1967), printed pamphlet, 3–4. Special thanks to Andrew Walder for sharing this document with me.

61. The poster was written by Kuai's friend Liu Caitang. Ibid., 4.

62. Kuai Dafu, "Ye Lin tongzhi, zheshi zenmo yihuishi?" [Comrade Ye Lin, what is going on?], in Qinghua daxue Jinggangshan hongweibing xuanchuandui, *Qinghua daxue dazibao xuan*, 7.

63. Tang Shaojie and Ji Peng, "Fengyu ru pan," 20.

64. Kuai Dafu, "6 yue 24 ri wan 7 dian ban Qinghua daxue 'geming zuopai' tong Kuai Dafu deng jinxing da bianlun: Kuai Dafu di yi ci fayan" [The great de-

bate between 'revolutionary leftists' and Kuai Dafu et al. on June 24 at 7:30 p.m.: Kuai Dafu's first speech], in Qinghua daxue Jinggangshan hongweibing xuanchuandui, *Qinghua daxue dazibao xuan*, 15.

65. Kuai Dafu interview (no. 13). Also, Tang Shaojie and Ji Peng, "Fengyu ru pan," 21–22.

66. Wang Fan interview (no. 5).

67. Kuai Dafu, "Kuai Dafu zai 6 yue 27 ri bianlun hui shang de fayan: Di er ci fayan" [Speeches of Kuai Dafu at the June 27 debate meeting: Kuai Dafu's second speech], in Qinghua daxue Jinggangshan hongweibing xuanchuandui, *Qinghua daxue dazibao xuan*, 30–31.

68. Kuai Dafu interview (no. 13); Wang Fan interview (no. 5); Interviews no. 2 and 12.

69. Tang Shaojie and Ji Peng, "Fengyu ru pan," 22. A ten-thousand-person demonstration was organized by the work team to attack Kuai after the June 24 debate.

70. Ibid., 21–22.

71. Shen Ruhuai, *Qinghua daxue wen'ge jishi*, 19.

72. Tang Shaojie and Ji Peng, "Fengyu ru pan," 25.

73. Kuai Dafu interview (no. 13). Kuai had a conversation with Wang Li, a member of the Central Cultural Revolution Small Group, after both of them were released from prison. Wang Li told Kuai that Mao personally notified his staff to let Kuai participate in the meeting of the Cultural Revolution activists.

74. Kuai Dafu interview (no. 13). At Kuai's July 30 meeting, which was held at Qinghua, He Pengfei stood guard outside and was extremely nervous about what Kuai was saying. He interrupted several times until Zhou Enlai, whom he addressed as "Uncle Zhou," got angry and ordered him out. This meeting lasted for three hours, but by the end Kuai had not finished the story of his conflicts with the work team. Thus, Zhou sent his chauffeur to pick up Kuai and bring him to meet with Zhou—the second time they had met—at the Great Hall of the People in the evening of August 1. Kuai brought two of his close comrades with him this time; two provincial CCP secretaries were also present. Kuai later realized that his story of the conflict between him and the work team was used by Mao Zedong as evidence to discredit Wang Guangmei and Liu Shaoqi. See also *Zhou Enlai nianpu* [A chronological biography of Zhou Enlai] (Beijing: Zhonggong zhongyang wenxian chubanshe, 1997), vol. 3, 44.

75. Interview no. 9. This interviewee refused to join Pinxie when she was invited.

76. Zhou Enlai, "1966 nian 8 yue 4 ri zai Qinghua daxue jianghua" [Speech at Qinghua University on August 4, 1966], at http://museums.cnd.org/CR/cdocs.htm (April 8, 2003).

77. Shen Ruhuai, *Qinghua daxue wen'ge jishi*, 20.

78. Shen Ruhuai interview (no. 10); Wu Dong interview (no. 12).

79. Shen Ruhuai, *Qinghua daxue wen'ge jishi*, 22.

80. "Zhonggong zhongyang guanyu wuchan jieji wenhua da geming de jue-ding" [Decision concerning the Great Proletarian Cultural Revolution], in Wang Nianyi, ed., *"Wenhua da geming" yanjiu ziliao*, vol. 1, 72–77. This document is also known as "the sixteen points." See also, Shen Ruhuai interview (no. 10).

81. Mao Zedong, "Paoda silingbu: Wode di yi zhang dazibao" [Bombard the headquarters: My first big character poster], in Wang Nianyi, ed., *"Wenhua da geming" yanjiu ziliao*, vol. 1, 70. See also, Liu Bing, *Fengyu suiyue*, 86.

82. "Women suo zhidao de 8.19 shijian" [The August 19 incident that we know], in Qinghua daxue Mao Zedong sixiang hongweibing Dongfanghong gongshe, ed., *Qinghua daxue dazibao xuanbian* [Selected wall posters of Qinghua University] (Beijing: 1966), mimeographed pamphlet, 1–3.

83. Sun Nutao interview (no. 6); Shen Ruhuai interview (no. 10); Shen Ruhuai, *Qinghua daxue wen'ge jishi*, 25–26.

84. Tang Shaojie and Ji Peng, "Fengyu ru pan," 50.

85. Shen Ruhuai, *Qinghua daxue wen'ge jishi*, 28.

86. Sun Nutao, "Geming shaoshu zan" [Praise for the revolutionary minority], in Qinghua daxue Mao Zedong sixiang hongweibing Dongfanghong gongshe, *Qinghua daxue dazibao xuanbian*, 24–25; Sun Nutao interview (no. 6).

87. Tang Shaojie and Ji Peng, "Fengyu ru pan," 127.

88. Ibid., 128.

89. Interviews no. 3 and 9.

90. Tang Shaojie and Ji Peng, "Fengyu ru pan," 43. On August 19, He Pengfei and other Qinghua University Red Guard leaders coauthored a poster targeting Wang Guangmei. This signified a policy shift of the children of high-level cadres.

91. "Zhonggong zhongyang guanyu wuchan jieji wenhua da geming de jue-ding," 72.

92. Tang Shaojie and Ji Peng, "Fengyu ru pan," 47; Interview no. 1.

93. Ji Peng interview (no. 4); Interview no. 1.

94. Shen Ruhuai, *Qinghua daxue wen'ge jishi*, 32.

95. Wang Fan interview (no. 5).

96. "Jinggangshan hongweibing choubei jianli weiyuanhui di yi hao jueyi" [The first resolution of the preparatory committee of the Jinggangshan red guards], in Song Yongyi, ed., *Zhongguo wenhua da geming wenku* [Chinese Cultural Revolution database] (Hong Kong: Xianggang Zhongwen daxue Zhongguo yanjiu fuwu zhongxin, 2002).

97. "Jinggangshan hongweibing choubei jianli weiyuanhui di er hao jueyi"

[The second resolution of the preparatory committee of the Jinggangshan Red Guards], in Song Yongyi, ed., *Zhongguo wenhua da geming wenku.*

98. "Jinggangshan hongweibing xuanyan" [The declaration of Jinggangshan Red Guards], in Song Yongyi, ed., *Zhongguo wenhua da geming wenku.*

99. "Zhonggong zhongyang pifa Junwei Zongzheng 'guanyu jundui yuanxiao wuchan jieji wenhua da geming de jinji zhishi'" [The Chinese Communist Party Central Committee transmits "The Central Military Committee's urgent directive concerning conducting the Cultural Revolution in military schools"], in Wang Niangyi, ed., *"Wenhua da geming" yanjiu ziliao*, vol. 1, 132–33.

100. Wang Fan interview (no. 5).

101. Shen Ruhuai interview (no. 10). Before the unification, the Eights' leaders Tang Wei and Chen Yuyan split with Wu Dong because they wanted to give Kuai's "rebellious spirit" more credit. They formed a subsection, the Eights' Headquarters, under the Mao Zedong Thought Red Guards.

102. Kuai Dafu interview (no. 13).

103. Qinghua daxue Jinggangshan lianhe zongbu yiwangxi zhandouzu, ed., *Qinghua daxue Jinggangshan bingtuan wuchan jieji wenhua da geming dashiji* [The chronology of the Qinghua Jinggangshan corps in the Great Proletarian Cultural Revolution] (Beijing: 1968), mimeographed pamphlet, December 25, 1966. Hereafter, *Dashiji.*

104. Tang Shaojie and Ji Peng, "Fengyu ru pan," 67.

105. *Dashiji*, December 30, 1966.

106. Shen Ruhuai, *Qinghua daxue wen'ge jishi*, 51; Interview no. 9.

107. Ji Peng interview (no. 4).

108. Shen Ruhuai, *Qinghua daxue wen'ge jishi*, 51.

109. *Dashiji*, January 6, 1967; Shen Ruhuai interview (no. 10).

110. *Dashiji*, December 20, 1966.

111. Wang Fan interview (no. 5); Sun Nutao interview (no. 6).

112. *Dashiji*, January 3, 1967; Ji Peng interview (no. 4). In Ji Peng's eyes, Kuai's only qualification was that he rebelled against the work team, which was not enough of a credential to be the commander in chief of all of Qinghua's red guards.

113. *Dashiji*, January 2–11, 1967; Shen Ruhuai interview (no. 10); Shen Ruhuai, *Qinghua daxue wen'ge jishi*, 57. These five regiments were: the Mao Zedong Thought Regiment (Mao Zedong sixiang zongdui), the Eights' Regiment (Baba zongdui), the East is Red Regiment (Dongfanghong zongdui), Chairman Mao's Guards (Mao zhuxi qingwei tuan), and the Tiananmen Regiment (Tiananmen zongdui).

114. *Dashiji*, January 22, 1967.

115. Ibid., January 26, 1967.

116. Ibid., January 22 and 26, 1967.

117. Ibid., February 7 and 15, 1967.

118. Ibid., February 26, 1967.

119. "Lun geming de san jiehe" [On the revolutionary "triple alliance" combination], *Hongqi* 5 (March 30, 1967).

120. *Dashiji*, March 1 and 7, 1967; Shen Ruhuai interview (no. 10).

121. "'Daji yidapian, baohu yixiaocuo' shi zichan jieji fandong luxian de yige zucheng bufen (1966 nian 6, 7 yue Qinghua daxue gongzuozu zai ganbu wenti shang zhixing zichan jieji fandong luxian de qingkuang diaocha)" ["Attacking many to protect a few" is the reactionary capitalist line (Investigation of the Qinghua University work team's reactionary capitalist line on the cadre problem during June and July 1966)], *Hongqi* 5 (March 30, 1967).

122. "Bixu zhengque di duidai ganbu" [We must treat cadres correctly], *Hongqi* 4 (March 1, 1967).

123. Shen Ruhuai interview (no. 10).

124. *Dashiji*, April 1, 1967.

125. Ibid., April 2, 1967. See also, Tao Dejian, *Tao Dejian huiyilu*.

126. Shen Ruhuai interview (no. 10); Ji Peng interview (no. 4).

127. *Dashiji*, April 13, 1967.

128. Ji Peng interview (no. 4); Sun Nutao interview (no. 6).

129. *Dashiji*, April 29, 1967.

130. Ibid., May 3, 1967.

131. Ibid., April 24, 1967. This argument was expressed in a poster by the Fourteens, titled "Long Live the Fourteens—on the New Stage of the Qinghua Cultural Revolution," written by Sun Nutao's battle team.

132. Ibid., April 22, 1967. This argument was expressed in a poster by the Fourteens entitled "Young Revolutionaries Should Have the Courage to Rehabilitate Cadres," written by Shen Ruhuai's battle team; Shen Ruhuai interview (no. 10).

133. Ibid., May 9, 1967. This argument was expressed in a poster by Jinggangshan Headquarters entitled "Completely Criticize the New-Stage Argument."

134. Ibid., May 10, 1967.

135. Ibid., April 22, 1967. This argument was expressed in a poster by the Fourteens titled "Young Revolutionaries Should Have the Courage to Rehabilitate Cadres," written by Shen Ruhuai's battle team.

136. Ibid., April 14, 1967, and May 29, 1967. On April 14, 1967, seven hundred people attended the founding meeting of the April Fourteen Liaison. On May 29, 1967, two thousand people attended the founding meeting of the April Fourteen Headquarters.

137. Shen Ruhuai, *Qinghua daxue wen'ge jishi*, 115.

138. Ji Peng interview (no. 4); Wang Fan interview (no. 5); Shen Ruhuai interview (no. 10); Interview no. 9.

139. Zhou Quanying, "Wo xinzhong de wen'ge" [The Cultural Revolution in my heart], *Ershiyi shiji* 52 (April 1999): 139–43. Zhou came from a very "bad" class background. His grandfather was a big landlord in Zhejiang, and his father was an officer in the army of the Nationalist general Fu Zuoyi and was persecuted in the rectification campaign in the 1950s. Also, interviewee no. 7 came from a "bad" class background and was consequently excluded from the Youth League. Still, he joined the Fourteens and stuck with the group till the last moment of the armed fight.

140. *Dashiji*, May 20, 1967.

141. Shen Ruhuai interview (no. 10).

142. Interview no. 7 and 9.

143. Ji Peng interview (no. 4).

144. *Dashiji*, July 21, 1967.

145. Ibid., July 29, 1967.

146. Shen Ruhuai interview (no. 10).

147. *Dashiji*, June 12, 14, and 17, 1967.

148. Ibid., August 22, 1967.

149. *Weida lingxiu Mao zhuxi he tade qinmi zhanyou Lin fuzhuxi zhaojian shoudu dazhuanyuanxiao hongdaihui fuzeren Nie Yuanzi, Kuai Dafu, Han Aijing, Tan Houlan, Wang Dabin tongzhi shi de zhongyao jianghua* [The important talk by the great leader Chairman Mao and his close comrade Vice-Chairman Lin in the meeting with leaders of the Beijing college red guards, Comrades Nie Yuanzi, Kuai Dafu, Han Aijing, Tan Houlan, and Wang Dabin] (Beijing: 1968), printed pamphlet, 3 and 20. Hereafter cited as *Jianghua*. Special thanks to Richard Siao for sharing his original document with me.

150. Zhou Quanying, "414 sichao bisheng!" [The Fourteens' Spirit Shall Win!], in Song Yongyi and Sun Dajin, eds., *Wenhua da geming he tade yiduan sichao* [Heterodox thoughts during the Cultural Revolution] (Hong Kong: Tianyuan shuwu, 1996), 390–408.

151. *Jinggangshan* (August 24, 1967), in Zhou Yuan, ed., *Xinbian hongweibing ziliao*, English title: *A New Collection of Red Guard Publications, Part I, Newspapers* (Oakton, VA: Center for Chinese Research Materials, 1999), vol. 8, 3890–92.

152. *Dashiji*, November 18 and 20, 1967.

153. Sun Nutao interview (no. 6). The first big armed battle took place in January 1968. Only after the intervention of the Beijing garrison under General Li Zhongqi did the two factions stop fighting. However, even at the negotiation table, in the presence of General Li, the two factions kept cursing each other.

154. Xu Youyu, *Xingxing sese de zaofan*, 178.

155. *Jianghua*, 4. Mao stated here that the center had already told students to stop fighting. On March 24 and 27, Lin Biao and Zhou Enlai respectively gave talks about stopping armed fights. Huang Yongsheng also later announced that order at a ten-thousand-person mass meeting.

156. Tang Shaojie, "Hongweibing de sangzhong: Qinghua daxue bairi da wu-dou" [The death knell of the red guard movement: The hundred day war in Qinghua University], in Liu Qingfeng, ed., *Wenhua da geming: Shishi yu yanjiu* [The Cultural Revolution: Evidence and analysis] (Hong Kong: Xianggang Zhongwen daxue chubanshe, 1996), 73–74.

157. *Jianghua*, 1.

158. Ibid., 2.

159. Ibid., 3.

160. Ibid., 16.

161. Red guard poem, written in 1968 by interviewee no. 2.

Chapter 3: To Protect and Preserve

ABBREVIATIONS USED IN THE NOTES

KFDJN   Ya Zi and Liang Zi, *Kongfu da jienan* [Great calamity of the Confucius Mansion] (Hong Kong: Tiandi tushu youxian gongsi, 1992)

WDGW   Song Yongyi, ed., *Zhongguo wenhua da geming wenku* [Chinese Cultural Revolution database] (Hong Kong: Xianggang Zhongwen daxue Zhongguo yanjiu fuwu zhongxin, 2002).

XBHZL   Song Yongyi, ed., *Xin bian hongweibing ziliao*; English title: *A New Collection of Red Guard Publications, Part II, vol. 29* (Oakton, VA: Center for Chinese Research Materials, 2001).

1. XBHZL, 11351; KFDJN, 27. Kong was the surname of Confucius (Kong Qiu). The three famed sites of Qufu, namely the Confucius Forest (Konglin), Confucius Mansion (Kongfu), and Confucius Temple (Kongmiao) are collectively known as the "Three Confucian Sites" (San Kong). When referring to all three as a whole, I will use this collective term. Since the sources use "Kongmiao," "Kongjia dian," and "Kongfu" interchangeably to designate both the Confucius Temple and Confucius Mansion—which are adjacent—I will refer to these two together as the "Confucius Temple complex." The Confucius Forest, home to the Kong family graveyard, is located about two kilometers north of the complex.

2. Michael Schoenhals, *China's Cultural Revolution, 1966–1969: Not a Dinner Party* (Armonk, NY: M. E. Sharpe, 1996), 3.

3. Barbara Barnouin and Yu Changgen, *Ten Years of Turbulence: The Chinese*

Cultural Revolution (London: Kegan Paul International, 1993), 98; Yan Jiaqi and Gao Gao, *Turbulent Decade: A History of the Cultural Revolution* (Honolulu: University of Hawai'i Press, 1996), 76; Yu Hui, ed., *Hongweibing mi lu* [Insiders' records of red guards] (Beijing: Tuanjie chubanshe, 1993), 193.

4. Yan Jiaqi and Gao Gao, *Turbulent Decade*, 72–73; Simon Leys, *Chinese Shadows* (New York: Viking, 1977), 99; Yang Kelin, ed., *Wenhua da geming bowuguan* [Cultural Revolution museum] (Hong Kong: Dongfang chubanshe youxian gongsi, 1995), vol. 1, 138–87.

5. Maurice Meisner, *Mao's China and After: A History of the People's Republic*, 3rd edition (New York: Free Press, 1999), 321.

6. Schoenhals, *China's Cultural Revolution*, 138.

7. Ibid., 212.

8. James C. Scott, *Weapons of the Weak: Everyday Forms of Peasant Resistance* (New Haven, CT: Yale University Press, 1985), xvi.

9. Ibid.

10. Dick Wilson, *Zhou Enlai: A Biography* (New York: Viking Penguin, 1984), 246.

11. Mao Zedong, "On New Democracy," in *Selected Works of Mao Tse-tung* (Beijing: Foreign Languages Press, 1967), vol. 2, 369.

12. Zhonggong zhongyang wenxian yanjiushi, *Zhou Enlai nianpu (1949–1976)* [A chronological biography of Zhou Enlai] (Beijing: Zhongyang wenxian chubanshe, 1997), vol. 3, 50. Also see Shan Shiyuan, *Wo zai gugong qishi nian* [My seventy years at the Imperial Palace] (Beijing: Beijing shifan daxue chubanshe, 1997), 400; and Yan Jiaqi and Gao Gao, *Turbulent Decade*, 70–71.

13. Xia Nai, "Yao jiaqiang wenwu baohu gongzuo" [We must improve the work of cultural protection], *Wenwu* 1 (1983): 10–11; Guojia wenwu shiye guanliju lilunzu, "Mianhuai Zhou zongli dui wenwu kaogu gongzuo de qinqie guanhuai" [Cherishing Premier Zhou's kind concern for cultural relics and archaeological work], *Wenwu* 1 (1977): 3; and "Zhou zongli guanhuai Dunhuang wenwu gongzuo" [Premier Zhou's concern for Dunhuang's cultural relics], *Gansu ribao*, December 1, 1972.

14. Author's experience on an eleven-day journey in Tibet in June 1999.

15. Some rather hagiographic accounts of Zhou Enlai's career can be found in compilations like *We Will Always Remember Premier Chou En-lai* (Beijing: Foreign Languages Press, 1977).

16. Li Tien-min, *Chou En-lai* (Taipei: Institute of International Relations, 1970), 346. This claim may exaggerate Zhou Enlai's ability to resist red guard activities, but it is important to consider just how positively Zhou has come to be viewed by commentators.

17. Wilson, *Zhou Enlai*, 248.

18. "Zhou Enlai jiejian zhongyang minzu xueyuan ganxun ban Xizang xuesheng tanhua jiyao" [Transcript of Zhou Enlai's talks at a reception for the Tibetan cadre training class at the Central Institute for Minorities] (October 15, 1966), in WDGW.

19. Ibid.

20. Wilson, *Zhou Enlai*, 253.

21. Conversation with Professors Paul Pickowicz and Susan Shirk (both members of that 1971 delegation of American scholars) at the University of California, San Diego, on February 24, 2003. Thanks to Professors Pickowicz and Shirk for sharing their experiences.

22. Wilson, *Zhou Enlai*, 247–48.

23. "Zhonggong zhongyang, guowuyuan, zhongyang junwei, guanyu baohu guojia caichan, jieyue nao geming de tongzhi," in Union Research Institute, comp., *CCP Documents of the Great Proletarian Cultural Revolution, 1966–1967* (Hong Kong: Union Research Institute, 1968), 365–68.

24. Ibid., 367.

25. Ibid., 366.

26. "Zhonggong zhongyang, guanyu zai wuchan jieji wenhua da geming zhong baohu wenwu tushu de jidian yijian," in Guojia wenwu shiye guanliju, comp., *Xin Zhongguo wenwu fagui xuanbian* [Selected laws and regulations on cultural relics in new China] (Beijing: Wenwu chubanshe, 1987), 87–88.

27. Ibid., 88.

28. Ibid.

29. "Mianhuai Zhou zongli dui wenwu kaogu gongzuo de qinqie guanhuai," 1–6.

30. Zhongguo bowuguan xuehui, *Zhongguo bowuguan zhi* [History of Chinese museums] (Beijing: Huaxia chubanshe, 1995), 25; Edward J. Malatesta and Gao Zhiyu, eds., *Departed, Yet Present: Zhalan, the Oldest Christian Cemetery in Beijing* (Macau: Instituto Cultural de Macau, 1995), 98.

31. Guojia wenwu shiye guanliju, comp., "Mianhuai Zhou zongli," 88.

32. Shoudu yuanlin pixiu lianluozhan, *Yuanlin geming, di san qi, Bei ba tian: Peng Zhen zhuanji* [Parks in revolution, third issue, Beijing domination: Peng Zhen special collection] (August 1967), 7; Beijing shi gongdaihui chengjian zu, *Chengjian zhanbao*, October 5, 1967: 2.

33. Beijing shi gongdaihui chengjian zu, *Chengjian zhanbao*, June 27, 1967: 1. Strangely, in the 1950s Mao had also rejected architect Liang Sicheng's idea that Beijing be kept small and beautiful. Mayor Peng Zhen had confided to Liang as they stood overlooking Tiananmen Square: "Chairman Mao wants a big modern city: he expects the sky there to be filled with smokestacks." Wilma Fairbank, *Liang and Lin: Partners in Exploring China's Architectural Past* (Philadelphia: Uni-

versity of Pennsylvania Press, 1994), 170. But both Peng and Liang suffered in the Cultural Revolution for "opposing Mao" with their urban planning ideas. Just whose side was Mao on?

34. Shoudu yuanlin pixiu lianluozhan, *Yuanlin geming*, 10.

35. Beijing shi gongdaihui chengjian zu, *Chengjian zhanbao*, June 27, 1967: 4.

36. Thanks to Michael Schoenhals for this insight and for the red guard source cited in Figure 3.2.

37. Li Xun and Elizabeth J. Perry, "Revolutionary Rudeness: The Language of Red Guards and Rebel Workers in China's Cultural Revolution," Indiana University East Asian Working Papers Series on Language and Politics in Modern China, 1993, www.indiana.edu/easc/resources/working_paper/noframe_2a-revol.htm (March 25, 2005).

38. Roxane Witke, *Comrade Chiang Ch'ing* (Boston: Little, Brown, 1977), 369.

39. Ibid., 370.

40. "Qi Benyu yu tushu wenwu kaogu bowuguan deng danwei geming zaofanpai daibiao zuotan jiyao" [Transcript of Qi Benyu's chat with revolutionary rebel representatives in library, cultural relic, archaeological, and museum units] (January 27, 1967), in WDGW.

41. Ibid. Qi was a historian by training and the author of critical essays like "Patriotism or National Betrayal?—On the Reactionary Film *Secret History of the Qing Court.*" See Harold C. Hinton, ed., *The People's Republic of China 1949–1979: A Documentary Survey* (Wilmington, DE: Scholarly Resources, 1980), 1686–96.

42. "Qi Benyu yu tushu wenwu kaogu bowuguan deng danwei geming zaofanpai daibiao zuotan jiyao."

43. Ibid.

44. "Qi Benyu zai Gugong de jianghua" [Qi Benyu's speech at the Imperial Palace] (December 1, 1966), in WDGW.

45. Witke, *Comrade Chiang Ch'ing*, 392.

46. "Qi Benyu zai Gugong de jianghua." My italics.

47. "Qi Benyu yu tushu wenwu kaogu bowuguan deng danwei geming zaofanpai daibiao zuotan jiyao."

48. Zhong Kan, *Kang Sheng ping zhuan* [Critical biography of Kang Sheng] (Beijing: Hongqi chubanshe, 1982), 262–69. As an "internal" (*neibu*) document and largely a polemic against Kang Sheng, this source may be biased, but the references to Kang's theft of cultural relics are corroborated in Zhang Jian, *Guobao jienan beiwanglu* [Memorandum of disasters to national treasures] (Beijing: Wenwu chubanshe, 2000), 284; *Wen'ge mi shi* [Secret history of the Cultural Revolution] (Hong Kong: Guoji zhengzhi yanjiushe, 1986), 230–33; and Li Luoli and Zhang Chunlei, eds., *Zhonghua renmin gongheguo quan jilu* [Chronicle of the People's Republic of China] (Shenzhen: Haitian chubanshe, 1999), vol. 3, 963.

49. *Wen'ge mi shi*, 231.

50. Zhong Kan, *Kang Sheng ping zhuan*, 263–64.

51. On his visit to China in 1971, journalist Tillman Durdin wrote that the Imperial Palace was "barred to protect it from rampaging Red Guards in pursuit of the directive to destroy the four olds. . . . To make doubly sure, truckloads of art treasures were hauled away to guarded warehouses." Tillman Durdin, "Peking: A Tense City for Foreigners," in Frank Ching, ed., *Report from Red China* (New York: Quadrangle Books, 1971), 145. But guarded warehouses were no hindrance to officials like Kang Sheng.

52. Zhong Kan, *Kang Sheng ping zhuan*, 268–69.

53. *Wen'ge mi shi*, 233.

54. An example of the first is Xie Chensheng, "Xin Zhongguo wenwu baohu gongzuo wushi nian" [Fifty years of cultural relic protection in new China], *Contemporary China History Studies* 9, no. 3 (May 2002): 64–65. On the other hand, an account from Hubei says the party center was ineffectual: Hubei sheng difang zhi bianzuan weiyuanhui, *Hubei sheng zhi: Wenwu ming sheng* [Hubei provincial history: Cultural relics volume] (Wuhan: Hubei renmin chubanshe, 1996), 828. Central effectiveness likely varied according to locality.

55. Field notes of Jiangsui He (Department of Sociology at the University of California, San Diego) based on research conducted in northern Shaanxi for the Beijing University Research Center for Oral History of Social Life. Notes dated May 7, 1998.

56. Beijing University Research Center for Oral History of Social Life, interview materials 199804253MZH and 199804262MPY. My thanks to Jiangsui He for this source.

57. Warren H. Phillips and Robert Keatley, *China: Behind the Mask* (Princeton, NJ: Dow Jones Books, 1972), 85. By 1972, when the authors visited the Summer Palace, the layer of whitewash had begun flaking away, revealing "faces of poets and generals, gods and demons, emperors and their ladies."

58. Chengdu shi Du Fu caotang wenguanchu, "Du Fu caotang" [Du Fu's thatched cottage], *Wenwu* 2 (1977): 89.

59. Louis Barcata, *China in the Throes of the Cultural Revolution: An Eyewitness Report* (New York: Hart, 1968), 174.

60. Malatesta and Gao, *Departed, Yet Present*, 29, 97.

61. Ibid., 95–101.

62. Simon Leys, *Broken Images: Essays on Chinese Culture and Politics* (London: Allison & Busby, 1979), 91. Maria Macchiocchi also wrote on her 1970 visit to China: "I have been told that the famous art works of the Summer Palace are all in the museums of the Forbidden City, carefully preserved and cataloged. I ask whether it is possible to see the museum which I visited in 1954 in the Forbidden

City. . . . I am told that it is still closed." Maria Antonietta Macchiocchi, *Daily Life in Revolutionary China* (New York: Monthly Review Press, 1972), 32–33.

63. Zhongguo bowuguan xuehui, *Zhongguo bowuguan zhi*, 4, 25, 537; Shanghai wenwu bowuguan zhi bianzuan weiyuanhui, *Shanghai wenwu bowuguan zhi* [History of Shanghai's cultural relics and museums] (Shanghai: Shanghai shehui kexue yuan chubanshe, 1997), 21.

64. Simon Leys, *Broken Images*, 91.

65. Ibid.

66. David Milton and Nancy Dall Milton, *The Wind Will Not Subside: Years in Revolutionary China, 1964–1969* (New York: Pantheon, 1976), 108.

67. Hubei sheng difang zhi bianzuan weiyuanhui, *Hubei sheng zhi*, 840.

68. Jacques Guillermaz, *The Chinese Communist Party in Power, 1949–1976* (Boulder, CO: Westview, 1972), 394. "Hutong" (here: *hutung*) refers to the narrow, often willow-lined lanes that were once typical in Beijing.

69. Xie Chensheng, "Renzhen zhixing wenwu baohu fa, kaichuang wenwu gongzuo xin jumian" [Diligently implement the cultural relic protection law, usher in a new phase of cultural relic work], *Wenwu* 1 (1983): 6–7.

70. Zhang Jian, *Guobao jienan beiwanglu*, 285–86.

71. Ibid., 287–89.

72. Hubei sheng difang zhi bianzuan weiyuanhui, *Hubei sheng zhi*, 20.

73. Conversation with Professor Zhang Yingjin at the University of California, San Diego, on March 3, 2003. Thanks to Professor Zhang for sharing this information about his hometown.

74. Simon Leys, *Chinese Shadows*, 101.

75. Tan Chung, ed., *Through the Eyes of Duan Wenjie* (New Delhi: Indira Gandhi National Centre for the Arts, 1994), appendix 2.

76. Chen Bohai, *Shanghai wenhua tong shi* [History of Shanghai's culture] (Shanghai: Shanghai wenyi chubanshe, 2001), 775.

77. Gao Yuan, *Born Red: A Chronicle of the Cultural Revolution* (Stanford, CA: Stanford University Press, 1987), 7–12.

78. Dong Ming, *Guodu fengyun* [The vicissitudes of the nation's capital] (Dalian: Dalian chubanshe, 1994), 227–28.

79. Wenwu bianji weiyuanhui, *Wenwu kaogu gongzuo sanshi nian* [Thirty years of cultural relic and archaeological work] (Beijing: Wenwu chubanshe, 1979), 409; *Historical Relics Unearthed in New China* (Beijing: Foreign Languages Press, 1972), 1–2.

80. Witke, *Comrade Chiang Ch'ing*, 370.

81. Gao Yuan, *Born Red*, 92. Gao notes in his preface (xxxi) that while the account is factual, "Yizhen" is not the actual name of his town in Hebei Province, and many of the names in his account have been disguised to protect anonymity.

82. Ibid., 93–94.

83. Ibid., 94.

84. Ibid.

85. Ken Ling, *The Revenge of Heaven: Journal of a Young Chinese* (New York: G. P. Putnam's Sons, 1972), 56. The city of Amoy (Fujian Province) is also known as Xiamen. I have used "Amoy" here for consistency with Ling's text.

86. Ibid., 56.

87. KFDJN, 15.

88. Ibid., 14–15; XBHZL, 11383.

89. KFDJN, 15.

90. In 1964, Li Xiu had personally supervised the Four Cleanups (*Siqing*) campaign as part of the Socialist Education movement. Author interview, Li Xiu, Ji'nan, September 5, 2003.

91. XBHZL, 11346.

92. Ibid., 11379.

93. Author interview, Li Xiu, Ji'nan, September 12, 2003.

94. Shandong sheng Qufu shi difang shi zhi bianzuan weiyuanhui, *Qufu shi zhi* [Qufu city annals] (Ji'nan: Qi lu shu she, 1993), front flap.

95. Shandong sheng Qufu shi, *Qufu shi zhi*, 42; KFDJN, 22.

96. The State Council declared the Three Confucian Sites among the first set of such national treasures on March 4, 1961. See Shandong sheng difang shi zhi bianzuan weiyuanhui, *Qufu shi zhi: Kongzi guli zhi* [Qufu city annals: Confucius's native place] (Beijing: Zhonghua shuju, 1994), 550.

97. KFDJN, 15.

98. Ibid., 24.

99. Shandong sheng Qufu shi difang shi zhi bianzuan weiyuanhui, *Qufu shi zhi*, inside front cover.

100. Liang Zi, "'San Kong' zaojie jishi" [Chronicle of calamity for the Three Confucian Sites], *Chunqiu* 49 (2002): 5. The conference was actually the second of such debates over Confucius and was attended by over 150 participants, including the later infamous red guard leader Tan Houlan. See KFDJN, 1–10.

101. KFDJN, 23.

102. Author interview, Li Xiu, Ji'nan, September 5, 2003; KFDJN, 18–19.

103. KFDJN, 27.

104. Ibid., 27–28.

105. XBHZL, 11351.

106. Liang Zi, "San Kong," 8. Although the official uses the term "Blood and Tears Palace" (Xieleigong) here, it was still being called the Imperial Palace (Gugong) in the 1967 polemics against Peng Zhen.

107. Zhonggong Qufu shiwei dangshi yanjiushi, *Zhongguo gongchandang Qufu*

shi lishi dashiji (1919.5–1996.12) [Historical chronology of the Chinese Communist Party in Qufu] (Beijing: Zhonggong dangshi chubanshe, 1998), 221; XBHZL, 11362. For the "Obliterate Confucius's Manor" theme song, see KFDJN, 147.

108. KFDJN, 14. Note that Qufu Normal School (Qufu shifan xuexiao) is different from Qufu Normal Institute (Qufu shifan xueyuan).

109. Liang Zi, "San Kong," 6; KFDJN, 14.

110. KFDJN, 28.

111. Ibid., 22.

112. Author interview, Li Xiu, Ji'nan, September 5, 2003; Liang Zi, "San Kong," 9; Zhonggong Qufu shiwei dangshi yanjiushi, *Zhongguo gongchandang Qufu shi lishi dashiji*, 221. Party leaders nationwide were also engaged in the "red sea." See Yan Jiaqi and Gao Gao, *Turbulent Decade*, 89–90. Some red guards saw the "red sea" for what it was, a resistance tactic aimed at dampening red guard spontaneity by denying them wall space for big character posters. See XBHZL, 11373, 11383.

113. XBHZL, 11373.

114. Ibid., 11350, 11351. The red guards viewed their humiliating defeat on August 26 as a "counterrevolutionary" and "revisionist" act akin to the 1956 Soviet crackdown on Hungary.

115. KFDJN, 77–78.

116. XBHZL, 11349, 11352.

117. Author interview, Li Xiu, Jin'an, September 12, 2003; Liang Zi, "San Kong," 11; KFDJN, 93–95. According to Secretary Li, the double-dealer may have been one Wang Xingquan, head of the agricultural work department, who was suspected of reporting on the actions of the party committee to the red guards.

118. KFDJN, 99. The relics of the Manchu Qing dynasty seem to have been singled out for destruction. Can we attribute this to Han nationalism? Why else would Han, or Ming dynasty artifacts for that matter, have been considered any more worthy of preservation, since they were all unequivocally "old" and "feudal" relics by the standards of the day?

119. Author interview, Li Xiu, Ji'nan, September 12, 2003; Liang Zi, "San Kong," 11. The exhuming of tombs, a terrible classical insult, turned into looting in the Confucius Forest from mid-November to December 1966. On December 6, Li Xiu angrily wrote a poem deploring these conditions: "Embroiled in revolution for twenty-eight years, from birth to death ne'er have I feared; in daring to carry out this Cultural Revolution, I'll brook no guilty conscience to the end." Zhonggong Qufu shiwei dangshi yanjiushi, *Zhongguo gongchandang Qufu shi lishi dashiji*, 222.

120. KFDJN, 109.

121. Zhonggong Qufu shiwei dangshi yanjiushi, *Zhongguo gongchandang Qufu shi lishi dashiji,* 222; XBHZL, 11351.

122. KFDJN, 252–54.

123. Ibid., 142–43.

124. According to one account, a former Shandong cadre named Di Jingxiang made a phone call to Zhou Enlai to plead for intervention against Tan Houlan's activities in Qufu. See Shandong sheng zhengxie wenshi ziliao weiyuanhui, *Shandong wenshi ziliao xuanji* [Selected personal histories of Shandong province] (Ji'nan: Shandong renmin chubanshe, 1992), vol. 32, 255–57. Also see Wenwu bianji weiyuanhui, *Wenwu kaogu gongzuo,* 195.

125. KFDJN, 211–13.

126. Zhonggong Qufu shiwei dangshi yanjiushi, *Zhongguo gongchandang Qufu shi lishi dashiji,* 222; XBHZL, 11354.

127. Xinhua tongxunshe, *Jue bu yunxu kai lishi daoche: Qufu renmin jiefa pipan Kongfu zui e* [We will never permit the return of past evils: The people of Qufu expose and criticize the crimes of the Confucius Mansion] (Beijing: Renmin meishu chubanshe, 1974).

128. Feng Jicai, *Ten Years of Madness: Oral Histories of China's Cultural Revolution* (San Francisco: China Books & Periodicals, 1996), 65.

129. Scott, *Weapons of the Weak,* 237.

130. Ken Ling, *The Revenge of Heaven,* 55–57.

131. Joseph R. Levenson, *Revolution and Cosmopolitanism: The Western Stage and the Chinese Stages* (Berkeley: University of California Press, 1971), 49.

132. Maurice Meisner, "Cultural Iconoclasm, Nationalism, and Internationalism in the May Fourth Movement," in Benjamin I. Schwartz, ed., *Reflections on the May Fourth Movement: A Symposium* (Cambridge, MA: Harvard University Press, 1972), 16.

133. Warren Tozer, "Taiwan's 'Cultural Renaissance': A Preliminary View," *China Quarterly* 43 (July–September 1970): 81.

134. Robert Jay Lifton, *Revolutionary Immortality: Mao Tse-tung and the Chinese Cultural Revolution* (New York: Random House, 1968), 145.

135. Ibid., 144.

136. John F. Burns, "Pillagers Strip Iraqi Museum of Its Treasure," *New York Times,* April 13, 2003: A1.

137. "Jim Clancy: Museum 'Shattered' by Looters," CNN (Cable News Network) Archives, April 16, 2003, www.cnn.com/2003/WORLD/meast/04/15/otsc.irq.clancy/index.html (May 19, 2003).

138. Philip Shenon, "U.S. Says It Has Recovered Hundreds of Artifacts and Thousands of Manuscripts in Iraq," *New York Times,* May 8, 2003: A12.

139. Burns, "Pillagers Strip Iraqi Museum," A6.

Chapter 4: Mass Killings in the Cultural Revolution

The author thanks Andrew Walder, Doug McAdam, Susan Olzak, Junling Ma, Dorothy Solinger, and Wang Feng for their support and assistance. He also thanks Joseph Esherick and Sigrid Schmalzer for their editorial assistance. An earlier version of this chapter was presented at the "UC San Diego–Stanford Conference on the Cultural Revolution," San Diego, California, 2003; the advice and fellowship of the participants are gratefully acknowledged. The research was supported by a Littlefield Dissertation Fellowship from the Stanford Institute of International Studies and a travel grant from the Social Science History Institute of Stanford University. Part of the data are from a larger project directed by Andrew Walder, supported by grants from the Henry R. Luce Foundation, and Stanford University's OTL Research Incentive Fund and the Asia-Pacific Research Center.

1. Wang Youqin, "1966: Xuesheng da laoshi de geming" [Nineteen sixty-six: A revolution of students beating teachers], in Liu Qingfeng, ed., *Wenhua da geming: Shishi yu yanjiu* [The Cultural Revolution: Evidence and analysis] (Hong Kong: Xianggang Zhongwen daxue chubanshe, 1996), 17–36; Wang Youqin, "Da laoshi yu da tongxue zhijian" [Between beating teachers and beating classmates], in ibid., 37–48.

2. Wang Shaoguang, *Failure of Charisma: The Cultural Revolution in Wuhan* (Hong Kong: Oxford University Press, 1995); Elizabeth J. Perry and Li Xun, *Proletarian Power: Shanghai in the Cultural Revolution* (Boulder, CO: Westview, 1997); Xu Youyu, *Xingxing sese de zaofan: Hongweibing jingshen suzhi de xingcheng ji yanbian* [Rebels of all hues: The formation and evolution of Red Guard mentalities] (Hong Kong: Xianggang Zhongwen daxue chubanshe, 1999).

3. Zhang Lianhe, "Wu jin Macun quan ting sha" [Five visits to Ma Village to dissuade killings], in Zhe Yongping, ed., *Nage shidai zhong de wo ming* [Our lives in that era] (Hohhot: Yuanfan chubanshe, 1998), 398–404.

4. Zhang Cheng, "Daoxian da tusha" [The Daoxian massacre], *Kaifang zazhi* (Hong Kong), in 4 parts: July, August, September, and December 2001.

5. Zheng Yi, *Hongse jinianbei* [Scarlet memorial] (Taipei: Huashi wenhua gongsi, 1993); Donald S. Sutton, "Consuming Counterrevolution: The Ritual and Culture of Cannibalism in Wuxuan, Guangxi, China, May to July 1968," *Comparative Studies in Society and History* 7, no. 1 (1995): 136–72.

6. Song Yongyi, ed., *Wen'ge da tusha* [Massacres during the Cultural Revolution] (Hong Kong: Kaifang zazhi she, 2002).

7. See the longer discussion in Andrew G. Walder and Yang Su, "The Cultural Revolution in the Countryside: Scope, Timing and Human Impact," *China Quarterly* 173 (March 2003): 74–99.

8. "Zhongguo gongchandang shiyi jie zhongyang weiyuanhui disanci quanti

huiyi gongbao" [Communiqué of the Third Plenum of Eleventh Central Committee of the CCP], December 22, 1978, in Song Yongyi, ed., *Zhongguo wenhua da geming wenku* [Chinese Cultural Revolution database] (Hong Kong: Xianggang Zhongwen daxue Zhongguo yanjiu fuwu zhongxin, 2002).

9. Zhonghua renmin gongheguo minzheng bu [Ministry of Civil Affairs, People's Republic of China], ed., *Zhonghua renmin gongheguo xingzheng quhua, 1949–1997* [Administrative jurisdictions of the People's Republic of China, 1949–1997] (Beijing: Zhongguo shehui chubanshe, 1998).

10. For further discussion of the data collection, see Yang Su, "Tumult From Within: State Bureaucrats and Chinese Mass Movements, 1966–1971" (Ph.D. dissertation, Stanford University, 2003); and Walder and Su, "The Cultural Revolution in the Countryside."

11. An earlier analysis of more than 1,400 counties showed that the numbers of victims (the persecuted, injured, and killed) are correlated with the number of words devoted to the Cultural Revolution in a county's gazetteer. When compared with reports from other sources for twelve counties, the underreporting of casualties was substantial. See Walder and Su, "The Cultural Revolution in the Countryside," 94, table 10.

12. Benjamin Valentino, *Final Solutions: Mass Killing and Genocide in the Twentieth Century* (Ithaca, NY: Cornell University Press, 2004), 1–90.

13. This quotation and others to follow are from the gazetteers. Translations are mine. *Quanzhou xian zhi* [Quanzhou county gazetteer] (Nanning: Guangxi renmin chubanshe, 1998), 17.

14. Ibid., 147.

15. Ibid., 565.

16. *Lingui xian zhi* [Lingui county gazetteer] (Beijing: Fangzhi chubanshe, 1996), 492.

17. One of the two major province-wide mass alliances.

18. *Guangxi wen'ge dashi nianbiao* [Chronology of the Cultural Revolution in Guangxi] (Nanning: Guangxi renmin chubanshe, 1990), 119.

19. *Mengshan xian zhi* [Mengshan county gazetteer] (Nanning: Guangxi renmin chubanshe, 1993), 27. Emphasis added.

20. *Hengxian xian zhi* [Hengxian county gazetteer] (Nanning: Guangxi renmin chubanshe, 1989), 19.

21. *Tianlin xian zhi* [Tianlin county gazetteer] (Nanning: Guangxi renmin chubanshe, 1996), 555.

22. These counties are Quanzhou, Wuming, Guixian, Lingui, Douan, Tiandeng, Luchuan, Luocheng, Mashan, Lingchuan, Guangning, Yishan, Liujian, Chongzuo, and Luzhai.

23. *Wuming xian zhi* [Wuming county gazetteer] (Nanning: Guangxi renmin chubanshe, 1998), 30.

24. These counties included Yangchun, Wuhua, Meixian, Lianjiang, Guangning, and Lianxian.

25. Among the three provinces, Hubei has the shortest average length of accounts of the Cultural Revolution.

26. *Xianfeng xian zhi* [Xianfeng county gazetteer] (Wuchang: Wuhan daxue chubanshe, 1990), 24–25.

27. Zhang Lianhe, "Wu jin Macun"; Yu Luowen, "Beijing Daxing xian can'an diaocha" [An investigation of the Beijing Daxing massacre], in Song Yongyi, ed., *Wen'ge da tusha*, 13–36.

28. The party center issued directives on July 3 and July 24, 1968, calling for mass organizations to be disbanded and for punishment of those who persisted in armed conflict. *Wenhua da geming yanjiu ziliao* [Cultural Revolution research materials] (Beijing: Zhongguo renmin jiefangjun guofang daxue dangshi dangjian zhenggong jiaoyanshi, 1988), vol. 2, 138–39, 152–53.

29. *Guangxi wen'ge dashi nianbiao*, 104–11.

30. Ding Shu, "Fengyu ru pan de rizi: 1970 nian 'yida sanfan yundong'" [Stormy days: The 1970 "one-strike three-anti campaign"], *Huaxia wenzhai* 343 (supplement issue, 2003): 1–14, online journal at www.cnd.org; Andrew Walder, "Anatomy of an Inquisition: Cleansing the Class Ranks, 1968–1971," paper presented at the conference, "The Cultural Revolution in Retrospect," Hong Kong University of Science and Technology, July 4–6, 1996; Walder and Su, "The Cultural Revolution in the Countryside."

31. Qujiang xian difang zhi bianzuan weiyuanhui, *Qujiang xian zhi* [Qujiang county gazetteer] (Beijing: Zhonghua shuju, 1999), 36. Emphasis added.

32. *Xinyi xian zhi* [Xinyi county gazetteer] (Guangzhou: Guangdong renmin chubanshe, 1993), 52; *Chenghai xian zhi* [Chenghai county gazetteer] (Guangzhou: Guangdong renmin chubanshe, 1992), 57; *Huazhou xian zhi* [Huazhou county gazetteer] (Guangzhou: Guangdong renmin chubanshe, 1996), 65. Emphasis added.

33. The table does not include the counties of Hubei since there were few mass killings in that province.

34. *Guangxi wen'ge dashi nianbiao*, 117.

35. See, for example, Zhang Cheng, "Daoxian da tusha," July 2001: 71; August 2001: 77; September 2001: 61; Zheng Yi, *Hongse jinianbei*, 48.

36. Zhang Cheng, "Daoxian da tusha," July 2001: 71.

37. *Guangxi wen'ge dashi nianbiao*, 53.

38. Zhang Cheng, "Daoxian da tusha," August 2001: 82.

39. Ibid., July 2001: 75.

40. Ibid., 73.

41. Ibid., August 2001: 81–83; Zheng Yi, *Hongse jinianbei*, 23–27.

42. *Guangxi wen'ge dashi nianbiao*, 132.

43. Stig Thogersen and Soren Clausen, "New Reflections in the Mirror: Local Chinese Gazetteers (*Difang zhi*) in the 1980s," *Australian Journal of Chinese Affairs* 27 (January 1992): 161–84; Eduard B. Vermeer, "New County Histories: A Research Note on Their Compilation and Value," *Modern China* 18 (October 1992): 438–67.

44. Walder and Su, "The Cultural Revolution in the Countryside," 81, table 1.

45. Xu Youyu, *Xingxing sese de zaofan*, 86–108.

46. Wang Shaoguang, *Failure of Charisma*, 149–202.

47. According to Xu, political events unfolded in a similar fashion in Jiangxi, although that province is not in a border region. See Xu Youyu, *Xingxing sese de zaofan*, 100–108.

48. *Guangxi wen'ge dashi nianbiao*, 61–63, 71, 75.

49. Barbara Harff, "No Lessons Learned from the Holocaust? Assessing Risks of Genocide and Political Mass Murder since 1955," *American Political Science Review* 97, no. 1 (February 2003): 57–73.

50. Walder and Su, "The Cultural Revolution in the Countryside."

51. Wang Shaoguang, *Failure of Charisma*, 181.

52. "Beijing daxue geming weiyuanhui shengli dansheng" [Victorious birth of the Beijing University Revolutionary Committee], *Renmin ribao*, October 6, 1969, in *Wenhua da geming yanjiu ziliao*, vol. 2, 373.

53. *Guangxi wen'ge dashi nianbiao*, 118–21.

54. Hai Feng, *Guangzhou diqu wen'ge licheng shulüe* [An account of the Cultural Revolution in the Canton area] (Hong Kong: Youlian yanjiusuo, 1971).

55. Ibid., 277–85, 342–45.

56. Wang Shaoguang, *Failure of Charisma*, 181–209.

57. *People's Daily*, *Liberation Army Daily*, and *Red Flag*, "The 1968 New Year Editorial," in *Wenhua da geming yanjiu ziliao*, vol. 2, 3.

58. Ibid., 4.

59. "Zhonggong zhongyang, guowuyuan, zhongyang junwei, zhongyang wen'ge zhuanfa Heilongjiang sheng geming weiyuanhui 'Guanyu shenwa pantu gongzuo qingkuang de baogao' de pifa" [CCP Central Committee, State Council, Central Military Commission, and Central Cultural Revolution Group authorize the circulation of the Heilongjiang Province Revolutionary Committee's "Situation report on rooting out traitors"], February 5, 1968, in *Wenhua da geming yanjiu ziliao*, vol. 2, 16.

60. "Zhonggong zhongyang, zhongyang wen'ge zhuanfa Mao zhuxi guanyu 'Beijing xinhua yinshuachang junguanhui fadong qunzhong kaizhan duidi dou-

zheng de jingyan' de pishi de tongzhi" [CCP Central Committee and Central Cultural Revolution Group transmit Chairman Mao's remarks on "Experience of the Beijing Xinhua Printing Plant Military Control Committee in mobilizing the masses to struggle against enemies"], in *Wenhua da geming yanjiu ziliao*, vol. 2, 126–30.

61. Wang Shaoguang, *Failure of Charisma*, 196–97.

62. The campaign was distinct from the national campaign with a similar name, the *yida sanfan* (One-Strike, Three-Anti). It occurred in numerous counties; see, for example, *Yunxi xian zhi* [Yunxi county gazetteer] (Wuhan: Wuhan cehui keji daxue chubanshe, 1995), 28.

63. *Guangxi wen'ge dashi nianbiao*, 96–99.

64. Wen Yuqiao, "Wen'ge 'qi er wu jiang hua': Bu jinjin shi Guangxi zaofan zuzhi de zongjie" [The Cultural Revolution "July 25 speech": Not merely the termination of the Guangxi rebel organizations], *Huaxia wenzhai* 287 (supplemental issue, 2003), online journal at www.cnd.org/cr.

65. *Guangxi wen'ge dashi nianbiao*, 53.

66. District here is an intermediate level of administration between county and commune. It was not very common in China. As discussed above, a typical county consists of three levels of governments: county, commune (township), and brigade (village).

67. Zhang Cheng, "Daoxian da tusha," July 2001: 68.

68. "Zhonggong zhongyang pizhuan Beijing shiwei zhongyao tongzhi" [CCP Central Committee transmits important notice of the Beijing Municipal Party Committee], November 20, 1966, in *Wenhua da geming yanjiu ziliao*, vol. 1, 163.

69. *Wenhua da geming yanjiu ziliao*, vols. 1 and 2.

70. The Chinese character *luan* has multiple meanings. It means random, indiscriminate, and chaotic. It also describes actions that violate law and order, particularly against or lacking proper authority.

71. *Guangxi wen'ge dashi nianbiao*, 58–127.

72. Zhang Lianhe, "Wu jin Macun."

73. Zhang Cheng, "Daoxian da tusha," December 2001: 71.

74. *Wenhua da geming yanjiu ziliao*, vol. 2, 119–20. Emphasis added.

75. Xie Fuzhi, August 7, 1967, in *Wenhua da geming yanjiu ziliao*, vol. 1, 530.

76. "Zhonggong zhongyang, zhongyang wen'ge zhuanfa Beijing shi geming weiyuanhui zhuanlai zhu Qinghua daxue de gongren, jiefangjun xuanchuandui guanyu 'Jianjue guanche zhixing dui zhishi fenzi zai jiaoyu gei chulu de zhengce' de baogao" [CCP Central Committee and Central Cultural Revolution Group transmit the report of the Qinghua University Worker–PLA Propaganda Team submitted to the Beijing Municipal Revolutionary Committee on "Resolutely and thoroughly implementing the policy toward intellectuals of reeducation and

providing a way out"], January 29, 1969, in *Wenhua da geming yanjiu ziliao*, vol. 2, 275–81.

77. Ibid., 281–83.

78. Hong Yung Lee, *The Politics of the Chinese Cultural Revolution* (Berkeley: University of California Press, 1978); Stanley Rosen, *Red Guard Factionalism and the Cultural Revolution in Guangzhou (Canton)* (Boulder, CO: Westview, 1982); Anita Chan, Stanley Rosen, and Jonathan Unger, "Students and Class Warfare: The Social Roots of the Red Guard Conflict in Guangzhou (Canton)," *China Quarterly* 83 (September 1980): 397–446; Wang Shaoguang, *Failure of Charisma*; Yin Hongbiao, "Wen'ge hongweibing yundong de liang da chaoliu" [Two streams of the red guard movement], in Liu Qingfeng, ed., *Wenhua da geming*, 231–48; and Hua Linshan, "Wen'ge qi jian qunzhong xin paixi chengyin" [The origins of mass factionalism during the Cultural Revolution], in Liu Qingfeng, ed., *Wenhua da geming*, 191–208.

79. Andrew G. Walder, "Cultural Revolution Radicalism: Variations on a Stalinist Theme," in William A. Joseph, Christine P. W. Wong, and David Zweig, eds., *New Perspectives on the Cultural Revolution* (Cambridge, MA: Harvard University Press, 1991), 41–62, 42.

80. Cui Zhiyuan, "Mao Zedong wen'ge lilun de deshi yu 'xiandai xing' de chongjian" [Losses and gains in Mao Zedong's theory of the Cultural Revolution and the reconstruction of "modernity"], *Zhongguo yu shijie* 2 (1997); Zheng Yi, "Liangge wenhua da geming chuyi" [A modest proposal on the two Cultural Revolutions], *Huaxia wenzhai* 83 (supplement, April 1996): 1–14, online journal at http://cnd.org.

81. Walder, "Cultural Revolution Radicalism," 42.

Chapter 5: The Death of a Landlord

1. In rural areas, a family grave is always a symbol of the wealth and power of the living members in the village. Huang Shumin, *Lincun de gushi* [The story of Lin village] (Taiwan: Zhanglaoshi chubanshe, 1994), 145–47. In Yangjiagou, the dilapidated cemetery of the Ma family and the magnificent graves of the new elites indicate the social changes and power transfer after land reform.

2. Susan L. Shirk, *Competitive Comrades: Career Incentives and Student Strategies in China* (Berkeley: University of California Press, 1982), 1.

3. Richard Madsen, *Morality and Power in a Chinese Village* (Berkeley: University of California Press, 1984), 4–6.

4. Discontent over the substantial inequalities between landlords and peasants existed in village life at that time. However, such inequalities were justified by such moral criteria as fate or industry. The notion of class and class struggle was not natural to the peasants. Guo Yuhua and Sun Liping, "Suku: Yizhong nongmin

guojia guannian xingcheng de zhongjie jizhi" [Telling of suffering: A method for forming a relationship between peasants and the state], in Yang Nianqun et al., eds., *Xin shixue* [New History] (Beijing: Zhongguo renmin daxue chubanshe, 2003).

5. Madsen, *Morality and Power*, 55–57.

6. Richard Solomon, *Mao's Revolution and the Chinese Political Culture* (Berkeley: University of California Press, 1971), 132; and Shirk, *Competitive Comrades*, 24.

7. Madsen, *Morality and Power*, 18–20.

8. Edward Friedman, Paul G. Pickowicz, and Mark Selden, *Chinese Village, Socialist State* (New Haven, CT: Yale University Press, 1991), xiv.

9. William Hinton, *Fanshen: A Documentary of Revolution in a Chinese Village* (New York: Vintage, 1966), x.

10. John Walton, "Making the Theoretical Case," in Charles Ragin and Howard Becker, eds., *What Is a Case?* (New York: Cambridge University Press, 1992), 121–23.

11. I would like to offer special thanks to Professor Sun Liping and all members of the Research Center for Oral History of Social Life.

12. *Fufengzhai Mashi jiazu zhi* [The genealogy of the Fufengzhai Ma] (complied by the offspring of the Ma family in spring 1997), 5.

13. Zhang Wentian, "Mizhi xian Yangjiagou diaocha" [Survey of Yangjiagou, Mizhi], in *Zhang Wentian Jin-Shaan diaocha wenji* [Collection of Zhang Wentian's investigations in Shanxi and Shaanxi] (Beijing: Zhonggong dangshi chubanshe, 1994), 135–40.

14. According to local tradition, in Yangjiagou servants and especially wet nurses were regarded as a kind of relative of the landlord families they worked for.

15. There are two stone tablets standing at the center of Yangjiagou to this day. One tablet records the building of the fortress against Moslem rebels, and the other is in honor of the distribution of relief food in the great famine at the beginning of the twentieth century.

16. A jingle about the Ma landlords popular among villagers in the 1940s made it clear that local people saw them as a colorful lot. Several Ma landlords described in these jingles were mean, while others were kind. The Ma family was not regarded as a one-dimensional moral or immoral entity. Neither was it held responsible for the poverty of other villagers. See Zhang Wentian, "Mizhi xian," 135.

17. As Madsen points out, "this ethos coincided nicely with the interests of China's rural gentry" (*Morality and Power*, 59). It is undeniable that the goodwill of the Ma landlords was in fact an investment to earn the villagers' loyalty, but we cannot deny that the ordinary peasants benefited from the patronage.

18. *Fufengzhai Mashi jiazu zhi*, 57.

19. In their research on social change in north China, Friedman, Pickowicz,

and Selden point out that children of the old elite became the activists of the communist revolution. Their parents' inability to defend the country against Japanese and other foreign invaders or to succor China's people destroyed their legitimacy. "These radicalized, patriotic, elite youth enlisted villagers from all strata to join them in a Communist Party led multiclass struggle." See Friedman, Pickowicz, and Selden, *Chinese Village, Socialist State*, xxi.

20. The records of party history in the *Mizhi xian zhi* [Mizhi county gazetteer] (Xi'an: Shaanxi renmin chubanshe, 1993) and *Zhongguo gongchandang Shaanxi sheng Mizhi xian zuzhi shi* [History of the party organization in Mizhi county, Shaanxi province] (Xi'an: Shaanxi renmin chubanshe, 1994) also document the fact that the youth of the Ma family were among the earliest party members. For instance, in *Mizhi xian zhi*, 718, an item about Ma Yuzhang specified that he joined the party in the late 1920s.

21. In 1934, Ma Ruyi, a member of another branch of the Mas, conducted his revolutionary activities publicly. Ruyi was from the Jingci branch of the family, whereas all the landlords belonged to the Ma Guangyu branch. An interview with Ruzhi, Ruyi's brother, revealed that the members of the Jingci branch thought they were suppressed by the Guangyu branch. Ruyi hailed from a small landlord family. In 1942, his father owned 16 *shang* (8 acres) of land. Ruyi's father was a teacher in the Ma landlords' family school. In such a close-knit community, the Ma landlords were well informed about Ruyi's revolutionary activities. Once Ruyi scattered some handwritten leaflets in the village. As soon as the Ma landlords read the leaflet, they recognized the handwriting of Ruyi. In February 1935, Ruyi was betrayed and killed.

22. Zhongtai's choice was very common among the Ma children. After studying outside, many returned to Yangjiagou. One of Zhongtai's uncles, Ma Xingmin, came back after studying architecture in Japan.

23. See Liu Xiaofeng, *Xiandaixing shehui lilun xulun* [Preface to the social theory of modernity] (Shanghai: Shanghai sanlian shudian, 1998), 496.

24. *Mizhi xian zhi*, 15.

25. Three representatives from the Ma family attended the second People's Assembly (Canyihui) of the Shaan-Gan-Ning Border Region.

26. The gravestone of Zhongtai records that he "took part in the revolution" (a term for government service under the communists) in February 1940, but we do not know what kind of job he had. The 1942 survey conducted by Zhang Wentian said that Zhongtai stayed at home managing family affairs. Zhang Wentian, "Mizhi xian," 134.

27. Zhonggong Mizhi xian Hecha quwei, "Guanyu Yangjiagou de tudi wenti" [About the land problem in Yangjiagou], August 9, 1948, Mizhi Archives.

28. Struggle played a central role in communist morality. From the 1930–31

great purge during the Soviet period in the south to the rectification movement in Yan'an, the party placed great hope on establishing a new society through struggle with various enemies who were said to represent the old society.

29. *Fufengzhai Mashi jiazu zhi*, 57.

30. Susan Shirk, "The Decline of Virtuocracy in China," in James L. Watson, ed., *Class and Social Stratification in Post-Revolution China* (New York: Cambridge University Press, 1984), 56–83.

31. Liu Xiaofeng discusses the difficulties the "masses" experienced in China, caught in the dichotomy between the "enemy of the people" and the "revolutionary masses." Liu Xiaofeng, *Xiandaixing*, 395–400.

32. Yu Luoke, "Chushen lun" [The theory of family origins] in Xu Xiao, Ding Dong, and Xu Youyu, eds., *Yu Luoke: Yizuo yu huiyi* [Yu Luoke: Posthumous work and reminiscences] (Beijing: Zhongguo weilian chubanshe, 1999).

33. Zhang Wentian, "Mizhi xian," 147.

34. After the establishment of the new state, Ma Mingfang became the top leader of Shaanxi Province, serving as its first governor and first party secretary in 1950–52. In the following two years, Ma was promoted to be a principal in the party's Northwest Bureau, which oversaw the administration of Shaanxi. He was in charge of the party, administration, and army affairs. Later, Ma Mingfang left Shaanxi, and worked as chief of the Organization Department of the party, and minister of Economics and Trade. After 1960, he became the highest leader in northeastern China, a status he enjoyed until the Cultural Revolution. Shaanxi sheng difang zhi bianzuan weiyuanhui, ed., *Shaanxi sheng zhi: Zhengwu zhi* [Gazetteer of Shaanxi province: Administration annals] (Xi'an: Shaanxi renmin chubanshe, 1997); *Zhongguo gongchandang mingren lu* [Chinese Communist Party who's who] (Chengdu: Sichuan renmin chubanshe, 1997).

35. *Fufengzhai Mashi jiazu zhi*, 57.

36. Unquestionably, Zhong Ling was an eminent figure since the Yan'an period. He is, in fact, the person who was criticized by Mao in "Fandui dang bagu" [Oppose party formulism], because of his adherence to traditional orthography in writing slogans. *Zhongguo dangdai mingren lu* [Contemporary Chinese who's who] (Beijing: Renmin chubanshe, 1991); Zhong Ling, "Zhong Ling pilu wushi'er nian qian Tiananmen qian liangtiao da biaoyu xiejiu shimo" [Zhong Ling talks about the process of writing two slogans on Tiananmen fifty-two years ago], in *Beijing qingnian bao*, October 10, 2001; He Fan, "Tiananmen biaoyu ceng liangci gaidong" [The slogans on Tiananmen have been changed twice], in *Zhongguo qingnian bao*, September 17, 2001.

37. *Fufengzhai Mashi jiazu zhi*, 7.

38. Bai Zhimin, "Bai Zhimin huiyi lu" [The memoirs of Bai Zhimin], in Zhonggong Mizhi dangshi yanjiushi, ed., *Jiefang zhanzheng shiqi Mizhi de tugai*

yundong [The Mizhi land reform movement during the Civil War], 1990, Mizhi Archives.

39. Gao Penggui, "Yangjiagou shejiao gongzuo zongjie" [Summary of the Socialist Education movement in Yangjiagou], 1964, Mizhi Archives.

40. Mao Zedong, "Guanyu nongcun shehuizhuyi jiaoyu deng wenti de zhishi" [Directives on socialist education and other issues in the rural areas] (May 1963), in Song Yongyi, ed., *Zhongguo wenhua da geming wenku* [Chinese Cultural Revolution database] (Hong Kong: Xianggang Zhongwen daxue Zhongguo yanjiu fuwu zhongxin, 2002).

41. "Hengsao yiqie niugui sheshen" [Sweep away all monsters], *Renmin ribao*, June 1, 1966; "A Call to Action," in Mark Selden, ed., *The People's Republic of China* (New York: Monthly Review Press, 1979), 545–48.

42. *Mizhi xian zhi*, 389.

43. In land reform, only the seventeen merit tablets memorializing the first three generations of the Ma landlord family, which stood at the entrance of Yangjiagou, were smashed by the residents of a neighboring village, who believed that these tablets limited their own fortune.

44. Even today, villagers born in the 1940s and 1950s still remember these relics of their childhood.

45. It was not easy for a youth from Yangjiagou to pass the entrance examination to the Mizhi Middle School, which was the best in the county. There were just a few Yangjiagou youths studying there in 1966. No evidence survives showing that there was a student from Yangjiagou among these radicals. Moreover, after studying outside the village for several years, even youths from Yangjiagou were relative strangers to other villagers.

46. Considering the location of the tablets, which was known to both villagers and outsiders, it is impossible to imagine that the young red guards were completely unaware of their existence. How could the Yangjiagou villagers hide the tablets with a thin layer of mud? Even if the mud worked, what were the bricks for? It is more reasonable for us to deduce that the villagers used some clever tactic to preserve these two tablets, such as arguing that by sealing the symbols of the landlord class with bricks, they would deny all sunshine to this evil class. See Chapter 3 in this volume by Dahpon Ho.

47. Zhonggong renmin bianxiu weiyuanhui, ed., *Zhonggong renming lu* [Chinese Communist Party who's who] (Taiwan: Guoli zhengzhi daxue guoji guanxi yanjiu zhongxin, 1978), 425–26.

48. In 1974 the county authorities decided to turn Mao's old residence into a museum. In the same year, the commune government moved out of Yangjiagou.

49. Zhonggong zhongyang, guowuyuan, zhongyang junwen, zhongyang wen'ge, "Guanyu jinji dongyuan qilai, xunsu xianqi chunji nongye shengchan gao-

chao de zhishi" [Directives on the swift peak of spring planting] (March 8, 1968), in Song Yongyi, ed., *Zhongguo wenhua da geming wenku.*

50. Madsen, *Morality and Power,* 179–80.

51. Zhonggong zhongyang ba jie shi'er zhong quanhui gonggao [Announcement of the Eighth Plenum of the Twelfth Congress of the CCP] (October 1968), in Song Yongyi, ed., *Zhongguo wenhua da geming wenku.*

52. At that time, Ma Mingfang was already suffering from an accusation by Kang Sheng, who had been digging out "betrayers" in the party since the 1940s. In 1941, on his way back from the Soviet Union to Yan'an, Ma Mingfang was arrested by the Xinjiang warlord Sheng Shicai. He was locked up in Sheng's prison for five years. In 1946, Ma was released with about 130 other revolutionaries during the short postwar united front. In 1967, these 130 people were accused of being set free after betraying the revolution. They were labeled the "Xinjiang traitor group"; Ma Mingfang was the most prominent of these betrayers. Shaanxi sheng, ed., *Shaanxi sheng zhi; Zhongguo gongchandang mingren lu.*

53. *Fufengzhai Mashi jiazu zhi,* 35, 42, 67.

54. *Mizhi xian zhi,* 497.

55. Zhongwen chubanwu fuwu zhongxin, ed., *Wenhua da geming zhong de renmin jiefangjun* [The People's Liberation Army in the Great Cultural Revolution] (Los Angeles: Zhongwen chubanwu fuwu zhongxin, 1996), 249–59.

56. "Zhonggong zhongyang, guowuyuan, zhongyang junwei, zhongyang wen'ge xiaozu guanyu renmin jiefangjun jianjue zhichi geming zuopai qunzhong de jueyi" [Decision of the CCP Central Committee, State Council, Central Military Committee and Central Cultural Revolution Small Group on the firm support of the leftist masses by the PLA], January 3, 1967, in Union Research Institute, ed., *CCP Documents of the Great Proletarian Cultural Revolution 1966–1967* (Hong Kong: Union Research Institute, 1968), 195–97.

57. In Yangjiagou today, some of the pictures and slogans are still preserved. The earlier red guards also might have left some pictures and slogans, but since memories of the red guards are focused on their destructive acts, all drawings and slogans were attributed to the army.

58. Zhang Ming was born in Yangjiagou in the 1940s, and moved out in the early 1980s. His son is now a famous *suona* player in Shaanxi Province. Yangjiagou villagers take delight in talking about his activities, despite his role as a rebel in the Cultural Revolution.

59. Shirk, *Competitive Comrades,* 19.

60. Martin King Whyte, *Small Groups and Political Rituals in China* (Berkeley: University of California Press, 1974).

61. In the 1990s, descendents of the Ma family came from Xi'an, Beijing, and even Hong Kong to visit their home village. In the view of the villagers, these Ma

offspring were as generous as their ancestors. They visited their acquaintances, such as their wet nurses and the family servants, and even provided them with some aid. They also donated books to the elementary school in Yangjiagou. One of Zhongtai's nieces helped Mizhi County get funds from the United Nations to support agricultural reform. *Fufengzhai Mashi jiazu zhi*, 17–18. As for the researchers, on one hand, the villagers are always inclined to believe that the researchers are offspring of Ma landlords; on the other hand, their research continuously refreshes the villagers' memories of the landlords.

62. In 1996–97, a new genealogy of the Ma landlords was compiled. Almost every villager knows this genealogy; several villagers who are not members of the Ma lineage even own a copy of the new family book. In the eyes of the villagers, the offspring of the Ma family are still distant relations whom they can ask for help. In 2000, when the villagers planned to reconstruct the theater stage in the village, which was also the place where the struggle against Zhongtai and other landlords occurred in the Cultural Revolution, the villagers still hoped to get some money from the Ma family.

63. Similar to the situation described by Richard Madsen in *Morality and Power in a Chinese Village*, there were two major, antagonistic leaders in Yangjiagou: Guo Chengming and Ma Rujun. Both rose to power after land reform, and they cooperated with each other during the collectivization period. But their conflicts were intense during and after the Socialist Education movement and the Cultural Revolution. Now, Guo Chengming is the organizer of folk religious activities, while Ma Rujun's son is the administrative leader of Yangjiagou.

64. The villagers criticized people who covertly dug up landlords' tombs. However, these persons still live in the village, and own luxury homes in the village, which other villagers believe were built using the income from looting the tombs. Thus, the demarcation between right and wrong remains unclear in the village today.

65. Shirk, *Competitive Comrades*, 1.

66. Ibid., 2, 4.

Chapter 6: Staging Xiaojinzhuang

ABBREVIATIONS USED IN THE NOTES

GJG:*1* Gao Jianguo, "Xiaojinzhuang de chenfu" [The rise and fall of Xiaojinzhuang], part one, *Sanyue feng* 15 (February 1986): 3–17.

GJG:*2* Gao Jianguo, "Xiaojinzhuang de chenfu" [The rise and fall of Xiaojinzhuang], part two, *Sanyue feng* 16 (March 1986): 6–20.

RMRB *Renmin ribao* [People's Daily].

TJRB *Tianjin ribao* [Tianjin Daily].

INTERVIEWS

Unless otherwise noted, all interviews were conducted in person between September 2002 and September 2003.

1. Taxi driver. Male. Baodi.
2. Village party secretary. Male. Baodi.
3. Former village party secretary. Male. Baodi.
4. Former county official. Male. Baodi.
5. Former municipal official. Male. Tianjin.
6. Former Liang Xiao writer. Male. California.
7. Former sent-down youth. Female. North China.
8. Former village party branch member. Male. Baodi.
9. Medical worker. Male. Baodi.
10. School teacher. Male. Baodi.
11. Village resident. Female. Baodi.
12. Taxi driver. Male. Tianjin.
13. Former Liang Xiao member. Male. Telephone conversation.

1. Names used in this chapter, with the exception of those of public figures and published authors (including prominent Xiaojinzhuang residents like Wang Zuoshan and Wang Du, who received extensive national press coverage during the 1970s), are not real.

2. Interview no. 1; Interview no. 2.

3. Edward Friedman, "The Politics of Local Models, Social Transformation and State Power Struggles in the People's Republic of China: Tachai and Teng Hsiao-p'ing," *China Quarterly* 76 (December 1978): 874.

4. For a persuasive argument linking Chinese ruralism with nationalism and outlining the Cultural Revolution's vision for rural China, see Maurice Meisner, *Marxism, Maoism and Utopianism* (Madison: University of Wisconsin Press, 1982), 63, 71. Of course, significant advances in rural education and health services during the Cultural Revolution must not be ignored.

5. Susan Mann, "Urbanization and Historical Change in China," *Modern China* 10, no. 1 (January 1984): 108.

6. See Tiejun Cheng and Mark Selden, "The Origins and Consequences of China's Hukou System," *China Quarterly* 139 (September 1994): 644–68; and Sulamith Heins Potter and Jack M. Potter, *China's Peasants: The Anthropology of a Revolution* (Cambridge, UK: Cambridge University Press, 1990), especially chapter 15.

7. Liu Bingrong, "Wo suo zhidao de Xiaojinzhuang" [What I know about Xiaojinzhuang], *Dangshi bolan* 6 (2002): 40.

8. Ibid., 40.

9. GJG:1, 5.

10. Interview no. 8.

11. GJG:2, 12.

12. Tianjin's main railway station was one of Jiang Qing's urban models, especially at the height of the campaign to criticize Lin Biao and Confucius in 1974. On Jiang's military models in the Tianjin region, see Ji Dengkui, *Ji Dengkui tongzhi zai "Tianjin shi ru fa douzheng shi baogao hui" shang de zhongyao jianghua* [Comrade Ji Dengkui's important talk at the Tianjin meeting on the history of the struggle between Confucianism and Legalism], internally circulated document, June 19, 1974; and Chen Xianrui, "Pi Chen pi Lin qijian de Beijing junqu" [The Beijing military district during "criticize Chen" and "criticize Lin"], *Bai nian chao* (May 2000): 49. I thank Michael Schoenhals for providing me with the first document and alerting me to the second.

13. GJG:1, 5.

14. Interview no. 4; Pien Tsai, "Peasant Poets of Hsiaochinchuang," *Chinese Literature* 10 (1974): 96–97.

15. On local honors, see TJRB, December 19, 1973; on grain yields see Ren Xizeng, "Jiang Qing shu Xiaojinzhuang de qianqian houhou" [The whole story of Jiang Qing establishing Xiaojinzhuang (as a model)], *Guoshi yanjiu cankao ziliao* 1 (1996): 18. My thanks to Michael Schoenhals for providing me with this source. See also Wang Yan, "Xiaojinzhuang yishi" [Xiaojinzhuang anecdote], *Lingdao kexue* (October 2002): 14; and GJG:1, 5. Before August 1973, when Tianjin became the administrative equivalent of a province (*zhixia shi*), Baodi County was part of Hebei Province's Tianjin Prefecture.

16. Interview no. 4.

17. Ren Xizeng, "Jiang Qing," 18; Interview no. 4. See also *Xiaojinzhuang zhengzhi yexiao ban de hao* [Xiaojinzhuang's political night school is good] (Beijing: Renmin chubanshe, 1974), 4.

18. Xie Xuegong became the undisputed leader of Tianjin in the aftermath of factional struggles between red guard groups in 1966 and 1967, while Wang Mantian emerged in Tianjin in 1967 and became a party secretary in charge of the city's cultural and educational affairs. As Mao's relative, Wang had special political capital; she was also a friend of Jiang Qing from their Yan'an days. Guoli zhengzhi daxue guoji guanxi xi yanjiu zhongxin et al., eds., *Zhonggong renming lu* [Chinese Communist who's who] (Taipei: Guoli zhengzhi daxue guoji guanxi xi yanjiu zhongxin, 1978), 63, 833; Interview no. 6.

19. Interview no. 5.

20. Gao Jianguo reports on the first visit of a general in a jeep from Beijing. GJG:1, 4. Wang Zuoshan told a reporter in March 2002 that Wu Dai inspected the village on several occasions. Wang Yan, "Xiaojinzhuang yishi," 14.

21. Interview no. 5.

22. Maurice Meisner, *Mao's China and After*, 3rd edition (New York: Free Press, 1999), 392–393.

23. Interview no. 5.

24. TJRB, February 12, 1974: 1; TJRB, March 1, 1974: 1.

25. Interview no. 5.

26. Ibid.

27. TJRB, June 11, 1974: 2; TJRB, January 29, 1974: 2.

28. "Liang Xiao" was the pen name under which articles by the writing group were published. This was a homonym for "two schools," meaning Qinghua and Beijing universities.

29. Fan Daren, *Wen'ge yubi chenfu lu: Liang Xiao wangshi* [The rise and fall of the Cultural Revolution's imperial scribe: A recollection of Liang Xiao] (Hong Kong: Mingbao chubanshe, 1999), 35–36.

30. Copies of her speech were first circulated as important study materials, but after 1976 were distributed again as examples of her ambitious "bid to be empress." Ross Terrill, *Madame Mao: The White-Boned Demon*, revised edition (Stanford, CA: Stanford University Press, 1999), 265.

31. A 1974 transcript of Jiang's speech indicates her repartee with Wang Mantian, Wu Dai, and Ji Dengkui. These details are missing in post-1976 versions of the speech. See Jiang Qing, *Jiang Qing tongzhi zai "Tianjin shi ru fa douzheng shi baogao hui" shang de zhongyao jianghua* [Comrade Jiang Qing's important talk at the Tianjin meeting on the history of the struggle between Confucianism and Legalism], internally circulated document, June 19, 1974, 1, 9, 11. Thanks to Michael Schoenhals for sharing this transcript with me. Also, Interview no. 6.

32. Jiang Qing, *Jiang Qing tongzhi*, 10.

33. Ibid., 1, 6.

34. Interview no. 5; Ren Xizeng, "Jiang Qing," 18. An internal, unpublished manuscript claims that this meeting happened at some point before June 19. See Baodi qu dang'anguan, *Xiaojinzhuang "dianxing" shimo* [Xiaojinzhuang as a model from start to finish], internal draft manuscript, 2004, 12.

35. GJG:1, 5.

36. Xiaomei Chen debunks the notion that Jiang Qing created the eight model works all by herself, but it is clear that Jiang was proud of her role in shaping and producing the operas, dramas, and ballet. Xiaomei Chen, *Acting the Right Part: Political Theater and Popular Drama in Contemporary China* (Honolulu: University of Hawai'i Press, 2002), 86, 105–7.

37. GJG:1, 6.

38. TJRB, June 21, 1974: 1.

39. Interview no. 3.

40. Interview no. 4; GJG:1, 6.

41. Hou Jun, *Jiang Qing san ci qu Xiaojinzhuang de bufen jianghua he huodong* [Parts of Jiang Qing's talks and activities during her three visits to Xiaojinzhuang], internally circulated document, October 14, 1976.

42. Wang Yan, "Xiaojinzhuang yishi," 14.

43. Liu Bingrong, "Wo suo zhidao de Xiaojinzhuang," 42.

44. Interview no. 6.

45. Hou Jun, *Jiang Qing*, 2.

46. Interview no. 4.

47. Ibid.

48. David Zweig calls the radicals' informal use of visits, model establishment, and press coverage "policy winds." David Zweig, *Agrarian Radicalism in China, 1968–1981* (Cambridge, MA: Harvard University Press, 1989), 35–38.

49. RMRB, August 4, 1974: 1.

50. Interview no. 4. Hu said that before Jiang Qing's visit he wrote up an article on Xiaojinzhuang's "Eight New Things," which was revised and augmented later in 1974.

51. Jiang Qing was following Mao's reversal of the Marxist idea that social being determines consciousness. Mao believed that instead of material advances leading to cultural change, only a remolding of people's consciousness through revolutionary cultural offerings could transform the other realms of Chinese society, including economic life. Meisner, *Mao's China and After*, 315. See also Roxane Witke, *Comrade Chiang Ch'ing* (Boston: Little, Brown, 1977), 3.

52. Gao Jianguo gathered these figures from documents he viewed in the Baodi County archives during the 1980s; GJG:1, 11.

53. RMRB, February 26, 1976: 1.

54. GJG:1, 11; RMRB, January 12, 1978: 2.

55. RMRB, January 12, 1978: 2.

56. Interview no. 9.

57. Respectively, Interview no. 3; Liu Bingrong, "Wo suo zhidao de Xiaojinzhuang," 42; GJG:2, 9.

58. Richard Madsen sheds light on the difficult position of village leaders, beholden to the competing demands of superiors and constituents. Richard Madsen, *Morality and Power in a Chinese Village* (Berkeley: University of California Press, 1984), 3. Here, I also consider the glorification of Mao a key element of Wang Zuoshan's script, given his village's identification with Jiang Qing and her connection to the supreme leader.

59. Interview no. 4; Interview no. 7.

60. Interview no. 3.

61. A group of former sent-down youth from Tianjin continue to visit Wang Zuoshan every Spring Festival. Interview no. 7; Interview no. 3.

62. Interview no. 3; Interview no. 8.

63. GJG:2, 7–8. A member of Jiang Qing's entourage described Wang Zuoshan as "fawning upon" (*bajie*), "pandering to" (*yinghe*), and "flattering" (*fengcheng*) Mao's wife, which must have been common responses to her commanding presence. Interview no. 6.

64. Interview no. 3; GJG:2, 8.

65. Interview no. 3.

66. *Xiaojinzhuang de shenke bianAge* [Xiaojinzhuang's profound change] (Changsha: Hunan renmin chubanshe, 1975), 62, excerpted from RMRB, October 1, 1974: 5.

67. Jiang Qing said as much during her first visit to Xiaojinzhuang. "I bring Chairman Mao's regards," she said. "I represent the party center and Chairman Mao in wishing you well." Ren Xizeng, "Jiang Qing," 18.

68. Interview no. 3.

69. Interview no. 8; GJG:2, 8.

70. GJG:2, 8.

71. Probably the Ministry of Agriculture. Interview no. 8; Zhonggong Tianjin shiwei zuzhibu, et al., *Zhongguo gongchandang Tianjin shi zuzhi shi ziliao, 1920–1987* [Materials on the history of the Tianjin CCP organization, 1920–1987] (Beijing: Zhongguo chengshi chubanshe, 1991), 392; GJG:2, 7.

72. RMRB, August 29, 1976: 1. Wang Zuoshan also criticized Deng in a poem published in the second Xiaojinzhuang poetry anthology, *Shi'er ji taifeng gua bu dao: Xiaojinzhuang shige xuan* [Even the fiercest typhoon cannot blow us down: Xiaojinzhuang poetry anthology] (Beijing: Renmin chubanshe, 1976), 12–13. For an English translation of the poem, "Every Single Victory Is Won Through Struggle," see *Chinese Literature* 9 (1976): 57–58.

73. Gao Jianguo viewed a transcript of this talk in the Baodi County archives. GJG:2, 8.

74. See Xiaomei Chen, *Acting the Right Part*, 33–46; and Xueping Zhong, Wang Zheng, and Bai Di, eds., *Some of Us: Chinese Women Growing Up in the Mao Era* (New Brunswick, NJ: Rutgers University Press, 2001).

75. This apparent attack on Premier Zhou Enlai was cited after Jiang Qing's arrest as one of her most heinous acts in Xiaojinzhuang. See RMRB, January 12, 1978: 2; and Hou Jun, *Jiang Qing*, 1. During the Criticize Lin Biao, Criticize Confucius movement, Jiang directed her writing groups to attack the Duke of Zhou and the Confucian rites (*zhouli*), both of which were alleged, after the arrest of the Gang of Four, to be attacks on Zhou Enlai.

76. All three women still live near Xiaojinzhuang, and people acquainted with

Zhou Kezhou and Wang Xian still refer to them by the names Jiang Qing gave them. Interview no. 8; Hou Jun, *Jiang Qing,* 1; GJG:1, 6–7.

77. Ban Wang argues that immersion in the model operas meant that "people no longer just performed the dramas and acted out the roles on the stage: they came to live these roles and act out the scenarios in daily life. . . . They even gesticulated and moved in the same heroic and theatrical way." Ban Wang, *The Sublime Figure of History: Aesthetics and Politics in Twentieth-Century China* (Stanford, CA: Stanford University Press, 1997), 214.

78. For these photos, see *Chinese Literature* 10 (1974): 98; and the front and back covers of *Xiaojinzhuang zhengzhi yexiao ban de hao,* respectively.

79. Interview no. 4; Interview no. 7.

80. RMRB, October 1, 1974: 5; *Xiaojinzhuang de shenke biange,* 64. Although Hao Ran does not identify the object of his gaze by name, numerous other published references name Yu Fang as Xiaojinzhuang's nineteen-year-old women's leader. See RMRB, August 6, 1974: 1.

81. Women were elevated to local leadership positions throughout China during the Criticize Lin Biao, Criticize Confucius campaign, but according to Friedman, Pickowicz, and Selden most men throughout north China were unenthusiastic about policies offering women equal pay. Outside of model villages, male leaders ridiculed and blocked measures promoting gender equality. Edward Friedman, Paul G. Pickowicz, and Mark Selden, *Revolution, Resistance, and Reform in Village China* (New Haven, CT: Yale University Press, 2005), chapter 12.

82. GJG:2, 13.

83. *Jianchi shangceng jianzhu lingyu geming fazhan shehuizhuyi tiyu: Xiaojinzhuang qunzhongxing tiyu huodong pengbo kaizhan* [Persist in the revolution of the superstructure, develop socialist sports: Xiaojinzhuang's mass character sports activities vigorously unfold] (Beijing: Renmin tiyu chubanshe, 1975). See inside of back cover for a photo of the women's volleyball team.

84. "Xiaojinzhuang de xinshi" [Xiaojinzhuang's new things], *Renmin huabao* (March 1975): 28.

85. Interview no. 8; GJG:2, 11.

86. Interview no. 8.

87. On Baodi's history of rhyming, see Liu Bingrong, "Wo suo zhidao de Xiaojinzhuang," 41; and Wang Yan, "Xiaojinzhuang yishi," 15. On Wang Du's role in writing and editing poetry, a Baodi man told me that Wang Du worked on many of the published poems attributed to Xiaojinzhuang residents. Interview no. 10. See also GJG:2, 11.

88. Oh, my first visit to Beijing,
impossible to calm my excited mood!
Thousands of hands embracing one another,

thousands of faces smiling in welcome.
So joyful and so proud,
we have arrived in the magnificent city of Beijing,
taking orders from Chairman Mao at his side,
researching this ever-important movement to criticize Lin and Confucius.

Excerpt from Tianjin renmin chubanshe, ed., *Xiaojinzhuang shige xuan* [Xiaojin-zhuang poetry anthology] (Tianjin: Tianjin renmin chubanshe, 1974), 20–21. My translation. An English translation of the entire poem can be found in *Chinese Literature* 4 (1975): 82–83.

89. Meisner, *Mao's China and After*, 362.

90. Interview no. 8; GJG:2, 11.

91. RMRB, August 29, 1976: 1; *Renmin wenxue* 3 (May 1976): 10; see also his three combative poems in *Shi'er ji taifeng gua bu dao*, 5–6, 12–13, 69–70.

92. RMRB, November 26, 1976: 3. For a text that depicts Wang Du encouraging Jiang Qing to criticize Deng Xiaoping, see Hou Jun, *Jiang Qing*, 5.

93. GJG:1, 10. This shunkouliu was not invented in Xiaojinzhuang, but at the time rhymes on the "ten ranks of people" were circulating throughout north China. Interview no. 4.

94. That subversive rhymes led to political criticism in Xiaojinzhuang is in accord with Link and Zhou's observation that shunkouliu could only be shared "in tightly guarded contexts" during the Cultural Revolution. Perry Link and Kate Zhou, "*Shunkouliu*: Popular Satirical Sayings and Popular Thought," in Perry Link, Richard P. Madsen, and Paul G. Pickowicz, eds., *Popular China: Unofficial Culture in a Globalizing Society* (Lanham, MD: Rowman & Littlefield, 2002), 89, 91.

95. On the long-term scapegoating of rural "class enemies," see Edward Friedman, Paul G. Pickowicz, and Mark Selden, *Chinese Village, Socialist State* (New Haven, CT: Yale University Press, 1991), xx, 270.

96. GJG:1, 10; GJG:2, 12.

97. GJG:2, 12.

98. GJG:1, 11.

99. Interview no. 2; Interview no. 8; GJG:1, 10–11.

100. RMRB, October 28, 1974: 1.

101. Interview no. 7.

102. Interview no. 4.

103. GJG:1, 14.

104. Interview no. 2.

105. GJG:1, 13.

106. Ibid.

107. Interview no. 11.

108. Ibid.

109. GJG:2, 12. According to Gao Jianguo, Wang Tinghe's point in telling this story was to show that Xiaojinzhuang indeed made mistakes but that much of its bad reputation came from people outside the village.

110. Television covered the Imelda Marcos visit and the village was also featured in a show entitled "Xiaojinzhuang jubian" [Xiaojinzhuang's tremendous changes]. RMRB, June 4, 1976: 1.

111. Interview no. 8.

112. Mao also complained to Jiang Qing, "we are lacking in poetry, novels, prose, and literary criticism." *Jianguo yilai Mao Zedong wen'gao* [Mao Zedong's manuscripts and drafts since the founding of the People's Republic] (Beijing: Zhongyang wenxian chubanshe, 1998), vol. 13, 443, 446.

113. Meisner, *Mao's China and After*, 401.

114. RMRB, December 27, 1975: 1.

115. Radicals like Yao Wenyuan treated it as such. On August 12, 1976, Yao instructed a team of *Red Flag* magazine editors and writers to cite Xiaojinzhuang when attacking Deng and praising earthquake relief. Yao Wenyuan, "Yao Wenyuan dui *Hongqi* zazhi bianji zu zhaoji ren tan pi Deng" [Yao Wenyuan talks to the *Red Flag* editorial group on criticizing Deng], August 12, 1976, in Song Yongyi, ed., *Zhongguo wenhua da geming wenku* [Chinese Cultural Revolution database] (Hong Kong: Xianggang Zhongwen daxue Zhongguo yanjiu fuwu zhongxin, 2002).

116. RMRB, January 12, 1978: 3.

117. Tianjin shi difang zhi bianxiu weiyuanhui, ed., *Tianjin tongzhi: Xinfang zhi* [Tianjin gazetteer: Letters and visits] (Tianjin: Tianjin shehui kexue yuan chubanshe, 1997), 29; RMRB, May 19, 1978: 2.

118. The poems that raised Han's ire were likely Li Shufeng's "Qinren lai zajia" [A dear person came to our home] and Wang Xinmin's "Qinren lai dao zamen cun" [A dear person came to our village], *Xiaojinzhuang shige xuan*, 15–16.

119. RMRB, May 19, 1978: 2.

120. *Tianjin tongzhi: Xinfang zhi*, 29. Han's letter to Xiaojinzhuang was only the first salvo in his purported battle against the Gang of Four. He also reportedly sent letters to Wang Hongwen, Zhang Chunqiao, Yao Wenyuan, and their supporters in the ministries of culture, public health, and sports warning that they would come to a bad end. RMRB, May 19, 1978: 2.

121. Baodi xian zhi bianxiu weiyuanhui, ed., *Baodi xian zhi* [Baodi county gazetteer] (Tianjin: Tianjin shehui kexue yuan chubanshe, 1995), 68. This number of visitors is not surprising, given Norma Diamond's report that provincial models could expect around fifty thousand tourists per year during the late 1970s. Norma

Diamond, "Model Villages and Village Realities," *Modern China* 9, no. 2 (April 1983): 164.

122. Ren Xizeng, "Jiang Qing," 19.

123. GJG:1, 10.

124. Interview no. 12.

125. Interview no. 6.

126. Liu Bingrong, "Wo suo zhidao de Xiaojinzhuang," 42.

127. Interview no. 13.

128. Friedman, Pickowicz, and Selden, *Revolution, Resistance, and Reform*, chapter 12.

129. See RMRB, October 13, 1974: 1, for an article on Hebei's Xiong County; and RMRB, December 8, 1974: 1, for a mention of how Hebei's Zhengding County managed to study both Dazhai and Xiaojinzhuang at the same time.

130. Propagandists awarded this label to such places as Shendaokou Brigade in coastal Shandong and an army unit in Lanzhou in an informal manner, much like Xiaojinzhuang itself rose without the benefit of official directives. RMRB, July 31, 1975: 5; RMRB, May 16, 1975.

131. Tang Tsou, Marc Blecher, and Mitch Meisner, "National Agricultural Policy: The Dazhai Model and Local Change in the Post-Mao Era," in Mark Selden and Victor Lippit, eds., *The Transition to Socialism in China* (Armonk, NY: M. E. Sharpe, 1982), 266–99.

132. Interview no. 8; GJG:2, 11.

133. Friedman, "The Politics of Local Models," 885.

134. Xiaojinzhuang literally means "Little Jin Village"; Dazhai means "Big Stockaded Village." RMRB, February 26, 1976: 1. Deng was blasted in 1976 for "putting the experiences of Dazhai and Xiaojinzhuang in opposition." RMRB, August 16, 1976: 3.

135. Zweig, *Agrarian Radicalism in China*, 65–69.

136. Jiang Qing, *Jiang Qing zai quanguo nongye xue Dazhai huiyi shang de jianghua* [Jiang Qing's speech at the national conference to study Dazhai], September 15, 1975, in Song Yongyi, ed., *Zhongguo wenhua da geming wenku.* See also Yan Jiaqi and Gao Gao, *Turbulent Decade: A History of the Cultural Revolution* (Honolulu: University of Hawai'i Press, 1996), 469.

137. RMRB, August 12, 1978: 3.

138. RMRB, May 21, 1978: 1; RMRB, December 11, 1978: 3.

139. Interview no. 7. The impact of lineage issues on Xiaojinzhuang politics deserves further investigation.

140. GJG:2, 6.

141. In late December 1976, *People's Daily* published an article by *Tianjin Daily* editors accusing Jiang Qing of "plucking peaches." RMRB, December 24, 1976.

This article, along with "Jiang Qing yu Xiaojinzhuang" [Jiang Qing and Xiaojin-zhuang], RMRB, January 12, 1978: 2, remains the official verdict about the village's model experience.

142. Interview no. 3; Wang Yan, "Xiaojinzhuang yishi," 14.

143. Liu Bingrong, "Wo suo zhidao de Xiaojinzhuang," 42.

144. *Baodi xian zhi*, 68. Wang Xian and Yu Ruifang are now schoolteachers in villages near Xiaojinzhuang.

145. Bruce Gilley, *Model Rebels: The Rise and Fall of China's Richest Village* (Berkeley: University of California Press, 2001), 106–7.

146. In Beijing in 2001, a television show host gave me an impromptu Chinese lesson. "Hey, you want to know a cool insult that you can use on anybody?" he asked. "Just call somebody a farmer. You can just tell people, 'you're a farmer'" (*ni shi ge nongmin*).

Chapter 7: Labor Created Humanity

1. See, for example, Victor Sidel and Ruth Sidel, *Serve the People: Observations on Medicine in the People's Republic of China* (New York: Josiah Macy, Jr. Foundation, 1973); Gordon Bennett, "Mass Campaigns and Earthquakes: Hai-Ch'eng, 1975," *China Quarterly* 77 (March 1979): 94–112; Science for the People, *Science Walks on Two Legs* (New York: Discus Books, 1974); C. K. Jen, "Science and the Open-Doors Educational Movement," *China Quarterly* 64 (December 1975): 741–47; Robert van den Bosch, *The Pesticide Conspiracy* (Garden City, NY: Doubleday, 1978).

2. W. W. Howells and Patricia Jones Tsuchitani, eds., *Paleoanthropology in the People's Republic of China: A Trip Report of the American Paleoanthropology Delegation* (Washington, D.C.: National Academy of Sciences, 1977). IVPP is the only scientific institute in China specifically charged with the study of paleoanthropology. It is one of many research institutes under the umbrella of the Chinese Academy of Sciences.

3. An early exception to this general trend is the work of Richard Suttmeier, a political scientist working with documents rather than a natural scientist on a tour of newly opened China. Suttmeier's 1974 *Research and Revolution* offers a thorough analysis of science policy beginning in 1949. Richard Suttmeier, *Research and Revolution: Science Policy and Societal Change in China* (Lexington, MA: Lexington Books, 1974).

4. The "Four Modernizations" referred to a state commitment to prioritizing the development of agriculture, industry, science and technology, and national defense. Although the concept had been a part of state discourse for many years, Deng's approach differed markedly from the earlier dominant view—found espe-

cially during the Cultural Revolution—that saw development as inextricable from revolutionary politics.

5. For examples of articles published in mainstream Chinese magazines soon after the Cultural Revolution criticizing Cultural Revolution–era treatment of scientists, see Li Zhong, "A Woman Engineer in an Oil Refinery," *Women of China* 10 (1976): 2–4; Lu Zhong, "A Woman Chemical Engineer," *Women of China* 7 (1980): 17–21. For an example of "scar literature" with a scientist protagonist, see Feng Jicai, *Voices from the Whirlwind: An Oral History of the Chinese Cultural Revolution* (New York: Pantheon, 1991), 224–43.

6. See, for example, Peter Neushul and Wang Zuoyue, "Between the Devil and the Deep Sea: C. K. Tseng, Mariculture, and the Politics of Science in Modern China," *Isis* 91, no. 1 (March 2000): 59–88; James H. Williams, "Fang Lizhi's Expanding Universe," *China Quarterly* 123 (September 1990): 459–84.

7. See, among others, Shuping Yao, "Chinese Intellectuals and Science: A History of the Chinese Academy of Sciences (CAS)," *Science in Context* 3, no. 2 (1989): 447–73.

8. Frederick Engels, *The Part Played by Labor in the Transition from Ape to Man* (New York: International Publishers, 1950).

9. Richard Suttmeier, writing in 1974, recognized the "two rather different premises underlying" science dissemination and mass science. He noted that the first was fundamentally a "'top-down' philosophy of knowledge" that saw expertise residing in scientific institutions, whereas the second was "bottom-up" and considered workers to be sources of "untapped expertise" based on their intimate understanding of production processes. See his *Research and Revolution*, 126.

10. It is conventional to consider 1976 the end of the Cultural Revolution, since in that year Chairman Mao died, and soon after the "Gang of Four" fell. For the history of science at least, however, it makes more sense to cap the period in 1978 with the implementation of Deng Xiaoping's Four Modernizations and the formal re-acknowledgment that science was a productive force rather than part of the "superstructure" and that intellectuals could thus be understood as part of the working class. See Shuping Yao, "Chinese Intellectuals and Science," 470.

11. Yan Jiaqi and Gao Gao, *Turbulent Decade: A History of the Cultural Revolution* (Honolulu: University of Hawai'i Press, 1996), xxiii. As Julia Andrews has documented, after 1971 Zhou Enlai was briefly able to encourage greater freedom in the world of art. Julia Andrews, *Painters and Politics in the People's Republic of China, 1949–1979* (Berkeley: University of California Press, 1994).

12. Merle Goldman, *China's Intellectuals: Advise and Dissent* (Cambridge, MA: Harvard University Press, 1981), 162–63.

13. *Evolution and Ethics* was first translated into classical Chinese by Yan Fu in 1898. According to paleoanthropologist Wu Xinzhi, the propagandist Yao

Wenyuan read *Man's Place in Nature* and wrote a positive review of it for Mao. Mao agreed with Yao's assessment, and subsequently the paleoanthropologist Wu Rukang and the paleontologist Zhou Mingzhen retranslated it. Author interview, Wu Xinzhi, January 17, 2002.

14. The first quotation was selected from Mao's 1940 *On New Democracy*. The second, "Use the past to serve the present, use the foreign to serve China" (*gu wei jin yong, yang wei zhong yong*), came from the 1964 "Chairman Mao's Talk to Music Workers."

15. Readership was much higher than 300,000, since friends, families, and even entire work units shared subscriptions. Precise subscription data are not available. Interview data, however, consistently put the figure at 300,000 before the increase in the number of popular science magazines in the late 1970s.

16. "Zheng gao jianze" [Guidelines for solicited articles], *Huashi*, trial issue (1972): 32. The origin of the "three great revolutionary movements" was a selection from an article Mao wrote in 1963 that became part of the famous "little red book" of the Cultural Revolution, *Quotations from Chairman Mao Zedong*. "Class struggle, the struggle for production and scientific experiment are the three great revolutionary movements for building a mighty socialist country. These movements are a sure guarantee that communists will be free from bureaucracy and immune against revisionism and dogmatism, and will for ever remain invincible." See Mao Tse-tung, *Quotations from Chairman Mao Tse-tung* (Peking: Foreign Languages Press, 1966), 40.

17. "Zheng gao jianze," 32. "Stratigraphy workers" (*diceng gongzuozhe*) presumably refers to all "science workers" (the politically appropriate term used collectively for scientists, technicians, and laborers engaged in scientific work) participating in stratigraphy, geology, paleontology, paleoanthropology, and any other study related to geologic strata.

18. Yang Jiao, *Zhongguo kepu zuojia cidian* [Dictionary of Chinese popular science writers] (Harbin: Heilongjiang kexue jishu chubanshe, 1989), vol. 1, 26–27.

19. Interview data on when Zhang Feng began working at *Fossils* and what position he held are contradictory, and I have been unable to find documentary evidence. Zhang Feng only recently agreed to be interviewed. The information he shared will be incorporated into future publications, while the information provided here was supplied by his former colleagues at IVPP.

This chapter relies extensively on interview data. However, the effects of trauma on memories of the Cultural Revolution compound the more general problem people have remembering specific details of events in the past. History teachers will not be surprised that dates and numbers are the most unreliable. Where I am unable to provide documentary evidence, I will be forced either to discuss the events in relatively general terms or to indicate that given information cannot be verified and must be treated with appropriate caution.

20. Chinese academic journals often use Latin for their preferred western name. This journal also sometimes used the more appropriate western name *Paleo-vertebrata et Paleoanthropologia.*

21. An interview subject remembers the large-print issue of *Fossils* having been prepared for Mao as a result of the inclusion in *Fossils* of a worker's criticism of an IVPP scientist (discussed below).

22. I have only recently found a copy of the original letter. A summary appears along with Mao's memo to Deng and Yao in Mao Zedong, *Jianguo yilai Mao Ze-dong wen'gao* [Mao Zedong's manuscripts since the founding of the PRC] (Beijing: Zhongyang wenxian chubanshe, 1998), vol. 13, 468.

23. "Speak bitterness" meetings date from revolutionary times. The Commu-nist Party encouraged peasants in communist-established soviets to attend meet-ings where they narrated long lists of grievances, particularly against landlords who had treated them unfairly.

24. This interview subject began working at IVPP several years after the Cultural Revolution. He remembers hearing about the incident at home from a family member who was then an employee of the Chinese Academy of Sciences. He originally said about 100,000 people participated, but then revised it down to 10,000.

25. The interviewee is a scientist who joined the institute in the 1950s. He was in the field when the events took place, but he remembers hearing about them from his colleagues. Hu Yaobang may be familiar to western audiences as the of-ficial whose death and memorial sparked the 1989 student protests in Tiananmen Square.

26. All three of these interviews were held while I was in Beijing in 2002.

27. "Genju Zhongguo kexue yuan qunzhong jiefa dazibao zhailu" [Extracts of big character posters in which the masses expose the Chinese Academy of Sci-ences], *Zhongyang shouzhang jianghua deng* [Central leadership speeches, etc.] 122–2 (Box 5, JC188Y), collected along with red guard materials at Harvard University's Fairbank Center.

28. Hu Qiaomu zhuan bianxiezu, ed., *Deng Xiaoping de ershisi ci tanhua* [Deng Xiaoping's twenty-four speeches] (Beijing: Renmin chubanshe, 2004), 76; "Guowuyuan lingdao tongzhi zai tingqu Hu Yaobang tongzhi huibao shi chahua (chuanchao gao)" [State Council leaders comment on Hu Yaobang's report (pri-vate draft)], *Zhongyang shouzhang jianghua deng* 122–3 (Box 5, JC188Y), collected along with red guard materials at Harvard University's Fairbank Center. This is the most conspicuous of several places in this chapter where I am heavily indebted to the kind guidance of Michael Schoenhals.

29. Hu Qiaomu zhuan bianxiezu, ed., *Deng Xiaoping de ershisi*, 76. See also "Guowuyuan lingdao tongzhi."

30. I found a copy of the six-page plan, entitled "*Huashi* yijiuqiliu nian xuan ti jihua" [Plan for the selection of topics for *Fossils* in 1976], and the letter (dated February 1976) in an unmarked box among Yang Zhongjian's books and papers in the IVPP library.

31. Dazhai was a model production brigade that had reportedly greatly improved the productivity of its land through the hard work and revolutionary fervor of its members.

32. Mao coined this phrase in response to a report on worker innovations during the Great Leap Forward (May 18, 1958). See Mao Zedong, *Jianguo yilai Mao Zedong wen'gao*, vol. 7, 236.

33. The Peking Man fossils were unearthed in the late 1920s and 1930s during excavations in which both western and Chinese scientists participated. At the time, they were widely regarded as the richest evidence on human evolution in the world.

34. I have no documentary confirmation for these dates, and the other people who participated are unclear about when the events took place.

35. Interview data. See also Xizang zizhi qu wenhuaguan [Tibet Autonomous Region Culture Center], "Bu yao shenquan yao kexue, bu xin 'tianming' gan geming—xi kan Lasa 'laodong chuangzao le ren' zhanlan" [We need science, not theocracy; we make revolution and don't believe in fate—Enjoying the Lhasa "Labor Created Humanity" exhibit], *Huashi* 1 (1977): 5–6, 2. Also see the inner front cover of *Huashi* 1 (1977) for photographs of the exhibit and accompanying activities.

36. Beijing bowuguan xiehui, *Beijing bowuguan nianjian (1912–1987)* [Yearbook of Beijing museums (1912–1987)] (Beijing: Beijing yanshan chubanshe, 1989), 509.

37. Xi'an Banpo bowuguan nianjian bianji weiyuanhui, *Xi'an Banpo bowuguan nianjian*, 1958–1998 [Xi'an Banpo Museum yearbook, 1958–1998] (no publication information), 118; author interview, Gao Qiang, April 13, 2002; author interview, Duan Shuqin, January 28, 2002; author interview, Zhang Lifen, February 4, 2002.

38. Author interview, Zhao Zhongyi, January 29, 2002; author interview, Gao Qiang, April 13, 2002.

39. Author interview, Lu Qingwu, June 3, 2002.

40. Jia Lanpo wrote these opinions in an informal document prepared for a meeting of the small group, and his son has preserved the document among his other papers, which are ordered chronologically and provided with page numbers. Jia Lanpo, "Dui Zhoukoudian xin chenlieguan fang'an de yijian" [Opinions on the plan for the Zhoukoudian exhibition hall], April 16, 1971, 117–20.

41. Information on the content of the exhibit provided here comes from a

pamphlet sold at the exhibit. Zhongguo kexue yuan gu jizhui dongwu yu gu renlei yanjiu suo, *Beijing yuanren yizhi jianjie* [A brief introduction to the Peking Man site] (Beijing: Zhongguo kexue yuan yinshuchang, 1972).

42. Zhongguo kexue yuan, *Beijing yuanren yizhi jianjie*, 5–6.

43. Shanghai ziran bowuguan, *"Cong yuan dao ren" zhanlan jieshao* [Introduction to the "From Ape to Human" exhibit] (no publication information, undoubtedly from the 1970s), 2.

44. Zhoukoudian Guest Book, June 14, 1956.

45. Author interview, Zhao Zhongyi, January 29, 2002. Zhao visited the exhibition hall before it was renovated.

46. For example, Wu Xinzhi designed a display in which casts of fossils were set within a painted silhouette to show the anatomical relationship of the bones and one depicting fossil evidence of fire with a painted backdrop representing smoke. Both displays were preserved in later renovations. Author interview, Wu Xinzhi, February 21, 2002. Reports conflict as to when Zhoukoudian first used statues of Peking Man, but there was certainly at least a small diorama.

47. The Upper Cave Man remains belong to the anatomically modern, Paleolithic humans found at Zhoukoudian.

48. See Josef Augusta and Zdeněk Burian, *Prehistoric Man* (London: Paul Hamlyn, 1960). At that time, there were no special classes or degrees available in scientific art. Li Rongshan had no training in science and no particular interest in science before being placed ("by chance," as he recalls) at IVPP. Author interview, Li Rongshan, January 24, 2002.

49. Author interview, Zhang Lifen, February 4, 2002. Zhang worked as a guide at Zhoukoudian until 1978, after which she transferred to IVPP proper to become a technician who creates casts and prepares fossils. The casts she and others make at IVPP have been used for research by scientists all over the world and have been widely displayed in schools, museums, and even the United Nations.

50. The quotation, originating in 1964, was included in *Quotations from Chairman Mao Zedong*. Mao Tse-tung, *Quotations from Chairman Mao*, 203–4.

51. Rules at Zhoukoudian were likely similar to those at Tianjin Natural History Museum, where visitors were required to have letters of introduction from their work units. Tianjin ziran bowuguan, ed., *Renlei de qiyuan zhanlan jianjie* [Introduction to the exhibit on human origins] (no publication information; undoubtedly from the late Cultural Revolution), 16.

52. Author interview, Zhao Zhongyi, January 29, 2002. (Zhao Zhongyi now works at IVPP producing reconstructions of prehistoric fauna and busts of modern-day scientists for the exhibition halls.) Members of the American Paleoanthropology Delegation who visited IVPP and Zhoukoudian in 1975 were told that Zhoukoudian then had "close to one thousand visitors" every day. Kwang-chih

Chang, "Public Archaeology in China," in Howells and Tsuchitani, eds., *Paleoanthropology in the People's Republic of China*, 136.

53. Author interview, Zhang Lifen, February 4, 2002. The Peking Man fossils were lost in 1941, ironically while being shipped to the United States for safekeeping during the war. Accusations that the Americans had stolen the fossils emerged during the Korean War and persisted throughout the Mao era. For an English-language treatment of the issue, see Harry L. Shapiro, *Peking Man* (New York: Simon and Schuster, 1974). For a recent, in-depth Chinese treatment, see Li Mingsheng and Yue Nan, *Xunzhao "Beijing ren"* [Searching for "Peking Man"] (Beijing: Huaxia chubanshe, 2000).

54. Author interview, Duan Shuqin, January 2002. Duan worked for many years in science dissemination at Zhoukoudian before transferring to IVPP's Paleoanthropology Museum after it opened in 1994.

55. Author interview, Zhang Lifen and Zhao Zhongyi, February 4, 2002.

56. Shanghai kexue jiaoyu zhipianchang [Shanghai Science Education Film Studios], *Zhongguo gudai renlei* [China's ancient humans] (1976).

57. Jia Lanpo, *Zhoukoudian: "Beijing ren" zhi jia* [Zhoukoudian: The home of "Peking Man"] (Beijing: Beijing renmin chubanshe, 1975), 21.

58. For a sympathetic foreigner's view, see C. K. Jen, "Science and the Open-Doors Educational Movement." Suzanne Pepper has written the most comprehensive overview of education in socialist China in *Radicalism and Education Reform in 20th-Century China: The Search for an Ideal Development Model* (Cambridge, UK: Cambridge University Press, 1996).

59. Zhang Yihong, "Kaimen ban keyan jiu shi hao" [Open-door science is a good thing], *Huashi* 2 (1976): 5.

60. Mao used this phrase in August 1971 to describe his diversification of the Military Affairs Committee to include people not affiliated with Lin Biao. See Mao Zedong, *Jianguo yilai*, vol. 13, 246–47.

61. Although scientists' elitism may well have contributed to their irritation over this policy, the noise of technicians engaged in fossil preparation undoubtedly hampered their work.

62. Shuping Yao very briefly defines "mixing sand" as it related to science: "While scientists were leaving the institutes, a host of workers and farmers were invited into them. This was called *chan shazi* (mixing sand)." Yao, "Chinese Intellectuals and Science," 465.

63. Liu Houyi, "'Yuanmou ren' kaocha ji" [Notes on the investigation of "Yuanmou Man"], *Yunnan wenwu jian bao* 4 (October 1974): 14–15.

64. Author interview, Jiang Chu, May 18, 2002.

65. Liu Houyi, "'Yuanmou ren' kaocha ji," 15.

66. Author interview, Jiang Chu, May 18, 2002.

67. Author interview, Li Zixiu, May 17, 2002; author interview, Jiang Chu, May 18, 2002.

68. Xinzhi Wu and Frank E. Poirier, *Human Evolution in China: A Metric Description of the Fossils and a Review of the Sites* (New York: Oxford University Press, 1995), 17.

69. Except where noted, the information presented here about Nihewan comes from Wei Qi, author interview, October 7, 2002.

70. Hebei sheng Yangyuan xian wenhuaguan [Cultural center of Hebei province, Yangyuan county], "Qunzhong ban kexue de daolu yue zou yue kuan'guang" [The road of mass science gets broader the more it is traveled], *Huashi* 2 (1975): 4–5; Xia Shufang, *Huashi mantan* [Conversations about fossils] (Shanghai: Shanghai kexue jishu chubanshe, 1978), 207–8.

71. No author, "Qunzhong bao huashi" [The masses report fossils], *Huashi*, trial issue (1972): 26–27.

72. Author interview, Yan Defa, December 2, 2001. Yan originally worked as a field researcher in paleontology, but because of poor health he was reassigned to a desk job in the 1960s.

73. Survey no. 39, 2002. I mailed a survey to people who responded to an advertisement I placed in *Fossils* magazine. Fifty-four people returned completed surveys.

74. Li Xuwen, survey no. 33, 2002; author interview, Li Xuwen, May 21, 2002; author interview, Ji Xueping, May 15, 2002.

75. See, for example, Gary Trudeau's depiction of bird watchers in his comic strip, *Doonesbury*. Gary Trudeau, *Doonesbury Dossier: The Reagan Years* (New York: Holt, Rinehart and Winston, 1984).

76. Such "workers" and "soldiers" may have been people who came from intellectual backgrounds but who had the necessary connections to obtain these desirable labels. In any case, anyone able to read and write about Marxist theory had almost certainly at least attended secondary school.

77. Zhou Guoxing, "Xiandai de yuan neng biancheng ren ma?" [Can modern apes become human?], *Huashi* 2 (1973), 10. The notion of history as a fixed entity whose tape could not be rolled back was not unique to socialist China, but it did well represent the rigidity of historical materialism as canonized there. The tape of history which cannot be rewound is found, for example, in Stephen Jay Gould's *Wonderful Life: The Burgess Shale and the Nature of History* (New York: Norton, 1989).

78. Yuan Hanxing and Zhang Jianpeng, "Women dui 'Xiandai yuan neng biancheng ren ma?' yi wen de yidian kanfa" [A few of our views on the article "Can modern apes become human?"], *Huashi* 1 (1975): 25.

79. Rather than retranslating this quotation, I have relied here on Mao Zedong, *Selected Works*, vol. 2, 314.

80. Ibid.

81. Chen Chun, "Zenyang lijie renlei qiyuan zhong de 'teding huanjing'" [How to understand the "specific environmental conditions" of human origins], *Huashi* 2 (1975): 22.

82. Zheng Hong, "Guanyu teding de huanjing ji qi zai renlei qiyuan zhong de zuoyong" [On the specific environment and its role in human origins], *Huashi* 2 (1975): 23.

83. Yuan Hanxing, "Cong renlei qiyuan kan fuzhi tiancailun de fandongxing" [A look from human origins at the reactionary character of reproducing the theory of innate genius], *Huashi* 3 (1976): 16, 5; Yuan Hanxing, "Duiyu renyuan huafen wenti yidian yijian" [A few opinions on the division between human and ape], *Gu jizhui dongwu yu gu renlei* 13, no. 2 (April 1975): 77–80; Yuan Hanxing, "Guanyu disiji mingming yu huafen tantao" [Inquiries into the naming and divisions of the quaternary], *Gu jizhui dongwu yu gurenlei* 14, no. 4 (October 1976): 222–27.

84. Author interview, Zhou Guoxing, January 7, 2002. Efforts to locate Yuan Hanxing have thus far failed.

85. Author interview, Zhou Guoxing, April 17, 2004.

86. See the editors' note introducing Dong Tiehan and Liu Guojun, "Guanyu cong yuan dao ren guodu jieduan de taolun" [Debate on the stages in the process from ape to human], *Huashi* 1 (1976): 25, which included two letters. Because of space limitations, I will not provide full citations for the other nine letters and articles. Please see *Huashi* 2 (1976): 23; 2 (1976): 31; 2 (1976): 31, 26; 3 (1976): 31 (three letters); 4 (1976): 14–16, 21; 1 (1977): 28–29; 3 (1977): 29–30.

87. Wu Rukang, "Ren yu yuan de jiexian wenti" [The problem of the boundary between human and ape], *Vertebrata PalAsiatica* 12, no. 3 (July 1974): 181–82, 186.

88. Frederick Engels, *Dialectics of Nature*, in E. J. Hobsbaum et al., eds., *Karl Marx, Frederick Engels: Collected Works* (Moscow: Progress Publishers, 1987), vol. 25, 493.

89. Deng was then undergoing his second round of formal criticisms. Xinhua she Nanjing, "Xiang gurenleixue zhong zichan jieji guandian yonggan tianzhan" [Bravely challenging the bourgeois viewpoint in paleoanthropology to battle], *Renmin ribao*, August 18, 1976: 3.

90. Lai Jinliang, "Ping 'yi yuan yi ren' jieduan lun" [Criticizing the "both ape and human" stage theory], *Huashi* 4 (1976): 14–16, 21.

91. Lai Jinliang, "Ping 'yi yuan yi ren' jieduan lun" [Criticizing the "both ape and human" stage theory], *Kexue tongbao* 21, no. 9 (1976): 404–9.

92. Wu Rukang, "Laodong chuangzao renlei—jinian 'Laodong zai cong yuan

dao ren zhuanbian guocheng de zuoyong' xie zuo yibai zhou nian" [Labor created humanity: Commemorating the hundredth anniversary of "The Part Played by Labor in the Transition from Ape to Human"], *Huashi* 2 (1976): 6–8.

93. Wu Rukang, "Guanyu cong yuan dao ren de guodu jieduan zhong 'yi yuan yi ren' de xingzhi wenti" [On the problem of the nature of "both ape and human" in the stages from ape to human], *Huashi* 1 (1977): 28–29; Wang Jianjun and Wang Anzheng, "Zenyang renshi 'fei ci ji bi' yu 'yi ci yi bi' de bianzheng guanxi" [How to identify the dialectical relationships between "either this or that" and "both this and that"], *Huashi* 3 (1977): 29–30.

94. This same point had been made in the post–Great Leap Forward reevaluation of science and scientists, and it was a key part of Deng's remarks after Hu Yaobang's September 1975 report to the State Council (see Note 28 above).

95. Author interview, Huang Weiwen, December 27, 2001. See also Jia Lanpo and Huang Weiwen, *The Story of Peking Man: From Archaeology to Mystery*, trans. Yin Zhiqi (Beijing: Foreign Languages Press, 1990), 217–18.

96. Nakayama Shigeru, "Grass-Roots Geology: Ijiri Shōji and the Chidanken," in Nakayama Shigeru, David L. Swain, and Yaga Eri, eds., *Science and Society in Modern Japan: Selected Historical Sources* (Cambridge, MA: M.I.T. Press, 1974), 270–90. I thank Nakayama Shigeru for alerting me to this source.

97. Ibid., 274.

98. Ibid., 277.

99. Hebei sheng Yangyuan xian wenhuaguan, "Qunzhong ban kexue," 5.

100. Author interview, Wei Qi, October 7, 2002. Wei Qi has recently published an article on Nihewan in which he includes a discussion of the lake legend. Wei Qi, "Zou xiang shehui, zou xiang qunzhong—Nihewan yanjiu ying xiang zhishi jingji zhuanhua" [Move in the direction of society, move in the direction of the masses—Nihewan research should turn to knowledge and economics], *Huashi* 1 (2001): 33–35.

101. Peasant knowledge of farming was an obvious well to tap in agriculture. Earthquake prediction efforts in the 1970s relied extensively on peasants' observations of livestock behavior. For something close to such a Marxist standpoint epistemology for industry, see Mao's memo of 1958 cited in Note 32 above.

Chapter 8: To Be Somebody

ABBREVIATIONS USED IN THE NOTES

FJRB *Fujian ribao* [Fujian Daily]
FPA Fujian Provincial Archives

While I assume complete responsibility for the research and findings of this chapter, I am greatly indebted to Dahpon Ho for his assistance in the writing of this final version. His help in working out the organization and correcting my English is particularly appreciated.

1. Mao himself only replied to two letters from the masses during the ten years of the Cultural Revolution. Besides Li, another favored addressee was a group of red guards at Qinghua Attached High School, whose rebellion was supported by Mao in the letter. So Li was the only individual from the masses to get a personal letter from Mao during the Cultural Revolution. See Zhonggong zhongyang wenxian yanjiushi, ed., *Jianguo yilai Mao Zedong wen'gao* [Mao Zedong's manuscripts and drafts since the founding of the People's Republic of China] (Beijing: Zhongyang wenxian chubanshe, 1987), vol. 12, 87–89.

2. Xiao Su, who was a Fujianese primary school student in 1973, could still recite Mao's thirty-character reply to Li Qinglin word for word when I met her at the University of California, San Diego, on June 10, 2003.

3. FPA, C157–1–10 (1973): "Quanguo zhiqing gongzuo huiyi huibao chuanda cailiao" [Materials on the 1973 national sent-down youth work conference], Document 1: "Zhongyang shouzhang zai zhongyang youguan bumen huibao zhishi qingnian shangshan xiaxiang gongzuo qingkuanghui shang de zhishi" [Orders from central leaders on the national sent-down youth work conference], 4. Also see FPA, C157–1–149 (1973): "Li Qinglin, Zhou Mantian jianghua" [The speeches of Li Qinglin and Zhou Mantian], Document 1: "Li Qinglin tongzhi zai Fuzhoushi qunzhong dahui shang de jianghua" [Li Qinglin's speech at the mass meeting in Fuzhou], 1.

4. FJRB, November 15, 1977: 1.

5. Mobo C. F. Gao, "Factional Politics in the CPC: A Case Study of the Rise and Fall of Li Qinglin," *China Report* 35 (January–March 1999): 58–59.

6. When I arrived at the Fujian Provincial Archives on August 4, 2003, the archives were launching a large project to convert the archives into PDF documents. All the volumes from the provincial office responsible for sent-down youth (category C157–1) had already been moved from storage to the computer room. Fortunately, the staff there allowed me take out the requested volumes. I noticed that the word "destroy" (*xiao*) had been marked on some volumes. The staff informed me that those were categorized as "unimportant" and would not be transferred to PDF format. This means that future visitors will not be allowed access to them anymore, as the selected electronic documents will be the only ones open to the public.

7. For a typical example of such accounts, see Xu Zhigeng, "Lishi de wanxiao: Li Qinglin ershinian chenfulu" [A historical joke: A twenty-year chronicle of the rise and fall of Li Qinglin], *Yuhua* (April 1994): 64–68.

8. Cai Tianxin, "Li Qinglin gei Mao Zedong xiexin shijian de qianyin houguo"

[The origin and result of Li Qinglin's letter to Mao], in Putian xian wenshiban, ed., *Bainian Putian* [The history of Putian county, 1900–2000] (Beijing: Zhongyang wenxian chubanshe, 2002), 315.

9. Author interview, Li Qinglin, Putian, August 17, 2003.

10. Author interview, Li Qinglin and Li Liangmo, Putian, August 12, 2003.

11. Ibid.

12. At that time the provision of food and daily necessities was mostly controlled by the state, and residents purchased these through tickets allotted by the government according to the number of mouths in the family. The average ration for each urban resident usually only met the basic living requirement. Thus youth, once rusticated in villages, were removed from the ration distribution lists, and their families could not provide for them in the city. This policy played a major role in preventing urban rusticated youth from unofficially returning to the city. Li Liangmo was removed from the ration list as soon as he became a sent-down youth in 1969. Author interview, Li Qinglin and Li Liangmo, Putian, August 12, 2003.

13. Li Songchen et al., eds., *Wen'ge dang'an* [Collection of Cultural Revolution documents] (Beijing: Dangdai Zhongguo chubanshe, 1999), 1090–91.

14. FPA, C157–1–270 (1974): "Jinian fuxin yizhounian" [Celebrating the first anniversary of Chairman Mao's reply to Comrade Li], Document 6: "Li Qinglin zai shengshi qingnian jinian Mao zhuxi gei Li Qinglin tongzhi zhongyao fuxin yizhounian dahui shang de jianghua" [Li Qinglin's symposium speech on the anniversary of Chairman Mao's reply], 8–9.

15. Author interview, Li Qinglin and Li Liangmo, Putian, August 12, 2003.

16. Author interview, Li Qinglin, Putian, August 17, 2003. An example of the swimming pool story (where Mao picks out Li's letter randomly after swimming in Zhongnanhai) can be found in Xu Zhigeng, "Lishi de wanxiao," 63. The volleyball story claims that Li Qinglin's daughter was on the national volleyball team and had a chance to meet Chairman Mao himself. This was recounted in conversation with former Fujian resident Xiao Su, in San Diego, California, June 10, 2003.

17. Li Songchen et al., eds., *Wen'ge dang'an*, 1090–91.

18. Ibid.

19. Cai Tianxin, "Li Qinglin shangshu yu zhiqing zhengce tiaozheng" [Li Qinglin's letter to Chairman Mao and the adjustment in party policy on sent-down youth], *Zhonggong dangshi yanjiu* 94 (April 2003): 31.

20. Zhonggong zhongyang wenxian yanjiushi, *Jianguo yilai Mao Zedong wen'gao*, vol. 13, 12, 115.

21. Ibid., 351, 349.

22. Cai Tianxin, "Li Qinglin shangshu yu zhiqing zhengce tiaozheng," 31. Also

see Zhonggong zhongyang wenxian yanjiushi, ed., *Zhou Enlai nianpu* [A chronological biography of Zhou Enlai] (Beijing: Zhongyang wenxian chubanshe, 1997), vol. 2, 589.

23. FPA, C157–1–7 (1973): "Zhonggong zhongyang guowuyuan wenjian" [Documents of the State Council], Document 1: "Zhongfa [1973] ershiyi hao" [Central document no. 21 (1973)], 1–10. Also see Zhonggong zhongyang wenxian yanjiushi, *Zhou Enlai nianpu*, vol. 1, 349–50.

24. FPA, C157–1–7 (1973), Document 1, 1.

25. Cai Tianxin, "Li Qinglin shangshu yu zhiqing zhengce tiaozheng," 32.

26. Ibid., 33.

27. Author interview, Zhang Jianhua, Fuzhou, August 25, 2003. Zhang Jianhua was a sent-down youth in Fujian Province.

28. FPA, C157–1–10 (1973), Document 7: "Zhongyang shouzhang zai zhongyang youguan bumen huibao zhishi qingnian shangshan xiaxiang gongzuo qingkuanghui shang de zhishi" [Orders of central leaders for reports on the national sent-down youth work conference], 1–3.

29. Cai Tianxin, "Li Qinglin shangshu yu zhiqing zhengce tiaozheng," 33–34.

30. In his letter, Li exhaustively described the food, housing, and income problems his son encountered. But except for the expression of his discontent over corruption, there was not a single word in the letter about other rusticated youth. See Li Songchen et al., eds., *Wen'ge dang'an*, 1090–91.

31. FPA, C157–1–153 (1973): "Guance 'fuxin'" [The study of Chairman Mao's reply to Li Qinglin in Fujian], Document 8: "Gedi xuexi Mao zhuxi gei Li Qinglin tongzhi de xin de qingkuang" [Reports on the study of Chairman Mao's reply to Comrade Li Qinglin from various places], 1.

32. FPA, C157–1–153 (1973), Document 5: "Fuzhoushi Chiwei qu, Chaoyang qu he Minhou xian xiangqian gongshe bufen ganbu qunzhong dui Mao zhuxi gei Li Qinglin tongzhi de xin de fanying" [The responses to Chairman Mao's letter to Comrade Li Qinglin from cadres and masses of Chiwei and Chaoyang districts in Fuzhou city and of Minhou county], 1–2.

33. FPA, C157–1–10 (1973), Document 1, 1.

34. FPA, C157–1–153 (1973), Document 1: "Putian xian chuanda Mao zhuxi gei Li Qinglin tongzhi huixin de yixie qingkuang" [Reports from Putian county on the circulation of Chairman Mao's reply to Comrade Li Qinglin], 1.

35. FPA, C157–1–269 (1974), "Pi Lin pi Kong" [The campaign to criticize Lin Biao and Confucius], Document 2: "Pi Lin pi Kong zhong youguan zhiqing wenti de dazibao zhaichao" [Selection of big character posters on the sent-down youth issue in the campaign to criticize Lin Biao and Confucius], 9. On May 3, *People's Daily* also published a very small picture of Putian sent-down youth on the third page. Yao Wenyuan immediately criticized this move, saying that it conflicted with Mao's reply to Li. Ibid.

36. FPA, C157–1–270 (1974), Document 6, 11–12.

37. FPA, C157–1–153 (1973), Document 1, 1–2.

38. FPA, C157–1–153 (1973), Document 2: "Putian diwei xuexi guanche Mao zhuxi de xin de qingkuang" [Putian municipal government report on the study of Chairman Mao's letter], 2.

39. FPA, C157–1–153 (1973), Document 1, 2.

40. FPA, C157–1–270 (1974), Document 6, 12.

41. FPA, C157–1–153 (1973), Document 1, 2.

42. FPA, C157–1–269 (1974), Document 2, 2–3.

43. FPA, C157–1–269 (1974), Document 1: "Han Xianchu dengren shi zenyang duikang Mao zhuxi gei Li Qinglin tongzhi fuxin de" [How Han Xianchu and his allies opposed Chairman Mao's reply to Comrade Li Qinglin], 3.

44. FPA, C157–1–153 (1973), Document 1, 2.

45. FPA, C157–1–153 (1973), Document 13: "Zhou Mantian tongzhi liuyue ershiyiri xiawu cong Beijing dalai dianhua" [Comrade Zhou Mantian's phone call from Beijing on June 21], 1–2; Document 15: "Zhou Mantian tongzhi liuyue ershi-wuri cong Beijing dalai de dianhua" [Comrade Zhou Mantian's phone call from Beijing on June 25], 3; Document 17: "Liuyue sanshiri Zhou Mantian tongzhi dalai dianhua yaodian" [Main points of Comrade Zhou Mantian's phone call from Beijing on June 30], 1–2.

46. FPA, C157–1–10 (1973), Document 2: "Quanguo zhishi qingnian shang-shan xiaxiang gongzuo huiyi qijian Mao zhuxi he dangzhongyang shouzhang de zhishi" [Orders from Chairman Mao and top party leaders on the national sent-down youth work conference], 1–2.

47. FPA, C157–1–153 (1973), Document 15, 1.

48. FPA, C157–1–270 (1974), Document 6, 12.

49. FPA, C157–1–269 (1974), Document 1, 3.

50. FPA, C157–1–270 (1974), Document 6, 12. Also see FPA, C157–1–269 (1974), Document 1, 4.

51. FPA, C157–1–270 (1974), Document 6, 14.

52. FPA, C157–1–270 (1974), Document 4: "Xu Huoqing tongzhi zai 'sheng xuexi Mao zhuxi gei Li Qinglin tongzhi zhongyao fuxin zhishi qingnian zuotanhui shang de jianghua'" [Xu Yuqing's symposium speech on the anniversary of Chairman Mao's reply to Comrade Li Qinglin], 3. Xu Huoqing was at that time the one of leading members of the provincial party committee.

53. FPA, C157–1–269 (1974), Document 1, 5.

54. FPA, C157–1–269 (1974), Document 2, 11.

55. Author interview, Li Qinglin and Li Liangmo, August 12, 2003.

56. FPA, C157–1–269 (1974), Document 1, 5.

57. FPA, C157–1–269 (1974), Document 1, 2–3.

58. FPA, C157–1–269 (1974), Document 1, 4.

59. Ibid.

60. FPA, C157–1–270 (1974), Document 6, 15.

61. FJRB, April 26, 1973: 1; April 26, 1973: 1.

62. FPA, C157–1–270 (1974), Document 15: "Xuexi Mao zhuxi gei Li Qinglin tongzhi zhongyao fuxin zhuankan" [Special symposium report on the anniversary of Chairman Mao's reply to Comrade Li Qinglin], 1.

63. FPA, C157–1–270 (1974), Document 15, 4.

64. FPA, C157–1–270 (1974), Document 6, 8. Also see FPA, C157–1–149 (1973), Document 1, 3–4.

65. FPA, C157–1–270 (1974), Document 6, 10.

66. Ibid., 8–9.

67. See "Jiefa pipan shengwei yuan zhuyao lingdaoren duikang Mao zhuxi gei Li Qinglin tongzhi fuxin de zuixing," and "Ganyu fanchaoliu, ganyu jianchi zhengque luxian," respectively, FJRB, April 28, 1974: 1.

68. FJRB, April 28, 1974: 1.

69. Chen Yichun, "Fujian wen'ge shinian shulüe" [The Cultural Revolution decade in Fujian], *Fujian dangshi yanjiu* (April 1992): 35.

70. Cai Tianxin, "Li Qinglin gei Mao Zedong xiexin shijian de qianyin houguo," 332.

71. Author interview, Cai Tianxin, Putian, August 18, 2003. Cai is currently in the Office of Party History in Putian County, and has published a series of articles on Li Qinglin.

72. Author interview, Zhang Yizhong, Fuzhou, August 13, 2003. Zhang had been a Putian county government cadre from 1971 to 1980. Furthermore, the house of Li Liangmo, Li Qinglin's eldest son, was crowded with peasants from various places in June 1973. Author interview, Li Liangmo, Putian, August 27, 2003.

73. Cai Tianxin, "Li Qinglin gei Mao Zedong xiexin shijian de qianyin houguo," 333.

74. Author interview, Li Liangmo, Putian, August 12, 2003.

75. Author interview, Zhang Yizhong, Fuzhou, August 13, 2003.

76. Author interview, Li Liangmo, Putian, August 17, 2003.

77. Author interview, Weng Zhijun, Putian, August 15, 2003. Wen is a former *Fujian ribao* correspondent who has spent years gathering material for a biography of Li Qinglin.

78. Author interview, Cai Tianxin, Putian, August 18, 2003.

79. "Li Qinglin jiaozi wunong songzi xiaxiang yi shiji xingdong pi Lin pi Kong" [Li Qinglin strongly supports the campaign against Lin Biao and Confucius by sending his son to the countryside], FJRB, December 22, 1974: 1.

80. Author interview, Weng Zhijun, Putian, August 15, 2003. This account was also confirmed in an interview with Zhang Yizhong, Fuzhou, August 18, 2003.

81. Chen Jianfu, untitled transcript of conversation dated April 29, 1975, in *Fujian ribao* archives. My gratitude to Weng Zhijun for sharing this transcript.

82. Cai Tianxin, "Li Qinglin gei Mao Zedong xiexin shijian de qianyin houguo," 332.

83. FPA, C-157–1–665 (1976): "Shengwei dangxiao jiepi sirenbang ziliao" [Materials for the campaign against the Gang of Four from the Fujian Party School], Document 3: "Chen Jiazhong, Li Qinglin yijiuqiliunian qiyue jiuri shangwu zai shengweiquanwei kuodahuiyi shang de jianghua" [Speech of Chen Jiazhong and Li Qinglin at the Fujian party committee meeting on July 9, 1976], 2.

84. Author interview, Li Qinglin and Li Liangmo, Putian, August 17, 2003.

85. Author interview, Zhang Yizhong, Fuzhou, August 13, 2003.

86. The six members of the special team were staff members from the court, the Disciplinary Inspection Committee (Jilüjiancha weiyuanhui), the Office of Mass Appeals (Xinfang bangongshi) and the Propaganda Department (Xuanchuanbu). Author interview, Zhang Yizhong, Fuzhou, August 13, 2003.

87. Author interview, Li Qinglin, Putian, August 17, 2003. For an example of Li's confession, see FPA, C157–1–665 (1976), Document 7: "Li Qinglin jiaodai yu Chen Jiazhong tanhua qingkuang" [Li Qinglin's confession of his talk with Chen Jiazhong], 2.

88. Author interview, Cai Tianxin, Putian, August 18, 2003.

89. Author interview, Li Qinglin and Li Liangmo, Putian, August 17, 2003.

90. The two rebels were Chen Jiazhong, former member of the Standing Committee of the Fujian party, and Zhuang Zhipeng, former vice president of the Fujian Revolutionary Committee. See Fujian sheng zhi bianzhuan weiyuanhui, ed., *Fujian sheng zhi* [Fujian provincial annals], vol. 10, *Dashiji* [Chronology] (Fuzhou: Fujian renmin chubanshe, 1994), 414.

91. Fujian sheng zhi bianzhuan weiyuanhui, ed., *Fujian sheng zhi*, vol. 1, *Zonggaishu* [General account], 131.

92. "Shengtao sirenbang zai Fujian de qinxin, xianxi fan'geming fenzi de taotian zuixing" [Condemnation of the followers of the Gang of Four in Fujian], FJRB, November 15, 1977: 1.

93. Fujian sheng zhi bianzhuan weiyuanhui, ed., *Fujian shengzhi*, vol. 10, 415.

94. Author interview, Li Qinglin and Li Liangmo, August 17, 2003. This account was also confirmed in interview with Zhang Yizhong, Fuzhou, August 13, 2003.

95. "Shengtao sirenbang zai Fujian de qinxin."

96. Author interview, Li Qinglin and Li Liangmo, Putian, August 12, 2003.

This account was also confirmed in an interview with Cai Tianxin, Putian, August 18, 2003.

97. Author interview, Li Qinglin and Li Liangmo, Putian, August 12, 2003.

98. Author interview, Li Qinglin and Li Liangmo, Putian, August 17, 2003.

99. Ibid.

100. Ibid.

101. Author interview, Weng Zhijun, Putian, August 17, 2003.

102. Author interview, Li Qinglin and Li Liangmo, Putian, August 12, 2003.

103. Author interview, Li Liangmo, Putian, August 17, 2003.

104. Ibid.

Chapter 9: The Sublime and the Profane

1. Liang Xiaosheng, *Jinye you baofengxue*, anthologized in his *Zhiqing xiaoshuo xuan* [Selected novels about sent-down youth] (Xi'an: Xi'an chubanshe, 1993), 388.

2. Quoted in Wang Ban, *The Sublime Figure of History: Aesthetics and Politics in Twentieth-Century China* (Stanford, CA: Stanford University Press, 1997), 21.

3. Wang Xiaobo believes that during the 1960s and 1970s, "China was in an anti-sex age. Only in such an age could sex become the main theme of life, just like only in a famine can eating become so prominent." See his "Cong *Huangjin shidai* tan xiaoshuo yishu" [On *Golden Age* and the novelistic art], in *Wang Xiaobo wenji* [Selected works of Wang Xiaobo] (Beijing: Zhongguo qingnian chubanshe, 1999), 318–19.

4. Quoted in Meng Fanhua, *Jiqing suiyue* [The passionate era] (Ji'nan: Shandong jiaoyu chubanshe, 1998), 118.

5. Quoted in ibid., 117.

6. Ke La, "Zai shijin de daode jiqing zhong zuoxiu" [Exhibiting undue moralistic passion], in Zhu Dake et al., eds., *Shi zuojia pipanshu* [Critiques of ten writers] (Xi'an: Shaanxi shifandaxue chubanshe, 1999), 92.

7. Liang Xiaosheng, *Jinye you baofengxue*, 359.

8. Ibid., 399–400.

9. Wang Xiaobo, *Huangjin shidai*, anthologized in his *Huangjin shidai baiyin shidai* [Golden age, silver age] (Beijing: Zhongguo qingnian chubanshe, 2002), 29.

10. Wang Xiaobo, *Huangjin shidai*, 29.

11. Ibid., 9.

12. Ibid.

13. Liang Xiaosheng, *Jinye you baofengxue*, 386.

14. Ibid., 330–31.

15. Ibid., 397.

16. Another sent-down youth dies when trying to protect the brigade bank

from a robber. Like Pei, this figure was once a substandard sent-down youth, and was only admitted into the mainstream later.

17. Liang Xiaosheng, *Jinye you baofengxue*, 281.

18. Its claim to an authentic depiction of history is borne out by historian Liu Xiaomeng, who quotes this novella in a chapter on how the sent-down youth in Heilongjiang returned to cities. See his *Zhongguo zhiqing shi* [History of China's sent-down youth] (Beijing: Zhongguo shehui kexue chubanshe, 1998), 732, 733.

19. Wang Xiaobo, *Huangjin shidai*, 3.

20. Liang Xiaosheng, *Jinye you baofengxue*, 399.

21. Ibid., 302.

22. My interpretation here may well clash with the author's intentions.

23. Wang Xiaobo, *Huangjin shidai*, 37.

24. Liang Xiaosheng, *Jinye you baofengxue*, 361, 293.

25. Ibid., 292.

26. Wang Xiaobo, *Huangjin shidai*, 4.

27. Ibid., 5.

28. On the difficulty Wang encountered in publishing his books in mainland China, and his unexpected stardom following his death, see Xie Yong and Ding Dong, "Wang Xiaobo: Yiwei zhishifenzi he yige shidai" [Wang Xiaobo: An intellectual and an age], in Ai Xiaoming and Li Yinhe, eds., *Langman qishi: Jiyi Wang Xiaobo* [A romantic knight: Remembering Wang Xiaobo] (Beijing: Zhongguo qingnian chubanshe), 238–56.

29. Wang Xiaobo's given name, meaning "a small ripple," was intended by his parents to commemorate this family event, in the hope that the disaster might finally turn out to be a ripple soon to pass.

30. See Ai Xiaoming's interview with Wang Xiaobo's mother and brother, in Ai Xiaoming and Li Yinhe, eds., *Langman qishi*, 80.

31. Laifang Leung, *Morning Sun: Interviews with Chinese Writers of the Lost Generation* (Armonk, NY: M. E. Sharpe, 1994), 112.

32. According to Wang Xiaobo's brother and mother, Wang went to Yunnan not against his will, but against the family's will. If that is true, it testifies to the widespread revolutionary enthusiasm of that period, which even consumed those at the margin. See Ai Xiaoming's interview with them, in Ai Xiaoming and Li Yinhe, eds., *Langman qishi*, 81.

33. Liang Xiaosheng, *Zibai* [Confessions] (Beijing: Jingji ribao chubanshe, 1997), 144–45.

34. Laifang Leung, *Morning Sun*, 272.

35. See Tian Song's interview with Wang Xiaobo, "Yi lixing de taidu" [With an attitude of reason], in Ai Xiaoming and Li Yinhe, eds., *Langman qishi*, 238.

36. Laifang Leung, *Morning Sun*, 180. The importance of age is emphasized by

many other sent-down youth too. A former sent-down youth reasons that "people may infer that there might not be much mental difference between two persons aged respectively forty-one and thirty-five; yet we have to admit that there is a big mental gap between two respectively aged twenty-one and fifteen." See Zhang Kai and Ji Yuan, *You shuo lao san jie* [Revisiting the sent-down high school graduates] (Beijing: Zhongguo qingnian chubanshe, 1997), 40.

37. Primary and junior middle school students tended to perceive the Cultural Revolution as a carnival during which they did not have to go to school and their parents were too busy with politics to discipline them. A testimony to this is the film *Yangguang canlan de rizi* [Days of sunshine], based on Wang Shuo's novella of the same name and directed by Jiang Wen.

38. Dai Jinhua, "Zhizhe xixue" [The wise man jokes], *Dangdai zuojia pinglun* 2 (1998): 22. Perhaps the sexual aspect of Wang Xiaobo's works is most vulnerable to misreading by the general public while contributing to his popularity. However, even misreading readers will not miss Wang's condemnation of the Cultural Revolution.

39. Wang Meng's article was published in the next issue of the same periodical in which *Snowstorm Tonight* appeared. Quoted in Meng Fanhua, *Jiqing suiyue*, 117–18.

40. Wang Meng, "Nande mingbai" [It's hard to grasp], *Dushu* 1 (1998): 29.

41. In fact, Dai Jinhua believes that the Cultural Revolution was the "subtext" of all subsequent literature and culture in the 1980s. See her "Zhizhe xixue," 25.

42. Li Jiefei, "Shinian yanyun guoyan" [Ten years in a flash], *Dangdai zuojia pinglun* 1 (1993): 28.

43. On the term "postmodern," see Tang Xiaobing, *Chinese Modern: The Heroic and the Quotidian* (Durham, NC: Duke University Press, 2000), 197. On "post-new era" (*hou xinshiqi*), see Zhang Yiwu, "Dui 'xiandaixing' de zhuiwen" [An inquiry into "modernity"], in Chen Sihe and Yang Yang, eds., *Jiushi niandai piping wenxuan* [Selected critical essays of the 1990s] (Shanghai: Hanyu dacidian chubanshe, 2001), 29–39. On "literature of a new state" (*xin zhuangtai wenxue*), see Wang Gan, Zhang Yiwu, and Zhang Weimin, "Xin zhuangtai wenxue san ren tan" [Three critics talk about the literature of a new state], in ibid., 434–51.

44. Zhang Zhizhong, *Shiji mo de xuanhua* [The fin-de-siècle uproar] (Ji'nan: Shandong jiaoyu chubanshe, 1998), 10. The "incident" mentioned here is of course the suppression of the democratic movement in 1989. Chinese critics have devised several ingenious ways to talk about 1989 without explicitly naming it.

45. Wang Jing argues that the market "certainly usurped the elite as the new legitimate maker of public opinions." See her *High Culture Fever: Politics, Aesthetics and Ideology in Deng's China* (Berkeley: University of California Press), 265. Another critic, Nan Fan, believes the market is an energetic and liberating force

compared to the grand but hasty narratives of the 1980s. See his "Bashi niandai yu 'zhuti' wenti" [The 1980s and the issue of "subjectivity"], *Dangdai zuojia pinglun* 5 (1998): 18.

46. See Zhang Kai and Ji Yuan, *You shuo lao san jie*, 10.

47. Wang Xiaobo, "Chengren de yongqi" [The courage to admit], in *Wang Xiaobo wenji*, 441.

48. Wang Xiaobo, "Guanyu chonggao" [On the sublime], in *Wang Xiaobo wenji*, 178.

49. Wang Xiaobo, "Chengren de yongqi," in *Wang Xiaobo wenji*, 442. Wang Shuo is another profane voice, yet he does not belong to the sent-down youth generation.

50. Dai Jinhua, "Zhizhe xixue," 22.

51. Quoted in Wang Xianghui, *Shangye shidai de yingxiong qingjie—Liang Xiaosheng lun* [Heroic complex in an age of commercialization: On Liang Xiaosheng] (Beijing: Huaxia chubanshe, 2000), 16–17.

52. On that famous exhibition, see Zhang Kai and Ji Yuan, *You shuo lao san jie*, 3–4.

53. Zhang Kangkang, *Dahuang bing he* [The wild north and the frozen river] (Changchun: Jilin renmin chubanshe, 1998), 2.

54. Ibid., 143.

55. Ah Cheng, *Xianhua xianshuo* [Idle talks on idle topics] (Taipei: Shibao chuban, 1994), 213.

56. It is not the case in other areas either. The official designation of the 1989 democracy movement as a "counterrevolutionary riot" (*fan'geming baoluan*) smacks of the Cultural Revolution.

57. Zhu Wei, an editor of *Renmin wenxue* and former sent-down youth, stated in a conference in 1994 that "all books on the sent-down youth are false, including Liang Xiaosheng's. Only the life of sent-down youth depicted by Wang Xiaobo is real." See Ai Xiaoming and Li Yinhe, eds., *Langman qishi*, 260.

Selected Bibliography

Ah Cheng 阿城. *Xianhua xianshuo* 閑話閑說 [Idle talks on idle topics]. Taipei: Shibao chubanshe, 1994.

Ai Xiaoming, and Li Yinhe 艾晓明, 李银河, eds. *Langman qishi: Jiyi Wang Xiaobo* 浪漫骑士：纪忆王小波 [A romantic knight: Remembering Wang Xiaobo]. Beijing: Zhongguo qingnian chubanshe, 1997.

Andreas, Joel. "Battling over Political and Cultural Power in the Cultural Revolution." *Theory and Society* 31 (August 2002): 463–519.

Andrews, Julia. *Painters and Politics in the People's Republic of China, 1949–1979.* Berkeley: University of California Press, 1994.

Barcata, Louis. *China in the Throes of the Cultural Revolution: An Eyewitness Report.* New York: Hart, 1968.

Barmé, Geremie, and Bennett Lee, eds. *The Wounded: New Stories from the Cultural Revolution.* Hong Kong: Joint Publishing Co., 1979.

Barnett, A. Doak, and Ezra F. Vogel. *Cadres, Bureaucracy, and Political Power in Communist China.* New York: Columbia University Press, 1967.

Barnouin, Barbara, and Yu Changgen. *Ten Years of Turbulence: The Chinese Cultural Revolution.* London: Kegan Paul International, 1993.

Baum, Richard. *Burying Mao: Chinese Politics in the Age of Deng Xiaoping.* Princeton, NJ: Princeton University Press, 1994.

————. "The Cultural Revolution in the Countryside: Anatomy of a Limited Rebellion." In *The Cultural Revolution in China*, ed. Thomas W. Robinson, 367–479. Berkeley: University of California Press, 1971.

"Beijing shi 'wenhua da geming' dashiji" 北京市'文化大革命'大事记 [Chronicle of events during the "Cultural Revolution" in Beijing]. *Beijing dangshi ziliao tongxun, zengkan* 17 and 18 (May and June 1987). Beijing: Zhonggong Beijing shiwei dangshi ziliao zhengji weiyuanhui, 1987.

Bennett, Gordon A. "Political Labels and Popular Tension." *Current Scene* (February 26, 1969): 1–15.

Bennett, Gordon A., and Ronald Montaperto. *Red Guard: The Political Biography of Dai Hsiao-ai.* New York: Doubleday, 1972.

Bernstein, Thomas P. *Up to the Mountains and Down to the Villages: The Transfer of Youth from Urban to Rural China.* New Haven, CT: Yale University Press, 1977.

Blecher, Marc J., and Gordon White. *Micropolitics in Contemporary China: The Cultural Revolution in a Technical Work Unit.* Armonk, NY: M. E. Sharpe, 1979.

Bo Yibo 薄一波. *Ruogan zhongda juece yu shijian de huigu* 若干重大决策与事件的回顾 [A review of certain major decisions and incidents]. Beijing: Renmin chubanshe, 1997.

Bu Weihua 卜伟华. "Qinghua fuzhong hongweibing chengli shimo" 清华附中红卫兵成立始末 [The story behind the founding of the Qinghua High School red guards]. *Zhonggong dangshi ziliao* 70 (June 1999): 96–127.

————. "Guanyu 'wen'ge' zhong Beijing de 'tianpai' he 'dipai'" 关于'文革'中北京的'天派'和'地派' [On the "heaven" and "earth" factions during Beijing's "Cultural Revolution"]. *Zhonggong dangshi ziliao* 73 (March 2000): 100–126.

————. "Qinghua fuzhong hongweibing chengli hou de yixie qingkuang" 清华附中红卫兵成立后的一些情况 [Some circumstances after the establishment of the Qinghua University red guards]. *Zhonggong dangshi ziliao* 80 (December 2001): 126–46.

————. "'Huoshao Yingguo daibanchu' shimo" '火烧英国代办处'始末 [The story behind "torching the British diplomatic offices"]. *Zhonggong dangshi ziliao* 86 (June 2003): 135–40.

Burns, John. *Political Participation in Rural China.* Berkeley: University of California Press, 1980.

Cai Tianxin 蔡天新. "Li Qinglin gei Mao Zedong xiexin shijian de qianyin houguo" 李庆霖给毛泽东写信事件的前因后果 [The origin and result of Li

Qinglin's letter to Mao Zedong]. In *Bainian Putian* 百年莆田 [History of Putian
county, 1900–2000], ed. Putian xian wenshiban 莆田县文史办, 310–41. Beijing:
Zhongyang wenxian chubanshe, 2002.

———. "Li Qinglin shangshu yu zhiqing zhengce tiaozheng" 李庆霖上书
与知青政策调整 [Li Qinglin's letter to Chairman Mao and the adjustment in
party policy on sent-down youth]. *Zhonggong dangshi yanjiu* 94 (April 2003): 30–
35.

Center for Chinese Research Materials. *Red Guard Publications*. 20 vols.
Washington, D.C.: Association of Research Libraries, 1975.

———. *Red Guard Publications, Supplement 1*. 8 vols. Washington, D.C.:
Association of Research Libraries, 1980.

———. *Red Guard Publications, Supplement II*. 8 vols. Oakton, VA: Center for
Chinese Research Materials, 1992.

Chan, Anita, Stanley Rosen, and Jonathan Unger. "Students and Class Warfare: The
Social Roots of the Red Guard Conflict in Guangzhou (Canton)." *China
Quarterly* 83 (September 1980): 397–446.

Chao Feng 巢峰, ed. *"Wenhua da geming" cidian* '文化大革命'詞典 ["Cultural
Revolution" dictionary]. Hong Kong: Ganglong chubanshe, 1993.

Chen Donglin 陈东林. "'Wenhua da geming' qunzhong zuzhi baokan yanjiu"
'文化大革命'群众组织报刊研究 [A study of the publications of mass
organizations during the "Cultural Revolution"]. *Zhonggong dangshi ziliao* 76
(December 2000): 137–52.

Chen Sihe 陈思和, and Yang Yang 杨扬, eds. *Jiushi niandai piping wenxuan*
九十年代批评文选 [Selected critical essays of the 1990s]. Shanghai: Hanyu
dacidian chubanshe, 2001.

Chen, Xiaomei. *Acting the Right Part: Political Theater and Popular Drama in
Contemporary China*. Honolulu: University of Hawai'i Press, 2002.

Chen Yichun 陈宜淳. "Fujian wen'ge shinian shulüe" 福建文革十年述略 [The
Cultural Revolution decade in Fujian]. *Fujian dangshi yanjiu* (April 1992): 34–37.

Cheng, Tiejun, and Mark Selden. "The Origins and Consequences of China's
Hukou System." *China Quarterly* 139 (September 1994): 644–68.

Ci, Jiwei. *Dialectic of the Chinese Revolution: From Utopianism to Hedonism*.
Stanford, CA: Stanford University Press, 1994.

Dittmer, Lowell. "Learning from Trauma: The Cultural Revolution in Post-Mao
Politics." In *New Perspectives on the Cultural Revolution*, ed. William A. Joseph,
Christine P. W. Wong, and David Zweig, 19–39. Cambridge, MA: Council on
East Asian Studies, Harvard University, 1991.

Esherick, Joseph W. "Revolution in a Feudal Fortress: Yangjiagou, Mizhi County, Shaanxi, 1937–1948." *Modern China* 24, no. 4 (1998): 339–77.

Falkenheim, Victor, ed. *Citizens and Groups in Contemporary China*. Ann Arbor: Center for Chinese Studies, University of Michigan, 1987.

Fan Daren 范達人. *Wen'ge yubi chenfu lu: Liang Xiao wangshi* 文革御笔沉浮录: 梁效往事 [The rise and fall of the Cultural Revolution's imperial scribe: A recollection of Liang Xiao]. Hong Kong: Mingbao chubanshe, 1999.

Fang Huijian 方惠坚, and Zhang Sijing 张思敬, eds. *Qinghua daxue zhi* 清华大学志 [Annals of Qinghua University]. Beijing: Qinghua daxue chubanshe, 2001.

Feng Jicai 冯骥才. *Yibaige ren de shinian* 100个人的10年 [One hundred persons' decade]. Nanjing: Jiangsu wenyi chubanshe, 1991.

Feng Jicai. *Voices from the Whirlwind: An Oral History of the Chinese Cultural Revolution*. New York: Pantheon Books, 1991.

———. *Ten Years of Madness: Oral Histories of China's Cultural Revolution*. San Francisco: China Books and Periodicals, 1996.

Forster, Keith. *Rebellion and Factionalism in a Chinese Province: Zhejiang, 1966–1976*. Armonk, NY: M. E. Sharpe, 1990.

Friedman, Edward. "The Politics of Local Models, Social Transformation and State Power Struggles in the People's Republic of China: Tachai and Teng Hsiao-p'ing." *China Quarterly* 76 (December 1978): 873–90.

Friedman, Edward, Paul G. Pickowicz, and Mark Selden. *Chinese Village, Socialist State*. New Haven, CT: Yale University Press, 1991.

———. *Revolution, Resistance, and Reform in Village China*. New Haven, CT: Yale University Press, 2005.

Fujian sheng zhi bianzhuan weiyuanhui 福建省志编撰委员会 [Fujian Provincial Gazetteer Editorial Committee], ed. *Fujian sheng zhi* 福建省志 [Fujian provincial gazetteer], vol. 1, *Zonggaishu* 总概述 [General account]. Fuzhou: Fujian renmin chubanshe, 1994.

———. *Fujian sheng zhi* 福建省志 [Fujian provincial gazetteer], vol. 10, *Dashiji* 大事记 [Chronology]. Fuzhou: Fujian renmin chubanshe, 1994.

Gao Jianguo 高建国. "Xiaojinzhuang de chenfu" 小靳庄的沉浮 [The rise and fall of Xiaojinzhuang], part one. *Sanyue feng* 15 (February 1986): 3–17.

———. "Xiaojinzhuang de chenfu" 小靳庄的沉浮 [The rise and fall of Xiaojinzhuang], part two. *Sanyue feng* 16 (March 1986): 6–20.

Gao, Mobo C. F. "Factional Politics in the CPC: A Case Study of the Rise and Fall of Li Qinglin." *China Report* 35 (January–March 1999): 41–60.

———. *Gao Village: a Portrait of Rural Life in Modern China*. Honolulu: University of Hawai'i Press, 1999.

Gao Yuan. *Born Red: A Chronicle of the Cultural Revolution*. Stanford, CA: Stanford University Press, 1987.

Garside, Roger. *Coming Alive: China after Mao*. New York: McGraw-Hill, 1981.

Gilley, Bruce. *Model Rebels: The Rise and Fall of China's Richest Village*. Berkeley: University of California Press, 2001.

Goldman, Merle. *China's Intellectuals: Advise and Dissent*. Cambridge, MA: Harvard University Press, 1981.

Goodman, David S. G. *Beijing Street Voices: The Poetry and Politics of China's Democracy Movement*. London: Marion Boyars, 1981.

Guangxi wen'ge dashi nianbiao bianxie xiaozu 广西文革大事年表编写小组 [Guangxi Cultural Revolution Chronology Editorial Group], ed. *Guangxi wen'ge dashi nianbiao* 广西文革大事年表 [Chronology of the Cultural Revolution in Guangxi]. Nanning: Guangxi renmin chubanshe, 1990.

Guo Yingqiu 郭影秋, with Wang Junyi 王俊义. "Guo Yingqiu linzhong koushu: 'Wen'ge' qinliji" 郭影秋临终口述：'文革'亲历记 [Guo Yingqiu's deathbed testimony: A personal account of the "Cultural Revolution"]. *Yanhuang chunqiu* 128 (November 2002): 44–53.

Guojia wenwu shiye guanliju 国家文物事业管理局 [State Cultural Relics Management Bureau], comp. *Xin Zhongguo wenwu fagui xuan bian* 新中国文物法规选编 [Selected laws and regulations on cultural relics in new China]. Beijing: Wenwu chubanshe, 1987.

Hai Feng 海丰. *Guangzhou diqu wen'ge licheng shulüe* 廣州地區文革歷程述略 [An account of the Cultural Revolution in the Canton area]. Hong Kong: Youlian yanjiusuo, 1971.

Han, Dongping. *The Unknown Cultural Revolution: Educational Reforms and Their Impact on China's Rural Development, 1966–1976*. New York: Garland, 2000.

———. "Impact of the Cultural Revolution on Rural Education and Economic Development in Jimo County." *Modern China* 27 (January 2001): 59–90.

Hao Ping. "Reassessing the Starting Point of the Cultural Revolution." *China Review International* 3, no. 1 (Spring 1996): 66–86.

He Luo 何洛, and Meng Jin 孟金. "Quanguo 'di yi zhang dazibao' chulong zhenxiang" 全国'第一张大字报'出笼真相 [The real story behind the nation's "first wall poster"]. *Zhonggong dangshi ziliao* 83 (September 2002): 113–27.

Hinton, William. *Hundred Day War: The Cultural Revolution at Tsinghua University*. New York: Monthly Review Press, 1973.

Huang Jiwei 黄集伟. "Wang Xiaobo: Zuichu de yu zuihou de" 王小波: 最初的与最后的 [Wang Xiaobo: The first and the last]. In *Langman qishi*, ed. Ai Xiaoming and Li Yinhe, 216–24.

Jen, C. K. "Science and the Open-Doors Educational Movement." *China Quarterly* 64 (December 1975): 741–47.

Jin Chunming 金春明, Huang Yuchong 黄裕冲, and Chang Huimin 常惠民, eds. *"Wen'ge" shiqi guaishi guaiyu* '文革'时期怪事怪语 [Odd episodes and terminology of the "Cultural Revolution" period]. Beijing: Qiushi chubanshe, 1989.

Jin Qiu. *The Culture of Power: The Lin Biao Incident in the Cultural Revolution*. Stanford, CA: Stanford University Press, 1999.

Kraus, Richard Curt. "Class Conflict and the Vocabulary of Social Analysis in China." *China Quarterly* 69 (March 1977): 54–74.

———. *Class Conflict in Chinese Socialism*. New York: Columbia University Press, 1981.

Lai Jinliang 赖金良. "Ping 'yi yuan yi ren' jieduan lun" 评"亦猿亦人"阶段论 [Criticizing the "both ape and human" stage theory]. *Huashi* 1976, no. 4: 14–16, 21.

Lee, Hong Yung. "The Radical Students in Kwangtung during the Cultural Revolution." *China Quarterly* 64 (December 1975): 645–83.

———. *The Politics of the Chinese Cultural Revolution: A Case Study*. Berkeley: University of California Press, 1978.

Leung, Laifang. *Morning Sun: Interviews with Chinese Writers of the Lost Generation*. Armonk, NY: M. E. Sharpe, 1994.

Levenson, Joseph R. *Revolution and Cosmopolitanism: The Western Stage and the Chinese Stages*. Berkeley: University of California Press, 1971.

Lewis, John. *Leadership in Communist China*. Ithaca, NY: Cornell University Press, 1963.

Leys, Simon. *Chinese Shadows*. New York: Viking, 1977.

———. *Broken Images: Essays on Chinese Culture and Politics*. London: Allison & Busby, 1979.

Li Chuanxin 李传信, ed. *Qinghua renwuzhi* 清华人物志 [Eminent people of Qinghua University]. Beijing: Qinghua daxue chubanshe, 1995.

Li Jiefei 李洁非. "Shinian yanyun guoyan" 十年烟云过眼 [Ten years in a flash]. *Dangdai zuojia pinglun* 1 (1993): 26–33.

Li Songchen 李松晨, et al., eds. *Wen'ge dang'an* 文革档案 [Collection of Cultural Revolution documents]. Beijing: Dangdai Zhongguo chubanshe, 1999.

Liang Xiaosheng 梁晓声. *Jinye you baofengxue* 今夜有暴风雪 [Snowstorm tonight]. In his *Zhiqing xiaoshuo xuan* 知青小说选 [Selected works about sent-down youth], 281–414. Xi'an: Xi'an chubanshe, 1993.

———. *Zibai* 自白 [Confessions]. Beijing: Jingji ribao chubanshe, 1997.

Lifton, Robert Jay. *Revolutionary Immortality: Mao Tse-tung and the Chinese Cultural Revolution.* New York: Random House, 1968.

Ling, Ken. *The Revenge of Heaven: Journal of a Young Chinese.* New York: G. P. Putnam's Sons, 1972.

Link, Perry, ed. *People or Monsters? and Other Stories and Reportage from China after Mao.* Bloomington: Indiana University Press, 1983.

———. *Stubborn Weeds: Popular and Controversial Chinese Literature after the Cultural Revolution.* Bloomington: Indiana University Press, 1983.

———. *Roses and Thorns: The Second Blooming of the Hundred Flowers in Chinese Fiction, 1979–1980.* Berkeley: University of California Press, 1984.

Liu Bing 刘冰. *Fengyu suiyue* 风雨岁月 [Years of hardship]. Beijing: Qinghua daxue chubanshe, 1998.

Liu Guokai. *A Brief Analysis of the Cultural Revolution,* ed. Anita Chan. Armonk, NY: M. E. Sharpe, 1987.

Liu Qingfeng 劉青峰, ed. *Wenhua da geming: Shishi yu yanjiu* 文化大革命: 史實與研究 [The Cultural Revolution: Evidence and analysis]. Hong Kong: Xianggang Zhongwen daxue chubanshe, 1996.

Liu Xiaomeng 刘小萌. *Zhongguo zhiqing shi* 中国知青史 [History of Chinese sent-down youth]. Beijing: Zhongguo shehuikexue chubanshe, 1998.

Liu Yigao 刘一皋. "Cong quanguo 'di yi zhang dazibao' he Xiaogang 'hongshou yin' tanqi" 从全国'第一张大字报'和小岗'红手印'谈起 [About the nation's "first wall poster" and the Xiaogang village "red fingerprint"]. *Zhonggong dangshi ziliao* 87 (September 2003): 144–60.

Liu Zhende 刘振德. "Jiyao mishu de huiyi" 机要秘书的回忆 [Reminiscences of a confidential secretary]. In *Liu Shaoqi de zuihou suiyue, 1966–1969* 刘少奇的最后岁月, 1966–1969 [Liu Shaoqi's final years, 1966–1969], ed. Huang Zheng 黄峥, 61–125. Beijing: Zhongyang wenxian chubanshe, 1996.

Liu Zhijian 刘志坚. "Dongluan zhichu de jingli he zaoyu" 动乱之初的经历和遭遇 [My experiences and misfortunes at the beginning of the turmoil]. *Zhonggong dangshi ziliao* 74 (June 2000), 23–59.

MacFarquhar, Roderick. *The Origins of the Cultural Revolution 1: Contradictions among the People, 1956–1957.* New York: Columbia University Press, 1974.

————. *The Origins of the Cultural Revolution 2: The Great Leap Forward, 1958–1960*. New York: Columbia University Press, 1983.

————. *The Origins of the Cultural Revolution 3: The Coming of the Cataclysm, 1961–1966*. New York: Columbia University Press, 1997.

MacFarquhar, Roderick, and Michael Schoenhals. *The Cultural Revolution: China in Turmoil, 1966–1976*. Cambridge, MA: Harvard University Press, 2006.

Madsen, Richard. *Morality and Power in a Chinese Village*. Berkeley: University of California Press, 1984.

Mao Tse-tung. *Quotations from Chairman Mao Tse-tung*. Peking: Foreign Languages Press, 1966.

Mao Zedong 毛泽东. *Mao zhuxi lun jiaoyu geming* 毛主席论教育革命 [Chairman Mao on revolution in education]. Beijing: Renmin chubanshe, 1966.

Mao Zedong 毛泽东, and Lin Biao 林彪. *Weida lingxiu Mao zhuxi he ta de qinmi zhanyou Lin fuzhuxi zhaojian shoudu dazhuan yuanxiao hongdaihui fuzeren Nie Yuanzi, Kuai Dafu, Han Aijing, Tan Houlan, Wang Dabin tongzhi shi de zhongyao jianghua* 伟大领袖毛主席和他的亲密战友林副主席召见首都大专院校红代会负责人聂元梓，蒯大富，韩爱晶，谭厚兰，王大宾同志时的重要讲话 [The important talk by the great leader Chairman Mao and his close comrade Vice-Chairman Lin at the meeting with leaders of the Beijing college red guards, comrades Nie Yuanzi, Kuai Dafu, Han Aijing, Tan Houlan, and Wang Dabin]. Beijing: 1968. Printed pamphlet.

Meisner, Maurice. *Marxism, Maoism and Utopianism*. Madison: University of Wisconsin Press, 1982.

————. *Mao's China and After: A History of the People's Republic*, 3rd ed. New York: Free Press, 1999.

Meng Fanhua 孟繁华. *Jiqing suiyue* 激情岁月 [The passionate era]. Ji'nan: Shandong jiaoyu chubanshe, 1998.

Mizhi xian zhi bianzuan weiyuanhui 米脂县志编纂委员会 [Mizhi County Gazetteer Editorial Committee]. *Mizhi xian zhi* 米脂县志 [Mizhi county gazetteer]. Xi'an: Shaanxi renmin chubanshe, 1993.

Mu Xin 穆欣. *Jiehou changyi: Shinian dongluan jishi* 劫後長憶：十年動亂紀事 [Memories of turmoil: An account of ten years of chaos]. Hong Kong: Xintian chubanshe, 1997.

————. "'Quanguo di yi zhang dazibao' chulong jingguo" '全国第一张大字报'出笼经过 [How the "the nation's first wall poster" was cooked up]. *Zhonggong dangshi ziliao* 75 (September 2000): 166–73.

Oi, Jean C. "Communism and Clientelism: Rural Politics in China." *World Politics* 37 (January 1985): 238–66.

———. *State and Peasant in Contemporary China.* Berkeley: University of California Press, 1989.

Oksenberg, Michel. "Occupational Groups in Chinese Society and the Cultural Revolution." In *The Cultural Revolution: 1967 in Review*, 1–44. Michigan Papers in Chinese Studies No. 2. Ann Arbor: Center for Chinese Studies, University of Michigan, 1968.

Pepper, Suzanne. *Radicalism and Education Reform in 20th-Century China: The Search for an Ideal Development Model.* Cambridge, UK: Cambridge University Press, 1996.

Perry, Elizabeth J. "Rural Violence in Socialist China." *China Quarterly* 103 (September 1985): 414–40.

———. "Shanghai's Strike Wave of 1957." *China Quarterly* 137 (March 1994).

Perry, Elizabeth J., and Li Xun. *Proletarian Power: Shanghai in the Cultural Revolution.* Boulder, CO: Westview, 1997.

Potter, Sulamith Heins, and Jack M. Potter. *China's Peasants: The Anthropology of a Revolution.* Cambridge, UK: Cambridge University Press, 1990.

Qinghua daxue Jinggangshan hongweibing xuanchuandui 清华大学井冈山红卫兵宣传队 [Qinghua University Jinggangshan Red Guard Propaganda Team], ed. *Qinghua daxue dazibao xuan (Kuai Dafu tongzhi de dazibao)* 清华大学大字报选 (蒯大富同志的大字报) [Selected wall posters of Qinghua University (wall posters by Comrade Kuai Dafu)]. Beijing: 1966. Printed pamphlet.

Qinghua daxue Jinggangshan lianhe zongbu yiwangxi zhandouzu 清华大学井冈山联合总部忆往昔战斗组 [Qinghua University Jinggangshan United Headquarters Recalling the Past Battle Team], ed. *Qinghua daxue Jinggangshan bingtuan wuchan jieji wenhua da geming dashiji* 清华大学井冈山兵团无产阶级文化大革命大事记 [The chronology of Qinghua Jinggangshan corps in the Great Proletarian Cultural Revolution]. Beijing: 1968. Mimeographed pamphlet.

Qinghua daxue Mao Zedong sixiang hongweibing Dongfanghong gongshe 清华大学毛泽东思想红卫兵东方红公社 [Qinghua University Mao Zedong Thought Red Guards East is Red Commune], ed. *Qinghua daxue dazibao xuanbian* 清华大学大字报选编 [Selected wall posters of Qinghua University]. Beijing: 1966. Mimeographed pamphlet.

Quan Yanchi 权延赤. *Yang Chengwu jianzheng wen'ge* 杨成武见证文革 [Yang Chengwu's testimony about the Cultural Revolution]. Beijing: Guangming ribao chubanshe, 2004.

Rosen, Stanley. "Comments: The Radical Students in Kwangtung during the Cultural Revolution." *China Quarterly* 70 (June 1977): 390–99.

———. *The Role of Sent-Down Youth in the Chinese Cultural Revolution: The Case of Guangzhou.* Berkeley: Institute of East Asian Studies, University of California, 1981.

———. *Red Guard Factionalism and the Cultural Revolution in Guangzhou (Canton).* Boulder, CO: Westview, 1982.

———. "Guangzhou's Democracy Movement in Cultural Revolution Perspective." *China Quarterly* 101 (March 1985): 1–31.

Schoenhals, Michael. "The Central Case Examination Group, 1966–79." *China Quarterly* 145 (March 1996): 87–111.

———. *China's Cultural Revolution, 1966–1969: Not a Dinner Party.* Armonk, NY: M. E. Sharpe, 1996.

Schurmann, Franz. *Ideology and Organization in Communist China.* Berkeley: University of California Press, 1966.

Science for the People. *Science Walks on Two Legs.* New York: Discus Books, 1974.

Selden, Mark, ed. *The People's Republic of China: A Documentary History of Revolutionary Change.* New York: Monthly Review Press, 1979.

"Shangfang tongxun" bianjishi '上访通讯'编辑室 ["Letters of Appeal" Editorial Office], ed. *Chunfeng huayu ji* 春风化雨集 [Spring breezes and rain: A collection]. Beijing: Qunzhong chubanshe, 1981.

Shen Ruhuai 沈如槐. *Qinghua daxue wen'ge jishi: Yige hongweibing lingdao de zishu* 清華大學文革紀事: 一個紅衛兵領袖的自述 [An account of the Cultural Revolution at Qinghua University: The personal account of a red guard leader]. Hong Kong: Shidai yishu chubanshe, 2004.

Shen Xueming 沈学明, and Zheng Jianying 郑建英, eds. *Zhonggong di yi jie zhi shiwu jie zhongyang weiyuan* 中共第一届至第十届中央委员 [Members of the first through fifteenth CCP Central Committees]. Beijing: Zhongyang wenxian chubanshe, 2001.

Shi'er ji taifeng gua bu dao: Xiaojinzhuang shige xuan 十二级台风刮不倒: 小靳庄诗歌选 [Even the fiercest typhoon cannot blow us down: Xiaojinzhuang poetry anthology]. Beijing: Renmin chubanshe, 1976.

Shirk, Susan L. *Competitive Comrades: Career Incentives and Student Strategies in China.* Berkeley: University of California Press, 1982.

Shoudu yuanlin pixiu lianluozhan 首都园林批修联络站 [Capital Parks Criticize Revisionism Liaison Station]. *Yuanlin geming, di san qi, Bei batian: Peng Zhen zhuanji* 园林革命, 第三期, 北霸天: 彭真专集 [Parks in revolution, third issue, Beijing hegemon: Peng Zhen special collection]. August 1967.

Sidel, Victor, and Ruth Sidel. *Serve the People: Observations on Medicine in the People's Republic of China.* New York: Josiah Macy, Jr. Foundation, 1973.

Solomon, Richard. *Mao's Revolution and the Chinese Political Culture.* Berkeley: University of California Press, 1971.

Song Yongyi 宋永毅, ed. *Wen'ge da tusha* 文革大屠殺 [Massacres during the Cultural Revolution]. Hong Kong: Kaifang zazhishe, 2002.

———, ed. *Xin bian hongweibing ziliao* 新编红卫兵资料. English title: *A New Collection of Red Guard Publications, Part II: A Special Collection of Newspapers in Beijing Area,* 40 vols. Oakton, VA: Center for Chinese Research Materials, 2001.

———, ed. *Zhongguo wenhua da geming wenku* 中国文化大革命文库 [Chinese cultural revolution database]. Hong Kong: Xianggang Zhongwen daxue Zhongguo yanjiu fuwu zhongxin, 2002. CD-ROM.

Song Yongyi 宋永毅, and Sun Dajin 孫大進, eds. *Wenhua da geming he tade yiduan sichao* 文化大革命和它的異端思潮 [Heterodox thoughts during the Cultural Revolution]. Hong Kong: Tianyuan shuwu, 1996.

Song, Yongyi, and Dajin Sun. *The Cultural Revolution: A Bibliography 1966–1976.* Cambridge, MA: Harvard-Yenching Library, 2001.

Su, Yang. "Tumult from Within: State Bureaucrats and Chinese Mass Movements, 1966–1971." Ph.D. dissertation. Stanford University, 2003.

Suttmeier, Richard. *Research and Revolution: Science Policy and Societal Change in China.* Lexington, MA: Lexington Books, 1974.

Tan Bin 谭斌 [Tan Lifu 谭力夫]. *Chizi baihua* 赤子白话 [Empty talk of an innocent]. Beijing: Beijing tushuguan chubanshe, 1996.

Tang Shaojie 唐少傑. "Hongweibing de sangzhong: Qinghua daxue bairi da wudou" 紅衛兵的喪鐘: 清華大學百日大武鬥 [The death knell of the red guard movement: The hundred day war in Qinghua University]. In *Wenhua da geming,* ed. Liu Qingfeng, 65–79.

———. "Cong Qinghua daxue de liangpai tan 'wenhua da geming' qunzhong zuzhi jiegou, gongneng" 从清华大学的两派谈'文化大革命'群众组织结构，功能 [Structure and function of "Cultural Revolution" mass organizations: The case of the two factions at Qinghua University]. *Zhonggong dangshi ziliao* 72 (September 1999): 66–81.

———. *Yiye zhichun: Qinghua daxue 1968 nian "Bairi da wudou"* 一葉知秋：
清華大學1968年'白日大武鬥' [An episode in the Cultural Revolution: the 1968
"hundred day war" at Qinghua University]. Hong Kong: Xianggang Zhongwen
daxue chubanshe, 2003.

Tang Shaojie 唐少杰, and Ji Peng 汲鹏. "Fengyu ru pan: Qinghua daxue
Jinggangshan bingtuan de xingshuai" 风雨如磐：清华大学井冈山兵团的
兴衰 [Stormy times: The rise and fall of Jinggangshan corps of Qinghua
University]. Unpublished manuscript. 2003.

Tao Dejian 陶德坚. *Tao Dejian huiyilu: Fengyu rensheng* 陶德坚回忆录：风雨
人生 [Memoir of Tao Dejian: A life of hardships], www.taosl.net/fy001.htm.
April 16, 2003.

Teiwes, Frederick, and Warren Sun. *The Tragedy of Lin Biao: Riding the Tiger
during the Cultural Revolution*. Honolulu: University of Hawaii Press, 1996.

Tianjin renmin chubanshe 天津人民出版社 [Tianjin People's Press], ed.
Xiaojinzhuang shige xuan 小靳庄诗歌选 [Xiaojinzhuang poetry anthology].
Tianjin: Tianjin renmin chubanshe, 1974.

Tozer, Warren. "Taiwan's 'Cultural Renaissance': A Preliminary View." *China
Quarterly* 43 (July–September 1970): 81–99.

Unger, Jonathan. *Education under Mao: Class and Competition in Canton Schools,
1960–1980*. New York: Columbia University Press, 1982.

———. "Cultural Revolution Conflict in the Villages." *China Quarterly* 153 (March
1998): 82–106.

Union Research Institute, comp. *CCP Documents of the Great Proletarian Cultural
Revolution, 1966–1967*. Hong Kong: Union Research Institute, 1968.

Vogel, Ezra F. "The Structure of Conflict: China in 1967." In *The Cultural
Revolution: 1967 in Review*, 97–125. Michigan Papers in Chinese Studies No. 2.
Ann Arbor: Center for Chinese Studies, University of Michigan, 1968.

———. *Canton under Communism: Programs and Politics in a Provincial Capital,
1949–1968*. Cambridge, MA: Harvard University Press, 1969.

Walder, Andrew G. *Chang Ch'un-ch'iao and Shanghai's January Revolution*.
Michigan Papers in Chinese Studies No. 32. Ann Arbor: Center for Chinese
Studies, University of Michigan, 1978.

———. *Communist Neo-Traditionalism: Work and Authority in Chinese Industry*.
Berkeley: University of California, 1986.

———. "Cultural Revolution Radicalism: Variations on a Stalinist Theme." In *New
Perspectives on the Cultural Revolution*, ed. William Joseph, Christine P. W.
Wong, and D. Zweig, 41–62. Cambridge, MA: Harvard University Press, 1991.

————. "Anatomy of an Inquisition: Cleansing the Class Ranks, 1968–1971." Paper presented at the conference, "The Cultural Revolution in Retrospect," Hong Kong University of Science and Technology, July 4–6, 1996.

————. "When States Unravel: How China's Cadres Shaped Cultural Revolution Politics." In *State Capacity in East Asia*, ed. Kjeld Erik Brødsgaard and Susan Young, 157–84. Oxford: Oxford University Press, 2000.

————. "Beijing Red Guard Factionalism: Social Interpretations Reconsidered." *Journal of Asian Studies* 61, no. 2 (2002): 437–71.

Walder, Andrew G., and Gong Xiaoxia, eds. "China's Great Terror: New Documentation on the Cultural Revolution." *Chinese Sociology and Anthropology* 26 (Fall 1993): 3–103.

Walder, Andrew G., Bobai Li, and Donald Treiman. "Politics and Life Chances in a State Socialist Regime: Dual Career Paths into the Urban Chinese Elite, 1949 to 1996." *American Sociological Review* 65 (April 2000): 191–209.

Walder, Andrew G., and Yang Su. "The Cultural Revolution in the Countryside: Scope, Timing and Human Impact." *China Quarterly* 173 (March 2003): 74–99.

Wang, Ban. *The Sublime Figure of History: Aesthetics and Politics in Twentieth-Century China*. Stanford, CA: Stanford University Press, 1997.

Wang Dongxing 汪东兴. *Mao Zedong yu Lin Biao fan'geming jituan de douzheng* 毛泽东与林彪反革命集团的斗争 [Mao Zedong's struggle with the Lin Biao counterrevolutionary clique]. Beijing: Dangdai Zhongguo chubanshe, 2004.

Wang Jianying 王建英, ed. *Zhongguo gongchandang zuzhishi ziliao huibian: Lingdao jigou yan'ge he chengyuan minglu (zengdingben)* 中国共产党组织史资料汇编：领导机构沿革和成员名录（增订本）[Collected materials on the organizational history of the Chinese Communist Party: A registry of office-holders and changes in leadership structures (revised and enlarged ed.)]. Beijing: Zhonggong zhongyang dangxiao chubanshe, 1995.

Wang, Jing. *High Culture Fever: Politics, Aesthetics and Ideology in Deng's China*. Berkeley: University of California Press, 1996.

Wang Li 王力. *Wang Li fansilu* 王力反思錄 [Wang Li's memoirs]. Hong Kong: Beixing chubanshe, 2001.

Wang Meng 王蒙. "Nande mingbai" 难得明白 [It's hard to grasp]. *Dushu* 1 (1998): 29–32.

Wang Nianyi 王年一. *Da dongluan de niandai* 大动乱的年代 [Turbulent decade]. Zhengzhou: Henan renmin chubanshe, 1988.

————, ed. *"Wenhua da geming" yanjiu ziliao* '文化大革命'研究资料 ["Cultural Revolution" research materials]. 3 vols. Beijing: Zhongguo renmin jiefangjun guofang daxue dangshi dangjian zhenggong jiaoyanshi, 1988.

Wang, Shaoguang. *Failure of Charisma: The Cultural Revolution in Wuhan.* Hong Kong: Oxford University Press, 1995.

Wang Xianghui 王向晖. *Shangye shidai de yingxiong qingjie—Liang Xiaosheng lun* 商业时代的英雄情结—梁晓声论 [Heroic complex in an age of commercialization: on Liang Xiaosheng]. Beijing: Huaxia chubanshe, 2000.

Wang Xiaobo 王小波. *Wang Xiaobo wenji* 王小波文集 [Selected works of Wang Xiaobo]. Beijing: Zhongguo qingnian chubanshe, 1999.

————. *Huangjin shidai* 黄金时代 [Golden age]. In his *Huangjin shidai baiyin shidai* 黄金时代白银时代 [Golden age, silver age], 3–53. Beijing: Zhongguo qingnian chubanshe, 2002.

Wang Xuezhen 王学珍, Wang Xiaoting 王效挺, Huang Wenyi 黄文一, and Guo Jianrong 郭建荣, eds. *Beijing daxue jishi (1898–1997)* 北京大学纪事 (1898–1997) [A chronology of Beijing University, 1898–1997]. 2 vols. Beijing: Beijing daxue chubanshe, 1998.

Wang Youqin 王友琴. "1966: Xuesheng da laoshi de geming" 1966：學生打老師的革命 [1966: A revolution of students beating teachers]. In *Wenhua da geming*, ed. Liu Qingfeng, 17–36.

————. "Da laoshi yu da tongxue zhijian" 打老師與打同學之間 [Between beating teachers and beating classmates]. In *Wenhua da geming*, ed. Liu Qingfeng, 37–48.

————. "Student Attacks against Teachers: The Revolution of 1966." *Issues and Studies* 37 (March–April 2001): 29–79.

————, ed. *Wen'ge shounanzhe: Guanyu pohai, jianjin yu shalu de xunfang shilu* 文革受難者: 關於迫害, 監禁與殺戮的尋訪實錄 [Victims of the Cultural Revolution: An investigative account of persecution, imprisonment, and murder]. Hong Kong: Kaifang zazhishe, 2004.

White, Gordon. "The Politics of *Hsia-hsiang* Youth." *China Quarterly* 59 (July–September 1974): 491–517.

————. *The Politics of Class and Class Origin: The Case of the Cultural Revolution.* Canberra: Contemporary China Centre, Australian National University, 1976.

————. "The Politics of Demobilized Soldiers from Liberation to Cultural Revolution." *China Quarterly* 82 (June 1980): 187–213.

White, Lynn T., III. "Workers Politics in Shanghai." *Journal of Asian Studies* 35 (November 1976): 99–116.

———. "The Road to Urumchi: Approved Institutions in Search of Attainable Goals during Pre-1968 Rustication from Shanghai." *China Quarterly* 79 (September 1979): 481–510.

Whyte, Martin King. *Small Groups and Political Rituals in China.* Berkeley: University of California Press, 1974.

Wilson, Dick. *Zhou Enlai: A Biography.* New York: Viking Penguin, 1984.

Witke, Roxane. *Comrade Chiang Ch'ing.* Boston: Little, Brown, 1977.

Wu De 吴德, with Zhu Yuanshi 朱元石. *Shinian fengyu jishi: Wo zai Beijing gongzuo de yixie jingli* 十年风雨纪事：我在北京工作的一些经历 [Ten years of trial: Some of my experiences working in Beijing]. Beijing: Dangdai Zhongguo chubanshe, 2004.

Wu Qingtong 吴庆彤. *Zhou Enlai zai "wenhua da geming" zhong* 周恩来在'文化大革命'中 [Zhou Enlai in the "Cultural Revolution"], expanded ed. Beijing: Zhonggong dangshi chubanshe, 2002.

Xi Xuan 席宣, and Jin Chunming 金春明. *"Wenhua da geming" jianshi* '文化大革命'简史 [Brief history of the "Cultural Revolution"]. Beijing: Zhonggong dangshi chubanshe, 2003.

Xiang Lin 湘霖, and Hong Yu 宏宇, eds. *Zhongguo xiandai yuanyu jishi* 中国现代冤狱纪实 [True accounts of unjust cases in contemporary China]. Hohhot: Nei Menggu renmin chubanshe, 1989.

Xiao Han 曉菡, and Mia Turner 米雅, eds. *789 jizhong ying: Zhongguo gaogan zinü zhong yige teshu qunti de gushi* 789集中營：中國高幹子女中一個特殊羣體的故事 [Concentration camp 789: The story of a special group of sons and daughters of Chinese high officials]. Ontario, Canada: Mirror Books, 1998.

Xu Jingxian 徐景賢. *Shinian yimeng: Qian Shanghai shiwei shuji Xu Jingxian wen'ge huiyi lu* 十年一夢：前上海市委書記徐景賢文革回憶錄 [Ten years' dream: The Cultural Revolution memoirs of former Shanghai party secretary Xu Jingxian]. Hong Kong: Shidai guoji chuban youxian gongsi, 2004.

Xu Youyu 徐友漁. *Xingxing sese de zaofan: Hongweibing jingshen suzhi de xingcheng ji yanbian* 形形色色的造反：紅衛兵精神素質的形成及演變 [Rebellion of all hues: The formation and evolution of red guard mentalities]. Hong Kong: Xianggang Zhongwen daxue chubanshe, 1999.

Xu Zhigeng 徐只耕. "Lishi de wanxiao: Li Qinglin ershinian chenfulu" 历史的玩笑：李庆霖20年沉浮录 [A historical joke: A twenty-year chronicle of the rise and fall of Li Qinglin]. *Yuhua* (April 1994): 64–68.

Ya Zi 亚子, and Liang Zi 良子. *Kongfu da jienan* 孔府大劫难 [Great calamity of the Confucius Mansion]. Hong Kong: Tiandi tushu youxian gongsi, 1992.

Yan Jiaqi, and Gao Gao. *Turbulent Decade: A History of the Cultural Revolution.*
  Trans. and ed. D. W. Y. Kwok. Honolulu: University of Hawai'i Press, 1996.
Yang Kelin 杨克林, ed. *Wenhua da geming bowuguan* 文化大革命博物馆
  [Cultural Revolution museum]. Hong Kong: Dongfang chubanshe youxian
  gongsi, 1995.
Yao, Shuping. "Chinese Intellectuals and Science: A History of the Chinese Academy
  of Sciences (CAS)." *Science in Context* 3, no. 2 (1989): 447–73.
Yin Hongbiao 印紅標. "Pipan zichan jieji fandong luxian: Zaofan yundong de
  xingqi" 批判資產階級反動路綫：造反運動的興起 [The starting point of
  the rebellion: The critique of the reactionary bourgeois line]. In *Wenhua da
  geming*, ed. Liu Qingfeng, 179–90.
———. "'Wenhua da geming' zhong de shehuixing maodun" '文化大革命'
  中的社会性矛盾 [Social contradictions in the "Cultural Revolution"].
  Zhonggong dangshi yanjiu 2 (1997): 77–82.
Zang, Xiaowei. *Children of the Cultural Revolution.* Boulder, CO: Westview Press,
  2000.
Zhang Cheng 章成. "Daoxian da tusha" 道縣大屠殺 [The Daoxian massacre].
  Kaifang zazhi 175 (July 2001): 63–80; 176 (August 2001): 76–85; 177 (Sept. 2001):
  59–63; 180 (Dec. 2001): 70–73.
Zhang Chengxian 张承先. "'Wenhua da geming' chuqi de Beida gongzuozu"
  '文化大革命'初期的北大工作组 [Beijing University's work team in the early
  stages of the "Cultural Revolution"]. *Zhonggong dangshi ziliao* 70 (June 1999): 16–
  44.
———. *Zhang Chengxian huiyilu: Wo qinli de dang de xuanchuan he jiaoyu
  gongzuo* 张承先回忆录：我亲历的党的宣传和教育工作 [Memoirs of
  Zhang Chengxian: My personal experiences in party propaganda and educational
  work]. Beijing: Renmin jiaoyu chubanshe, 2002.
Zhang Hua 张化, and Su Caiqing 苏采青, eds. *Huishou "wen'ge": Zhongguo shinian
  "wen'ge" fenxi yu fansi* 回首'文革'：中国十年'文革'分析与反思 [The
  "Cultural Revolution" in retrospect: Analysis and reflections on China's ten-year
  "Cultural Revolution"]. 2 vols. Beijing: Zhonggong dangshi chubanshe, 1999.
Zhang Kai 张凯, and Ji Yuan 纪元. *You shuo lao san jie* 又说老三届 [Revisiting the
  sent-down high school graduates]. Beijing: Zhongguo qingnian chubanshe, 1997.
Zhang Kangkang 张抗抗. *Dahuang bing he* 大荒冰河 [The wild north and the
  frozen river]. Changchun: Jilin renmin chubanshe, 1998.
Zhang Wentian 张闻天. "Mizhi xian Yangjiagou diaocha" 米脂县杨家沟调查
  [Survey of Yangjiagou, Mizhi]. In *Zhang Wentian Jin-Shaan diaocha wenji*

张文天晋陕调查文集 [Collection of Zhang Wentian's investigations in Shanxi and Shaanxi], 123–287. Beijing: Zhonggong dangshi chubanshe, 1994.

Zhang Yiwu 张颐武. "Dui 'xiandaixing' de zhuiwen—jiushi niandai wenxue de yi ge quxiang" 对现代性的追问—九十年代文学的一个趋向 [An inquiry into "modernity": A tendency of literature in the 1990s]. In *Jiushi niandai piping wenxuan* [Selected critical essays of the 1990s], ed. Chen Sihe and Yang Yang, 29–39.

Zhang Zhizhong 张志忠. *Shiji mo de xuanhua* 世纪末的喧哗 [The fin-de-siècle uproar]. Ji'nan: Shandong jiaoyu chubanshe, 1998.

Zheng Yi 鄭義. *Hongse jinian bei* 紅色紀念碑 [Scarlet memorial]. Taipei: Huashi wenhua gongsi, 1993.

———. "Liangge wenhua da geming chuyi" 两个文化大革命雏议 [A modest proposal on the two Cultural Revolutions]. *Huaxia wenzhai* 83 (Supplement, 1996): 1–14. Online journal at http://cnd.org.

Zheng Yi. *Scarlet Memorial: Tales of Cannibalism in Modern China*. Trans. T. P. Sym. Boulder, CO: Westview, 1996.

Zhong, Xueping, Wang Zheng, and Bai Di, eds. *Some of Us: Chinese Women Growing Up in the Mao Era*. New Brunswick, NJ: Rutgers University Press, 2001.

Zhonggong Mizhi xianwei zuzhibu, Zhonggong Mizhi xianwei dangshi yanjiushi, and Mizhi Dang'anju 中共米脂县委组织部，中共米脂县委党史研究室，米脂档案局 [CCP Mizhi County Party Committee Organization Department, Party History Office, and Bureau of Archives]. *Zhongguo gongchandang Shaanxi sheng Mizhi xian zuzhi shi* 中国共产党陕西省米脂县组织史 [Historical materials on the party organization in Mizhi county, Shaanxi province]. Xi'an: Shaanxi renmin chubanshe, 1994.

Zhonggong zhongyang wenxian yanjiushi 中共中央文献研究室 [CCP Central Documents Research Office], ed. *Zhou Enlai nianpu* 周恩来年谱 [A chronological biography of Zhou Enlai]. Beijing: Zhongyang wenxian chubanshe, 1997.

———, ed., *Jianguo yilai Mao Zedong wen'gao* 建国以来毛泽东文稿 [Mao Zedong's manuscripts and drafts since the founding of the People's Republic of China] vol. 12. Beijing: Zhongyang wenxian chubanshe, 1995.

Zhonggong zhongyang zuzhibu, zhonggong zhongyang dangshi yanjiushi, zhongyang dang'an guan 中共中央组织部，中共中央党史研究室，中央档案馆 [CCP Central Organization Department, Party History Office, and Central Party Archives]. *Zhongguo gongchandang zuzhishi ziliao 1921–1997* 中国共产党组织史资料 1921–1997 [Materials on the organizational history of the Chinese

Communist Party, 1921–1997]. 19 vols. Beijing: Zhonggong dangshi chubanshe, 2000.

Zhonghua renmin gongheguo minzheng bu 中华人民共和国民政部 [Ministry of Civil Affairs, People's Republic of China]，ed. *Zhonghua renmin gongheguo xingzheng quhua, 1949–1997* 中华人民共和国行政区划, 1949–1997 [Administrative jurisdictions of the People's Republic of China, 1949–1997]. Beijing: Zhongguo shehui chubanshe, 1998.

Zhongyang shouzhang jianghua deng 中央首长讲话等 [Central leaders' speeches, etc.]. In Harvard University's Fairbank Center collection of red guard materials.

Zhou Enlai 周恩来. "1966 nian 8 yue 4 ri zai Qinghua daxue de jianghua" 1966年8月4日在清华大学的讲话 [Speech at Qinghua University on August 4, 1966]. http://museums.cnd.org/CR/cdocs.htm. April 8, 2003.

Zhou Quanying 周泉缨. "Wo xinzhong de wen'ge" 我心中的文革 [The Cultural Revolution in my heart]. *Ershiyi shiji* 52 (April 1999): 139–43.

Zhou, Xueguang, and Liren Hou. "Children of the Cultural Revolution: The State and the Life Course in the People's Republic of China." *American Sociological Review* 64 (February 1999): 12–36.

Zhou Yuan, ed. *Xinbian hongweibing ziliao* 新编红卫兵资料. English title: *A New Collection of Red Guard Publications, Part I, Newspapers.* 20 vols. Oakton, VA: Center for Chinese Research Materials, 1999.

Zweig, David. *Agrarian Radicalism in China, 1968–1981.* Cambridge, MA: Harvard University Press, 1989.

Index

History / China

Based on a wide variety of unusual and only recently available sources, this book covers the entire Cultural Revolution decade (1966–76) and shows how the Cultural Revolution was experienced by ordinary Chinese at the base of urban and rural society. The contributors emphasize the complex interaction of state and society during this tumultuous period, exploring the way events originating at the center of political power changed people's lives and how, in turn, people's responses took the Cultural Revolution in unplanned and unanticipated directions. This approach offers a more fruitful way to understand the Cultural Revolution and its historical legacies.

The book provides a new look at the student Red Guard movements, the effort to identify and cultivate potential "revolutionary" leaders in outlying provinces, stubborn resistance to campaigns to destroy the old culture, and the violence and mass killings in rural China.

STANFORD UNIVERSITY PRESS *www.sup.org*

JOSEPH W. ESHERICK *holds the Hwei-chih and Julia Hsiu Chair in Chinese Studies and is Professor of History at the University of California, San Diego.*

PAUL G. PICKOWICZ *is Professor of History at the University of California, San Diego.*

ANDREW G. WALDER *is Professor of Sociology at Stanford University.*

ISBN 0-8047-5350-4

Cover photograph: Buddhist sculptures ablaze on the streets of Hefei, Anhui Province, in September 1966.

90000

9 780804 753500